DEVISING, DYING AND DISPUTE

For the women in my life:

My mother Libby,

my wife Adriana

and my daughter Lisa

Devising, Dying and Dispute

Probate Litigation in Early Modern England

LLOYD BONFIELD
New York Law School, USA

Routledge
Taylor & Francis Group

LONDON AND NEW YORK

First published 2012 by Ashgate Publishing

Published 2016 by Routledge
2 Park Square, Milton Park, Abingdon, Oxon OX14 4RN
711 Third Avenue, New York, NY 10017, USA

First issued in paperback 2017

Routledge is an imprint of the Taylor & Francis Group, an informa business

British Library Cataloguing in Publication Data
Bonfield, Lloyd, 1949–
    Devising, dying and dispute : probate litigation in early modern England.
    1. Wills – England – History – 17th century. 2. Probate law and practice – England – History – 17th century.
    I. Title
    346.4'2054'09032–dc23

Library of Congress Cataloging-in-Publication Data
Bonfield, Lloyd, 1949–
    Devising, dying and dispute : probate litigation in early modern England / Lloyd Bonfield.
        p. cm.
    Includes bibliographical references and index.
    ISBN 978–1–4094–3427–6 (hardcover : alk. paper)
    (ebook) 1. Probate law and practice – England – History – 17th century. 2. Wills – England – History – 17th century.
    I. Title.
    KD1518.B66 2012
    346.4205'2–dc23   2011044378

ISBN 13: 978-1-138-11705-1 (pbk)
ISBN 13: 978-1-4094-3427-6 (hbk)

Contents

List of Tables

Preface

This book has been 'a long time coming.' Its genesis was in an observation by my M.A. supervisor, later colleague and friend, Professor Henry Horwitz who, to paraphrase, remarked – you teach modern wills, why not look at will contests in the past? The records of the Prerogative Court of Canterbury are extensive; they would provide evidence for an interesting study in social, economic and legal history. Indeed. A decade and a half later I am able to offer this volume. The delay can be explained by the usual academic laments: too many courses to teach, too many exams to grade, too many committee meetings to attend, too many administrative chores to shoulder. To that I can add the unique challenge of living in New Orleans: too many hurricanes. Progress was impeded by numerous storms: Georges and Ivan and Lily and Ike and, of course, Katrina. Multiple back-ups were generated that later required reconciliation; lost notes needed to be reclaimed. Academic and climactic challenges aside, both the shear mass of documentation and the intellectual challenge of presenting effectively law to historians and history to lawyers was for me a daunting task. On one level, the endeavour should be straightforward: lawyers have respect for the past, and historians realize how important it is to understand the law. In practice, however, the disciplinary divide is not so easily broached. This volume is my modest offering.

Many conferences and colleagues have borne the burden of boredom and respectfully listened to presentations and read all or parts of this volume. Chapters of this volume were presented at the annual meetings of the American Society for Legal History and the Social Science History Association. Another helpful venue for developing a presentation strategy was Professor William Nelson's Golieb seminar at New York University Law School where the multitude struggled with pre- and post- Katrina versions of the work. I'd like particularly to thank Bill's own unflagging efforts to make sense of the morass, and those of my New York Law School colleagues who regularly participate, Professors Bill LaPiana and Richard Bernstein. Professor Tom Green read the manuscript twice, and while the evidence never said quite enough for him, his perceptions on what could be teased out of the documents were invaluable. My former Tulane colleague, Professor Felice Batlan, read many chapters, and I thank her for making me understand more, though perhaps not enough, about gender and power-relations past and present.

Continuity and Change has been an endeavour that has governed much of my academic life for over a quarter-century. It has also provided me with enduring friendships. My Founding Co-editor of *Continuity and Change*, Richard Wall, sadly gone, patiently honed his legal history skills on various versions of chapters, as did our Founding Associate Editor, Professor (now Dean) Larry Poos, and his successor, Professor Phillipp Schofield. Whatever Richard perused Beatrice Moring also read; I am certain her insightful remarks were incorporated into his now-cherished scribbles. Maureen Street, *Continuity and Change*'s long-suffering copy editor, read the entire storm-ridden text, pencil in hand and, as she has always done, insisted that thoughts flow logically and grammatically. Thanks to one and all.

As my current dean Rick Matasar reminds my colleagues frequently, we conduct our research largely at the expense of our students. My two academic homes, Tulane Law School and New York Law School, have both generously supported this mission with sabbaticals, summer grants and travel stipends. I was also fortunate enough to be honored with a John Simon Guggenheim Fellowship which allowed me a year in the then Public Records Office, now the National Archive.

To teach and write about death and the property transmission that it occasions is not always an agreeable task. If not present at the onset, which in my case it was, a certain degree of moroseness invades the recesses of the psyche. The support of my family, my wife Adriana and my daughter Lisa, in bearing with a difficult individual obsessed with the deaths and estates of others he never knew was invaluable. My mother passed away during the course of the project. From the very beginning of my career as a lawyer-historian, her confidence in my ability and memories of her own determination has sustained me. One supportive woman in a life is more than one can expect; I have been blessed with three to whom I gratefully dedicate this work.

Finally, those engaged in archival research lead a decidedly solitary life. One is never more alone than when seated in the reading room of any archive, let alone, the mighty National Archive. Sadly, it is no more salubrious to while away countless hours in Kew than it was in the neo-gothic tomb at Chancery Lane. To deal with the inherent loneliness, I purchased for a pound in Shaftesbury in Dorset a small hand-carved wooden English sparrow, improbably called Carlo. He has been my constant companion and 'best buddy' ever since, joining me on my transatlantic expeditions. He is witty, urbane, intelligent, even-tempered, shares my passion for micro-brews, and what's best, we hardly ever disagree. I thank him for his company. A 'polite and industrious' fellow, he is already at work on another project.

List of Cases

Introduction

Devising, Dying, and Dispute
in Early Modern England

Introduction

This is a book about devising, about dying, and finally, about dispute. Probate courts, then as now, generally focused on an individual's final legal acts. But through the evidence generated by the contested probates observed in my research, litigation over the particular validity of wills, this book is able to proceed further: it also chronicles the last words, and the last moments, of a group of now-deceased property owners. Narratives of living, will-making and dying are constructed by employing the Prerogative Court's record, and they shed light upon how its judges made the often difficult (though for the parties involved crucial) choice between will validity and will nullification. Because these documents depict deaths, the disposition of estates and, above all, the disputes that wills engendered, much can be learned from them about property law, and about the interplay between law and society in past time.

A book that focuses upon death presents some obvious drawbacks: this is not a happy narrative. It is written at a time when the sudden demise of individuals is commonplace and seems even mundane. Recent events, from terrorism to tsunami, have reminded us that death can strike suddenly and unexpectedly, leaving individuals with insufficient time to settle their worldly affairs soberly and with deliberation.[1] So it was for many of the players whose passing came to the attention of the Prerogative Court of Canterbury in the late seventeenth century. Unhappily, the mortality portrayed in the court record did not amount to what contemporaries described as the 'good death,' a proposition that is perhaps questionable to the twentieth-first-century Western mind.[2] The will-makers whose last words and acts are considered here did not die in the dignified manner of James I, or at least not in the stylized version that has come down to us thanks to

---

[1] In fact will-making seems to be on the rise as a result of the attack on the World Trade Center. 'Jolted by September 11, Many Rush to Make Wills,' *New York Times*, December 13, 2001. New York Region.

[2] For a discussion of the 'good death,' see Ralph Houlbrooke, *Death, Religion and the Family in England, 1480–1750* (Oxford, 1998), ch. 7.

the artistic mastery of Rubens who, slightly earlier in time, painted the monarch's passing in the center oval in the ceiling of the Banqueting Hall in the Palace of Whitehall.[3] Our will-makers were not kings nor did they depart this life flanked by angels. Rather, the court records reveal far more grim deaths, as in reality was James's own, the product of debilitating and painful illness, with what passed for 'medical science' offering very little in the way of relief. Those who clustered around the unfortunate souls who were about to pass on were hardly angels; indeed, they often seem to have been more interested in securing the payment of debts owed to them, and ensuring themselves an adequate legacy, than in comforting the unhappy person soon to be dispatched. The narratives presented in the following pages are therefore harrowing, but they are informative, and they shed light on a multitude of themes in social and in legal history.

The Historical Moment Observed: Property Law Theory in Transition

The vignettes of dying that emerge from the legal record provide a unique opportunity to view a variety of themes located on the disciplinary divide between legal and social history. For through the lens of devising, dying and dispute, this book observes the impact of two fundamental legal changes that came about during the late seventeenth century: first, an alteration in the manner in which property was defined; and second, a change in the requirements mandated in order to transmit property. Of course, in most societies law is in an ongoing process of revision: any historian focusing upon a particular culture and era may generally argue comfortably that the society under his or her observation is one in transition, but for historians of seventeenth-century England the claim for legal change during the period is more easily substantiated. A lot transpired: after all, the monarchy was removed and then restored, and in a scant dozen years. The English Revolution, whether it was launched over religion or the balance of political power between monarch and subject, could not, and did not, leave the law unchanged, because law was crucial to the debate over both, and indeed to other revolutionary discourse, and therefore was integral to the underlying conflict.

This volume is not a comprehensive study of law in the run-up to the civil war, and its aftermath, or in those years in between when 'the world was turned

---

3   In the 'Apotheosis of James I,' the dying king is lifted majestically heavenward surrounded by angels. I owe this reference to remarks made in lecture by Professor Neil Shipley who introduced me to early modern English history as an undergraduate. I have been drawn to the masterwork ever since then.

upside down,' though that story has not yet been fully told.[4] Rather my concern is more targeted; I focus upon a fiefdom in law's kingdom fondly known as property law and, in particular, the ability to devise personal property by will in the second half of the seventeenth century. The law of property, itself an 'alterable social institution,'[5] is a major player in the narrative, as it was during the Revolution.[6] I argue that the notion of property experienced one of its most significant alterations during the period, a transition that had a considerable effect on testamentary disposition at the time.

This movement can be illustrated by the changing definition of property during the period. Decades ago, G.R. Aylmer examined law dictionaries printed in the seventeenth and early eighteenth centuries and noted a transition in the later seventeenth century from what might be termed property law's 'feudal' underpinnings to more modern Lockean ones.[7] Early seventeenth-century treatments of the law first noted that a property right was a right in a thing 'which is in no way depending upon any other mans courtesie,' but they go on to indicate that such dominion could not exist in land, because all lands in the realm were held of the crown. By the end of the century, however, the feudal connotation of real property (all lands held of the crown) disappeared, and the term was defined more broadly, with ownership rights unqualified: property was the 'highest' right in a thing, coupled with the holder's ability to defend 'Life, Liberty, and Estate' by a legal action if that right was violated.

What Aylmer's discussion curiously omits is the very dangerous conversation over the definition of property rights that engaged radicals during the Revolution, and that must have inspired, at least in part, the transition towards embracing individualism within the definition of property.[8] Much discussion in the pamphlet literature of the period was devoted to ownership rights. Gerrard Winstanley, perhaps the most prolific of the revolutionary writers, is frequently

---

[4]   C.W. Brooks, *Law, Politics and Society in Early Modern England* (Cambridge, 2008) is an admirable recent attempt to grapple with these issues. I recognize that in my treatment of property law theory and its link with will-making and probate in these next few pages, I am open to the charge that I have said both too much and too little about the connection between property law and inheritance practice. My suggestion here is simply that a study of probate litigation that commences after the Restoration is defensible because fundamental notions about the nature of property ownership had been challenged and rebuffed.

[5]   The characterization of Andrew Reeve in his *Property* (Atlantic Highlands, NJ, 1986), p. 39.

[6]   Christopher Hill, *The Intellectual Origins of the English Revolution* (Oxford, 1997), p. 89 and ch. 5.

[7]   G.E. Aylmer, 'The meaning and definition of property in seventeenth-century England,' *Past and Present*, vol. 86, (1980) pp. 87–97.

[8]   See Christopher Hill, *The World Turned Upside Down* (New York, 1972), especially ch. 5.

dubbed a 'communist' by modern historians, for maintaining that all property should be held as common stock.[9] He was not alone in this radical view, and the collectivist ideas of property rights that were mooted were dangerous to the interests of the traditional propertied class. It is thus not difficult to understand why the victorious elite would want to adopt a more stridently individualistic definition of property upon the Restoration: it made explicit that which they believed was implicit.[10]

Linked ideologically with the proposed common ownership of land, a heightened sense of what has been termed 'self-ownership' also emerged in revolutionary thought. Unlike collectivist property ownership, this concept survived the Restoration and became merged into the contemporary understanding of property rights.[11] It was comprised of two intertwined strands: the spiritual and the secular. Much of the religious dispute, both before and during the Revolution, revolved around liberty of conscience: the right of persons to define their own religious precepts without the interference of others, particularly the state. This theme is frequently expressed in the pamphlet literature.[12] But self-ownership also entailed secular rights: to manage one's own productive capacity, itself deemed to be a property right, and to deal with its fruits free of the will of others.[13] Combined with the expanding notions of property ownership, the concept of self-ownership was exceedingly dangerous to the propertied classes during the Interregnum.

While the mantra of liberty of conscience did not survive the Restoration, self-ownership did. It emerged, for example, as a dominant theme in John Locke's treatment of property in his *Two Treatises of Government*.[14] His writings reveal much about the link between self-ownership and freedom of disposition of property in the late seventeenth-century psyche. In Locke's view, law existed to 'preserve and enlarge freedom,' with personal rights conflated with property rights. A person had the right to manage both his person and his productive

---

[9]   See George H. Sabine (ed.), *The Works of Gerrard Winstanley* (Ithaca, 1941), pp. 2–6.

[10]   While historians have perceived evidence of this 'individualistic' nature of property rights in England as early as the Middle Ages, its extent remains a matter of debate. See Alan Macfarlane, *The Origins of English Individualism* (Oxford, 1978). The precise language of late-seventeenth-century property discourse, however, left little room for doubt. Ownership of property was intrinsically individualistic.

[11]   Laura Brace, *The Idea of Property in the Seventeenth Century* (Manchester, 1998), pp. 1–6.

[12]   Hill, *The World Turned Upside Down*, ch. 5.

[13]   C.B. Macpherson, *The Political Theory of Possessive Individualism: Hobbes to Locke* (Oxford, 1962), pp. 142–53.

[14]   Ian Shapiro (ed.), *Two Treatises of Government and a Letter Concerning Toleration* (New Haven, 2003).

capacity, and to deal with them free of the will of others; Locke wrote that an individual should be able to 'dispose and order as he lists his actions, possessions and his whole property ... and not to be subject to the arbitrary will of another.'[15]

The theme of free will is related to, and indeed provides the backdrop for, Locke's discussion of inheritance, in which freedom to control the devolution of property was linked to self-ownership. But this consideration created a conundrum: in order to protect individualistic rights in property, some members of society had to be deprived of their rights of disposition in their material estate. Locke reasoned as follows. Property owners have by law broad powers of free disposition. He wrote that 'a father may dispose of his own possessions as he pleases.'[16] But the right to do so was limited, and vested only in those to whom God gave 'understanding.' Such individuals had the 'freedom of will' to dispose of their property according to the procedures set out by law. Yet Locke noted that not all persons were competent; some lacked 'sufficient understanding' and thus with respect to property were 'not to have any will.'[17] He placed property owners without capacity in two camps: those under the control of others and those who had once had reason but somehow lost it. He discussed each group in turn. First, those under the will of others:

> But if, through defects that may happen out of the ordinary course of Nature, any one comes not to such a degree of reason wherein he might be supposed capable of knowing the law, and so living within the rules of it, he is never capable of being a free man, he is never loose to the disposure of his own will ... because he is under the government of others.[18]

He then placed in a second group idiots and lunatics, who 'for the present cannot possibly have the use of right reason to guide themselves.'[19] Thus to protect free disposition it needed to be removed from the mentally deficient who were unable to exercise it rationally; their wills must be annulled, and their property should pass by the pattern of intestate succession set out by law.

---

[15]   Ibid., II, sec. 57.

[16]   Ibid., II, sec. 65. Locke's distain for primogeniture is well known (*Two Treatises*, I, sec. 91; see also James Tully, *A Discourse on Property: John Locke and his adversaries* (Cambridge, 1980), pp. 133–140). In his discussion of parental duties, Locke focused on the mutual support obligations that bound parent and child, sometimes suggesting that children have present rights in parental property (*Two Treatises*, I, secs. 88–90).

[17]   Ibid., II, sec. 58. The coincidence of terms, the word 'will' signifying both volition, and a testamentary act, should not be forgotten.

[18]   Ibid., II, sec. 60.

[19]   Ibid., II, sec. 60.

These two categories of persons – those under the control of others and the mentally infirm – were both denied self-ownership in this emerging rights-based, individualistic property regime. It is not by coincidence that these unfortunate souls will figure prominently in the testamentary litigation studied here. The newly-forged individualistic gloss on property rights made it even more imperative for probate courts to struggle with assessing the mental capabilities of will-makers, and to ponder Locke's conundrum, consciously or otherwise, when the wills of those who were alleged to be mentally deficient came before the court. It was the business of probate courts to remove freedom of disposition from those who were not competent to exercise it.

Their task was rendered even more difficult in the late seventeenth century, the historical moment observed in this study, for another reason: this was the time of the beginnings of the scientific study of mental illness. In his seminal study, Keith Thomas has argued that the period was one in which religion and magic could no longer provide adequate explanations for individual disease or other misfortune, and when the mystical was giving way to rationalism and science.[20] And so it was with mental illness. Michael MacDonald has documented that the repudiation of 'supernatural explanations' for 'distracted' minds was yielding to secular diagnosis and treatment.[21] Accordingly, physicians were studying, and attempting to treat, the mental diseases that had hitherto been in the domain of clerics and astrologers.[22]

To be sure, the movement towards the rationale approach to mental disease was incomplete. Even at the close of the period under study, John Brydall of Lincoln's Inn, in his book *Non Compos Mentis*, could still opine that a mental disease he called 'furor' was caused by the 'overheating' or 'combustion' of 'animal spirits,' and that lunatics had the misfortune of being born during the 'Interlune,' so that 'if the Moon be ill-sett ... it causeth Men to be subject, either to Convulsions, to Lunacy, or to the Falling sickness,' at which time their testamentary capacity should be removed.[23] Few 'distracted' or melancholy English folk actually received treatment, and only scant numbers were deprived of their legal capacity during their lives through formally constituted 'commissions of lunacy.' They went about their business free from legal constraints, and they also made their wills.

---

[20]   *Religion and the Decline of Magic* (New York, 1971), pp. 13–14, 643–4.

[21]   Michael MacDonald, *Mystical Bedlam: madness, anxiety and healing in seventeenth-century England* (Cambridge, 1981), pp. 10–12.

[22]   This point will be demonstrated below by reference to a collection of tracts on mental disease compiled in Richard Hunter and Ida MacAlpine (eds.), *Three Hundred Years of Psychiatry: 1535–1860* (London, 1963).

[23]   John Brydall, *Non Compos Mentis: or the law relating to natural fools, mad -folks and lunatic persons* (London, 1700), pp. 53, 94–5.

But when their testamentary acts were offered for probate, their conduct might be alleged by contestants of the will as grounds for denying validity to a will. Through observing these causes, ones that alleged a lack of capacity and undue influence, we may attempt to discern whether the emerging trend towards more rational views of mental illness influenced the court in its decisions.

The Authenticity of Legal Acts: the Statute of Frauds

In addition to ascertaining the impact on property law of these two intellectual trends – transitions in concepts of ownership rights and in perceptions of mental diseases – this book also focuses on a change in the law in microcosm by examining the 'Act for the prevention of Frauds and Perjures' adopted by Parliament in 1677.[24] The Statute of Frauds is arguably the most significant piece of English legislation governing the transmission of property ever adopted,[25] because its guiding principle, novel in the late seventeenth century though commonplace in our own time, was the insistence upon formality in the transfer of property by requiring a written document for particular types of transactions to be binding.

The adoption of the statute by Parliament comports well with theories of the modernization of the law. It is perhaps the most important 'way station' in the progress in English law from an oral legal culture to one based upon the written word, a transition so aptly described by Jack Goody in his gloss on Sir Henry Maine's progress from 'status to contract.'[26] By the 1670s, Parliament no longer perceived that a scant handful of statutes supported by judge-made law was sufficient to deal with the increasing complexity of property transactions constructed by a burgeoning segment of the legal profession specializing in land conveyancing. Likewise, the growing importance of personal wealth prompted Parliament to intervene to tidy the process by which the church courts governed the testamentary transmission of personal property. With respect to the succession to both types of property, then, real and personal (land and chattels) Parliament must have believed that more formality was warranted, and set about to achieve it.

The modern lawyer will conclude that the statute only tinkered around the edges of reforming the law governing property transfer, both *inter vivos*

---

[24]   29 Car. II, c. 3 (1677), secs. 18–23.

[25]   Or at least most frequently rehearsed in our own day: no law student navigates the first year without acquaintance with the statute. Its notoriety should not, as we shall see, assume that the law achieved its ends.

[26]   Jack Goody, *The Logic of Writing and the Organization of Society* (Cambridge, 1986), pp. 147–58. Henry Maine's seminal work is *Ancient Law* (London and New York, 1864).

and testamentary. With respect to the transmission of personal property, the primary concern in this volume, Parliament was unwilling to remove the probate of wills and the administration of estates from the church courts, a step it took only in 1857.[27] Perhaps the elimination of ecclesiastical jurisdiction was too much linked in Parliament's collective psyche with the excesses of the Revolution and Interregnum, periods in which a revamp of probate jurisdiction was mooted but ultimately never came to fruition. Yet probate procedure *was* significantly revamped. The Statute of Frauds, which largely focused on land transfers, also included provisions on the validity of nuncupative (oral) wills of personal property. This marriage between the two hitherto separate fields has gone unnoticed by historians, but it has much to tell us about law reform in early modern England. Because the records of the most important probate court in the realm, the Prerogative Court of Canterbury, are unusually rich, I have marshaled them in considering whether the legislation governing wills of personalty was likely adopted in response (or at the very least was addressed) to vexing issues raised in probate litigation. Finally, I evaluate the statute's success in easing the court's load of troublesome cases.

Although the statute's efficacy may be doubted, not much more progress in setting out workable rules governing will validity has been made in the following three centuries. Indeed the modern wills and estates lawyer should find in these testamentary 'causes,' the term employed to connote will contests in the Prerogative Court, much that is familiar. Mental capacity and undue influence were, and remain, unending grist for the probate courts' mill; authenticity issues not dissimilar from the ones that surface in our causes are likewise raised in our own time.[28] Successive chapters discuss how the court came to grips with each legal issue in light of the emerging focus on self-ownership and the individualist cast of rights in property; the observed transition in medicine's approach to mental illness; and Parliament's concern for the authenticity of acts transmitting property rights.

A Social History of Will-Making and Will-Makers

In addition to the legal transitions mapped above, important social themes also have emerged from the exploration of probate litigation undertaken for

---

[27] 20 and 21 Vict., c. 77 (1857).

[28] The new millennium brought with it a flurry of scholarly articles on these age-old subjects in the English law reviews. See Roger Kerridge, 'Wills made in suspicious circumstances: the problem of the vulnerable testator,' *Cambridge Law Journal*, vol. 59 (2000), pp. 310–34, and Andrew Brokowki, 'Reforming section 9 of the Wills Act,' *Conveyancer and Property Lawyer*, (2000), pp. 31–42.

this volume. This is also a book about women and gender relations in late-seventeenth-century England. Testamentary causes provide a multitude of unique insights into women as legal actors. In the first place, we can document women playing a direct role in the process of will-making and in testamentary litigation, as testatrixes and as parties to disputes. Women often played a vital part in the preparation of the wills of others, as advisors, scriveners and witnesses. Perhaps more crucially, however, they also often found themselves in the church court as witnesses to will execution ceremonies, to the mental state of the will-maker, to family relations between property holder and heir, and to the oft-times crucial issue of whether a couple had been legally joined in marriage. Consequently, women were key players in the process of will-making and probate, empowered and indeed powerful, in a position to play crucial roles in determining the outcome of testamentary litigation. Of course, they did not decide whether an individual will was valid. That was a matter for the court. But they did provide much of the evidence on the formulation and execution of particular wills to the judge who did, because women were frequently present when wills were contrived and executed.

In addition, this is a book about families and the law, and about family law. The disputes observed here most often occurred between and amongst family members. Indeed a substantial number of the disputes involve what in modern legal systems is clumped under the term 'domestic relations law.' The Prerogative Court was called upon to consider the validity of a particular marriage, whether family members had engaged in domestic violence, and whether guardians had adequately cared for their wards.

The Narrative

The shear bulk of the evidence exhumed and the multifaceted arguments set out in the succeeding chapters create a rich story of devising, dying, and dispute. Many of the causes raise multiple themes discerned above, and the themes themselves are interrelated. We begin with a description of 'the culture of will-making' in the seventeenth century. This culture – how English men and women actually went about their testamentary business – was governed by what Peter Laslett called 'noumenal normative rules,' 'programmatic principles embedded in collective attitudes.'[29] These social mores were fostered by taboos surrounding will-making, fears that inclined individuals to avoid undertaking testamentary

---

[29]   Peter Laslett, 'Demographic and microstructural history in relation to human adaptation: reflections on newly established evidence,' in D.J. Horner (ed.), *How Humans Adapt: a biocultural odyssey* (Washington, 1983), pp. 343–70.

acts until the last possible moment, when they were therefore *in extremis*. Scant attention has been devoted to probate litigation, and this study demonstrates the unique insight that conflicts over wills can provide into the complicated 'culture of will-making.' Chapter 1 both synthesizes the impressive quantity and quality of the secondary literature on will-making, and supplements it with evidence about will-making teased from the litigation studied in the Prerogative Court. It answers a number of questions that historians have asked about will-making: about what proportion of English folk wrote wills; for what reasons they did so; and how they undertook their testamentary acts. The conclusion that emerges from my study of the Canterbury testamentary causes is that by the last quarter of the seventeenth century, the law of wills and ecclesiastical court supervision of probate must have seemed to Parliament unsatisfactory and inefficient, as untidy as were the deaths reported in the causes, and certainly in need of reform.

The narrative then turns to probate jurisdiction in England, and to the reforms proposed during the Interregnum and the Restoration, in particular, the Statute of Frauds. Thereafter the legal issues presented by the litigants during the period 1660–1700 are tabulated to demonstrate that the Parliamentary reforms were calculated to resolve the problems that plagued the court. Yet this attempt at legislative tidying appears to have addressed only a modest proportion of the types of disputes that cluttered the court's docket. The testamentary causes observed here illustrate that the provisions on the validity of oral wills, though drafted by the Prerogative Court's long-serving judge, Sir Leoline Jenkins, met with only mixed success. Causes raising questions about the authenticity of oral and written wills plagued the court even after the statute was adopted. Viewed from the perspective of probates judges, the process of will-making must have seemed haphazard, and the resultant documents were often of dubious validity. But the process also empowered them. After all, whether a will was admitted or denied probate turned on the narrative that the judge created from scraps of evidence produced by the parties. Parliamentary reform and its effects, as well as the exercise of judicial power, are thus observed in this volume.

Light having been shed on the issue of the link between the Statute of Frauds and the testamentary causes, the two broad legal themes discussed above will be addressed through the litigation. First, how the court responded to Locke's conundrum is considered. My focus turns to the causes in which a lack of mental capacity and coercion were alleged. Thereafter, attention shifts to authenticity issues that are raised, in order to ascertain the extent to which the statute actually lessened the court's burden when wills of doubtful appearance and provenance came before it.

Having addressed the legal themes, I investigate three areas of concern to social historians that emerge from the litigation: marriage, family discord, and the role of women in the culture of will-making. The value of the evidence for furthering the debate on the legal role of women is remarkable. In their synthetic work on *Women in Early Modern England*, Sara Mendelson and Patricia Crawford sum up their agenda with a single question: what was women's experience of life and the world in early modern England?[30] This study supplies some answers. First, the records confirm the view of Amy Erickson that, while seventeenth-century law treated men and women (in particular married women) differently, women participated in the process of property transmission and sought to manipulate the law in their own interest.[31]

Second, historians have assumed rather than demonstrated that early modern England's lax marriage-formation law gave rise to disputes over property.[32] The causes observed here illustrate that the issue of marriage validity was raised with considerable frequency in the Prerogative Court. The records provide unique insight into the circumstances in which so-called 'clandestine marriages' occurred, how they were alleged, and how litigants attempted to prove or to deny the validity of an alleged union.

Finally, historians have unearthed scant evidence of family discord in early modern England.[33] Because the pattern of testamentary disposition of property is often an indication of familial concord or conflict, testamentary disputes provide useful windows into the familial relations of will-makers. The causes allow the historian to probe the darker side of family relations in the past, and they demonstrate that while some testators during our period engaged in verbal abuse of both their spouses and their children, little record of actual physical violence remains.

---

[30] (Oxford, 1999), p. 2.

[31] Amy Erickson, *Women and Property in Early Modern England* (London, 1993), Introduction.

[32] The literature is surveyed in the introduction to Chapter 10, below.

[33] Even Lawrence Stone, who agreed with Thomas Hobbes' verdict in *Leviathan* (London, 1651), Chapter 13, paragraph 9 that life in this period was 'nasty, brutish and short' (Hobbes actually prefaced those words with the more even more despondent 'solitary' and 'poor'), was unable to find much evidence of familial violence in contemporary diaries and court records. Lawrence Stone, *The Family, Sex and Marriage in England 1500-1800* (London, 1977), p. 223. More recent work by Elizabeth Foyster, *Marital Violence* and Joanne Bailey, *Unquiet Lives: marriage and marriage breakdown in England, 1660–1800* (Cambridge, 2003) has rethought questions of spousal violence. See the discussion below, Chapter 11, and Macfarlane, *The Origins of English Individualism*, pp. 152–4.

The Timeless Struggle between Generations

Litigation, like that observed in this volume, is a process that places linen, dirty or otherwise, on public display; disputes shed much light upon the human condition in the past and reveal aspects of the private lives of the players who were involved. In my careful study of the records of the Prerogative Court, the timeless struggle between the generations over property is revealed, illuminating the counterpoised interests of property owners and those whom society regards as (as wills and trust lawyers elegantly christen) the 'natural objects of their bounty.' An interplay amongst a variety of social and legal norms is revealed: the strongly held regard for freedom of disposition mandated by the emerging rights-based understanding of property; the context in which dying and will-making occurred; the demands imposed by familial obligations; and the nature of family relations, be they hostile or affective.

This volatile mix raised problems for those lawmakers who might have liked to fashion a rational framework for rules governing testation, because the countervailing interests of will-maker, legatee, and heir made it difficult to determine whether reform was necessary and if so precisely how the law should be changed. Thus (to use colloquial phraseology) even if the system was 'broke,' it was not clear how should Parliament 'fix' it. The narrative below observes, through the testamentary causes, both the demands and the limits that societal norms place on the law that governs property transmission.

And the Timeless Nature of the Law

This study, although it is a work of legal history, has some modern relevance. A book that focuses upon litigation is also a study of the exercise of power, and in particular the exercise of judicial power. It is axiomatic, though simplistic, to assert that judges apply law; they do not make it. While that principle may be qualified by lawyers who study other areas of law, it certainly is misplaced in the context of seventeenth-century probate. Probate court judges were powerful men. The rather malleable law governing will-making, even though altered by Parliament, bestowed considerable latitude on them in disposing of contentious estates. Whether an individual satisfied the mental and physical requirements for making a valid will depended upon the narrative of a particular will-making scenario that had to be pieced together by the judge from the assertions of the parties and the testimony of witnesses. Ultimately, it was that process, selecting proffered fact from alleged fancy, which steered the judge to a verdict on a will's validity. For, as we shall see, the omission of a requirement or two was not always deemed fatal to a will if, and though only if, the narrative constructed led the judge to the conclusion that the now-deceased really did want (or perchance even should have wanted) his or her otherwise ambiguous act to stand as a will. Perhaps because of its difficult charge, the Prerogative Court seems to have been very lenient in applying the rules regarding will validity. Indeed, the court only very infrequently relied upon legal technicality to find a will invalid. The impression I am left with, after struggling with the evidence, is that the court was less concerned with form and formality than it was with facilitating testamentary intentions; if the court was persuaded that a testamentary act represented the volition of the will-maker, it was prepared to admit it to probate. More frequently than not, what the court strained to do was to figure out what actually had transpired, rather than to scrutinize the will to determine whether it adhered to formalities.

That approach has a modern ring. Although English law has remained faithful to a literal interpretation of the formalities of due execution embodied in the Wills Act, the former colonies have strayed.[34] American and Canadian probate law (influenced by Australian law) seems inclined to return to these roots.[35] In a recent 'revolution' nearly as profound as the one occasioned by the Statute of Frauds, and later by its successor which focused more explicitly on testamentary acts, the Wills Act of 1837,[36] judges are granted increased power to validate wills. The formalities of execution for wills first mandated by the Statute of Frauds have been relaxed by statute and by common law, through the adoption of the dispensing power for harmless error in the American Uniform Probate Code[37] and the application of the contract doctrine of substantial compliance to the formalities of will execution.[38] What goes around comes around: the effect of these reforms is once again to empower modern probate judges (as, it is argued here, were seventeenth-century brethren similarly enabled) by allowing them to go beyond merely determining whether a will conforms to statutory formalities. These so-called 'remedial' doctrines permit modern courts to construct a narrative of will-execution through the testimony of witnesses, to determine whether the document offered for probate reflects the deceased's testamentary

---

[34] The Law Reform Committee's 22nd Report, *The Making and Revocation of Wills* cmnd. 7902, 1980 considered and then rejected substantial compliance.

[35] Inspired by experiences in other jurisdictions that derived their law from England. See J. Garth Miller, 'Substantial compliance and the execution of wills,' *International and Comparative Law Quarterly*, vol. 36, pp. 559–88.

[36] 7 Will. IV and 1 Vict., c. 26 (1837).

[37] Sec. 2–503.

[38] For a discussion see John Langbein, 'Substantial compliance with the wills Act,' *Harvard Law Review*, vol. 88, (1975) pp. 489–532; and the Restatement (Third) of Property, Wills and Other Donative Transfers sec 3.3 (1999).

desires. Thus this 'modern' process has a 'seventeenth-century ring,' and this study provides a salutary reminder of some of the potential consequences of these modern reforms.

Chapter 1
The 'Culture of Will-Making' in Early Modern England

Introduction

Ours is a narrative based upon wills probated in the Prerogative Court of Canterbury from the Restoration of the Stuart monarchy in 1660 until the end of the seventeenth century. Its mission is twofold: first, to observe how and upon what grounds wills were executed and disputed, and second, to marshal court documentation to illuminate social and familial relations. But before litigation over will validity can be examined, we must consider the document that gave rise to the disputes studied – the will – and grapple with a triad of fundamental questions about will-making during the period. Which individuals wrote wills? How did they do so? For what reasons did they undertake their testamentary acts?

The answers to these questions shed light upon the 'culture of will-making' that obtained during the period. This culture – the societal backdrop against which wills were made – and the contemporary process of testation, together comprise a collective narrative that can be reconstructed from the observation of a large number of separate and discrete legal acts. The conduct of individuals can be explored through the litigation, and further understanding of it provides crucial insights into the process of property transmission in past time. The litigation observed, I would argue, demonstrates that this 'culture of will-making' gave rise to numerous dubious testamentary acts which in turn spawned disputes. The enactment of the Statute of Frauds in 1677 was intended to create a very different culture (though it did not fully accomplish this), a more orderly one that should have produced fewer problematic wills.[1] Its mixed success will be examined in subsequent chapters.

---

[1] Some modern commentators on the law of wills argue that a set of clear formalities of execution encourages will-making because property owners can rest easy knowing that their property will pass according to their will if they adhere to the formalities. See the classic discussion of A.G. Gulliver and C.J. Tilson, 'Classification of gratuitous transfers,' *Yale Law Journal*, vol. 51 (1941), pp. 1–10, and my own 'Reforming the Requirements for

Historians have provided some qualified answers to this triad of questions on contemporary will-making, thanks largely to the pioneering work and active encouragement of Joan Thirsk, who, almost a half-century ago issued a summons to social historians to dash to the archives in order to exploit these hitherto ignored documents.[2] Indeed, so successful was her plea that a collected volume of research papers that rely upon probate records produced by a broad array of courts has been published.[3] Most of the scholarship using probate documents, however, focuses upon records produced in undisputed probates: upon the wills, inventories, and accounts routinely produced in uncontentious testamentary successions.[4] Scant attention has been focused on the wills and administrations that were contested,[5] and this is unfortunate, for the simple reason that disputed wills produced mounds of evidence illuminating how and why they were drafted and executed. Court in contested probates documents are therefore crucial to understanding the impetus behind will-making, and the context in which wills were made. This study therefore aims to fill a significant historical gap in understanding the crucial process of intergenerational property transmission in early modern England.

How Many Englishmen and Women Wrote Wills?

Those who wish to study wills in early modern England are not at a loss for sources. Estimates for the number of wills that survive for the early modern

---

Due Execution of Wills: Some Guidance from the Past,' *Tulane Law Review*, vol. 70 (1995), pp. 1893–1920.

  [2] 'Unexplored sources in local records,' *Archives*, vol. vi (1963) 29, pp. 8–12. Peter Spufford has produced an excellent 'history' of the labors of antiquarians and genealogists to make wills accessible. 'A printed catalogue of the names of testators' in G.H. Martin and Peter Spufford (eds.), *The Records of a Nation* (Woodbridge, 1990), pp. 167–86.

  [3] Tom Arkell, Nesta Evans, and Nigel Goose (eds.), *When Death Do Us Part: understanding and interpreting the probate records of early modern England* (Oxford, 2000). It also contains a comprehensive 20-page bibliography of publications whose documentary sources include wills.

  [4] Christopher Marsh, 'In the Name of God? Will-making and Faith in Early Modern England,' in Martin and Spufford (eds.), *The Records of a Nation*, pp. 217–26; and Ralph Houlbrooke, *Death, Religion and the Family in England 1480–1750* (Oxford,1998), an extension of his section in his *Church Courts and the People during the English Reformation* (Oxford, 1979), pp. 89–116.

  [5] Like all historians, I stand on the shoulders of others. Both John Addy (*Death, Money, and the Vultures: inheritance and avarice 1660–1750* (London, 1992) and Jane Cox (*Hatred Pursued beyond the Grave; tales of our ancestors from the London church courts* (London, 1993) pp. 67–113.) have found themselves steeped in probate litigation.

period in England vary widely. Using the nominative listing of will-makers found in the Index Library volumes, Motoyasu Takahashi counts over 750,000 registered wills for the sixteenth and seventeenth centuries.[6] Peter Spufford regards this number as a serious underestimate, reckoning that upwards of 1,750,000 wills were registered, while Amy Erickson, using a different time-span, the mid-sixteenth to the mid-eighteenth centuries, sets her tally at over 2 million.[7] Whatever number proves to be the most accurate guess for a nation that numbered about 4½ million souls, suffice it to say that probated wills of the early modern period are not in short supply.[8]

Two questions come to mind immediately if we are to place these stark numbers in context. The first is, about what percentage of the population made wills during the period, and the second is whether that proportion was increasing or declining. Unhappily, neither calculation is a straightforward one to make. In order to compute the percentage of those who died leaving wills, deaths in parish registers must be linked with entries in will registers. To undertake this exercise requires having both reliable will and parish registers for a particular probate jurisdiction.[9] But even where these documents survive, other aspects of the early modern probate regime render the calculations problematic. In the first place, the geographical extent of probate jurisdictions did always not correspond to single parishes with easily recoverable age-specific mortality data.[10] Moreover, some individuals who died in any parish doubtless had a will probated in another jurisdiction, because their property was located elsewhere, or because the extent of their estate satisfied the jurisdictional requirements of another, and perhaps

---

[6]   Arkell, Goose and Evans, 'Wills as an Historical Source,' p. 39.

[7]   A.L. Erickson, *Women and Property in Early Modern England* (London, 1993). Peter Spufford, 'A printed catalogue of the names of testators,' in Martin and Spufford (eds.), *The Records of a Nation*, p. 170.

[8]   Moreover, when the near inexhaustible supply of wills are exhausted, there are administrations of intestate estates to consider. According to J.S.W. Gibson, one administration was undertaken for every two wills probated during the period 1558–1600 in the Prerogative Court of Canterbury and in the Prerogative Court of York 1514–1680 as well as the Consistory Courts of Lincoln and of Chichester. *Wills and Where to Find Them* (Chichester, 1974), p. 2.

[9]   Local historians can attest to the proposition that even well documented sources have their inexplicable missing time spans. Even jurisdictions with efficient record-keeping, like the Prerogative Court of Canterbury, suffer from missing documentation, as I have learned in chasing down documents and entries that are mentioned in the record but do not seem to exist.

[10]   In an ideal world one would like to look at the trend in adult mortality in the probate jurisdiction, and more specifically consider the trend amongst males and widows, the two most likely groups of will-makers.

more 'prestigious,' probate court (like the Prerogative Court of Canterbury, the jurisdiction studied here).[11] Finally, calculations made from the will registers are based on probated wills rather than executed testamentary acts. Thus they may greatly underestimate the number of wills actually executed. Not all wills made were offered for probate, because the heirs, creditors, and executors of these wills might choose not to bother. Indeed, in a significant number of the causes observed here, probate was abandoned in mid-course, and the will was not proved.[12] In neither circumstance would notice of these wills appear in the probate registers.

Studies that have struggled with calculating the percentage of those dying testate suggest that, while the incidence of will-making clearly varied, the proportion of those whose wills were probated were lower than a third of those whose deaths were recorded in the corresponding parish register.[13] However, a third must be regarded an unusually high incidence of will-making, and was probably related to particular local factors, such as religious persuasion, wealth, or agricultural regime.[14] While Takahashi claims that about 18 percent of adults who died left wills that were probated,[15] a survey of the numerous extant local studies indicates that a more likely ratio might be around one in ten.[16]

Likewise, it is not an easy task to determine trends over time in the percentage of those dying who made wills. While it has been suggested that there was an increase in will-making in the seventeenth century, driven by increased economic

---

[11] See the discussion on this issue in the Appendix.

[12] Indeed, many of the wills in our sample did not proceed to sentence, and there is no record in the will registers. Of the 184 causes observed, 139 (75.5 percent) either proceeded to sentence, or the wills were noted as proved in the will registers; 45 (24.5 percent) disappear from the record prior to sentence and there is no indication in the will registers that these wills were probated.

[13] I rely here on the summary in Goose and Evans, 'Wills as an historical source,' pp. 46–7, and in Houlbrooke, *Death, Religion and the Family*, pp. 84–6.

[14] This figure is for Kirkby Lonsdale in Cumbria, where the Quaker influence is said to explain the high percentage of will-makers. See also the research of Sarah Harrison noted in S. Coppel, 'Wills and the community: a case study of Grantham,' in P. Riden (ed.), *Probate Records and the Local Community* (Gloucester, 1985), p. 78.

[15] Motoyasu Takahashi, 'The number of wills proved in the sixteenth and seventeenth centuries: graphs, with tables and commentary,' in Martin and Spufford (eds.), *The Records of a Nation*, p. 212.

[16] See for example the studies of Earls Colne (8 percent), Grantham (10 percent), Cambridge (12 percent) and Reading (10 percent) summarized in Goose and Evans, 'Wills as an Historical Source,' p. 45. For London, Jane Cox speculated that in the late seventeenth century about 2 percent of the population died leaving wills. *Affection Defying the Power of Death: wills, probate, and death duty records* (Birmingham, 1993), p. 9.

prosperity,[17] it is also necessary (in addition to respecting the above caveats) for the researcher to correct for demographic trends. Wills enrolled in the registers cannot merely be counted to determine the movement in rates of testation; population trends within the jurisdictional boundaries must be considered. If the number of wills probated increased by a quarter over a 50-year period but the number of recorded adult deaths rose similarly, the proportion of will-makers to those who died intestate would have remained constant, even though there are more extant wills.[18] With demographic trends in mind, Nigel Goose and Nesta Evans offer a crude aggregative comparison of population increase and will survival for the whole of England. They conclude that more wills per capita survive for the early seventeenth century than for the previous hundred years, but that the growth spurt in the ratio of will probates to adult deaths occurred before 1570.[19] Ralph Houlbrooke concurs, and believes that the percentage of will-makers may well have declined during the later seventeenth and eighteenth centuries as a growing proportion of the population had little or no property to bequeath, and as the ability of the church courts to compel probate diminished.[20] However, the overall stagnation or even decline in will-making was not evident in other probate jurisdictions. Indeed, there was a dramatic shift of business towards the Prerogative Court of Canterbury. According to Takahashi, the number of wills probated there doubled between 1620 and 1690, a period of relatively modest population increase.[21]

Why Did Englishmen and Women Write Wills?

The studies that calculate the extent of will-making thus indicate that relatively few early modern Englishmen and women died leaving wills. Assuming, as was probably the case, that the modest numbers cannot be attributed to the failure of executors or beneficiaries to probate wills that were made, other factors must

---

[17]   Addy, *Death, Money and the Vultures*, p. 12.

[18]   Adult mortality rose in the period 1611–1676, and then was constant until 1691 when it began to fall. E.A. Wrigley and R.S. Schofield, *The Population History of England 1541–1871: a reconstruction* (Cambridge, 1982), p. 236.

[19]   Goose and Evans, 'Wills as an historical source,' p. 40.

[20]   Houlbrooke, *Death, Religion, and the Family*, p. 85.

[21]   Takahashi, 'Number of wills,' pp. 198, 212. Admittedly, adult male deaths in England is a crude measure. The Prerogative Court of Canterbury was situated in London, and many of the wills probated were those of Londoners. Ideally, then, trends in London adult mortality would be a more useful index. On the other hand, many London deaths would have been of minors and those in service, both of whom were unlikely to leave wills. It is difficult to imagine that the numbers of propertied adult males doubled in the years 1620–90.

be considered: those that prompted some individuals to order their estate by will, while disinclining others to undertake the trouble and the expense of will-making. Four reasons may be offered to explain will-making: first, the desire to craft an individualized inheritance strategy; second, the exhortations of others, particularly clerics, to do so; third, for the avoidance of family discord; and finally, for the selection of an executor.

The Desire to Craft an Individualized Inheritance Strategy

One way of determining why some individuals left wills while others did not might be to consider the practical effects of dying without a will. In the absence of a will, the law resolved two of the above concerns regarding the devolution of the dead person's property, the first and the fourth: to whom it should pass; and who should supervise its disposition. Arguably, if an individual was content with the stipulated distribution and the administrator provided by law to wind up the estate, there was little incentive to bother with a will.[22] At least some property owners probably understood the pattern of disposition directed by the laws of descent, and decided to leave well enough alone. For example, when John Jennyns (one of the will-makers whose estate became embroiled in probate litigation in the Canterbury Prerogative Court) was pressed to make a will, it was alleged that he became angry and said, 'I have noe need to trouble myself or you about ye Settlement of my Estate. The law settles it for me and let it goe where it ought to goe (meaning his Brother) next heir at Law.'[23]

Not all property owners were as content with allowing the law of descent to take its course as was John Jennyns.[24] Indeed, historians generally agree that many property owners in England were inclined to follow their own minds rather than the default rules on the matter of inheritance.[25] If there is a single generalization that can stand about inheritance strategies fashioned during the period, it is that they defy generalization. For example, Keith Wrightson and David Levine

---

[22] 23 and 24 Car. II, c. 10 (1670).

[23] *Jennyns contra Jennyns*, Allegation, PROB 18/6/45.

[24] Although it was slightly more complex in practice, the Statute of Distributions (23 and 24 Car. II c. 10, sec. 3) directed that one-third of the personal estate of an individual pass to the surviving widow, and two-thirds to the children, the surviving heirs of a deceased child taking the ancestor's share by representation. If the intestate died without there being children or their representatives, one-half of the estate passed to the surviving widow and the remaining one-half to the next of kin. If the intestate had no widow, then the entire estate passed to his children and their representatives or to his next of kin.

[25] For a summary, see Lloyd Bonfield, 'Seeking connections between law and kinship in early modern England,' *Continuity and Change* vol. 24 (2009), pp. 49–82.

find a 'bewildering variety of inheritance strategies' in the village of Terling in the sixteenth and seventeenth centuries from their survey of its wills.[26] And the will was merely one vehicle for implementing intergenerational transfer; linking *inter vivos* transfers of copyhold land in manorial court rolls with bequests in wills would likely have illuminated even more complex inheritance strategies.[27]

Most research indicates, not unexpectedly, that individuals were more likely to write wills when their wealth was more extensive and their family responsibilities more complex. In Terling, it was the better-off males who tended to make wills, while the very poor did not.[28] Perhaps those men with more property wanted to 'customize' the division to be made between their widow and children, as well as the mix between or among children, rather than relying upon the pattern mandated by the particular local inheritance custom that controlled the descent of property. Wrightson and Levine assert that there was a tendency to use wills to equalize the shares of children where advancements to some children had already been made. Men in the lower-middle group tended to do so when they had unmarried children to endow, suggesting that they wanted to ensure that each child received some economic start in life.[29] While other studies confirm the link between wealth and testation, there is at least one that does not. In her pioneering work on Chippenham in Cambridgeshire, Margaret Spufford finds that it was the poor with family responsibilities, rather than the better-off, who disposed of what little they had by will.[30]

Gender was another variable in the mix in considering why some of the dying made wills to pass on their property while others did not. Women made wills far much less frequently than did men, and married women rarely made wills. At least in the eyes of the law, a married woman could not execute a will without the consent of her husband, permission that could be withdrawn until the point in time at which property was actually delivered to her executors after her death.[31] Mary Prior's work demonstrates that by the late seventeenth century

---

[26] Keith Wrightson and David Levine, *Poverty and Piety in an English Village: Terling 1525–1700* (Oxford, 1995), p. 95.

[27] In my 'Normative rules and property transmission, in Lloyd Bonfield, Richard Smith, and Keith Wrightson (eds.), *The World We have Gained* (Oxford, 1985), pp. 161–64, I stress the potential for life-time gifts of personal property from parents to their children, transfers that would likely escape probate records.

[28] Wrightson and Levine, *Terling*, p. 37.

[29] Their groups 3 and 4; Wrightson and Levine, *Terling*, pp. 94–9.

[30] For a summary see Goose and Evans, 'Wills as an historical source,' p. 44, and Houlbrooke, *Death, Religion, and the Family*, pp. 85–6.

[31] Henry Swinburne, *A Brief Treatise of Testaments and Last Wills* (Garland Reprint of 1590 edition, New York, 1978), pp. 83–6. The reason for this was simple – a married woman's person property became that of her husband upon marriage, and if he survived her,

consent was not infrequently given by husbands, though married women's wills amounted to well under 1 percent of all wills registered in the Prerogative Court of Canterbury.[32] Widows, on the other hand, figure rather more prominently in the record than do their married counterparts. A number of studies of probate registers of the sixteenth through the early eighteenth centuries place the proportion of widows' wills at around 20 percent of the total listed.[33] Widows found themselves in a pivotal role in the process of devolution, for their will was the final opportunity for the senior generation to pass on property to the successor generation, as the once nuclear family finally dissolved. If relative equality between the children was the overriding goal for most families, it was the death of the longer-living parent that would provide the final opportunity to achieve it, or indeed to realize an alternative inheritance strategy.

The Exhortations of Others

While it is tempting to attribute will-making to a desire on the part of property owners to fashion individualized inheritance strategies, it must be remembered that the will made directions other than about the disposition of property. Death occasioned the transmogrification of body and soul, as well as the passage of property; thus secular and spiritual concerns intersected at the moment of will-making. Before temporal matters were resolved in a will, religious ones were usually first addressed. In the opening passages of the document, the will-maker generally committed his or her soul and directed burial of the body. The former has captured the attention of historians, because many wills contained statements in which will-makers (or their scribes) offered detailed expositions upon the destiny that would await their souls.[34] Arguably, analysis of these

---

she could not 'give that away which was hers without the sufferance or graunt of the owner.' Some exceptions were noted. Perhaps the most significant was the property a married woman held as an executrix; if a widow served as executrix of her deceased husband, she could will that property even if she subsequently remarried.

[32]   Mary Prior, 'Wives and wills 1558–1700,' in John Chartres and David Hey, *English Rural Society, 1500–1800: essays in honour of Joan Thirsk* (Cambridge, 1990), pp. 201–25.

[33]   For a summary see Goose and Evans, 'Wills as an Historical Source,' pp. 46–7, and Houlbrooke, *Death, Religion, and Family*, p. 87. Erickson reckons that women, largely widows, executed about one in five of the wills probated in the seventeenth century. Erickson, *Women and Property*, pp. 204–5.

[34]   In this book, I have not offered my own analysis of the religious preferences of the will-makers whose wills were litigated because of the nature of the 'sample.' Ours is really too small and far too diverse a group. Most studies of the spiritual content of wills are much larger, and focus on a particular locale in which there is other evidence of the religious persuasion of the population. For a discussion see Margaret Spufford, 'Religious preambles and the

directions provides insights into the religious beliefs of the will-maker (or the scribe). Moreover, will-makers also usually specified the resting-place for their corporeal remains, and sometimes directed the manner, and the cost, of their funerals.[35]

Clerical concern, and indeed intervention, then, may account for testation. As Christopher Marsh notes, some individuals felt that it was their Christian duty to settle their worldly affairs by will.[36] A passage in the 'Visitation of the Sick' admonished the dying to consider their obligations both 'toward God and man.'[37] The reason for clerical intervention might be multi-faceted, and perhaps self-interested. In the mid-seventeenth century, some considered charity the 'virtue' that granted to the dying 'hopes of heaven and pardon.'[38] The will provided the dying with an opportunity to make a final round of charitable bequests.[39]

Arranging for the disposition of property by will, then, took on the guise of a religious duty. The solution of religious commentators to reconciling competing claims for the dying person's attention was to urge the settling of affairs at the onset of illness, or even in advance thereof, well before the end was near, as the 'Visitation of the Sick' prescribed.[40] In his treatment of the obligations of the

---

scribes of villagers' wills in Cambridgeshire'; and Christopher Marsh, 'Attitudes towards Will-making' both in Arkell, Evans and Goose (eds.), *When Death Do Us Part*, pp. 144–57, 158–75, as well as Houlbrooke, *Death, Religion and the Family*, pp. 110–34.

[35] Wills generally specified the parish churchyard where the deceased wished to be buried. In our eclectic collection of wills, will-makers frequently left funeral arrangements to their executors (for example William Almond (*Almond contra Almond*, PROB 11/349, 1); Stephen Parks (*Parks contra Boughey*, PROB 11/349, 190); William Sherman (*Sherman contra Millner*, PROB 11/350, 50). Thomas Frere expressed a ceiling, no more than £50 (*Frere contra Frere per curator*, PROB 11/349, 305), while Thomas Comber merely directed that he be interred without 'pompe or costly funeral' (*Comber contra Comber*, PROB 11/349, 295).

[36] Marsh, 'Attitudes towards Will-making in Early Modern England,' pp. 174–5. One of our will-makers Vere Gerard noted in the introductory clause of her will that she was 'willing to make a Christian declaration of my Mynde and will.' *Gerard v. Blackston*, PROB 11/350, 125.

[37] Canon 67 of the Canons of 1604 in Gerald Bray (ed.), *The Anglican Canons 1529–1947* (Woodbridge, 1998).

[38] Jeremy Taylor, *The Rule and Exercise of Holy Dying* (London, 1674), p. 179.

[39] M.M. Sheehan, *The Will in Medieval England: from the conversion of the Anglo-Saxons to the end of the thirteenth century* (Toronto, 1963).

[40] Although this has been much noted by historians the admonition itself was very bland. After directing the minister to advise those who had not done so to make a will, there follows: 'But men should often be put in remembrance to take order for the settling of their temporal estates, whilst they are in health.' Arguably having already made a will did not

pious, Anthony Sparrows, the Bishop of Exeter and later of Norwich, noted that the dying ought to 'bestow their whole time and care, as it is fit, about settling and securing their future estate.'[41] With this advice lay commentators concurred.[42] Writing towards the close of the period, William Assheton, a prominent Oxford theologian, referred to a person's will as 'not only the most solemn but also the Concluding Act of his whole life: And as such should be managed with the greatest Deliberation and Prudence.' However, in his view, individuals were by nature 'inconsiderate.' He noted that they either failed to write a will, or left it to be done 'amidst the pains and distractions of a Sick Bed, resulting in a will that was not only imperfect and defective in itself, but very disturbing to the Dying Testator.'[43]

The testamentary litigation provide evidence that some clergy did indeed do their duty and advise dying members of their flock to write their wills, though it is not clear that they did so in order to secure charitable bequests. Three weeks before his death, one Mr. Read, styled 'minister' of Windsor in the record, reminded one of our will-makers that 'You are a weake man and God knows how it may please him to dispose of you,' and advised him to settle his estate without delay.[44] Similarly, when the Bishop of Hereford came to see the Countess of Somerset to pray with her, he was alleged to have asked her if she had settled her estate.[45] Likewise, William Colett, a 'minister,' testified that he discussed will-making with Thomas Gollibrand 'according to his Duty.'[46]

Another cleric who was present at a deathbed consoling a dying man (whose will was subject to testamentary litigation) seems to have played rather an active role in a will-making. Robert Lord, the Rector of Sutton in Norfolk, visited Sir Thomas Pettus at his house during his last illness and remained with him for a week. According to Lord, he asked Sir Thomas if he had a will. Sir Thomas indicated that he had executed one in favor of his wife, Lady Elizabeth, but had reconsidered its terms and decided to revoke it. To do so, he asked his wife to

---

exempt the ill individual from rethinking his estate plan. In a an earlier part of the visitation the minister was to implore the sick person as follows: 'I require you to examine yourself and your estate both toward God and man.' The Visitation of the Sick, *The Book of Common Prayer* (London, 1669). See also Canon 67 of the Canons of 1604 in Bray (ed.), *The Anglican Canons*, p. 359.

[41]   *A Rationale upon the Book of Common Prayer of the Church of England* (London, 1668), p. 330.

[42]   Houlbrooke, *Death, Religion and the Family*, pp. 82–3.

[43]   *Theological Discourse of Last Wills and Testaments* (London, 1696), pp. 1–2.

[44]   Or at least so Mary Holford reported in a deposition, *Niblett contra Thonold*, PROB 24/14, 357.

[45]   *Thyn et Gregory contra Somerset*, PROB 18/7/27.

[46]   *Gollibrand contra Gollibrand*, PROB 24/14, 214.

throw it into the fire. When Pettus expressed some doubt about whether the document she burned in his presence was in fact his will, the clergyman turned lawyer: Lord advised Pettus to make another will, and then sent for an attorney whom he believed would draft a replacement. But the lawyer, who arrived surreptitiously, was unable to prepare a draft will in time. Perhaps this was because at the same time Lady Elizabeth summoned a different scrivener who actually did produce a new will. The Reverend Lord was present at the execution of that will, one contested by Pettus's daughter on various grounds.[47] He testified against the will's validity by observing that Pettus had signed a document prepared by his wife's lawyer without him having even read it.[48]

Minimizing Family Discord

Some English folk regarded will-making as a way to minimize unchristian familial conflict; they clearly sensed that dissension over their estate might follow their death, and believed that a will might quell dispute. The following examples from the testamentary litigation observed in this study document such concern. Edward Twyne's will, written while he was in 'good and perfect health and sound memory,' explained that he wished to dispose of his property 'seeing by dayly experience the trouble strife and controversies which arise between Friends by reason of their estates.'[49] Sir John Lee, who had three daughters, devised his estate to them in equal shares. The will nominated his eldest daughter, Katherine, as his executrix, and left his 'gold and plate' to her. A clause in the will noted that he had executed the document while in good health 'so that noe differences or questions may arise about the same after my death.'[50] James Burton hoped that his will, written in good health, might promote 'perfect Amity and affection ... between my Relations.'[51] In a last example, William Halley did similarly, 'for the pease and welfare of my family.'[52]

Some will-makers were aware that their estate plans might dissatisfy their relatives and resorted to rudimentary 'no-contest' provisions.[53] To minimize

---

[47] This case is further discussed in Chapter 9.

[48] *O'Keever alias Pettus contra Pettus*, PROB 24/14, 221–2.

[49] *Rivey contra Twyne*, PROB 11/374, 341.

[50] *Lee contra Lee*, PROB 11/342, 59.

[51] *Brace alias Burton contra Burton*, PROB 11/352, 40.

[52] *Halley contra Halley*, PROB 11/349, 319.

[53] In the modern probate law in most states in the United States, a clause in a will that provides that a legatee under a will who contests the validity of the will forfeits the legacy is generally valid. This puts the legatee to a gruesome choice: accept the legacy (which is presumably less than was expected or less than the legatee would receive under intestacy)

potential conflict, William Sherman left £30 to his daughter Mary on condition that she not 'molest hinder or trouble my s[ai]d Executrix [his wife Elizabeth] but shall and doe peaceably and quietly permitt and suffer my said Elizabeth take out Letters of Administration ... [if she is troublesome] she receives 12d in full satisfaction of all legacies and claims.'[54] Likewise, Ellen Steele made bequests to her niece Anne Johnson and her daughter (also Anne) conditional upon the legatees accepting the sums (land was devised to a nephew) and also disclaiming bequests made to them under the will of her deceased husband.[55]

The Selection of an Executor

A final reason for writing a will was to select an individual to deal with the will-maker's property at death: the executor or executrix. In the absence of a direction by will, the ordinary was permitted to exercise discretion in selecting as administrator the deceased's widow/widower, his next of kin, or both as specified by statute.[56] Churchmen were wary of both executors and administrators, and their perceived proclivity towards avoiding the payment of charitable bequests. Jeremy Taylor, Bishop of Down and Conner, and a protégé of Archbishop Laud, admonished the faithful to 'Let the dispensation of Our Alms be as little entrusted to our Executors as may be [*excepting the lasting and successive portions*]' on the grounds that executors might be tempted to avoid the charitable obligation by claiming that the estate was impoverished.[57] Visitation articles addressed to the clergy directed priests to monitor the actions of executors and administrators in order to insure that charitable bequests were paid over by executors.[58]

---

or contest and risk losing the legacy if the will and the no-contest clause are held valid. See the Uniform Probate Code, secs. 2–517 and 3–905 (1990) and the Restatement (Third) of Property: Wills and Other Donative Transfers, sec. 8–5 (2003).

54   *Sherman contra Millner*, PROB 11/350, 50.

55   *Bernard contra Johnson*, PROB 11/349, 284.

56   An ordinary was the official (of varying clerical rank) who had jurisdiction in will probate and intestate administration that was held in a given church court jurisdiction. In cases in which a husband survived his wife, he was to be granted administration of her estate. 21 Hen. VIII, c. 5 (1529).

57   Ibid., p. 177–9.

58   Although the bishops were concerned with other matters concerning probate, in particular the demanding of fees in excess of amounts stipulated, the visitations also manifest concern that executors and administrators were less than punctilious in fulfilling charitable bequests. A good example is that of Bishop Godfrey Goodman recommended the following: 'That the Church and the poore not be defrauded of their legacies ... the church-wardens ought to be very careful to present ... executors. as are faulty ... '. Kenneth Fincham, *Visitation Articles and Injunctions of the Early Stuart Church* (Church of England Record Society,

Lawyers echoed these cautionary sentiments. Henry Swinburne entreated will-makers to select an executor carefully because the 'ignorant, negligent, or unfaithful' might find the office 'troublesome peradventure also discommodious.'[59] Moreover, the executor undertook a number of very personal tasks, most significant amongst them arranging burial; it was the executor who was charged with the responsibility to ensure that the deceased was properly interred.[60] These two tasks were so linked in the mind of contemporaries that if it could be shown that oversight of the burial without objection was undertaken by a person claiming executorship, this fact could be used as evidence that a will nominating him or her was indeed valid. For example, Benjamin Bradbourne was alleged to have made two wills, each naming a different executrix, his sister and his widow.[61] In her allegation, the widow claimed that the one she promoted had been recognized as valid shortly after his death because she had buried her husband according to the instructions therein without objection.[62] Likewise, two witnesses testified that they regarded Sir William Turner as executor of Phillipa Brooke's estate because they were employed by him to make a coffin for her.[63]

Executors had other important duties to perform after the deceased was buried: to collect the debts owed to the deceased, to discharge any debts owed, and to distribute property according to the will-maker's direction. Thus a desire to choose an honest and competent individual to wind up one's worldly affairs may well have prompted some to make a will. The testamentary causes I have studied here reveal some detailed questioning of the activities of executors and administrators, and other scholars have uncovered significant allegations of chicanery on their part.[64]

Studies suggest that by the seventeenth century married men most frequently chose their surviving spouse as executrix, followed by their children.[65] While

---

1994), vol. II, p. 54. It should be noted that the officials of the various probate jurisdictions were not without suspicion. Archbishop Laud's 1634 articles includes the question as to whether a judge or other ecclesiastic office holder had retained sums 'taken out of the estate of any dying intestate ... upon the same to bestow, in *pios usus*.' Ibid., p. 95.

[59] Swinburne, *A Brief Treatise*, p. 45.

[60] Many of our will-makers left the manner of their burial to their executors. See above, footnote 35.

[61] *Bradbourne contra Townsend*, PROB 18/8/106 and PROB 18/8/116.

[62] Ibid., PROB 25/2/187.

[63] *Turner contra Fretwell*, PROB 24/15, 173, 197.

[64] See for example, Addy, *Death, Money and the Vultures*, ch. 7, tellingly entitled 'Fraudulent Executors.'

[65] See especially Erickson, *Women and Property*, pp. 156–60, and Susan Amussen, *An Ordered Society: gender and class in early modern England* (Oxford, 1988), pp. 81–5, cited in Houlbrooke, *Death, Religion and the Family*, pp. 137.

these choices parallel the statutory mandate in successions where the deceased left no will,[66] the ordinary was permitted to constitute both spouse and children as joint administrators. If the surviving spouse was a child's step-mother rather than the natural mother, there was evidently potential for conflict over the distribution of the estate. Moreover, not all individuals died leaving a spouse and/or children; for some, collateral relatives were next of kin. The litigation observed here suggests that while will-makers did indeed select spouses and children to execute their wills, others were also nominated; perhaps these testators' selections explain, at least in part, why their wills were made, and then why they became the subject of contest.

The Canterbury testamentary causes indicate that the selection of a trusted executor or executrix should have been an important concern, at least for some will-makers. At times an executor might be called upon to exercise discretion and judgment on matters left vague or unresolved in a will. For example, it was alleged that Robert Markham at some time before the will was executed gave his brother and executor George precatory directions 'that certain legacies be paid though not expressed' (presumably in the writing) from property that he appointed for that purpose.[67] For Joan Smith, a widow without children, the problem of the selection of an executor was particularly poignant. She had learned by her own experience with the estate of her husband that discord between executors might arise to burden the estate's beneficiaries if more than one was selected. Citing those unhappy circumstances, the proponents of Smith's will alleged that she had made clear her desire to burden her own legatees with only a single executor.[68]

While the extant record does not state explicitly the nature of the troubles that Smith endured, two causes in which the judgment of joint executors was required can be cited, and both indicate that the co-executors differed on how their charge ought to be exercised so that probate court intervention was required. In one cause, three executors quarreled over whether to deviate from what appears to have been the expressed terms of a will. Two executors of the will of Thomas Pitt conceded that the deceased had not left a legacy to his grandson 'who is forced to maintain his father having dissipated his estate.' According to the allegation, an arbitrator had awarded the grandson £200 to be paid to him at the age of 21, and each executor was to make a proportional contribution from the property under his control.[69] Apparently one executor had a change of heart

---

[66] 21 Hen. VIII, c. 5 (1529).

[67] *Markham et Carrington contra Markham*, PROB 18/1/46.

[68] *Elson contra Ayliff et Hayes*, PROB 18/7/87.

[69] *Lowder et Impey contra Pitt*, PROB 18/10/83.

about the proposed resolution of the dispute because three witnesses confirmed both the agreement to arbitrate and the amount of the arbitrator's award.[70]

A further cause dealt with the exercise of discretion by more than a single individual acting as executor, albeit in a different context. When Robert Morefield made his will, he appointed his minor son, also Robert, to serve as executor and residuary legatee.[71] Although the will did not explicitly create a trust, the court, because the executor was under the age of majority, created one: four trustees were named to act on behalf of the son during his minority. John Partridge was one of the trustees so named, and he brought suit to take control of Morefield's estate, charging his fellow trustees with misfeasance. According to his allegation, both Henry Sammards, the 'attorney' who had drawn up the will, and Benjamin Stoodley were unfit to serve as co-trustees. In general terms, the allegation claimed that Sammards was 'likely to damage the estate,' and both he and Stoodley had made 'improper use of the deceased's property.' A specific charge was also made: that Sammard and Stoodley had carried off the dead man's property. A third trustee, one Samuel Dorme, who was married to Morefield's sister, refused to serve as trustee because he felt that the will had been drawn 'contrary to [the testator's] intent,' and that he 'would not want to be in a law suit.' Although no documentation appears to have survived, Partridge's written allegations submitted to the court might have been made in response to discord between the trustees. Partridge was careful to note that while the deceased's will had empowered the trustees to exchange lands, the sales had occurred with the consent of only two, Sammard and Stoodley.[72]

Indebted testators might have had greater reason to select an executor, because a creditor who was so constituted had a better chance of having a debt owed to him or her repaid. The probate of the will of Dudley Rowse provides an example of one in which the will's promoter alleged that he had been constituted executor for just that reason. According to the allegation of one Marmaduke Darell, his 'intimate friend' for 30 years, Rowse was a Receiver of the Royal Aid for Buckinghamshire, and in order to secure performance of his obligation he 'took on a bond' for £10,000 and he had not 'acquitted all sums.' Thereafter, presumably upon default, Rowse was imprisoned for debt, and Darell had provided a loan in order to have him released. Further loans were made upon a bond co-signed by Darell. In order to satisfy all these debts, Darell alleged

---

[70]   Ibid., PROB 24/17, 135, 136.

[71]   The residuary is the testator's remaining property after specific bequests of personal property, and general bequests of cash sums has been made. The residuary, percentage-wise, frequently amounted to a large proportion of the estate.

[72]   *Partridge contra Samwaies et al.*, PROB 18/21/85.

that Rowse had executed the holographic will[73] that he offered for probate, a document in which Darell was named executor.[74]

Debt also lingers in the testamentary litigation over the estate of Richard Hussey. Samuel Pitt petitioned the court to have letters testamentary (documents issued by a probate court empowering an individual to deal with an estate as executor or administrator) that had already been issued to William Knowles, the administrator of the estate, revoked, and then offered for probate an oral will naming him executor of his cousin Richard's estate. Pitt alleged that Hussey owed him at least £100, and that he was obligated by a bond to act as surety for Hussey's debts to the sum of £700. Accordingly, Hussey 'out of kindness' had uttered an oral will making him executor.[75] Knowles, Hussey's nephew, denied the validity of the oral will, and in an allegation countered that an arbitrator had awarded Pitt only £40.[76] The will was not admitted to probate, and Pitt, presumably, had to be content with the more modest arbitration ward.[77]

A final detailed example of the relationship between debts owed and a creditor's claim that he had been constituted executor to satisfy them comes from the cause between Samuel Ellis and Andrew Parsons over the estate of Richard Parsons, the latter's nephew. Both sides agreed that Richard was deeply in debt at the time of his death. In challenging Ellis's allegation that statements made by Richard constituted an oral will, Andrew Parsons charged that his dying nephew had uttered the words rashly, and in response to a demand by Ellis for the repayment of some longstanding debts.[78] There was some logic to Ellis's claim. Having passed considerable periods of time in prison for debt, Richard may well have wished to placate the man who had arranged for his freedom.[79] Indeed, Andrew Parsons alleged that Richard had told others that he was frightened of Ellis, had asked him to pay off the debt that he owed to Ellis, and had vowed to move to the country and live off the income that his father had left him. Beholding to Ellis he no doubt was, but the issue between the parties was a legal one: did Richard intend to make Ellis his executor by an oral will, thereby

---

73 A holographic will is one entirely in the hand of the will-maker, and requires no witnesses for it to be valid. See Chapter 7.

74 *Darrell contra Rowse*, PROB 18/7/21. A witness, Samuel Sewell, confirmed the substance of the allegation PROB 24/15, 3. The parties must have settled, because the cause did not proceed to sentence.

75 PROB 18/3c/65.

76 *Pitt contra Knowle*, PROB 18/3c/60.

77 Ibid., PROB 11/338, 323.

78 *Ellis contra Parsons*. Ellis's allegation is PROB 18/6/23. Parsons submitted a number of allegations; the reference for the statement above is PROB 18/7/14.

79 Ibid., PROB 18/7/22.

ensuring that the debt owed to him would be satisfied? Uncle Andrew denied the testamentary validity of his nephew's utterance. Moreover, he claimed that Ellis had already conceded that the words were insufficient to amount to an oral will. According to Parsons, when one Richard Aldworth (styled in a court document 'one of His Maj. Auditors') told Ellis that he had heard that Ellis did 'pretend to have a will of Richard Parsons,' he noted that Ellis did not claim that he was the executor of Richard's estate. Rather Ellis had merely said that he wanted to make certain that the debt owed to him by Andrew would be repaid.[80] This Ellis denied, and he further alleged that he had not only satisfied debts that Parsons owed to others, but he had also paid medical expenses incurred in the course of Richard's last illness, as well as the costs of his funeral.[81] As I noted above, this last contention, oversight of the funeral, was regarded as evidence that the person undertaking the burden was recognized as executor.[82]

In addition to satisfying a debt that was a binding legal obligation, an individual might wish to repay kindness or hospitality by nominating the generous benefactor as executor. Examples can be found in the Canterbury causes. Hugh Nauney noted in his will that he wished that his cousin Ann be made his executrix, 'because she is so engaged to me and lent me so much money without writings.'[83] Likewise, Thomas Turner offered for probate a will alleged to be that of Robert Fretwell. He explained his selection as executor over that of Fretwell's kin by explaining that the testator had declared him to be his 'only friend in the world,' and that 'the kindred who contest the will did not take care of him.'[84]

Selecting an executrix, however, might not always result in the person nominated winding up the estate. In one cause, choosing a married woman landed her husband as executor. One of the more detailed allegations of dereliction of duty by an executrix involved the inventory produced by Robert Mascall, the husband of Jane Mascall, who was nominated as executrix in her father's will. Although the initial inventory submitted does not seem to have survived, Thomas Spenser, Jane's son, challenged the inventory of his grandfather's estate prepared by Robert. It was alleged that Mascall omitted items of property from the inventory to the value of at least £2,000, overlooked a mortgage owed to the deceased of at least £400, and neglected to list ready money in hand amounting to £25: a considerable oversight indeed! In addition, it was claimed that Mascall charged the estate with legacies that were not owed, because some of the beneficiaries had predeceased the testator. The contestants

---

[80] Ibid., PROB 18/7/14.

[81] Ibid., PROB 18/7/56.

[82] See footnote 35 above.

[83] *Nauney contra Nauney*, PROB 11/310, 164.

[84] *Turner contra Brook* cited in *Turner contra Fretwell*, PROB 18/1/84.

believed that he intended to pocket them, because it was noted that the will did not direct that the legacies should pass to the estate of the deceased beneficiaries. According to the inventory produced by Robert, the estate was insufficient to satisfy all the legacies specified. Thomas's revisions, however, produced an estate in surplus: one valued at over £1,804, with the legacies actually due amounting only to £1,391.[85]

A person nominated as executor in a will might find it necessary to resign his or her post if the estate was overburdened by debt. John Dyamond was a factor to Bartholomew Collyer and William Skinner, and died in Barbados while employed by them, leaving a will naming his wife executrix. The two merchants alleged that he had a quantity of their goods in hand, as well as debts owed to them in the amount to £1,040. Unhappily it was asserted that the value of Dyamond's estate amounted to about one-quarter of that sum. The widow reached an agreement with the two men in which she renounced the executorship, and allowed the creditors to be constituted administrators in return for the right to retain possession of her husband's household goods.[86]

The wrapping up of Dyamond's estate was complicated because, in common with other will-makers involved in trade, it was difficult to ascertain both the extent and the value of the personal property that he actually owned. In the cause involving Dyamond's estate, witnesses were called to try to sort out his personal debts and credits from those he had assumed on behalf of his employers and clients.[87] Similarly, the estate of Joseph Skutt was complicated because it was not clear to what extent the goods in his warehouse had already been sold, and were therefore not his property at his death.[88] Frequently, it was difficult to estimate the value of a merchant's estate. What his stock was actually worth might be questionable, particularly when the executrix had to rely upon the judgment of appraisers to determine a price. Moreover, the quality of the stock was related to its value, and might be a subject of debate between executor and heirs. The questioning of the inventory produced upon the death of Thomas Atkinson, a wine merchant, provides an example of differing calculations. The executrix, his widow, claimed that a lower appraisal inserted by her in the inventory was justified because some of the wine had gone off, and was therefore 'fitt only for vinegar.'[89]

85   *Mascall contra Spenser*, PROB 18/3c/40.

86   *Dyamond alias Webber contra Collyer et Skinner*, PROB 18/7/42.

87   Ibid., PROB 24/14, 208, 227.

88   *Baden alias Harward et al. contra Skutt*, PROB 18/4/40.

89   *Austin contra Smith con Atkinson*, PROB 18/21/63. Lest it be thought that only those named as executors or executrices were alleged to be dishonest, it should be noted that many of the same charges were lodged against administrators and adminstratrices.

One final allegation of malfeasance that emerges from the Canterbury litigation observed is particularly telling because it not only charged that a wide array of property was omitted or fraudulently calculated by the executrix but it also detailed precisely how she concealed some of the property. In his will, Richard Delves nominated his widow as his executrix, not an uncommon choice, as I have noted. The deceased man's sister, Mary Godfrey, challenged her sister-in-law's actions as executrix. First, she charged the widow with failing to include a variety of items in her inventory, from the value of a lease to 'three quarters and a half of meale.' Second, it was claimed that the widow had understated the actual value of the debts collected, the value of molasses resold, and the cash that Delves had on hand. Finally, she was alleged to have moved goods to the value of £20 from the dead man's chamber shortly after his death into her own, and then proceeded to sell them on her own account.[90]

In sum, the testamentary litigation I have analyzed suggests that there was reason for a testator to select an executor to wind up his or her 'commercial' affairs, and also to choose carefully when so doing. Of the 15 litigated causes in which the activities of personal representatives were questioned, 11 involve the activities of executors nominated in the will and 4 question the actions of administrators appointed by the court. In most of the causes, it was the inventory prepared by the personal representative that was challenged, because it was alleged that he or she undervalued or failed to include (usually not inadvertently) specific items of personal property: some debts owed to the

---

Inventories that they produced were challenged on the grounds that goods were omitted and undervalued (or both), sometimes with remarkable specificity. See for example the estate of Lady Mason alias Hussey (*Collier alias Hussey et Walls alias Hussey contra Hussey*, PROB 18/7/47) in which her eldest son gave bond for double the estimated value of the estate but seems to have undervalued his mother's goods, and according to a witness summoned by the administrator's younger brother, did not accurately calculate the value of debts owed to the deceased. PROB 24/14, 402. An amusing example comes from the estate of Arthur Pulter. In addition to other valuation concerns lodged against the inventory produced by John Buxton, his administrator, was that he appropriated a horse (because he did not include it in his inventory) worth from as much as £40 to no less than £10. *Needham contra Pulter et Buxton*, PROB 18/13/70. Two witnesses were called upon to confirm that Buxton had sold the horse for £25 and appropriated the proceeds. PROB 24/20, 106, 108.

90   *Godfrey contra Delves*, PROB 18/7/58.

deceased,[91] particular personal items,[92] or more generic specifications of the value of 'goods,' that is, miscellaneous items of personal property.[93] Inventories prepared by administrators were likewise also challenged.[94]

How They Made Their Wills

A very different culture of will-making exists in modern Britain (and its former colonies) than the one that obtained in the seventeenth-century past. Modern estate planning is generally done well in advance of death. After consultation with clients, lawyers draft papers; statutes specify the requirements of due execution that must be observed in order for a document to be probated as a valid will.[95] While not without its rules, church court practice in the early modern period was considerably more flexible in determining the validity of testamentary acts than is modern law. Both oral and written wills were recognized in the seventeenth century, and wills written in the hand of the will-maker rather than by another were valid even in the absence of attestation by witnesses.[96] In his survey of the survival of the Roman canon law after the Reformation, Richard Helmholz concludes that with respect to probate the church courts established less stringent requirements for will validity than those prescribed by formal law, and then proceeded to interpret those accommodating rules rather leniently. If

---

[91]   See the allegation promoted in Robert Morefield's will (*Partridge contra Samwaies et al.*, PROB 18/21/85) where a 'notebook of debts' disappeared, the probate of Nicholas Keale's will (*Brire et Chamberlayne contra Bryant*, PROB 18/12/93), the probate of Thomas Gold's will (*Mascall contra Spenser*, PROB 18/3c/40), and the probate of Francis Blagrave's will (*Blagrave contra Quarrington*, PROB 18/7/80).

[92]   See the probate of Phillip Warwick's will in which 'jewels, rings diamonds and peerless, point lace and rich items of greate value' were excluded. (*Clarkeson contra Darcy alias Warwick*, PROB 18/18/30); or that of Joseph Skutt's will (*Baden alias Harward et al. contra Skutt*, PROB 18/8/40), and that of John Clay's will, in which a variety of jewelry was alleged to have been omitted (*Draper contra Clay*, PROB 18/24/35).

[93]   See the probate of the will of Thomas Pettus in which goods to the value of £5,000 were alleged to have been excluded (*O'Keever alias Pettus contra Pettus*, PROB 18/8/43).

[94]   See, for example, *Collier alias Hussey et Walls alias Hussey contra Hussey*, PROB 18/7/47; and *Needham contra Pulter et Buxton*, PROB 18/13/70.

[95]   See, for example, Uniform Probate Code sec. 2–202.

[96]   Swinburne, *A Brief Treatise*, p. 341, noted that holographic wills were valid in the absence of witnesses. Richard Burn, *Ecclesiastical Law* 3rd edn (London, 1775), vol. iv, p. 93 notes a cause in the Court of Delegates in 1696 that acknowledges this proposition. The formalities of will execution are further discussed below in Chapter 6 and 7.

the judges were satisfied that the testamentary act represented the volition of the will-maker, he concludes, they were inclined to admit it to probate.[97]

The causes analyzed here confirm his view.[98] They also suggest that the events surrounding the execution of wills were rather like snowflakes: largely similar, but with no two exactly alike. A common theme in our causes is haste, frequently, though not invariably, because the will-maker appears to have been at death's door.[99] It is possible that this factor might render their typicality suspect: perhaps the fact that the testamentary act was made at or near the time of death made our wills more susceptible to contest. When time was short, the mental capacity of the dying person might be more questionable, undue influence was more easily brought to bear, and conformity with legal formality might be less possible to achieve.[100] So the causes observed here may depict atypical vignettes of will-making, unless of course many of those wills that were not the subject of contest (or at least a fair number of them) were also contrived on the deathbed. In his study of death and dying, Ralph Houlbrooke notes an increased tendency away from deathbed will-making in the century and a half after the Reformation. Although he argues that the ties between death and will-making may have been 'loosened,' Houlbrooke does cite a number of studies that show remarkably high percentages of deathbed will-making even into the mid-eighteenth century.[101] Moreover, it must be remembered that even if a person on the deathbed had already made a will, the church's 'Visitation of the Sick' (as noted above) advised the dying to reconsider its terms. In the Canterbury causes, examples of will-makers *in extremis* altering or supplementing an existing testamentary act can be found.[102] In short, while the evidence presented in the causes ought not to be regarded as typical of the way wills were made in the late seventeenth century, much can be deduced about the process of will-making from considering the circumstances in which the wills in this study were executed.

The admonition to execute wills while in good health appears to have had little effect upon late seventeenth-century Englishmen and women. Even a century after our period, legal commentators, including Sir William Blackstone,[103] continued to express a similar lament. They urged the clergy to

---

97 Richard Helmholz, *Canon Law and the Law of England* (London, 1988), p. 7.

98 We shall see that few wills were set aside for want of due execution. See below, Chapter 7.

99 See discussion accompanying footnotes 37–48.

100 These issues are addressed in Chapter 6 below.

101 Houlbrooke, *Death, Religion, and the Family*, pp. 88–107.

102 See below, text accompanying footnotes 106 and 107.

103 William Blackstone, *Commentaries on the Laws of England*, 4 vols. (Chicago, 1979), Vol. 4, pp. 500–501. My current research on the formulation of the Wills Act of 1837

turn the attention of the infirm to tidying their worldly affairs earlier on in their illness. But legal writers seem resigned to deathbed wills; one even went so far as to propose that physicians and apothecaries should learn the rudiments of will-making in order to advise their patients![104]

The advice offered by the clergy and legal commentators to write a will while in good health, however, may have flown in the face of a popular belief that to do so was to tempt fate.[105] This conviction supported a culture of last-minute will-making. Even those in dire straits were reluctant to make a will in the hope that they might recover, regarding the 'making of a Will as a mortal sign.'[106] Examples of the hopelessly ill refusing to except that their end was near abound.[107] Indeed the testamentary litigation observed by others, and the causes analyzed here, suggest that reluctance to plan in advance did result in suspect testamentary acts, wills that could be challenged on the grounds of lack of capacity and/or undue influence, or ones that might fail to adhere to the proper formalities of execution.[108]

To be sure, the causes observed in this study confirm the contemporary view that many testators were unprepared for death, and that substantial numbers had insufficient time at their disposal to make a written will. While wills routinely assert that their makers were of sound mind, not all wills describe the physical health of their author. Forty-two of the 184 wills observed here make clear expressions of their maker's physical state; of those that do mention condition 34 indicate that the will-maker was in ill health, while the remaining 8 assert good health. These will-makers seem more robust than were those observed by Stephen Coppel, who found that only 7 of 97 will-makers who divulged their

---

suggests that deathbed wills continued to be common well into the 19th century.

[104]   *A Familiar, Plain and Easy Explanation of the Law of Wills and Codicils* (London, 1785).

[105]   Marsh, 'In the Name of God,' pp. 217–26.

[106]   Taylor, *Holy Dying*, p. 167. Taylor believed that one ought to presume the opposite, that all illness would be fatal.

[107]   Both Addy and Marsh cite examples of unwarranted optimism amongst the dying. For example, during what proved to be his final illness, Cuthbert Burrell was urged a number of times to make a will, but he was said to have replied that the next day or following week would 'do fine' (Addy, *Death, Money and the Vultures,* pp. 92–4). Marsh quotes Thomas Willows who told a neighbour he would write his will if his health did not improve in three days; it did not, but by then he was unable to have a will written. Marsh, 'In the Name of God?' in Martin and Spufford, eds. *The Records of a Nation*, p. 242.

[108]   See for example, that of Addy, *Death, Money and the Vultures*; Houlbrooke, *Death, Religion, and Family,* pp. 80–109; and Marsh, 'In the Name of God,' pp. 217–26.

state of health noted that they were in good health.[109] The percentage of the unhealthy in his study (and perhaps those in the Prerogative Court sample) are skewed towards the unhealthy since will validity is at issue; his findings may well be an underestimate, because some will-makers who died in the same week that their wills were written did not mention that they were in ill health.

Yet the causes observed here demonstrate that advanced planning did not always lead to non-contentious probates.[110] A number of the will-makers did plan ahead, and explained in their documents why they did so, but their estates were still enmeshed in controversy. For example, Joan Smith noted that, while she wrote her will while 'in health of body,' she did so considering 'the certainty of death and the incertainty of life, the blessings of Immortality and the Myseries of this Mortality.'[111] Likewise, Thomas Colwell proclaimed his good physical condition, but was 'desirous in my health to sett my house and heart in order before the day of my visitation shall come and my earthly Tabernacle of my body shall be dissolved.'[112]

The wills embroiled in testamentary causes confirm another of Houlbrooke's contentions: that the drafting of written wills was no longer the exclusive province of clerics by the later seventeenth century.[113] Indeed, the wills that were the subject of the Canterbury litigation do not appear to have been written by clerics, at least to the extent that the scrivener can be determined from the record. The causes I have observed resulted in 184 testamentary acts.[114] Twenty-eight were oral wills, and 17 were self-penned. Of the remaining 139, the scrivener cannot be ascertained for 70 wills, but of the 69 wills whose drafters can be

---

[109] 'Will-making on the deathbed,' *Local Population Studies*, vol. 40 (1988), p. 43. I particularly like Jane Cox's imagery that wills were not made until individuals were 'pinched by the messengers of death.' See her *Affection Defying the Power of Death*, p. 25.

[110] See the Tables accompanying Chapter 3.

[111] *Elson contra Ayliff et Hayes*, PROB 11/350, 49.

[112] *Colwell contra Colwell*, PROB 11/349, 320. See also the wills of Gerard Lane (whose will was not the subject of litigation but whose will is mentioned in *Roope et Wakeham contra Jones et al.*) who wrote a will in good health 'considering his age' (PROB 11/382, 325) and of Clement Pragell who 'considered the incertainty of this transitory life and that all flesh must yield to death.' (*Hill contra Bond*, PROB 11/365, 128). Though not in good health, Thomas Lodge noted 'how certain we are to dye and the incertainty of the tyme and manner of its approach.' As a 'chirugion,' he must have had first-hand knowledge of the deaths of others (*Lodge contra Lodge et Lodge*, PROB 11/382, 343).

[113] Ralph Houlbrooke, *Death, Ritual and Bereavement* (London, 1988), pp. 99, 107.

[114] I have observed 184 causes. Ten were petitions to take up administration in which no wills were alleged to have been made, and 12 involved petitions for accountings in which the origin of the will is not specified. Twenty-two of the causes allege a second testamentary act.

deduced, 38 were produced by friends or neighbors, while 31 were written by those styled 'lawyer,' 'attorney,' or 'scrivener.'[115] Not a single cleric appears to have been a draftsman of any of the wills offered for probate in the collection.[116]

'Legal professionals' thus produced many of our contested wills. Whether these documents were subject to different standards than those produced by the non-lawyer, lay or clergy, cannot be ascertained. But when one lawyer produced his own will, and a questionable one according to the contestants, the court was urged to look carefully at the document, because it did not appear to conform to legal niceties. The will of Thomas Hoare, an attorney, provides this example: in the testamentary litigation involving the authenticity of his will, some doubt was raised over its validity, because it appeared to have been drafted 'without form or fashion.'[117]

Of course, because the wills observed herein are derived from testamentary litigation, they demonstrate that a will-maker might not be able to rest easy even in cases in which a lawyer was involved in crafting a will. For example, Lawrence Alcocke, an attorney, prepared the will of Joan Smith. In common with many of the testamentary acts in these causes, haste is evident; although the will offered for probate was drafted about a month before her death, it was not duly executed (if indeed it was at all!) until Smith was on her deathbed.[118] When it was contested, Alcocke equivocated as to his own view of its validity, and was alleged to have said 'that she had done something that might amount to a will.'[119]

---

[115]   As we shall see, there are two groups of wills, a quinquennial sample commencing with 1661, and all the testamentary litigation for 1676. Of the 100 causes in our sample years, 95 testamentary acts were alleged to have been undertaken. We arrive at this figure by deducting 15 (seven were petitions to take up administration in which no will was alleged and eight were petitions for accountings in which the will itself was not admitted); and adding 10 because in 10 of our causes a second act was alleged. Twelve were oral wills, so we are thus left with 83 written documents. It is not possible to ascertain the person who wrote 40 of these wills, but 21 were penned by friends or neighbors, while 19 were written by those styled 'lawyer' 'attorney' or 'scrivener,' and three were holographs. Likewise our 1676 causes produced 89 testamentary acts. We again reduce by 7 because 3 were petitions to take up administration; and 4 were petitions for accountings while adding 12, causes in which a second testamentary act was alleged. Sixteen were oral wills, and 14 were holographs. The drafters of 30 of the wills cannot be ascertained. Of the remaining 29 causes, 17 were drafted by neighbors and friends, with 12 penned by those with varying degrees of legal acumen.

[116]   Though a minister did draft a testamentary document for the Countess of Somerset, it appears to have been superseded by the will drafted by Bridgeman (*Thyn et Gregory contra Somerset*, PROB 11/7/27).

[117]   *Hoare contra Hoare*, PROB 18/13/11.

[118]   *Elson contra Ayliff et Hayes*, PROB 18/6/73.

[119]   Ibid., PROB 18/7/87. He conceded this in his deposition, PROB 24/14, 267–9. The will was admitted. The sentence is PROB 11/349, 266.

His doubts may be attributed to the will's only very casual adherence to the formalities of execution. According to the contestant's answer, Alcocke – who as an attorney should have known 'what is requisite for the making of a will' – conceded after Smith's death that he was uncertain whether 'one Witness would be the Sufficient to prove the same at Common Law so would one witness be sufficient in this Court without the hand or Seal of the Testator or Testatrix.'[120]

Sometimes a will-maker might lament the fact that he could not draft his own will and was forced to summon a scrivener. For example, in her allegation, Elizabeth O'Keever (styled in the litigation as 'alias Pettus') maintained that her father, Sir Thomas Pettus, declared on his deathbed that he had no will, 'and if he knewe how to make one he would.'[121] Other will-makers thought that they knew a fair bit of the law, or at least enough to produce their own will.[122] Two wills were offered for probate as the last will of Benjamin Bradbourne, one by his sister Elizabeth Townsend[123] and the other by his widow, Katherine.[124] The will offered by the widow, already probated in the Prerogative Court in the less formal 'common form,' had been written by the now-deceased in his own handwriting shortly before he died. While this will was neither signed nor witnessed, her husband believed – or so it was alleged – that the will was valid; when he was asked if he wanted the earlier will retrieved, the deceased opined that it was unnecessary because 'another will in writing would make the other will void.'[125] The dead man's sister agreed that he possessed the requisite legal acumen, but argued his skill or knowledge to a different conclusion. In her answer, she claimed that had her brother wanted to revoke his will he would have done so unambiguously, 'he being one that understood such things.'[126] Indeed the records reveal much discussion around the deathbed about whether the dying man properly understood the way in which wills could be revoked.[127]

Lay persons also wrote wills for their friends and neighbors. The desire for economy might incline people to select a non-lawyer. For example, when Richard Hodgekinson made his will, he asked one John Langston to perform the task, according to a witness, to 'save charges.'[128] However, it might be false economy

---

[120] Ibid., PROB 25/2/120.

[121] *O'Keever alias Pettus contra Pettus*, PROB 18/7/13.

[122] Given the number of holographs in our collection, we can confirm that it was not uncommon for a will-maker to settle his or her own affairs. See below, Chapter 7.

[123] *Bradbourne contra Townsend*, PROB 18/8/106.

[124] Ibid., PROB 18/8/116.

[125] Ibid., PROB 18/8/116.

[126] Ibid., PROB 25/2/187.

[127] In addition to the above, see Ibid., PROB 25/2/186.

[128] *Hodgekinson contra Hodgekinson*, PROB 24/14, 309.

to avoid professional assistance, because selecting a layman rather than a lawyer to draft a will could result in technical mistakes that might affect the pattern of distribution. George Aberry, who drafted a deathbed will for Francis Lewin, inadvertently (or so it was claimed) 'left out the christian names' of his brother's children, a mistake that would render their legacies 'lost,' or so it was alleged. It was also suggested by the contestants that other pieces of copyhold land that were to pass by will were mis-described, likewise invalidating the bequests. Some doubt about the accidental nature of Aberry's handiwork was raised; as executor he would have far more leeway in dealing with the will-maker's property if these bequests were found void.[129] Sometimes more than just the skills of lay drafters might be questioned. Doubt was cast on the will of Abagail Hardwick, penned from oral instructions by her lodger Jane Bennet. Contestants alleged that Bennet was 'very deafe,' and that the weakened testatrix could not have spoken with sufficient volume for her to have heard the terms of her will.[130]

Some wills were a joint effort between will-maker and scrivener. A scrivener might prepare the equivalent of the modern form will, setting out the formalities but leaving blanks for the dispositions and other specific provisions. For example, according to a deposition of one Somerset Fox, Vere Gerard, her kinswoman, 'had a mind to make a will,' and asked her to 'gett ye forme of a will.' She obtained a writing in which the scrivener set out a preamble, with spaces left for the legacies, and indeed even a blank for her to specify the place for her burial.[131] Even in wills in which a scrivener was more directly employed, the will-maker might still take an active role. According to the allegation of the proponents who promoted the will of John Cox, the testator noted that in a will he was about to sign 'the usual clause putt into wills was left out vizt. after my debts and funeral expenses are paid and discharged.' The scrivener, Richard Herbert, an attorney, replied that this was unnecessary: he counseled his client that it was 'only a matter of form.'[132]

The continuing practice of some will-makers to make or revise wills on the deathbed, or very close thereto, made it more difficult for property owners to wind up their affairs with privacy. In principle, by committing a will to writing in one's own hand, a person could keep the desired pattern of distribution secret. Even if the document was witnessed, it was not necessary for the will-maker to divulge its contents to those attesting it; Swinburne noted that a will-maker might 'keepe secret the tenour or contents of his Will.'[133] It was necessary, of

---

[129]   *Aberry con How contra Aldine*, PROB 18/21/18. In fact the will was denied probate; the sentence is PROB 11/407, 349.

[130]   *Hardwick contra Holland*, PROB 18/1/15.

[131]   *Gerard v. Blackston*, PROB 24/14, 391.

[132]   *Cox et Tompkins contra Cox*, PROB 18/18/90.

[133]   Swinburne, *A Brief Treatise*, pp. 40–41.

course, for the witnesses to oral wills to have heard their contents. Wills drafted by others were somewhere in the middle of the privacy continuum. In written wills produced by others, the will-maker might swear the scrivener to secrecy. The Countess of Somerset, for example, was sequestered during the period when her codicil was alleged to have been drafted, because she was 'a verie private person.' In communicating the terms of an earlier will, she had cautioned the minister who drafted it 'not to tell what he did.'[134] Privacy might also be compromised given the close quarters in which our ancestors resided. Neighbors might overhear, observe, and even intervene when they discovered that a will-making was underway. William Price was a grain factor who resided in the parish of St Giles in the Fields in London. Although he had already executed a will, he determined to make another on his deathbed, at least according to his two sisters who promoted the document. A scrivener was summoned, and a will was drafted. According to his sister's allegation, there was commotion outside his bedroom while the will was being read back to him. His kinsman, also named William Price, reported that a 'mealeman' (whose name is omitted) was 'much concerned that the deced should make his will having a wife or words to that effect the s[ai]d dece[eas]ed. being very much displeased and angry said he wondered anyone should concern or trouble themselves about his business saying that they might mind their own.'[135]

Conclusion

The evidence I have uncovered through the exploration of probate litigation adds to the store of knowledge exhumed by other historians relying on other less rich types of probate documents, allowing us to illuminate the culture of will-making that obtained in the late seventeenth century. Individuals made wills (or chose not to bother) for a variety of reasons, and most of them are discernible only by way of inference. Of course wills were made to accomplish the specific directions made. Thus a will could be its maker's last religious affirmation, manifest ultimate charitable bequests, direct final distributions of wealth, satisfy debts (pecuniary or otherwise) owed, select an executor or executrix, or as we shall see (in the chapter on family discord) settle old scores.[136] At the very least, it was sensible to make a will to nominate a trusted individual to wind up one's

---

134 *Thyn et Gregory contra Somerset*, PROB 18/6/73.
135 *Price contra Price*, PROB 18/13/15.
136 See Chapter 9.

worldly affairs, though not all of our will-makers were able to achieve the goal of efficient probate by selecting a particular individual as executor.

Those who decided to make wills undertook the act in a variety of ways. Some used trained lawyers, others neighbors. Others were satisfied with their own drafting skills and made holographs, and still others took advantage of the ability to make testamentary directions by word of mouth.

The causes exhumed here document a 'culture of will-making' that was in fact in need of reform. The circumstances under which many wills were drafted gave rise to wills of dubious validity. Will-makers, such as Joan Smith who had 'done something that might amount to a will,' also empowered probate courts judges like those in the Prerogative Court to determine the validity of a will against the charges of others, to apply the amorphous legal rules to a narrative of will-making that the judge stitched together from scraps of evidence submitted. Perhaps the adoption of more rigorous validity rules would assist them with their labour. But before one can be certain of the court's dilemma, a more complete observation of the causes is in order. It is the law and the probate litigation that it spawned that the following two chapters address.

PART I
The Forum and its Litigation

That the probate of wills in early modern England was largely reposed in ecclesiastical courts was a peculiarity of English legal practice. This section, comprised of the following two chapters, recounts the hazy origins of church court probate and outlines proposed reforms before, during, and after the civil wars. Its goes on to analyze the probate litigation in the Prerogative Court in the second half of the seventeenth century squarely within the context of the major Restoration reform in property transmission, the adoption of the Statute of Frauds. Though a sketch of probate procedure is provided in the narrative, those readers who require a fuller description should consult the Appendix. Likewise the methodology employed in selecting and analyzing the cases is therein provided.

Chapter 2

Probate Jurisdiction in Early Modern England: England's Own 'Peculiar Institution' in Crisis

Introduction

In modern Western legal systems, both secular law and courts largely govern family and property relations. In early modern England, however, it was ecclesiastical law and the church courts that controlled crucial areas of family and property law, most notably marriage-formation law and the probate of wills, and the intergenerational devolution of personal property.[1] This chapter charts the history of probate in England, and argues that, by the second half of the seventeenth century, England's 'peculiar institution,' ecclesiastical probate, was in crisis. While Parliament made some attempt during the Interregnum to revamp probate jurisdiction, the reforms instituted were not comprehensive and they did not survive the Restoration. Nevertheless, Parliament tried again in the 1670s and eventually enacted significant reform with the adoption of the Statute of Frauds in 1677. This chapter provides evidence that there was a considerable quantity of probate litigation in which a variety of issues of will validity were raised. It analyzes probate litigation both before and after the statute was adopted, and suggests that the reforms made were probably undertaken in reaction to perceived shortcomings in the probate system. The chapter then goes on to consider whether the reforms actually lightened the Canterbury Prerogative Court's burden after 1677.

---

[1] Though far-reaching, ecclesiastical jurisdiction was not exclusive. Borough and manorial courts also probated wills. In England, wills were usually proved in church courts, where issues of will validity might be raised. The transmission of personal property directed in the will or, if the deceased property-owner died intestate, the administration of his or her goods was supervised by the church courts. The application of the will or succession to land was governed by Chancery or the common-law courts. King's Bench heard testamentary litigation involving land, and testamentary directions over the disposition of land by use were under the purview of Chancery. Indeed, some of the wills that we shall observe in Prerogative Court of Canterbury litigation had already been or were simultaneously being heard in royal courts.

The Origins of Testamentary Jurisdiction

If having probate jurisdiction delegated to church courts seems anomalous to the modern observer, it certainly was of ancient vintage. That testamentary business is found in the earliest surviving church-court records makes it difficult to ascertain precisely when ecclesiastical probate was first established in England. Church-court intervention in testamentary matters appears in the earliest extant records of the Province of Canterbury, which date from the beginning of the thirteenth century.[2] While causes heard by the Archbishop of Canterbury or his court in the course of the thirteenth century largely concerned testamentary debt and the collection of legacies owed from executors, other matters were raised.[3] One cause involved jurisdictional quarrels between church courts. It concerned the collection of a legacy, and was brought in the first instance to the archbishop's court rather than to a diocesan court; it became enmeshed in procedural issues before it disappeared from the record.[4] Another recorded cause probably involved the validity of a particular will, since six witnesses appeared in court to testify that a document offered for probate was the one that they had witnessed.[5]

Likewise, the earliest commentators on the common law, Glanvill and Bracton, acknowledged that testamentary jurisdiction, proof of will validity, rested with the church courts. Yet they offer only very limited insight on the origins of testamentary jurisdiction. By the time of Glanvill, the late twelfth century, probate of wills and the administration of estates of personal property was firmly established. In his discussion of wills in his section on inheritance,[6] Glanvill acknowledged that heirs were 'bound to observe' the testaments of their ancestors and to pay their debts. He then considered freedom of testation, the capacity to make a will, and the will-making process. When he turned to the central concern of his work, the royal jurisdiction, he acknowledged that proof of will validity lay in the church courts: if a person detaining a dead person's property did so because he questioned the validity of a will on the grounds of improper execution, or if he disputed specific terms, the issue, Glanvill wrote, should be heard in the church courts and 'determined ... by the evidence of those who were present at the making of the testament.'[7] Thus proof of will

---

2   Norma Adams and Charles Donahue, Jr., *Select Cases from the Ecclesiastical Courts of Canterbury c.1200–1301*, Selden Society, London, vol. 95 (1981), pp. 3, 10.

3   Ibid., pp. 88–93.

4   Ibid., Case C.7.

5   Ibid., Case C. 8.

6   G.D.G. Hall (ed.), *The Treatise on the Laws and Customs of the Realm of England Commonly called Glanvill* 2nd edn (Oxford, 1993), Book VII.

7   Ibid., p. 81.

authenticity – probate – was firmly under church court jurisdiction by the close of the twelfth century.

Although Bracton's discussion of wills is more complete, and he confirmed that probate jurisdiction reposed in the church courts, he was likewise silent on the origins of ecclesiastical control over will validity, writing only that 'the royal court meddles in testamentary matters no more than in matrimonial.'[8] Indeed for Bracton the dividing line between ecclesiastical and lay jurisdiction over a testator's estate was firmly fixed. He noted that those debts of the deceased that were acknowledged or proved prior to his or her death (and therefore the estate's assets) should be pursued by executors in the church courts. However, for debts not acknowledged or proved during the dead person's lifetime, the heirs of the deceased had to bring an action in the secular court.[9]

Thus early commentators on English law recognized that probate of wills was under spiritual court control, but they had little to say about the origins of this ecclesiastical jurisdiction. Later writers are no more enlightening. For example, Sir Edward Coke imagined a time in which probate jurisdiction was in lay hands. In *Hensloe's Case*,[10] an action in debt was brought by a creditor of a deceased debtor against the executor of the debtor's will. In order to resolve the case, it was necessary to consider the powers of ordinaries, and the historian in Coke could not resist the opportunity to inquire into the origins of their jurisdiction. Coke first noted the rather inconsistent view of Lynwoode regarding the origins of probate jurisdiction in church courts: that it reposed therein both *consuetudine Anglae* and *per consensum Regis*. Relying on the writing of Archbishop Matthew Parker, Coke seemed to favor the latter view: that the king had delegated authority to the Bishops to probate wills. But he did not speculate upon precisely when and by what means this jurisdiction was obtained.[11]

Thus neither Coke nor Parker specified when the transition from lay to spiritual control occurred. Other commentators assumed that there had been a transfer. For example, John Selden wrote that clerical jurisdiction dated from 'ancient times' in most of England, though in certain places secular jurisdiction obtained by custom. Selden observed, however, that testamentary jurisdiction could not be intrinsic to Christianity because lay probate existed in most other parts of Europe. Because ecclesiastical jurisdiction was not pervasive in Christian Europe, Selden therefore concluded that the origins 'not being sufficiently found in either of these laws [the civil or the canon] diverse parts of which … have been

---

[8]   Samuel E. Thorne, trans., *Bracton on the Laws and Customs of England* (Cambridge, MA, 1968), vol. II, p. 181.

[9]   Ibid.

[10]   (1600) 9 Co. Rep. 36b.

[11]   Ibid., 38a.

much dispersed through Christendom,' church court oversight in England was 'now exercised by imitation among us.'[12]

Other writers were equally perplexed by the anomaly of ecclesiastical probate jurisdiction and similarly confounded by its origins. For example, the antiquary Sir Henry Spelman believed that probate was always in the hands of the clergy, though he added: 'I must confess it be hard to find manifest proof in those ancient days of the Conquerer and his sons.'[13] John Ayliffe likewise remarked upon the uniqueness of such ecclesiastical jurisdiction in England, and found its origins in 'custom.'[14] Writing in the eighteenth century, the ecclesiastical lawyer Richard Burn reasoned that because there were wills before there were ecclesiastical jurisdictions, probate jurisdiction must have originally reposed in lay hands: in the county court or the court baron.[15]

Legal writers were more comfortable in offering the rationale for, rather than explaining the origins of, testamentary jurisdiction in church courts. Here consensus was achieved amongst the commentators, though largely because subsequent authors seem merely to have reiterated the speculation of their learned predecessors. For example, William Perkins, writing in the seventeenth century, offered as justification for ecclesiastical jurisdiction the dubious proposition that 'spiritual men have better consciences than laymen.'[16] In the early eighteenth century, Burn found Perkins's logic compelling, citing him for the proposition that the clergy were more diligent supervisors of probate.[17] Sir William Blackstone followed on, but he provided no novel insight into either the origins or the logic of church-court oversight. In summarizing testamentary jurisdiction, Blackstone concurred with Perkins that, with respect to the goods of intestates, the clergy were 'of better conscience' than laymen, so the crown wisely vested probate jurisdiction in an ecclesiastic, the ordinary.[18]

Better consciences aside, the scattered thoughts of Sir Thomas Ridley may provide a more satisfying conceptual justification for ecclesiastical jurisdiction.

---

12   *Of the Original of Ecclesiastic Jurisdiction of Testaments* (London, 1683), p. 4.

13   Henry Spelman, 'Of the Origins of Testaments and Wills,' in *The English Works of Sir Henry Spelman, Kt.* (London, 1727), p. 132. Spelman was more certain when it came to Scotland. According to him, by the time of the conquest, Scottish kings had granted probate jurisdiction to the bishops.

14   John Ayliffe, *Parergon Juris Anglicani: or a commentary by way of supplement to the canon and constitutions of the Church of England* (London, 1724), p. 535.

15   Richard Burn, *Ecclesiastical Law* 6th edn (London, 1797), pp. 229–30.

16   John Perkins, *A Profitable Book* (15th edn Garland Reprint, 1978), sec. 486.

17   Burn, *Ecclesiastical Law*, p. 233.

18   William Blackstone, *Commentaries on the Laws of England*, 4 vols. (University of Chicago Reprint, 1979), vol. II, p. 494.

According to Ridley, the implementation of provisions in wills was the enforcement of a trust: had men understood that their executors would not perform their wills, 'they would never have putt their trust as they did.'[19] In the formative period of the common law, the royal courts provided no specific actions for breach of trust, and aggrieved parties would need to go elsewhere. The ecclesiastical courts provided an apt tribunal. While the unavailability of recourse to royal courts might not explain fully the origins of church-court probate jurisdiction, it may help to account for its continuance.

Modern scholars who have worked on the ecclesiastical courts note the peculiarity of church-court probate jurisdiction in England, but have likewise shed little light on its genesis. F.W. Maitland speculated upon the origin of manorial-court probate jurisdiction over the estates of villeins. Because the lordship of a number of manor courts that exercised probate jurisdiction was or had previously been in the hands of religious houses, Maitland suggested that it might be found in privileges granted by Bishops to the spiritual lords of the manor.[20] When a manor holding probate jurisdiction came into lay hands, the privilege passed to the temporal lord. The manor of Chippenham provides such an example. In 1465, the homage claimed that the lord (a layman) held probate jurisdiction 'by the confirmation and ratification of various popes of Rome, as appears by bulls sealed under lead and shown to the ministers of the bishop of Norwich.'[21] Although Chippenham had been in ecclesiastical hands, the manorial court rolls suggest that its probate of wills had fallen into desuetude long before 1465. The reassertion of the custom replete with the allegation of origins was probably an attempt by a vigilant steward to reassert jurisdiction, and thereafter probate was a regular feature of business in the manor court. Spiritual origins, however, cannot account for all examples of manorial-court probate, because manor courts exercising probate jurisdiction can be found that had never been in spiritual hands.[22]

---

[19]   Thomas Ridley, *A View of the Civil and Ecclesiastical Law* (Oxford, 1675), p. 380.

[20]   Frederick Pollock and Frederick W. Maitland, *The History of English Law* (Cambridge, 1968), vol. II, pp. 341–2.

[21]   L.R. Poos and Lloyd Bonfield, *Select Pleas in Manorial Courts 1250–1550: family and property law* (Selden Society, London, vol. 114, 1998), case no. 222.

[22]   An example of manorial-court probate illustrates its hazy origins, even to contemporaries. In Barnet in Hertfordshire, manor court jurors proclaimed in 1349 that the court had jurisdiction to prove wills of naïf tenants while free tenants had their wills probated before the archdeacon of St. Albans Monastery; when asked from 'what time this custom began,' the jurors recited the well-worn refrain 'from time out of mind.' Ibid., case no. 212 and pp. cxlvi–ii.

The most venerated modern student of English wills, Michael Sheehan, traced developments in testamentary practice in England from the ability of an Anglo-Saxon property owner to make *post obit* gifts (ones that would take effect at death) through to the readily recognizable pattern of the medieval will. According to Sheehan, the church's interest in testamentary matters can be explained by the presence of clergy at the deathbed, and the need to protect bequests to the poor. Thus the church's earliest intervention in the area of 'probate' was to assist the dying person in fulfilling an intention to make a gift to the church: to make certain that property, both real and personal, bequeathed for the good of his soul would pass free from the claims of his heirs or creditors.[23]

Yet, as Sheehan noted, it was not necessary for the church to garner probate jurisdiction to ensure that pious bequests were honored. While Christian teaching may have provided the motive for bequests outside the recognized line of succession, and the church initially strove to protect them, English church-court intervention went further. Eventually clerics or their surrogates found themselves engaged in a wide-ranging administrative role. Church courts considered the validity of wills and monitored the succession to personal property in circumstances in which the issues in controversy bore little relation to pious bequests.[24] By the mid-seventeenth century, the Prerogative Court was probating thousands of wills, and supervising nearly the same number of administrations of intestate estates.[25]

Unlike Jack Goody, who argued that the church maintained control over probate to secure and to protect the flow of legacies for spiritual purposes,[26] Sheehan cast the survival and strengthening of clerical intervention in the process of probate in a far less conspiratorial fashion. He rejected Goody's notion that ecclesiastical control over will-making was a result of the church lawyers 'bullying' their lay brethren; after all, most secular administrators were clerics, and were aware of temporal 'claims and resources.'[27] Sheehan merely concluded that, once allocation of probate jurisdiction to the church had been made, it was regarded as a franchise. In common with much English justice in the twelfth and thirteenth centuries, the ability to prove wills was just one of many other privately

---

[23] Michael Sheehan, *The Will in Medieval England from the Conversion of the Anglo-Saxons to the Thirteenth Century* (Toronto, 1963), pp. 11–8.

[24] Ibid., 3–4.

[25] Motoyasu Takahashi, 'The number of wills proved in the sixteenth and seventeenth centuries: graphs, with tables and commentary,' in G. H. Martin and Peter Spufford (eds.), *The Records of a Nation* (Woodbridge, 1990), p. 212.

[26] Jack Goody, *The Development of the Family and Marriage in Europe* (Cambridge, 1986), ch. 6.

[27] Sheehan, *The Will in Medieval England*, pp. 137–8.

held rights to dispense justice. By the time royal justice made inroads into areas of private jurisdiction, probate was well-ensconced in the church courts, and it was never absorbed by the royal courts. As intriguing as Sheehan's view of the origins and continuation of ecclesiastic court jurisdiction over wills may be, it does not explain why it endured until the nineteenth century, particular since other areas of private jurisdiction were challenged and successfully absorbed in the thirteenth century.[28] Yet when the boundary between spiritual and temporal jurisdiction was fixed by the writ *Circumspecte agatis* in the thirteenth century, probate remained within the purview of the church courts.[29]

Perhaps such speculation as to pedigree is the closest the historian can come to understanding precisely why probate jurisdiction was originally garnered by the church courts. Its survival, however, is more interesting than its genesis. Why did secular jurisdiction not take control of probate, except with respect to disputes over freehold land when it became devisable by will,[30] and for all property briefly during the Interregnum?[31] Perhaps attending to the sheer mass of testamentary business was a daunting prospect for the royal courts which had in the course of the Middle Ages acquired jurisdiction over other subject matter. Even as avid a law reformer as Sir Mathew Hale admitted that to place the probate of wills 'under the Examination of Temporal courts ... perchance, would be thought to be great a Charge.'[32] Lack of interest, and perhaps despair, rather than design, may account for the survival of this peculiarity of the English legal system. But the less cynical might explain the absence of pressure for reform (with the exception of concerns over excessive fees) by arguing that the system to administer estates implemented by the church courts was serviceable, at least until pressure for reform began to mount in the seventeenth century. Prior

---

[28]   See D.W. Sutherland, *Quo Warranto Proceedings in the Reign of Edward I* (Oxford, 1963).

[29]   Peter Heath, *Church and Realm, 1272–1461* (London, 1988), pp. 39–42; David Millon, '*Circumspecte Agatis* Revisited,' *Law and History Review*, vol. 2 (1984), pp. 105–17.

[30]   32 Hen. VIII, c. 1 (1540).

[31]   'An Act for the probate of Wills, and Granting Administrations in' C.H. Firth and R.S. Rait (eds.), *Acts and Ordinances of the Interregnum 1642–1660*, 3 vols. (London, 1911), vol. 2, pp. 702–3 and pp. 564–6.

[32]   I have a reference in my notes to a pamphlet version of Sir Mathew Hale, *Two Tracts on the Benefit of Registering Deeds in England* (London, 1756), pp. 44–5. However, the same work can more readily be found as *A treatise, shewing how usefull, safe, reasonable and beneficial, the inrolling & registring of all conveyances of lands, may be to the inhabitants of this kingdom by a person of great learning and judgment* (London, 1756).

thereto, the major objections to ecclesiastical-court probate, at least so far as Parliament was concerned, were largely related to procedural delay and to cost.[33]

Probate in the Early Modern England

From the Reign of Elizabeth to the Civil Wars

Until the flurry of activity during the civil wars and Interregnum, Parliament seemed content to allow probate jurisdiction to remain largely in the hands of church courts and left it largely untouched. Between the Statute of Wills (1540),[34] which sanctioned and governed the testamentary disposition of lands and tenements, and the Restoration (1660) only one statute was enacted that dealt with succession to personal property. The thrust of this late Elizabethan statute (1601), as amply articulated in its verbose preamble (which runs to approximately half the length of the entire statute!), was to protect the creditors of those who died intestate rather than to improve the process by which their estates were distributed. In order to do so, the statute held the administrator of an intestate's estate accountable for the property of deceased person that came into his or her hands.[35]

Likewise, there was little change in probate practice in the prior century from within the Prerogative Court of Canterbury. In his study of the court in the sixteenth century, Christopher Kitching discerned only modest reforms and 'minor procedural adjustments.'[36] Richard Helmholz agreed, remarking upon a certain 'timelessness' to probate jurisdiction in the church courts during the sixteenth century.[37] Helmholz regarded changes during the period as minimal, and suggested that those that did occur were directed towards ensuring that

---

[33] Heath, *Church and Realm*, 212, 288. See generally, Richard Helmholz, *Canon Law and the Law of England* (London, 1988), and Ralph Houlbrooke, *Death, Ritual and Bereavement* (London, 1989).

[34] 32 Hen. VIII, c. 2 (1540).

[35] 43 Eliz. I, c. 8 (1601). The statute did so by charging the administrator of the goods of an intestate individual with personal liability for the fraudulent discharge of debts. In substance, then, the statute merely extended the liability already imposed upon the executors of wills to the administrators of intestates' estates.

[36] Christopher Kitching, 'The Prerogative Court of Canterbury from Warham to Whitgift,' in Rosemary O'Day and Felicity Heal (eds.), *Continuity and Change: personnel and administration of the Church of England, 1500–1642* (Leicester, 1976), p. 213.

[37] Helmholz, *Canon Law*, p. 78.

probates were not granted without due deliberation, and that the required fees were collected in accordance with (and not in excess of) statutory mandates.[38]

Parliamentary Reform: the First Era

During the civil wars and the Interregnum, however, Parliament was required to turn its attention to probate, due in large measure to its assault upon the episcopacy and its jurisdiction. Donald Veale, in his study of law reform during the period, maintained that the focus of reform in the area of probate was upon forum rather than upon procedure and substantive law.[39] Law reformers sought to replace church courts with secular courts, but they put forward only modest proposals to alter the established requirements for the due execution of wills. With respect to forum, Parliament retained both a preference for localized probate jurisdiction (as opposed to a single centralized court) and a partiality towards retaining the procedural status quo. But some change in the latter was mooted, and indeed implemented, and the aspirations of the reformers provide useful insights into contemporary perceptions of the probate system.

The process of reform began in November 1644, when Parliament deprived William Merrick of his office as Commisary General or Keeper of the Prerogative Court of Canterbury and replaced him with Sir Nathaniel Brent.[40] Merrick, a Royalist, was removed primarily because had 'absented himself from due attendance on the said Office ... by reason whereof, the Administration of the estates of such persons who died intestate could not be taken, nor the Wills of others ... duly proved.'[41] Yet it was not until April of 1646 that, Parliament selected a committee that was charged with the reform of probate jurisdiction.[42] The committee did not report back to Parliament until 1649, when a second committee, headed by Sir Peter Wentworth and Miles Corbet, was constituted to bring forward a reform bill. This measure was read twice, but went no further.[43] In the meantime, in October 1646, Parliament abolished both the episcopacy and all jurisdictions held by their authority.[44] While Brent's jurisdiction was

---

[38] Ibid., p 87.

[39] Donald Veale, *The Popular Movement for Law Reform 1640–1660* (Oxford, 1970), pp. 193–4.

[40] 'An Ordinance for the constituting of Sir Nathaniel Brent Judge of the prerogative Court of Canterbury', in Firth and Rait (eds.), *Acts and Ordinances*, vol. I, pp. 564–6.

[41] Ibid., p. 564.

[42] Henry Parker, *Reformation in Courts and Cases Testamentary* (London, 1650), p. 2.

[43] Ibid., pp. 2–3.

[44] 'An Ordinance for the abolishing of Archbishops and Bishops within the Kingdom of England, and the Dominion of Wales, and for settling of their Lands and Possessions upon

exempted by the ordinance, it became necessary to consider alternatives to probate in the now defunct Bishops' courts, and in the lesser ecclesiastical jurisdictions that probated wills and administered estates.

It was one matter to abolish existing probate jurisdictions, but quite another to reconstruct them. The pamphlet literature produced during the period suggests that there were deep divisions within Parliament over the appropriate structure that probate jurisdiction should henceforth assume. A pamphlet written by the staunch Parliamentarian Henry Parker in 1650 set out two 'extreme' alternatives that were apparently under consideration, and added a third that he argued 'mitigates both these extremes.'[45] The first plan was to create a set of at least 20 probate courts manned by 'civilians,' lawyers trained, like their church-court predecessors, in the civil law, while another proposal advocated the vesting of probate jurisdiction in the common-law courts. According to Parker, while both options raised political concerns, the second was more palatable to some for partisan reasons: the common lawyers had supported Parliament, while the civilians were largely Royalists.

Parker's third option granted comprehensive probate jurisdiction to a secularized Prerogative Court, and then went on to create a court to which appeals from its judgments might be lodged. This solution was attractive to Parker, because he wanted to retain the civil – law nature of probate jurisdiction. In the first place, Parker noted that England had hitherto never regarded probate jurisdiction as 'municipal.' Moreover, England required lawyers conversant with the civil law to deal with a variety of other legal matters. According to Parker, without probate business there would be insufficient income for the civilians. As a consequence, England would cease to produce its own lawyers trained in the civil law, and soon thereafter all such practitioners would be foreigners, an unsatisfactory state of affairs. Finally, Parker noted that sufficient punishment had already been visited upon the civilians, because matrimonial causes and questions of 'canonical obedience' had already been secularized.[46]

In his tract, Parker raised objections to both the 'civilian' and the 'common – law' solutions to probate. In the first place, he believed that there was insufficient business for 20 probate courts; secondly, he argued that the courts at Westminster were already overburdened with cases, and therefore unable to entertain probate jurisdiction.[47] To create probate courts with insufficient business would be dear in terms of money; to bestow more business on already clogged royal courts

---

Trustees, for the use of the Commonwealth,' in Firth and Rait (eds.), *Acts and Ordinances*, vol. I, pp. 879–83.

[45] Parker, *Reformation in Courts*, pp. 3–4.

[46] Ibid., pp. 3–5.

[47] Ibid., pp. 7–9.

would be costly in terms of time. Under his plan, routine probate would be moved to the localities by requiring judges to send deputies to 'the chiefe Town or City of each County' that was located at least 60 or 70 miles distant from London. Contested wills and other testamentary disputes would, however, be heard exclusively in London, where a probate registry would be created.[48]

William Sheppard, the prolific legal treatise writer of the mid-seventeenth century, offered a quite different proposal. His scheme would create a central probate court for those who died in the area around London (including Westminster, Middlesex, Kent, Surrey, Essex, and Hertfordshire) as well as at sea and abroad, with local registries in the other counties. Sheppard also envisaged an appellate structure. Only one appeal to a higher court was to be permitted, with the forum of resort dependent upon the place of probate: those in the home counties (and therefore in proximity to London) would have appeals heard in the courts at Westminster; those probates or administrations heard in the provincial registries would be appealed to provincial courts and, in the absence of provincial courts, appeal would be to the General Sessions.[49]

Not everyone agreed that such elaborate court systems were required. Hugh Peters, more a preacher than he was a lawyer, promoted a decidedly simpler solution, arguing that it should be sufficient for wills to be proved before two justices of the peace without charge and to be registered in the parish register or another book 'kept in everie parish to that purpose.'[50] In a tract written in response to Peters, Rice Vaughn, of Gray's Inn, acknowledged that wills without controversy might be so serviced, but scoffed at Peters's naïveté. Vaughn noted that probate affairs could be far more complicated than merely the registration of wills or the straightforward administration of intestate estates. His reservations against placing jurisdiction in the hands of justices of the peace summarized the complexities of probate that the Prerogative Court dealt with regularly, and it is worth setting out at length:

> But what then? when they are acknowledged, Do you suppose all wills to be good then? and must the Justices be Judges and **Interpreters of the Wills and Testaments of such as devise** estates? Are they all throughout the Nation so quicksighted, as to discern the Intentions of Testators in their Wills? and

---

[48] Ibid., pp. 6, 10.

[49] William Sheppard, *England's Balme* (London, 1656), pp. 140–42. Sheppard also offered some suggestions on how to regulate recalcitrant executors more effectively, pp. 105–8, 210, and noted that it was advisable to clarify the pattern of intestate distribution, p. 142.

[50] Hugh Peters, *Good Work for a Good Magistrate* (London, 1651), p. 33. Fortunately, his proposal to 'burn all the old Records' upon the creation of the will register was not implemented.

Judges fit to decide whether men make their Wills with disposing memories and understandings, or no? can they with ease reconcile the seeming contradictions that often happen in dying mens Wills, by reason of those ignorant persons that many times they are necessitated to imploy to write down their Wills? are they so able Judges, where several Wills arise in competition one with the other to decide the controversie aright, which should take place? and do they know how to determine, whether, and when a Nuncupative, or a Verbal Will shall avoid a written Will or no? If so then let the design of your proposal prosper.[51]

Parliament's eventual solution to the question of probate jurisdiction more resembled the visions of Parker or Sheppard than that of Peters. But the plan adopted was incomplete. In the first place, attention was focused on the highest level of probate court, while lesser jurisdictions were ignored. An act was adopted in 1653 that abolished probate jurisdiction in the Prerogative Courts of Canterbury and of York and replaced them with a Central Probate Court.[52] Twenty men were constituted by Parliament to serve as Judges of the Probate Court. This court was vested with all of the 'jurisdiction and powers to probate wills and grant administration for the whole of England and Wales that had lawfully been held by Sir Nathaniel Brent (now deceased) for the Province of Canterbury.' The judges were authorized, though they were not bound, to sit in groups of five at any place in England and Wales. Because they assumed the powers of both Prerogative Courts, Canterbury and York, the Central Probate Court's jurisdiction was limited to estates with a value over £5. The lesser probate jurisdictions, to the extent that they were not previously dissolved, were unaffected by the act. Interestingly, no guidance was given respecting the procedural or substantive law to be applied in the new forum. Was the court to resemble its predecessor, an ecclesiastical jurisdiction reconstituted with lay judges? What law would resolve the myriad of probate disputes that Vaughn recognized were the mainstay of probate jurisdiction? These two vital questions were not addressed, perhaps suggesting that, unlike the ecclesiastical control over forum, probate procedure and law were not areas of popular discontent.

Incomplete though the act was, Parliament went no further. While the act establishing the Central Probate Court was revived and confirmed several times during the Interregnum,[53] no attempt was made to extend its jurisdiction to the kingdom's less wealthy subjects. In short, Parliament was more concerned to

---

[51]   Rice Vaughn, *A Plea for the Common Laws of England* (London, 1651), pp. 10–11.

[52]   Firth and Rait (eds.), *Acts and Ordinances*, vol. II, p. 702.

[53]   Ibid., vol. II, p. 824 (Dec. 24, 1653); p. 869 (Apr. 3, 1654); p. 1131 (June 26, 1657); p. 1272 (May 19, 1659); p. 1317 (July 22, 1659).

disband old institutions, the Prerogative Courts of Canterbury and York, than it was to revamp probate jurisdiction and procedure.

The Second Era of Parliamentary Reform

Thus, personnel aside, one might conclude from Parliament's modest tinkerings that there was reasonable satisfaction with the way in which testamentary business was handled in the kingdom. Indeed, after the Restoration Parliament revived probate jurisdiction in those church courts that had been deprived of it by statute. William Merrick returned to the revived Prerogative Court of Canterbury, and by the close of 1660 the court's probate business had returned to levels that existed before the court was dissolved.[54]

If Parliament's intervention in the area of probate jurisdiction during the Interregnum was limited to fashioning a replacement for the Prerogative Courts of Canterbury and of York, its attention turned squarely to matters of probate procedure rather than to forum in the following decade. In the 1670s, Parliament passed two acts that covered a number of critical areas of the probate of wills and intestate administration.

The first post-Restoration reform statute, enacted by Parliament in 1670, was styled 'An Act for the better settling of Intestates Estates,' commonly referred to as the Statute of Distributions.[55] While the statute is perhaps best remembered for the pattern of descent and distribution to property directed therein,[56] its primary thrust was to govern the conduct of administrators and protect the deceased individual's creditors.[57] Like its Elizabethan predecessor, the statute

---

[54]   I.M. Green, *The Re-establishment of the Church of England, 1660–63* (Oxford, 1978), pp. 132–3.

[55]   22 and 23 Car. II, c. 10 (1670).

[56]   The statute mandated the following distribution: one-third to the widow, and the remaining two-thirds to the children of the intestate. If the intestate died without issue the widow received one-half, with the residue descending to the next of kin. Amy Erickson notes that the statute disadvantaged widows by reducing their share of an intestate husband's estate to one-third if the intestate had children and one-half if he did not. Practice prior to 1670 in some areas allowed the widow a larger share. Dr. Erickson suggests the treatment of widows was separated in the statute between those with children and those without. Strictly speaking, this is incorrect; the distinction was between intestates that died with or without children regardless of whether the children were also those of the widow. *Women and Property in Early Modern England* (London, 1993) 29, pp. 178–81. It must be noted, however, that the statute expressly allowed the customs of London and the Province of York to stand. 22 and 23 Car. II, c. 10 (1670) (Sec. 2).

[57]   At least if the structure of the statute is relevant. The statute begins (ibid., Sec. 1) with administration procedure and then addresses the pattern of distribution (ibid., Sec. 3).

directed that sufficient performance bonds be taken of administrators, and in fact the legislation even commenced with a recitation of the proper form that such instruments should assume. The act also empowered the ordinaries to compel administrators to account for goods that came into their hands, and to direct administrators to pay the balance to the appropriate distributees specified, after debts and expenses were paid. Parliament also provided that no distribution should be made until one year after the intestate's death and that, upon disbursement, the recipients of payments from an administrator were required to undertake to reimburse him or her if a debt owing to the intestate was thereafter recovered against the administrator.[58]

The second statute, 'An Act for the prevention of Frauds and Perjuryes,' enacted in 1677, tightened the requirements for will validity.[59] First, this Statute of Frauds required that all directions made governing the descent of lands and tenements should be in writing, signed by the testator, and witnessed by three or four credible witnesses.[60] If the directions were made by will, the statute also prescribed the means by which such testamentary acts were to be revoked.[61] A second, and less studied, set of provisions governed the validity of oral wills of personal property.[62] So comprehensive was the statute that, although it was modified in the nineteenth century by the Wills Act of 1837,[63] it set the requirements for the validity of wills that remained essentially in effect in England until the reforms of the twentieth century. Because the statute had an extensive impact on testamentary litigation in the Prerogative Court, it will be necessary to consider carefully the debate on its adoption and the detail of its provisions.

The Parliamentary Adoption of the Statute of Frauds

As Lord Nottingham noted in a speech delivered in a committee of the whole House of Commons in February 1671, the issue regarding the registration of property transfers 'hath been for so many years the discourse of wise and knowing men that one would think by this time the question should be thoroughly

---

58   Ibid., Sec. 5.
59   29 Car. II, c. 3 (1677).
60   Ibid., Sec. 5.
61   Ibid., Sec.6.
62   Ibid., Secs. 18–23.
63   7 Will. IV and 1 Vict., c. 26 (1837).

understood.'[64] One might say the same for the adoption of the Statute of Frauds.[65] Yet the path to Parliamentary adoption was tortuous. Two crucial alterations from earlier drafts, an addition and a deletion, appear in the Lords' Bill passed in May 1675, the immediate predecessor to the statute adopted, changes which have attracted relatively scant attention from historians.[66] First there is what the May 1675 bill did not contain: it omitted a section that had invalidated deathbed wills, a provision that had been included in earlier drafts. Secondly, there is what was added: six new paragraphs appeared that established requirements for the validity and probate of nuncupative wills of personal property.

While the inclusion of the sections governing the validity and probate of nuncupative wills is often noted, it is the eliminated section that seems more critical, particularly in light of the testamentary litigation in the Prerogative Court that will be explored in the next chapter. The earlier Lords' Bill of 1673 contained a provision that voided a will in writing that was made in a person's last illness, unless the will-maker recovered and, in the words of the bill, 'shall after the making thereof Live to go abroad again and bee seene in some Church in the time of divine Service or in some publique and open markette place.'[67] This mandate was followed in the same paragraph by a prohibition against the oral revocation of wills that disposed of lands and tenements, and a further clause that held that wills of land should remain in force unless altered by a written document. Taken together, these provisions suggest that there was some concern that property-holders were being induced to modify their wills by both documents and utterances made on their deathbed. Indeed, Nottingham had noted the link between the deathbed and the oral utterances in his speech, arguing that 'men are drawn into unwary discourses upon their deathbeds and one or two words amount to a revocation.'[68] However, Lord Chief Justice North must have thought that the tightening up of the requirements for revocation was a sufficient safeguard against rash revisions on the deathbed. When he was summoned before the Lords' Committee in April 1675, he suggested a revision: deathbed wills would be permitted, but existing wills should only be revoked by

---

[64]   D.E.C. Yale (ed.), *Lord Nottingham's Chancery Cases*, 2 vols. (Selden Society, London, 1954 and 1961), vol. 79, p. 966.

[65]   Crawford Henning, 'The original drafts of the Statute of Frauds (29 Car. II c. 3) and their authors,' *University of Pennsylvania Law Review*, vol. 61 (1913), pp. 283–316. Philip Hamburger, 'The Conveyancing Purposes of the Statute of Frauds,' *American Journal of Legal History*, vol. xxvii (1983), pp. 354–85.

[66]   *Ninth Report of the Royal Commission on Historical Manuscripts*, Part II, Appendix, p. 48.

[67]   Henning, 'Original Drafts,' p. 289.

[68]   Yale (ed.), *Nottingham's Chancery Cases*, vol. 79, p. 978.

a subsequent writing or 'by burning, canceling, tearing, or obliterating the same by the Testator himself, or in his presence by his direction and consent.'[69] This second means of revocation – by a physical act done to the document – a process which is familiar to the modern student of wills – was not specified in the earlier bill. Thus the revised bill of May 1675 contained an important innovation, but also a revision: the means by which a person could revoke by physical act done to the document was clearly specified, and the ability to bequeath on the deathbed was preserved.

But what of oral wills? Neither the 1673 draft bill nor indeed any of its predecessors had addressed the question of the validity of oral wills of personal property. However, shortly after North's revisions were approved, the committee asked Sir Leoline Jenkins to offer articles on the 'better Ascertaining of nuncupative wills.'[70] An eminent civil lawyer, Jenkins had followed Sir William Merrick as Judge of the Prerogative Court, and though he was frequently out of the country on diplomatic missions, he retained his position into the next decade.[71] Thus the provisions dealing with nuncupative wills came from the hand of one who was well-versed in the actual issues that arose in probate and estate administration. His six proposals, produced in less than a week, were annexed to the bill that was adopted by the Lords. The bill was subsequently dropped in the Commons, only to be revived in the following year.[72]

The provisions drafted by Sir Leoline were largely the ones finally enacted in 1677, the particulars of which will be discussed below. The most significant difference between the two drafts was the ambit of the document. While the validity requirements in his draft applied to all oral wills, Parliament limited the statute's reach to oral wills of personal property where the value of the estate of personal property was in excess of £30. Most estates of this magnitude were likely to come before one of the two Prerogative Courts, rather than the lesser probate jurisdictions. Yet the Prerogative Courts could probate wills of lesser value, and the proposal therefore created dual standards for oral wills even within the same jurisdiction. Secondly, though it contained a limitation on the time period in which an oral will could be introduced into probate after its utterance, Sir

---

[69] *Ninth Report*, Part II, Appendix, p. 48.

[70] Ibid., p. 49. William Wynne, Jenkins's biographer, noted only that he had 'some Word' in the matter and refers specifically only to the section that makes an exception from the requirements regarding nuncupative wills for the wills of soldiers and seamen. *The Life of Sir Leoline Jenkins*, 2 vols. (London, 1724) p. liii. Unlike for the Statute of Distributions (vol. 2, pp. 695–7), there is no extant document penned by Jenkins that explains his draft.

[71] Ibid.

[72] *Ninth Report of the Royal Commission on Historical Manuscripts*, Part II, Appendix, p. 49.

Leoline's draft left blank the precise number of months. Parliament filled in the term: only six months could transpire between the time the words were spoken and the offer of probate. Parliament, however, added a qualification; the six-month time period was waived if the oral will had been redacted within six days of its utterance. With these modest amendments, the actual statute adopted closely followed Jenkins's proposals.

Regardless, it remains unclear why the Lords' Committee decided to marry requirements for the validity of oral wills of personal property to those dealing with land transfers by deed or will. After all, while the particulars may have come from an expert, the inspiration for inclusion seems to have emanated from the Lords' Committee rather than a probate court. Moreover, the inclusion of the requirements governing the validity of nuncupative wills in the statute, though not without its logic, is enigmatic. First, if the purpose of the bill was to regularize all property transfers so as to minimize the potential for fraud and perjury, it is odd that the very same draft that regulated oral wills excluded trusts of personal property from its ambit. While a provision in the 1673 Lords' Bill that required that declarations of trusts be in writing regardless of whether the trust corpus was personal or real property, it was eliminated in the 1675 draft.[73] So one circumstance in which fraud and perjury might be curtailed came within the purview of the bill – nuncupative wills of personal estates in excess of £30 – while another avenue for chicanery that had previously been blocked – trusts of personal property – was reopened. Second, if the drafters of the bill were concerned only with the conveyancing of freehold land, and not with transfers of personal property, why did they include a section on wills of personalty?[74] Indeed, the provisions on nuncupative wills were far-reaching: both their validity and the procedure by which they could be probated were addressed in the sort of detail that is absent from the other sections of the bill.

Though the response to these questions may only be speculation, and the historian is on less firm ground when dealing with the inspiration for legislation in the absence of specific references in the statute, one may be slightly more bold in resolving the latter point: the detail in which the matter of oral wills was addressed. Once he was summoned, Sir Leoline, who, according to his biographer, was a reformer who 'framed many Good Rules and Orders,' may have decided to seize the opportunity to legislate in a difficult area of probate.[75] Or was the eminent civilian perhaps taking the opportunity to secure his turf, and ensure that jurisdiction over wills would not be removed from his court? It

---

73   Henning, 'Original drafts,' p. 290.
74   Hamburger, 'Conveyancing purposes,' p. 373.
75   Wynne, *Life of Sir Leoline Jenkins*, p. xvii.

should be recalled that another clause was added to the draft bill, one that was 'to preserve the jurisdiction of the Prerogative Courts and other Ecclesiastical Courts in these cases.'[76] What is clear is that Parliament was reluctant to mandate drastic changes to the 'culture of will-making' of the time. After all, deathbed wills, written and oral, remained valid, though both were subject to tighter requirements.

The Statute's Mandates on Oral Wills

The Statute of Frauds created a set of substantive requirements for the validity of oral wills of personal estates valued in excess of £30. Its terms may now be addressed. First, the statute required an affirmation from three persons 'that the Testator at the time of pronouncing the same [his oral will] did bid the persons present or some of them beare wittnesse that such was his Will.' Secondly, the words had to have been spoken in the last illness of the deceased. Thirdly, there was a 'venue' requirement: with regard to nuncupative wills of those with an estate in excess of £30, the words alleged to be a will had to have been spoken in the dying person's

> habitation or dwelling or where he or she hath beene resident for the space of ten dayes or more next before the makeing of such Will except where such person was surprized or taken sick being from his owne home and dyed before he returned to the place of his or her dwelling.[77]

In addition to setting the requirements for the validity of oral wills, the statute also regulated two aspects of procedure in the church courts with regard to the proof of nuncupative wills. Testimony proving the validity of nuncupative wills had to be received by the court within six months of the deceased's death, except if the testimony 'or substance thereof' had been committed to writing within six days of the making of the will.[78] A further section of the statute required that the court grant letters testamentary that would authorize executors to deal with the estate no earlier than 14 days after the death of the testator. It also provided that the widow or next of kin be summoned to court to have the opportunity to contest the probate of an oral will.[79] Finally, the statute limited the ability to

---

[76]   *RCHM Ninth Report*, Part II, Appendix, p. 49.

[77]   All these requirements, although they were in separate sections of Sir Leoline's draft (points 1, 2 and 4 *RCHM Ninth Report*, Part II, Appendix, p. 49) were collapsed into a single section, 29 Car. II, c. 3 (1677), sec. 18.

[78]   Ibid., Sec 19.

[79]   Ibid., Sec 20.

revoke a clause, devise, or bequest in a written will by 'word of mouth.' According to the statute, the words spoken that were purported to have revocatory force had to have been reduced to writing in the lifetime of the will-maker, been read to him or her, and been assented to by the will-maker.[80]

Conclusion

Until the Interregnum, complaints about the fees that probate occasioned aside, Parliament seemed generally content with England's 'peculiar institution' – probate of wills and the administration of estates in the church courts. That jurisdiction was never fully removed from church courts during the Interregnum, and that it was so quickly returned at the Restoration suggest that there was some satisfaction (or at least no great dissatisfaction) with the ecclesiastical administration of personal estates. But the contentment may have been wearing thin, because by the 1670s Parliamentary interest had been piqued, and what emerged in the Statute of Frauds was a rather comprehensive 'reform' in the area of will-making with respect to land, as well as with regard to the probate of personalty in the church courts.

Very little direct evidence survives to shed light on precisely why Parliament became interested in succession to personal property in the 1670s, so inferences must be drawn more indirectly. Two points seem certain. The first was that Parliament did not seek a root and branch reform of the 'cultural of will-making'; even after the Statute of Frauds property could pass through deathbed directions. Second, because the author of the reform was the leading figure of the Prerogative Court of Canterbury, it is likely that the changes were framed in response to difficult issues that had been raised in litigation. The investigation of litigation both before and after the legislation that follows in the next chapter may confirm whether Parliament, through Sir Leoline Jenkins, was responding to actual problems in the probate process in the church courts.

---

[80] Ibid., Sec 21.

Chapter 3
Disputes: The Subject Matter of Testamentary Litigation

Introduction

This chapter is both deceivingly modest and unabashedly bold in scope. On the one hand, it seeks simply to outline to the reader that which counsel in the Prerogative Court of Canterbury presented to the judges: the legal issues that arose in testamentary litigation. Yet it unlocks, on the other hand, a significant evidentiary vault: the documents produced by probate litigation.[1] No comprehensive study of probate litigation has been hitherto undertaken. The significant quantity of evidence that these disputes produced – records that shed light on the processes of will-making and dying, as well as on the dynamics of family relations – has not therefore been exploited.

In this chapter I consider the hypothesis that was proffered in the previous one: that the reforms of the Statute of Frauds of 1677 were promulgated to address vexing questions of will validity heard in the probate courts, in particular, the most important venue, in the Prerogative Court of Canterbury. Cause and effect is not always easy to prove, but if the statute addressed problems with will validity that resulted in testamentary litigation that can be discerned by our survey of litigation,

---

[1]   There was a significant amount of testamentary business in the Prerogative Court of Canterbury. Each year thousands of wills were proved in common form and administrations granted. In addition to these will probates, somewhere between 75 and 200 (or more) wills were proved in solemn form. These probates are the ones studied in this volume. The validity of wills offered for probate in solemn form could be challenged and, as we shall see in this chapter, on a variety of grounds. Some solemn-form probates were more vigorously pursued, others less so. Even eliminating the probates in solemn form that were largely uncontested, causes that were largely contests in form rather than in substance (at least so far as the extant record suggests) 54 wills were actively engaged in litigation in 1676. Moreover, the sampling process for other years, though no doubt unscientific, suggests an even greater frequency of actively contested causes in the years observed. Four of five causes in our sample years were not simply routine offers of probate in solemn form; since on average about 80 to 200 wills were offered for probate in solemn form each year, somewhere in the neighborhood of 65 to 160 causes were probably actively pursued each year during the period. For a more detailed discussion see the Appendix. Similarly, for a discussion of the procedure involved in solemn-form probates, see the Appendix.

one may at the very least suggest that the Parliamentary intervention discussed in the last chapter was undertaken in response to troublesome causes. This inference may be the stronger because, as we noted, Sir Leoline Jenkins was actively involved both in the Canterbury court's business and in drafting an important part of the statute. Finally, the chapter considers whether the reforms actually adopted in the statute eased the court's burden. Were fewer troublesome causes litigated because of the statute's more rigorous validity requirements for oral wills? Meeting the burden of proof with respect to each of these queries is not easy, but analyzing the legal issues raised by the disputes that were brought both before and after the statute sheds some light on its aspirations, as well as upon its success. The straightforward should precede the complex, so a categorization and tabulation of the legal issues that were raised in the Prerogative Court of Canterbury will be addressed first, followed by the analysis of the impact of the statute.

The Categories of Testamentary Litigation

No preconceived classification scheme of the subject matter of testamentary disputes was initially framed by me for this study. Rather, the causes themselves were allowed to determine the categories: as the documents were examined, the issues that were litigated over naturally fell into distinct groups. The allegations offered by the will's promoter were the first documents I studied; but as additional categories of court documents came under my scrutiny, the legal aspects of the narratives presented to the court by the parties were further elaborated, and the often complex and multi-faceted basis for a contest became clearer. The litigants who became enmeshed in some of the causes raised more than a single legal issue, and a number of interrelated (or sometimes unrelated) legal problems and deficiencies of the will or wills offered for probate were frequently alleged.

Uncontested Offers of Probate in Solemn Form

About a quarter (23.9 percent) of the 184 causes analyzed here began and ended their 'careers' in court as straightforward offers of probate in solemn form (see Table 3.1). One may speculate upon the reasons why these seemingly non-controversial wills were promoted in solemn form. While it was more costly and time-consuming, probating a will in solemn form offered both the executor and the distributees of the estate more security in dealing with the deceased's property. Probate in solemn form required the will's proponent to serve notice of the offer of probate to the intestate heirs (the issue of the deceased or, in the event of no surviving issue, collateral heirs) and the surviving spouse: the persons who would take the estate if no will was executed, or if the will being promoted was found to be invalid.[2] Once a sentence in solemn form was issued, the executor's distribution of property in accordance with the will's terms could not be contested.[3] In probates in which the executor was neither the surviving spouse nor the heir, he or she might deem it prudent to probate a will in solemn form to establish a claim to administer the estate more securely, and with finality.

Table 3.1   Will contests by issues raised: Prerogative Court of Canterbury 1660–1700

	N = 184		
	N	percent (all cases)	percent (actively contested)
'Uncontested' Probates in Solemn Form	44	23.9	–
Mental elements			
Testamentary capacity	44	23.9	31.4
Undue influence	34	18.5	24.3
Authenticity issues			
Authentic legal act	21	11.4	15
Irregular execution	10	5.4	7.1
Conflicting wills	22	12	15.7
Nuncupative (oral) wills	29	15.8	20.7
Account	15	8.2	10.7
Petition to take up administration	10	5.4	7.1
Miscellaneous	5	2.7	3.6

Note: Because many of the causes raised more than one issue, the totals in the first column exceed the actual number of causes. In each table, two columns follow that calculate the percentage of causes in which each issue was raised. The first column of percentages includes all causes; the second attempts to make it easier to discern the relative frequency of contested issues by excluding the 'probates in solemn form,' probates that were largely uncontested.

---

[2]   The vagaries of probate procedure is sketched in the Appendix .

[3]   Indeed, some of the probates in solemn form might have been initiated by the ordinary who was empowered to require that a will be so promoted if he had qualms about its validity. Henry Swinburne, *A Brief Treatise of Testaments and Last Wills* (Garland Reprint of 1590 edition, 1978), pp. 224–5.

These uncontested probates in solemn form are themselves of two types, based largely upon the extent of the contest that can be gleaned from the record. The first group of solemn-form probates were of the shortest duration in court. In these causes, the promoter (usually an executor, a creditor or an heir) filed an allegation, but the cause, at least so far as the record reveals, went no further. No additional documents exist, and the cause frequently did not proceed to sentence. Each allegation recited that the will-maker was of sound mind at the time the testamentary act was formulated and executed, and that the will, if written, had been duly executed – that is to say, signed and published by the will-maker, and witnessed (unless it was a holograph) by at least two persons who were present at the time of its execution. In these causes, there is no evidence that an answer (a formal reply presented to the court and introduced by a party who had been served with notice that an estate in which he or she might have interest in (that is, he or she would take some or all of the deceased's property if the will was not proved) was submitted by the party or parties informed of the proceedings. The interrogatories (a series of questions addressed by the party to witnesses he or she called, or those summoned by the other side) filed by the promoter with the allegation were addressed exclusively to the witnesses of the will, and touched only upon questions relating to the will-maker's capacity and (if it had been written by another) the will's due execution; no depositions were taken in response to the interrogatories.[4] It may well be that the parties cited – the widow and/or heirs – never appeared. It is likely that the promoter saw no reason to occasion further expense by producing witnesses and deposing them. The promoter thereafter either dropped the cause (and presumably retained the personal property, the goods and money that constituted the deceased's estate) or the will proceeded to sentence and the property was distributed according the directions therein. Presumably the dispository provisions of the deceased's will were observed. But it is of course possible that the executor, heirs, and beneficiaries worked out their own settlement of the deceased's estate, paying debts, collecting credits, and distributing the remaining property.

A second type of cause that falls into the category 'uncontested probate in solemn form' produced some further documentary record than did the first group of causes discussed above, albeit a scant one. Here the contestant presented interrogatories, the witnesses to the will were called and deposed (required to respond orally to the questions directed to them), but no dispute over the pattern of distribution mandated or the due execution/authenticity of the will emerged. The cause proceeded to sentence; the will was 'proved.'

---

4   Most (but not all) of the allegation files also contain interrogatories submitted by the same party; others also contain interrogatories submitted by the opposing party.

Thus, much of the testamentary business – slightly less than a quarter of the wills observed in my study – consisted of these routine 'uncontested offers of probate.' What the two types of causes share – hence the logic of collapsing them together in a single category – is that they were largely uncontested. While in the latter kind of cause the contestant made an appearance, no effort seems to have been made to have the promoted will set aside. Precisely why an executor felt compelled to incur the expense of initiating or pursuing the probate of the will in solemn form cannot be ascertained directly from the surviving record; why the heirs or spouse bothered to put in an appearance if they had neither inclination nor justification to contest the will is likewise unclear.

One may speculate, however, upon the reasons why some of these wills were promoted in solemn form. As we noted above, it was more costly and time-consuming to probate a will in solemn form. But the additional expense provided greater protection to both the executor and the distributees of the estate when dealing with the deceased's property. Recall that once a sentence in solemn-form had been issued, the executor's distribution of property in accordance with the will's terms could not be contested.

There is evidence that solemn form probates might have been undertaken to ensure such finality. Although most of the executors who probated one of the wills in our study were related to either the deceased or the surviving spouse, about a third of the executors (54 out of 181 or 29.8 percent) were unrelated to the deceased, and only 6 of these 54 probates by unrelated executors (11.2 percent) went uncontested. In her study of will-making, Amy Ericson found that roughly three-quarters of the wills that she surveyed appointed a surviving spouse as executrix.[5] Surely some heirs in her study must have also been appointed as executors; thus the percentage of executors related by blood or marriage must have been well above the 75 percent mark. Using these figures as a benchmark, executors in our causes therefore probated wills in our solemn-form probates much more frequently than their numbers would suggest, and they were far more likely to be engaged in disputes than their nominations justify. Thus savvy non-heir executors probating wills in solemn form had reason to be cautious before undertaking their charge. Still, many of our solemn-form probates are of wills in which the executor was a spouse, an heir, or a co-heir. For motives that remain obscure, these related executors, like many of those unrelated, were more circumspect in dealing with estates, and were sufficiently concerned to use the solemn form of probate to establish their authority to deal with the deceased's property, and with finality.

---

[5]   Amy Erickson, *Women and Property in Early Modern England* (London, 1993), Table 9.1.

The Contested Wills

The promoters of the other wills observed here, also solemn-form probates, did not fare as well; in this far larger number of causes – over three-quarters of those studied – parties with an interest in the deceased's estate – a widow, an heir, or a creditor – challenged the validity of the will that the promoter offered for probate, and did so actively, by submitting to the court answers, counter-allegations, and interrogatories. The legal basis for these contests will be discussed in detail in succeeding chapters, but first a tabulation of the various grounds of contest that were alleged is necessary, in order to consider whether the litigation may have been the inspiration for parliamentary adoption of certain provisions of the Statute of Frauds. The contested causes fell into three main groups: those that challenged whether the will-maker had the requisite mental state to make a will and that he or she was free from coercion; those challenging whether the document promoted was an authentic legal act of the deceased; and those that queried whether words spoken by the deceased amounted to an oral will.

Mental Elements: Capacity and Coercion

The most common will challenges focused upon the mental state of the testator at the time the will was executed: these were contests either on the grounds of undue influence (18.5/24.3 percent) or on issues of testamentary capacity (23.9/31.4 percent) (see Table 3.1). In these causes, the contestant alleged either that the will-maker did not have the presence of mind to undertake a testamentary act, or that even if he or she did, that the will in question was the product of the coercion of others. Both grounds were alleged in many causes.[6]

Contestants who regarded the testator as mentally diseased or defective, and therefore unable to appreciate the nature of the testamentary act he was making, challenged the will-maker's mental capacity. Because this lack of capacity had to be inferred from behavior, the variety of bizarre conduct that was alleged, and frequently described in considerable detail, is to the modern observer both heartbreaking and amusing. Most importantly, however, the narratives presented by the parties, though they often conflicted, offer insights into the processes of dying and of will-making. These narratives reveal much about the bittersweet nature of family relations in the past, topics to be considered in succeeding chapters.[7]

6　These issues are discussed in Chapter 4, below.
7　In particular, Chapters 8 and 9, below.

Likewise, the circumstances that contestants of a will put forward to support allegations of undue influence varied greatly. A contestant might relate dubious conduct on the part of the will's proponent or beneficiary (or indeed others) in securing the writing or execution of the will that they offered for probate. The coercion proffered might be overt or covert. For example, the will-maker may have been confined in the promoter's house, whereas others, relations and/or 'friends' (a word of art frequently employed by the proctors who drafted the allegations and interrogatories to indicate non-relations who had the best interests of the dying person at heart, as opposed to the promoter of the will) were denied access to the will-maker, thereby allowing the promoter (or another person) sufficient latitude to craft the imposed testamentary plan. Alternatively, the intervention of others that was related by the contestant could be subtler; for example, the proponent (or another), rather than the will-maker, had 'instructed' the scrivener as to the terms to be included in the will.

Issues of Will Authenticity

A second group of controversies focused on the authenticity of the document itself: whether the will offered for probate was actually the deceased's last will. In a fair number of causes (12/15.7 percent; see Table 3.1), conflicting wills appeared before the court. The promoter offered a testamentary act for probate, but another person alleged that a different will should be probated instead of (or in addition to) the one initially introduced. The contestant might allege that the document in his or her possession (or the words uttered that amounted to a nuncupative will) was of later date, and therefore it revoked, or should be read in tandem with, the promoted will. In some causes, the contestant alleged that the will promoted by the other side was flawed. For example, it was charged that the will was not properly executed, or was the product of undue influence, or had been executed by a person of unsound mind. 'But the will I promote,' it was alleged, 'is untarnished.'

In addition to causes involving conflicting wills, the testamentary litigation raised more directly significant numbers of other authenticity questions (11.4/15 percent; see Table 3.1). Questions of whether the will offered for probate was the final testamentary volition of the deceased arose in a myriad of contexts. For example, questions of whether stray papers in a doubtful hand that were found under dubious circumstances but that were nevertheless styled 'last will' should be probated figure prominently in litigation. The causes reveal that recourse to rudimentary handwriting analysis was sometimes undertaken to determine whether a will was actually a holograph. Likewise, with respect to written wills, interlineations were perplexing: who had crossed out words, or who might have added language to the document, and when the changes occurred (before, during, or after death) could be at issue. Where and by whom the will was found might also raise authenticity questions.

Certain formalities were required for a will to be duly executed, and a number of contests (5.4/7.1 percent; see Table 3.1) were lodged on the grounds that a will had been 'irregularly executed,' that is, it was not signed, published, and witnessed in conformity with ecclesiastical law. Causes were brought before the Prerogative Court in which will-makers (or witnesses) for one reason or another had failed to sign or to publish a will, that is, to express clearly that the document in question was to stand as a testamentary act. Failure to conform to the formalities of due execution required might be inadvertent – an accident or an oversight – or death might have intervened before the execution of the will was concluded.

Oral Wills

Although oral wills frequently raised authenticity questions, they merit their own category, in part due to their numbers but also because they were singled out for specific treatment in the Statute of Frauds. For these reasons, the particular concerns raised by wills made by 'word of mouth,' as contemporaries so styled them, will be addressed more fully in a separate chapter.[8] In the last half of the seventeenth century, oral wills were what modern lawyers call 'litigation breeders.' About one in six (15.8 /20.7 percent) of the Canterbury will contests involved nuncupative wills (see Table 3.1). In 1676 (a year which I reviewed all the catalogued contests because it was when Statute of Frauds was under final consideration) oral wills provided the court with the most common subject of testamentary business; almost one will in three testamentary acts was nuncupative (Table 3.2).

Prior to the statute, oral wills were only very loosely subject to formality requirements, and the circumstances in which they were uttered were explored in detail by litigants because a contestant often challenged the will promoter's contentions that the now-deceased had intended the declarations to have testamentary effect. The words alleged to be nuncupative wills were, after all, just words. To be a valid testamentary act, they had to be uttered with the intent to make a will. In addition, someone had to hear, and to recall, the precise words spoken. How else might the expression be implemented? The alleged testamentary act could only be proved by the recollections of witnesses. Thus their memory, character, and honesty were crucial, and all were delved into in

---

8   Chapter 5, below.

Table 3.2   Actively contested wills by issues raised: pre and post Statute of Frauds

N=140*				
	1661–1676**		1681–1696***	
Mental Elements	N	percent	N	percent
Testamentary Capacity	22	25.9	22	40
Undue Influence	21	24.7	13	23.6
Authenticity Issues				
Authentic Legal Act	10	11.8	11	20
Irregular Execution	4	4.7	6	10.9
Conflicting Wills	14	16.5	8	14.5
Nuncupative (Oral) Wills	27	31.8	2	3.6
Account	8	9.4	7	12.7
Petition to Take up Administration	4	4.7	6	10.1
Miscellaneous	3	3.5	2	3.6

*   Recall that of the 184 causes 44 are regarded as 'uncontested.'
**   Eighty-five causes.
*** Fifty-five causes.

detail through interrogatories and the ensuing depositions. Context did indeed matter. Where the words were spoken was relevant; the alehouse, for example, was not an uncommon venue for tidying worldly affairs, and one that disgruntled heirs held suspect.[9]

Thus while the law recognized the will by word of mouth, and therefore sanctioned its inherent informality, nuncupative wills were scrutinized to ensure that their orators had intended the utterance to be a valid testamentary act. After the Statute of Frauds was adopted, oral wills of estates valued over

---

[9]   Amongst others, the will of Gregory Thorned discussed in Chapter 4 (*Cooke contra Batty*, PROB 18/3c/28), that of John Singleton (*Hicks et Meggs contra Singleton*, PROB 18/18/15) and one of the many alleged wills of Richard Parsons (*Ellis contra Parsons*, PROB 18/6/23, PROB 24/14, 195) both discussed in Chapter 7 were made in alehouses.

£30 were subject to specific requirements, and the focus of the litigation turned
to whether the will fell within the ambit of the statute and, if so, whether its
mandates had been satisfied.

Miscellaneous Issues

In addition to the three main groupings of legal issues discussed above, some
of the litigation observed revolved around other questions. For example, a
significant number of the testamentary causes in the Canterbury Prerogative
Court did not involve the proving of wills. Rather, petitioners in a number
of causes sought a grant of administration of the deceased's goods in intestate
successions (5.4/7.1 percent; see Table 3.1), usually based upon an alleged
marriage. Causes in which marriage was raised as an issue assumed one of two
patterns: either the party alleging marriage sought to take up administration
of the deceased's goods on the grounds that, as surviving spouse, he or she had
priority to do so as the law directed[10] or the putative surviving spouse alleged
that a marriage had taken place in order to justify the execution of a will that
nominated him or her as executor. The former causes were classified as petitions
to take up administration; the latter usually figure as causes relating to undue
influence, mental capacity, conflicting wills, or authenticity. The causes in which
marriages were alleged and contested offer fascinating insights into marriage
processes in the past, and will be discussed in a subsequent chapter.[11]

A second type of cause that is not a contest over a will but a different form
of testamentary litigation is those in which the petitioner sought an accounting
from an executor, an administrator, or a third party with custody of the deceased's
goods. Given the financial interests at stake, and the control the executor of a will
or administrator of an intestate estate held over the assets of the estate, it is not
surprising that a number of causes heard by the court dealt with the monitoring
of these assets (8.2/10.7 percent; see Table 3.1). Unfortunately, the records
provide only a catalogue of objections lodged by creditors and beneficiaries and
the responses made by executors; this genre of testamentary litigation does not
seem to have resulted in a sentence in any of the causes.

Finally, a number of causes defy categorization and are tabulated as
'miscellaneous.' Either it is impossible from the state of the evidence to discern
precisely what was at issue, or the issue defies simple categorization. Happily this
particular dilemma, and the odd cause that just doesn't fit in, was faced only very
infrequently (2.7/3.6 percent of all causes; see Table 3.1).

---

[10]   23 and 24 Car. II, c. 10 (1670).

[11]   See Chapter 8, below.

Analysis of the Canterbury Prerogative Court Causes

The thrust of the Statute of Frauds was to authenticate legal transactions. To what extent does the probate litigation observed here suggest that it reduced the number of dubious testamentary acts? This question can be resolved by surveying the evidentiary issues that each type of cause engendered. We have seen that, uncontested probates aside, the causes naturally fall into three broad categories (with some 'outliers' -the odd cause), and this is most easily expressed by the following questions. First, was the **mental state** of the will-maker sufficiently robust to undertake **freely** a testamentary act? Second, was a written document and its extant provisions the **authentic legal act** and, in some causes, the final testamentary direction of the deceased? And finally, did the words uttered amount to an **oral will**, and if so what were its provisions?

With respect to the first question, about the will-maker's mental capacity, a will was a legal act and the law required that its author be both of sound mind to undertake it and free from the coercion of others at the time of its execution. The fact that written wills were often deathbed documents contributed to qualms and quibbles about capacity (was the will-maker on his or her 'last legs' mentally, as well as physically?) and undue influence (were others allowed to overwhelm the testator's volition and substitute it for their own volition).[12] Each side substantiated its case through interrogatories presented to the witness summoned, and through the depositions produced. Because will-making was an act generally undertaken before a limited number of individuals, the evidence required to demonstrate either a lack of capacity or undue influence in each type of cause was similar: the 'non-expert' opinion testimony of those who had surrounded the will-maker at the time the will was contrived and executed. In interrogatories, witnesses were asked to relate facts: to describe the will-making drama and to illuminate the roles of the participants. What was the role of the alleged 'undue influencer' in securing the will? Who had dictated the dispositions in the will? Likewise, witnesses were asked to state conclusions: was the will-maker of sound mind and did the will represent the volition of another rather than that of the will-maker?

The second group of written wills is comprised of those that directly raised a variety of authenticity issues. In what I have called the 'culture of will-making,' the context in which wills were executed, testamentary acts were produced that often lacked formality, or that appeared dubious on the face of the document. Unlike the modern pattern of testation in which there is professional oversight of a process undertaken in advance of death, the last-minute and haphazard nature

---

[12]   See Chapter 1, especially footnote 39.

of many of the will executions described in these records frequently resulted in the omission of certain of the requisite legal formalities. Moreover, multiple testamentary acts were undertaken, some as 'corrections' in the texts of existing wills. The probate court had to sift through evidence to determine the validity of these testamentary acts, and of the dispositions contained therein. While some of the authenticity questions raised in written wills might be resolved by examining the documents themselves, the court was again largely dependent upon the testimony of witnesses to resolve conflicts.

A final group of causes involved so-called nuncupative, or oral, wills. Indeed, the testamentary validity of utterances and their exact terms was the single most common ground for dispute in 1676 (the year in which I read all surviving allegations): 16 of the 54 (27.1 percent) actively contested wills were oral. Wills by word of mouth had inherent authenticity problems: 'Who said what to whom, and did she mean it to be a will?' Often the circumstances surrounding the making of an oral will were crucial to its validity, and they could only be recounted by witnesses. The court had the unenviable task of assessing the reliability of the witnesses and piecing together a narrative of the alleged will-making by separating fact from fancy. The court exhibited a greater propensity to nullify oral wills brought before it than with respect to written wills: only 7.4 percent of written wills were nullified, while the figure is 17.2 percent for oral wills.[13]

Testing the Hypothesis

To what extent may we conclude that the Statute of Frauds was adopted in response to vexing issues that arose in testamentary causes? Recall that although there is little direct evidence of a connection in the record, Sir Leoline Jenkins, Judge of the Prerogative Court of Canterbury, was actively involved in the recasting of the final draft. Surely he was aware of the testamentary business we have observed here. Before deciding, however, we must undertake one further tabulation, and separate the causes that transpired prior to the statute and those litigated thereafter.

Table 3.2 illustrates the breakdown of the testamentary causes by subject matter litigated before and then after the adoption of the Statute of Frauds. Because many of the causes raised more than one issue, the totals in the first 'N' columns often exceed the actual number of causes. In the table, there are two columns that calculate the percentage of causes in which each issue was raised.

---

[13]   See Table, Chapter 5. Only 7.4 percent of written wills were nullified, while 17.2 percent of oral wills were nullified.

The most striking difference between the pre- and post-statute causes is the near disappearance of oral wills after its passage.

Considering the Impact of the Statute of Frauds

The Statute of Frauds mandated written documentation for land transfers (both *inter vivos* and by will), as well as tightening the requirements for the validity of oral wills of personal property. The marriage of the two provisions by Parliament was rational because the causes described above illustrate that oral wills of personal property raised almost the same question as did oral land transfers: how can reliable evidence of the authenticity of legal acts be secured?

Yet the statute was a mixed success. With respect to the thorny issues of validity raised by nuncupative wills, Parliament made some inroads into lightening the court's burdens. By 1680, the first sample year in the study after the adoption of the Statute of Frauds, the number of oral wills in litigation had declined precipitously. In fact, all but two of the nuncupative wills in the data set (27 out of 29) were offered for probate before the statute, and the two thereafter were those of mariners,[14] whose wills (along with those with estates below the £30 threshold) were exempted from its terms. The tightening up of the requirements had the effect of either limiting the making of oral wills or at least preventing executors and legatees from offering utterances that did not conform to the statutory mandate for probate in the Prerogative Court of Canterbury. While oral wills did not disappear altogether from the court's docket,[15] their validity was subject to the stricter rules of the statute, and advocates must have realized the futility of bringing causes involving them to the court in instances in which the statute's provisions had not been followed.

But it must be stressed that it was a mixed success: the Statute of Frauds did little else to lighten the burden of the Prerogative Court. The statute is more notable for issues that it did not confront: it addressed neither issues of mental capacity and undue influence nor the variety of authenticity issues of written wills that plagued the Canterbury court. Causes involving written wills raising mental capacity and undue influence remained robust throughout the period; litigation continued to arise with respect to written wills in which the court had to determine questions of will authenticity, and whether someone had tampered with a testamentary document.

---

[14] *Williams contra Phillips*, PROB 18/24/20; *Bush contra Couzens*, PROB 18/24/65.
[15] See Chapter 5, below.

Conclusion

While Parliament seems to have considered challenging the contemporary 'culture of will-making', it ultimately relented. The provision invalidating the deathbed wills included in the 1673 draft of the statute but mysteriously eliminated from the final bill, would certainly have limited much of the post-1677 testamentary litigation observed here.[16] English folk continued to settle their affairs by will on the deathbed, and that predisposition often led to testamentary litigation. If the statute was intended to remove the burden of contested wills from the court's docket, its effect was like much pre-nineteenth-century law reform: rather limited.

It remained up to the court to frame most of the requirements for will validity, and the outcome of the causes suggests that these were flexible. This approach provided only very modest disincentives to contest. But the judges may have discouraged contests to some extent by creating a healthy presumption of will validity. The contestant in probate proceedings probably had a difficult row to hoe. Fewer than one-in-ten will contests observed here proved successful. This ratio suggests that the judges accorded wills a healthy presumption of validity, and that approach may have deterred some from undertaking the expense of a contest. Why other individuals were prepared to take on the odds, assuming they actually were aware of them, can best be ascertained by detailed investigation of the causes, the subject of the succeeding chapters.

---

[16] See Chapter 2, above.

PART II
The Legal Issues: Mental Element in Will-Making and the Authenticity of Legal Acts

Having broadly categorized the causes that came before the Prerogative Court of Canterbury by legal issue raised, the following chapters examine the strategy used by litigants to raise each of the issues. Mental capacity or undue influence actions consider the extent to which emerging theories on property rights, self-ownership, and mental disease and disability in seventeenth-century England were reflected in probate litigation, while the following three chapters investigate questions that confronted the court over the authenticity of testamentary legal acts, oral and written. While the latter aspect, authenticity, will be presented in a number of different categories, the causes are all interrelated, because in each doubts were raised as to whether the testamentary act being promoted was the genuine and legally binding act of the will-maker. The purpose of the Statute of Frauds was to require specific formalities of due execution for certain legal acts to be valid. The discussion of the litigation in the chapters allow us to consider whether the safeguards that were included in the Statute may have been prompted by the causes that the court was actually confronting, and whether in fact the provisions actually diminished the quantity of testamentary litigation in the years following its adoption.

Chapter 4
'Of Sound and Disposing Mind and Memory': Testamentary Capacity and Undue Influence

Introduction

The greatest proportion of wills observed in my collection of Prerogative Court of Canterbury causes was challenged on the grounds either that the testator lacked testamentary capacity at the time of execution, or that the testamentary act offered for probate was procured by undue influence. These two bases for contest – discrete ones in the law of wills – are nevertheless interrelated: in both, the will-maker's mental state at the time the will was executed is at issue. At first glance, what was at stake in each of these testamentary causes was the validity of a single will, and the court was presented with a simple decision: should it confirm the will offered for probate and allow an individual's estate to pass according the terms set out therein; or should the court invalidate the will and mandate that the deceased's property should descend by the laws of intestate succession?

A straightforward choice to be sure, yet these causes raised a fundamental question regarding the nature of the property-ownership rights of those who through age or infirmity had weakened intellect: under what circumstances should an individual's ability to dispose of his or her property by will be curtailed? With only very vague legal benchmarks to serve as a guide, the Prerogative Court was charged to determine, in the light of the evidence presented by the parties, whether the will offered for probate was a 'reasoned' legal act. If it was, the will would be probated; if it was not, the will was not valid, and the default rules of intestate succession would govern the transmission of the deceased's estate.

The Counterpoised Interests: Property Rights and Personhood

However, much more than a single, simple disposition of property was at stake when a will offered for probate was challenged on the grounds of mental capacity or undue influence. Broader jurisprudential considerations were in play. Setting aside a testamentary act removed from a person control over the transmission of his or her property after death, and thereby conflicted with two closely held contemporary societal norms. First, to remove freedom of disposition clashed with the 'individualistic' conception of property rights that obtained in early modern English law and culture.[1] By our period, a rights-based property law theory had emerged that regarded ownership as squarely and absolutely grounded in individuals and not held collectively by a family or by society; under this legal regime, property should not descend to kin unless the owner so specified, or failed to make a direction.[2] To set aside a testamentary act that left property to strangers, as did many a will that was contested on the grounds of lack of capacity or undue influence, resulted in the substitution of heirs specified by the law of intestate succession (family members) for the beneficiaries named by the will-maker. Thus the effect of a will's nullification restored a familial character to a will-maker's property (or at the very least removed its individualistic stripe), and substituted for individual volition society's conception of preferred property-devolution patterns, that mandated by intestate succession law.

Setting aside a will thus removed a significant aspect of control over the individual's own destiny, what contemporaries deemed 'self-ownership'[3] and what Margaret Radin has more recently coined 'personhood.'[4] It did so in a pernicious fashion. The court acted after the will-maker's death, and without the usual legal process and safeguards when 'madness' – admittedly just cause to limit self-ownership – was at issue.[5] Few relatives undertook the expense and bother of taking out commissions of lunacy for their relation during the life of an alleged mad person, a determination that would restrain an individual's ability to dispose of property;[6] rather, the same end might be achieved by waiting until the property-owner's death and using examples of irrational conduct in order to have an unwanted will set aside at probate on the grounds of a lack of mental capacity.

---

[1]   Alan Macfarlane, *The Origins of English Individualism* (Oxford, 1978).

[2]   See Introduction, above, specifically the text at footnotes 10–18.

[3]   Laura Brace, *The Idea of Property in the Seventeenth Century* (Manchester, 1998), pp. 1–5.

[4]   Margaret Radin, 'Property and Personhood,' *Stanford Law Review*, vol. 34 (1982), pp. 964–70.

[5]   Michael MacDonald, *Mystical Bedlam: madness, anxiety, and healing in seventeenth-century England* (Cambridge, 1981); H. Horowitz and P. Polden, 'Continuity or change in the Court of Chancery in the seventeenth and eighteenth centuries?' *Journal of British Studies*, vol. 35 (1996), pp. 24–57.

[6]   MacDonald, *Mystical Bedlam*, pp. 142–50; Roy Porter, 'Madness and the Family before Freud,' *Journal of Family History*, vol. 23 (1998), pp. 159–72, especially, p. 169.

Depriving an individual of testamentary freedom was therefore serious business, a judicial determination that should not be undertaken lightly. In my introduction, I noted how Locke grappled with the dilemma of removing freedom of disposition from a person who 'through defects that might happen out of the ordinary course of nature ... comes not to such a degree of reason ... that he is never let loose to the disposure of his own will'[7] and from those susceptible 'to the arbitrary will of another.'[8] That Locke's struggle was shared by the legal community can be demonstrated by reference to the work of John Brydall. His treatise, *Non Compos Mentis*, published at the close of our period, was the standard work on testamentary capacity, and it proclaimed that for a will to be valid it must 'imply an Act of Will guided with Reason.'[9] Accordingly, control over the transmission of property at death was accorded to its owner if he or she was 'rational.'[10]

In our own time, probate courts are assisted by mental health professionals and there is broad agreement (though perhaps not absolute) upon what constitutes rational and irrational conduct. In the seventeenth century, however, the court was without such a consensus. While the burgeoning medical literature of the period explored the nature of both 'melancholia' and madness, and had begun to consider them as diseases in which there was some hope of treatment, the more time-honored explanations of the 'distracted' and the 'distempered' were still being offered by astrologers and demonologists.[11] But 'medical progress' did not escape the lay community. Roy Porter has argued that Locke, in his *Essay concerning Human Understanding*, used contemporary medical advances to demonstrate how the 'incoherent' ideas of madmen could lead them through rational analysis to 'jumbled conclusions.'[12] Likewise, Brydall, our contemporary legal authority on capacity issues in will-making, cited medical literature and used prevalent medical terms such as 'furor,' 'distraction,' and 'melancholia' to describe and discuss the impact of mental diseases on will-making.[13]

---

[7] Ian Shapiro (ed.), *Two Treatises of Government and a Letter Concerning Toleration* (New Haven CN, 2003), Book II, sec 59.

[8] Ibid., Book II, sec. 57.

[9] John Brydall, *Non Compos Mentis: or the law relating to natural fools, mad folks and lunitick persons explored* (London, 1700), p. 2.

[10] Shapiro (ed.), *Two Treatises*, Book II, sec. 58.

[11] These conclusions are based upon a survey of the medical literature in Richard Hunter and Ida MacAlpine (eds.), *Three Hundred Years of Psychiatry, 1535–1860* (London, 1963). In the second half of the seventeenth century, medical writers such as Sydenham, King, Morton, and Boyle wrote about diagnosis and cures that have a decidedly modern ring. See for examples, see pp. 221–36.

[12] Roy Porter, *Madness* (Oxford, 2002), pp. 238–9.

[13] Brydall, *Non Compos Mentis*, pp. 52–3.

The Probate Court's Conundrum

These strands of property law 'theory' created a conundrum for the court. To promote and to preserve freedom of disposition, a cherished cultural norm in early-modern English society, it had to be removed on an individual basis from a person who was devoid of 'reason.' In short, the mentally frail had to be protected from themselves – to be restrained from crafting an estate plan that they would not have undertaken had they been of sound mind or free from coercion. The court's role, then and now (for there is a timeless character to the controversies observed here), was as gate-keeper. It applied its notions of capacity and undue influence to factual situations, the narratives presented to it by the parties and their witnesses in each contest. In order to perform its function, the court had to sort fact from fancy: first, to ascertain what had actually transpired and then to determine whether the will-maker's personhood should be respected by admitting his or her testamentary act to probate.

This process of review empowered the judges. After all, the legal actor, the will-maker, was dead. What the Prerogative Court had to work with was the evidence that others presented to the court, the allegations of the parties and the depositions of witnesses whom they called. These individuals had been present at the time of execution of the will or at other crucial moments in the will-making drama. Their reliability, however, had to be in question: their assertions were made by individuals with varying degrees of interest in the litigation, and had therefore, perhaps, been embellished to promote or challenge a testamentary act. So piecing together what had actually happened was no mean task.

The causes observed here suggest that the judges in the Canterbury Prerogative Court used their power to strike a balance that supported personhood, individualism, and freedom of disposition, because they set aside wills only very reluctantly. In this way, the court may have admitted to probate some wills that had in fact been made by those of doubtful capacity and/or free will. This was a risk that the judges were prepared to take to permit a property-holder to direct transmission until the very end of life. And it was one that Parliament must have tacitly approved: had the proposal to limit the validity of deathbed wills survived in the 1676 draft of the Statute of Frauds, many of the vexing causes explored below would not have plagued the court after the statute had been adopted.

Legal Standards for Testamentary Capacity

Church-court law defined both testamentary capacity and undue influence, albeit with an annoying lack of precision. To be of sound mind, to have sufficient mental capacity to make a valid will, the will-maker had to understand that the act being undertaken had legal significance. For John Ayliffe, like John Locke, sound mind was a question of reason and of volition:

> For the Act of Making a Will is a human Act, which ought to be executed *in humano modo*: But a human Act can not be executed by him that hath not sufficient Judgement and Will to make a Testament.[14]

Reason and volition, judgment and will: the will-maker must have the mental presence both to appreciate that the act undertaken directed the transmission of property upon death and to be able to construct a logical pattern of disposition. Ayliffe provided an example of how sound mind might be measured. It was not 'sufficient' that the testator 'answer to usual and ordinary questions'; rather he or she 'ought to have disposing Memory ... to make a Disposition of his Estate with Reason and Understanding, and such a Memory is called a sound and perfect Mind or Memory.'[15] Other commentators set the bar less high; as William Sheppard put it in the mid-seventeenth century, only 'mean' understanding was sufficient, 'of the middle sort between a wise man and a fool.'[16] A century later, a discourse on sound mind agreed, noting that 'the law will not scrutinize into the depth of a man's capacity, particularly after his death,' and conceded that an individual need only 'conduct himself in the common course of life' to execute a valid testamentary act. This rather low threshold was justified because to hold otherwise 'might be opening a wide door to support pretensions of fraud or imposition on the testator.'[17]

Emerging trends in medicine were likely percolating from the minds of doctors to those of lawyers. By our period, the guidance of Henry Swinburne, whose sixteenth-century treatise remained the most prominent work on testaments into our century, on the issue seems decidedly antiquated and simplistic. Swinburne had defined sound mind in the negative, by enumerating those individuals who lacked it: 'madd folkes and lunaticke persons'; 'Idiots'; 'olde men'; 'Of him that is drunke'; and 'Of him that is at the very point of Death.'[18] John Brydall's treatise

---

[14] John Ayliffe, *Parergon Juris Anglicani: or a commentary by way of supplement to the canon and constitutions of the Church of England* (London, 1724), pp. 530–31.

[15] Ibid., p. 533.

[16] William Sheppard, *The Touchstone of Common Assurances*, 6th edn (Dublin, 1785), p. 389.

[17] *A Familiar Plan and Easy Explanation of the Law of Wills and Codicils* (London, 1785), p. 16.

[18] Henry Swinburne, *A Brief Treatise of Testaments and Last Wills* (Garland Reprint of 1590 edition, 1978), pp. 36–42; 61–4.

Non Compos Mentis penned a century or so thereafter, at the close of our period, has a decidedly more modern ring, and reveals a more nuanced treatment of mental disease. Consistent with the emerging medical literature, its author observed a bewildering variety of diverse mental conditions. Perhaps the most serious malady was 'furor,' a condition of madness that a person suffers 'through some Sickness, Grief, or other Accident,' and 'utterly loseth his Memory and Understanding.'[19] Unhappily, furor was usually permanent. 'Distraction,' on the other hand, was a less serious condition in which 'Reason being thus set aside Fancy gets the Ascendant.'[20] In both a fever might be present, but the 'rage' which accompanied distraction was more likely to pass. An individual suffering from either condition could not make a valid will. 'Lunacy,' however, was a more transient condition in which the individual navigated between *compos* and *non compos mentis*. The malady was likened to convulsions and the falling sickness, conditions in which doctors agreed that on certain days sufferers 'are not counted whole.'[21] Yet those with any of the mental conditions set out by Brydall could have lucid intervals in which their testamentary capacity was restored: 'in Calm Intermissions during of the time such of their Quietness and Freedom of Mind' ... [they might] make a valid will.[22]

At a number places in his discourse, Brydall raises the important question of upon which party the burden of proof lies in testamentary causes where the mental capacity of will-makers are at issue. Will-makers were presumed to be *compos mentis*, and their testamentary acts to be valid, regardless of whether the document itself so proclaimed, that clause asserting sound mind being 'more usual than necessary.'[23] Yet once a mental disease was proved at a particular point in the individual's life, the madness was presumed to be ongoing, unless the proponent of the will showed that the symptoms that had been observed were 'short-lasting' or 'a long time dispatched.'[24]

Finally, the commentators, including Brydall, did not clearly specify the actual conduct of an individual that would render him or her *non compos mentis*. To the court that must have seemed unfortunate, because that was what the judges usually had as evidence: the testimony of ordinary folk who described the will-maker's actions. From such testimony, it had to determine whether the stories related actually had transpired and, if so, whether the conduct as related rendered an individual incapacitated. Brydall wrote that he must do 'such things

---

19   Brydall, *Non Compos Mentis*, p. 52.
20   Ibid., p. 53.
21   Ibid., pp. 94–5.
22   Ibid., pp. 103–4.
23   Ibid., p. 67.
24   Ibid., p. 68.

or heard speak such words as a man having Wit and Reason would not have done or spoken'; his modest catalogue of conduct that indicated madness included throwing stones at windows, spitting on another man's face, and making animal sounds.[25] But, as Brydall noted, the court might also surmise capacity from the dispositions in the will: 'if a Testament be wisely and orderly framed,' it should be held valid, while one 'with a mixture of Wisdom and Folly' would be presumed to a product of mental disability.[26]

This standard permitted a good deal of subjectivity and empowered judges, because the court (and not the will-maker) became the arbiter of what dispositions were rational. The judge in each cause first had to separate truth from fancy, sorting through the testimony of witnesses who described the will-maker's mental state prior to and after the testamentary act in question in order to create a narrative. Then he had to measure the conduct reconstructed against the legal benchmark. The sentences issued by the court (either confirming the will on the grounds that the contestant had failed to substantiate the claim of incapacity or setting aside the will) merely state whether or not the contested will was admitted to probate: the reasoning of the judges is absent. The disposition of the causes, however, does suggest that contestants of wills on the grounds of incapacity had a tough row to hoe: judges were reluctant, though not completely unwilling, to set aside wills on capacity grounds. The mental capacity of the will-maker was challenged in 44 of our causes;[27] 34 of them proceeded to sentence, 25 wills (73.5 percent) were admitted to probate and only 9 were nullified (26.5 percent).[28]

Legal Standards for Undue Influence

While the will-maker's state of mind was also relevant in a contest on the grounds of undue influence, it was the conduct of others that was the main focus of inquiry. Personhood, individualism, and freedom of disposition mandated that a valid will should represent the volition of the will-maker, and not that of another. Thus the legal issue to be considered was (and remains in modern law) whether another individual had coerced the will-maker: whether pressure

---

[25]   Ibid., pp. 67–8.

[26]   Ibid., pp. 104–6.

[27]   See Chapter 3, Table 3.1.

[28]   In two causes, conflicting wills were offered; one of the wills was admitted, but the other seven did not proceed to sentence. Arguably, the percentage of wills nullified on the grounds of capacity was greater than those nullified on other grounds. Whether the contests were abandoned because the challenge was a weak one cannot be ascertained; if such were the case a much higher percentage of wills had been admitted.

to influence the will-maker had been sufficiently extensive to overwhelm his or her volition, thereby substituting another person's testamentary preferences for those of the will-maker.[29] Because an individual in a less than robust mental state might be susceptible to the influence of others, the grounds of undue influence and testamentary capacity were often linked in the Canterbury causes that I observed (or at least they were in the minds of contestants). Hence both might be asserted in the same allegation.[30] The words of one witness in a testamentary cause are helpful in illustrating the connection between capacity and influence. John Bailey testified that he had known will-maker Benjamin Hubbard since his childhood; he regarded him as a person who was 'of weak capacity and understanding' (lack of sound mind), and one that 'might be easily persuaded by faire words and for a glass of wine or other trivial thing that pleased him' (susceptibility to undue influence).[31] This blending often renders it difficult in an individual cause to determine precisely whether undue influence or want of testamentary capacity was being asserted by a contestant, and if the will was successfully contested it may not be clear which theory (or both) actually prevailed.

To be sure, the use of the term, undue influence, in this chapter is anachronistic: neither Swinburne or Brydall in their treatises (or other commentators) nor the contestants themselves in their allegations employ it. Given the relative frequency with which this ground for contest was raised, it is surprising that Swinburne devoted rather little discussion to the circumstances in which a person 'doth not of his own accord make or declare his testament.'[32] He noted that:

> those in extremitie ... therefore are readie to answere (yea) to anie question almost, that they may be quiet: which advantage, craftie and covetous persons knowing very well, are then most busie, and doo labour with toothe and naile to procure the sicke person to yield to their demands.[33]

Swinburne postulated that the circumstances under which undue influence would be brought to bear were at the deathbed (or very near thereto). Most of the observed causes substantiate his view; undue influence was usually raised

---

[29]   The classic discussion in American law is Ashbel Gulliver and Catherine Tilson, 'Classification of gratuitous transfers', *Yale Law Review*, vol. 51 (1941), pp. 1–39.

[30]   In fact, both claims were raised in 18 causes. About half of the undue influence claims also raised the issue of capacity (18 of 39) and about four in ten of the capacity causes (18 of 43) also raised undue influence.

[31]   *Whitelocke contra Hulburd*, PROB 24/35, 185.

[32]   Swinburne, *Brief Treatise*, p. 62.

[33]   Ibid., p. 63.

when a physically weakened will-maker was winding up affairs at the end of his or her life.[34] Swinburne stressed the coercive element in his treatment of the subject: another person in some manner 'procured' the will by forcing its maker to execute the testamentary act in question.[35] Undue influence might affect (or infect) the entire will or only certain bequests therein; it might be perpetrated by a lone legatee, to augment his bequest, or by another to promote a legacy to a third party.[36]

What constituted 'free consent,' like what constituted 'sound mind,' was frequently expressed in the negative: consent was not freely given and a will, either oral or written, was deemed to be void as the product of undue influence where the will-maker had been compelled to execute it by fear, by fraud, or by 'immoderate flattery.' Each of these elements was distinct, though parties in the causes often regarded them as interrelated. Fear might be generated by actual physical force or by threat of future violence. Fraud sufficient to void a will occurred when a testator was deceived by another, and where the deception was substantial and for an evil purpose.[37] Flattery was considered immoderate when a person of 'weak judgment and easie to be perswaded' gave an individual a large bequest; it also occurred when a testator in a weakened condition was under the 'government' or control of the persuader.[38] This latter variety of undue influence – when control by another overwhelmed the volition of the testator - was (and remains in modern law) difficult to delineate.[39] Ordinary 'fair and flattering speeches to move the will-maker' which led to a bequest were not regarded as immoderate, and would not therefore invalidate a will. On the other hand, if the will-maker was in a weakened position and friends would 'press him much and so wrest words from him, especially if it be in advantage

---

[34] Of the 34 causes in which undue influence is raised by contestants, 25 involved wills made at or very near the deathbed. Only 5 were made while the will-maker was alleged to be in reasonable health, while in the remaining 9 it is not possible to ascertain whether or not the will-maker was at death's door. See Chapter 1 above, text at footnotes 98 through 105.

[35] The exercise of undue influence might be a course of conduct over time rather than as a single event. As such a variety of kinds conduct, explored below, was said to give rise to a claim that the will was the volition of another.

[36] Swinburne, Brief Treatise, p. 240.

[37] According to Swinburne (ibid., pp. 242–3), a will was not void if the perpetrator of a fraud had saved the testator from making an unwise bequest, for example, leaving property to a 'vile and naughty person omitting his honest wife and dutiful children.'

[38] Ibid., pp. 242–3.

[39] For a recent treatment in American law, see Melanie Leslie, 'The Myth of Testamentary Freedom,' Arizona Law Review vol. 38 (1996), pp. 235–90. For English law, see Roger Kerridge, 'Wills made in suspicious circumstances: the problem of the vulnerable testator,' Cambridge Law Journal, vol. 59 (2000), pp. 310–34.

of them,' the will was 'very suspicious.'[40] Accordingly, it was recognized that those who were ill at the time a will was executed might be willing to yield to the 'desires of another person ... to be at quiet and rest.'[41]

As with capacity issues, the devil was in the detail: the question turned on the facts of each individual cause presented by the parties and their witnesses. The judges were also left to determine from the evidence presented what had actually happened, and whether it amounted to the requisite level of coercion given the will-maker's proffered temperament. As we have seen with contests on the grounds of mental capacity, it was not easy, though not impossible, to set aside a will on the grounds of undue influence. Of the 26 causes in this study that proceeded to sentence in which undue influence was alleged the will was admitted to probate in 20 (76.9 percent).[42]

Testamentary Litigation and Capacity

The Strategies of the Proponents

More detailed discussion of the Canterbury causes provides insights into the strategies of counsel to substantiate or contest capacity, and highlights the court's role as arbiter of what constituted 'sound mind.' Proponents of wills offered in solemn form routinely asserted that the will-maker was of 'sound mind and memory' at the time of execution.[43] Other allegations described their testators as 'sensible.'[44] Instead of merely asserting a conclusion, however, the proponent's counsel might (perhaps sensing a contest) describe specific conduct that would lead to a finding of mental capacity. For example, in the allegation promoting the will of Simon Leach, it was noted that he could 'compte or tell ... English money.'[45] Likewise, in promoting the will of Richard Barret, the allegation contended that, although he had 'palsey,' he was of sound

---

⁴⁰   Sheppard, *Touchstone of Common Assurances*, p. 399.

⁴¹   George Meriton, *The Parson's Monitor consisting of such Cases and Matter as principally concern the Clergy* (London, 1681), p. 29.

⁴²   Of the total of 39 causes brought, 4 involved conflicting wills, and 9 did not proceed to sentence. Again, as with nullifications on capacity grounds, the percentage of wills nullified on the grounds of undue influence was greater than those nullified on other grounds. What led the contestants to drop the 9 causes is uncertain.

⁴³   Examples are *Nauney contra Nauney*, PROB 18/1/35; *Bourden contra Bourden*, PROB 18/1/54 and *Bradford contra Crisp*, PROB 18/1/70.

⁴⁴   See for example, an allegation in *Thyn et Gregory contra Somerset*, PROB 18/7/27.

⁴⁵   *Croke contra Drewry alias Leach*, PROB 18/19/74.

mind; to substantiate this conclusion, it was asserted that he 'discoursed well' on the day that the will was executed, that within days of his death he had attended to the buying and selling of cattle and other business matters, and that on the day the will was executed he offered a learned disquisition on his hobby, the operation of clocks.[46] Similarly, it was alleged that John Cox had read over his will and noticed that the clause requiring the executor to pay his debts had been omitted. According to the proponent of the will, the attorney who had written the will was present, and had indicated that the clause 'was merely a matter of form.' In addition, the testator was also concerned about the fact that one of his witnesses was not literate, and could make only a mark.[47] That these testators were able to discourse on the law amongst other more mundane matters certainly suggested, at least according to the proponents, both the reason and the clarity of mental processes that constituted 'sound mind.'

To bolster conclusions of capacity, proponents phrased interrogatories that asked witnesses to relate facts or draw conclusions regarding the will-maker's mental state. For example, witnesses to the will of Priscilla Rogers were asked to relate the ceremony of its execution.[48] They testified that when her will was 'laid before her' for execution, though she was 'very weake and infirmed,' she asked for spectacles, because she could not write her name without them, suggesting perhaps a certain presence of mind. A pair was provided to her.[49] Likewise, to substantiate the notion that Charles Woodward had sufficient capacity, a witness to his will was asked to relate the ceremony;[50] he recalled that after execution the will-maker 'called for a pint of Canary [wine] to make Dep[onen]t and the others Drink.'[51] Thus, through interrogatories, the proponent led the witnesses summoned to construct a narrative that was calculated to furnish the court with evidence that the deceased had been lucid at the very moment the will was executed, and that the will was in Ayliffe's words 'a human act' or, as Locke or Brydall required, had been crafted by a person with a 'rational mind,' one to whom 'self-ownership' or 'personhood' ought to be accorded.

---

46 *Owen contra Barrett*, PROB 18/24/5.
47 *Cox et Tompkins contra Cox*, PROB 18/18/88.
48 *Davis et al. contra Rogers*, PROB 18/1810.
49 Ibid., PROB 24/25, 246, 258.
50 *Wise contra Woodward*, PROB 18/24/70.
51 Ibid., PROB 24/35, 205.

The Strategies of Contestants

Contestants likewise framed various arguments in their attempts to set wills aside. Because 'sound mind' was a legal rather than a medical conclusion, allegations of incapacity were put forward in sophisticated medical terms only relatively infrequently. Rarer still was the use of the legal word of art 'insanity'; only one allegation in the group specifically used this term.[52] In the litigation examined here, the contestant of a will on capacity grounds would often eschew both Brydall's classifications and Ayliffe's standard in favor of far more descriptive characterizations: that the will-maker was a 'fickle and uncertain person';[53] 'of shallow understanding';[54] 'childish';[55] 'melancholy';[56] or simply 'crazy.'[57] Specific incidents might be related; William Balle fell off a scaffold that caused his 'memory and judgment to be so impaired that he was incapable of managing his estate.'[58] The contestant of the will of John Gore proffered – and a witness confirmed – that at the time the dying man made his will he was asked if one Mr. Osborne, a friend of Gore, had come to visit him; Gore replied 'I know him not.'[59]

Other allegations eschewed specific incidents of behavior that suggested unsound mind, and only offered the legal conclusion of incapacity. John Williams was 'so dozed, stupid and distempered ... that he was not fit to do any serious or judicious act.'[60] Francis Lewin was 'by reason of his great age and infirmity so decayed in his understanding' that he could not execute a will.[61] Thomas Day, who died 'suddenly,' was not in 'the right frame of mind to make a will.'[62]

This deference to lay rather than technical conceptualizations (be they legal or medical) may be explained because the court was required to rely on the observations and conclusions of ordinary persons though the depositions. The exception was 'distemper,' a medical condition that was sometimes asserted. Thus James Campion was alleged to have been 'distempered in his braine.'[63] According to the contestants of the will of Sir William Willoughby, Bart., he

---

52   *King et Taylor contra Jepp*, PROB 18/7/64 208.
53   *Nauney contra Nauney*, PROB 18/1/35.
54   *Marshall contra Oakley*, PROB 18/18/40.
55   *Owen contra Barrett*, PROB 24/35, 77.
56   *Hill contra Bond*, PROB 24/20, 161.
57   *Marshall contra Oakley*, PROB 18/18/40.
58   *Washington contra Balle*, PROB 18/21/7.
59   *Land et Barnaby contra Burt*, PROB 18/3b/40.
60   *Williams contra Williams*, PROB 18/18/87.
61   *Aberry con How contra Aldine*, PROB 18/21/90.
62   *Day contra Day*, PROB 18/4/37.
63   *Campion per curitrix contra Thomas*, PROB 18/13/90.

had been 'seized of a violent distemper' and for two weeks prior to his death was 'devoid of reason not capable of discourse etc ... not of sufficient apprehension' to make a will.'[64] Christopher Jones must have been 'void of understanding' to have struck his wife with his fist while they were lying in bed together, and also to have uttered 'many extravegant and senseless words.'[65] Another deponent perceived him to be 'much distempered in his brains,' and to have often talked 'idley and senselessly.'[66]

Inferences of Incapacity: Physical Debilitation

Although it was mental rather than physical vigor that was at issue, a debilitated physical condition might be used to imply a lack of sound mind. For example, the Countess of Somerset 'had a great sore upon her groin which must [have been] painful'; that she did not complain was instructive, at least to the contestant: 'but not being very sensible she never mentioned it.'[67] William Balle had 'grown so weake that he made water and it run through the seate of his breeches.'[68] Moreover, it was contended that Balle was 'unable to hold a pen to sign' his will.[69] The inability of the will-maker to grasp a writing instrument firmly during will-execution was also used to question mental capacity; in a number of other cases it was noted that the will-maker's hand had been guided when the document was signed,[70] or 'had his fingers moved to seal' the will.[71] Other telltale signs of physical weakness were described: during the execution ceremony, the will-maker was 'so feeble that she could not sit up,'[72] or spoke so softly that a witness remarked that he could hardly 'tell whether it was a man or a woman.'[73] Thus the strength, posture, and position of the body both at the time of the will's execution and at the moment when the terms of the will were dictated were considered relevant to the issue of testamentary capacity.[74]

---

[64] *Dixie alias Willoughby contra Slater*, PROB 18/3b/4.

[65] *Leslow alias Jones contra Jones*, PROB 18/6/10.

[66] Ibid., PROB 24/13, 53.

[67] *Thyn et Gregory contra Somerset*, PROB 18/7/27.

[68] *Washington contra Balle*, PROB 24/30, 92–3.

[69] Ibid., PROB 24/30, 92.

[70] *Povey contra Povey*, PROB 18/24/15; PROB 18/24/42.

[71] Ibid., PROB 18/24/42.

[72] *Thyn et Gregory contra Somerset*, PROB 18/6/22.

[73] *Long contra Martin*, PROB 24/30, 114.

[74] *Conway contra Huddle et Starr*, PROB 18/6/79, PROB 18/6/24; *Mullen contra Netter*, PROB 18/21/94.

Physical diseases that affected the brain were likewise alleged to put testamentary capacity in issue. For example, the contestant of the will that Richard Barret executed on his deathbed charged that he had had 'apoplectick fitts' prior to his death.[75] Similarly, Anne Povey was alleged to have been 'lightheaded.'[76] Sometimes witnesses were at pains to explain precisely the physical condition in which they found the testator. Mary Sleight, a domestic servant, noted that Povey was 'dozy,' and at the time the will was executed was much 'given to dozing,' but was not 'lightheaded.'[77]

Physical evidence might also be used to support allegations of incapacity. To support a contention that Sir William Willoughby, Bart., was not of sound mind when he executed his will on his deathbed, it was noted that when his body was embalmed his head was opened and fluid was observed on his brain. The doctors present commented upon 'the serious humours and water on the brain.'[78] Yet the proponents did not regard this piece of medical evidence as dispositive of the cause. While they agreed that the will-maker had suffered from 'watery humours,' they denied that the doctors concluded, as the contestants had alleged, that the dying man's condition would 'destroy understanding.'[79]

Inferences of Incapacity: Quirky Behavior

Lack of capacity was frequently inferred from behavior, rather than from medical evidence of physical or mental illness.[80] Although Brydall offered a handful of examples as benchmarks of a lack of capacity, the Canterbury causes illustrate in more detail how capacity issues were raised. It requires reference here to a series of examples of bizarre conduct that were alleged by the contestants and refuted by the promoters. The resulting litany of accounts that follows is instructive, and also both poignant and amusing. In contesting the will of Simon Leach on the grounds of lack of testamentary capacity, for example, three interrogatories illuminate the contestant's strategy, which was to demonstrate that the will-maker was rather more quirky and peculiar than was typical even for an aged Englishman. First, the deponent was asked if Leach was only allowed pocket money by his wife Anne; second, he was pressed to reveal if it was not true that Leach preferred the company of boys to that of men and women; and finally, the

---

75 *Owen contra Barrett*, PROB 18/24/28.

76 *Povey contra Povey*, PROB 18/24/15.

77 Ibid., PROB 24/35, 56.

78 *Dixie alias Willoughby contra Slater*, PROB 18/3c/4.

79 Ibid., PROB 18/3c/100.

80 William McGovern, Sheldon Kurtz, and Jan Ellen Rein, *Wills, Trusts and Estates* (St. Paul, MN 1988), pp. 272–6.

deponent was asked if it was true that when a question was posed to the will-maker he would grin and not answer, and 'sometimes pull out his yard to piss and never putt the same up again.'[81]

Outrageous commands to servants made by the will-maker might be used to support an allegation of unsound mind. Mary Culver, Richard Barret's domestic servant, deposed that he 'caused many silly things to be done.' If ordering his dairy maid to wash his pigs in a tub in his kitchen was not sufficiently suspect, Barret asked her to 'cut some pork from off the spit as it was roasting and throw it down before the piggs to see whether they would eat some of their grandfather or grandmother.'[82] Another example of how commands to servants might support an assertion of lack of capacity comes from litigation over the will of Francis Lewin. According to the allegation of his two daughters contesting his will, which had been executed shortly before his death, and promoting one executed a decade earlier, Lewin was 'aged,' 'infirmed,' and 'unable to manage affairs.' As evidence of his mental state, the allegation offered a variety of specifics; for example, after 48 years of marriage to his wife, Joanne, who had recognized his 'childishness,' Lewin decided that he no longer wished to live with her, and 'turned her out.' The conclusion of childishness was bolstered by the allegation that he

> would several times command his servants to draw him about his house and
> grounds in a wheelbarrow and would make a noise and use the actions of children,
> and was in a childish foolish sorte of way altogether voyd of any understanding.[83]

In addition, the allegation claimed that Lewin had been unable to contract business by the beginning of 1688, about two years before his deathbed will was executed. To support this contention, the allegation noted that he was 'so voyd of understanding' that he was alleged 'to have put his sheepe into a close of pease which he said would do the pease a great deal of good.'[84] As further testimony to his failure to observe good farming practice, a witness deposed that he 'locked cows in the cow house the whole day.'[85]

Some allegations point to deranged behavior at the time of a testamentary act in rather a straightforward way. As evidence of the will-maker's unsound mind, this time to prove that a revocation of a will executed about a month before his death

---

[81] *Croke contra Drewry alias Leach*, PROB 18/19/74.

[82] *Owen contra Barrett*, PROB 24/35, 77.

[83] *Aberry con How contra Aldine*, PROB 18/21/16. This allegation of infantile behavior was supported in the deposition of at least one witness. See ibid., PROB 24/30, 17.

[84] Ibid., PROB 18/21/16.

[85] Ibid., PROB 24/30, 17.

was invalid for lack of capacity, it was alleged by Margaret, the wife of Edmund Medlicott, that her husband 'wanted to leave his bed to save the King from a murder plot'; when she showed the dying man his will, he ripped it up, and this action accounted for the piecemeal nature of the document that she nevertheless offered for probate. According to her allegation, the dying man thereafter regained his senses, and when he was asked if the will should stand, he replied in the affirmative.[86] Exactly how odd the behavior had to have been to invalidate a will remains unclear. Yet the allegations and interrogatories suggest, consistent with Brydall's contentions, that assessments and scrutiny of the will-maker's behavior both prior to and after the will were executed were regarded by advocates as relevant evidence of sound mind or unsound mind at the time the will was made.

Inferences of Incapacity: Elderly Will-Makers

Advanced age, another ground for lack of sound mind discussed by Swinburne, was raised in fashioning allegations in the Canterbury causes. An example is the will of Richard Delves who, according to one deposition, was alleged to be 'above fourscore years'; he was also said to be 'much decayed in his memory judgement and understanding ... by reason of his great age.'[87] On the other hand, in causes in which capacity was at issue, deponents sometimes noted the age of testators, though usually in general terms. For example, Richard Barret was said to have been of 'great age ... near four score,'[88] and Priscilla Rogers was between 'three and four score years.'[89] Witnesses might not always agree precisely on the will-maker's age: while two witnesses deposed that Clement Pragell was an 'old man,' one witness reckoned him to be 'near three score,'[90] another 'between three and four score.'[91]

Inferences of Incapacity: The Inebriated Testator

Both Brydall and Swinburne noted that a testator who was drunk at the time a will was executed should be deemed to have lacked the requisite sound mind.

---

[86] *Medlicott contra Medlicott*, PROB 18/7/25.

[87] *Godfrey contra Delves*, PROB 24/15, 232.

[88] *Owen contra Barrett*, PROB 24/35, 79.

[89] *Davis et al. contra Rogers*, PROB 24/25, 247.

[90] *Hill contra Bond*, PROB 24/20, 66.

[91] Ibid., PROB 24/20, 69. Likewise another witness in *Davis et al. contra Rogers* (footnote 89 above) estimated Davis' age in a slightly more youthful range of between 50 and 60. PROB 24/25, 250.

Brydall had little sympathy for the drunkard who, unlike a madman, 'brought himself into the necessity.' The quantity of drink consumed, however, had to be excessive, leading to a deprivation of intellect and reason.[92] Will-makers who were alleged to be under the influence of drink surface in a number of our causes. Sir William Willoughby, Bart., whose will contest has been described previously, was alleged to have drunk 'immoderately' at the time his will was executed.[93] A witness might be interrogated regarding the testator's alcoholic consumption at the time the will was drafted or executed. One interrogatory directed that witnesses be asked if the testator had 'drunk hard' prior to having made his will.[94]

A person who had consumed alcohol in significant quantities might also be susceptible to persuasion, creating another link between sound mind and undue influence. For example, in one allegation it was maintained that the proponent had traveled with the now-deceased to the country, plied him with drink, and had him write his will.[95] Then as now, strange things might be done under the influence of alcohol. Take, for example, the will of Gregory Thorned, styled in the document as a 'Gentleman of the Chappel Royal' and rather a hale and hearty fellow. In challenging his nuncupative will, which was according to the contestant uttered in an alehouse, it was alleged:

> If someone flattered him he might say he would give him estate and if asked the day after Gregory Thorned would smile and say 'you know that when I am merry I doe talk of things I never intend to doe and would bid them not take any notice of wt hee then said.'[96]

Medical Evidence of Mental Capacity

Given that both the promoters and the contestants of wills on testamentary-capacity grounds frequently alleged the debilitated physical condition of the will-maker as evidence of a weakened mental state, it is surprising that there is little evidence of 'expert' medical opinion on states of mind in the litigation observed. As I have noted, a number of allegations charged that a will-maker was distempered, 'light-headed,' or the like in order to suggest that he or she lacked competence. But relatively few litigants corroborated lay persons' conclusions with a doctor's statements or depositions.

---

[92]   Brydall, *Non Compos Mentis*, pp. 123–4.
[93]   *Dixie alias Willoughby contra Slater*, PROB 18/3b/4.
[94]   *Sherman et Pratt contra Green*, PROB 18/5/106.
[95]   *Whitelocke contra Hulburd*, PROB 18/24/55.
[96]   *Cooke contra Batty*, PROB 18/3c/28.

Both sides in the litigation surrounding the validity of the codicil to the will of the dowager Countess of Somerset, however, did resort to statements by physicians. In his allegations, the Duke of Somerset, her eldest son and the primary beneficiary under her first will, challenged the offer of probate of a codicil executed on her deathbed. Somerset claimed that his mother's physician, Dr. Thomas Cox, had determined that the countess had suffered from a 'Lethargy or an Apoplecticall distemper or a Lethargy Joyned with Apoplectical distemper.'[97] According to the duke, Cox had settled on that opinion when he was first summoned, and indicated that her 'braine was seised.' Later the doctor reported to the duke that his mother had 'lost reason from the time she had first fell ill until her death.' It was maintained that the doctor had indicated at the onset of treatment that the malady was so severe that those who suffer from it generally did not recover and died within the first few days after diagnosis. Cox told the countess that she had a 'Lethargy or Apoplexy,' and asked her if she had made her will; another attending physician, Dr Willis, advised her to do so with dispatch 'because the disease could take away ... reason.'[98]

Thyn, her son-in-law and executor of the deathbed codicil, contradicted Somerset's medical evidence with his own. He submitted interrogatories to the attending apothecary to show that even though the countess's condition had been costly (the value of the potions prescribed was impressive) it was not so grave, at least earlier in the course of the illness. First, the apothecary was asked to confirm whether he had prepared the medicines in accordance with the directions of her doctors. Thereafter, he was invited to give his own 'expert medical opinion' as to whether a person with the 'apoplectic disorder could live for six or seven days and still be of sound mind.' Finally, a question was posed that attempted to draw a distinction between the countess's need for medicine and the severity of her illness at the time the potions were ordered:

> Do you know that Physicians in the beginning of distemper prescribe some Physic to them wch may be preventitive to diseases w[hi]ch may come upon their patients in such sickness notwithstanding their patients do not actually labour with such disease at that time when they prescribe that physicke and by such preventing physicke such diseases w[hi]ch otherwise might come upon their patients have been prevented?[99]

---

[97]   *Thyn et Gregory contra Somerset*, PROB 18/8/114.

[98]   Ibid., PROB 18/7/27.

[99]   Ibid., PROB 18/8/114.

Other Canterbury causes likewise produced medical testimony through interrogatories directed to doctors. In litigation surrounding the will of Anne Povey, one doctor was asked if she were 'light headed,' and whether 'water' shown to him (presumably drained from her head) would support such an opinion. In addition to querying her 'lightheadedness,' another question in the same interrogatory (though directed to a different doctor) asked from which type of 'distemper' she suffered.[100] In another cause, a physician was asked if the now-deceased had the 'bloody flux,' and whether it was usual for persons who suffered from the malady to have it for weeks and to lose their senses while the illness ran its course.[101] The medical evidence in the following two cases was probably solicited from the attending physicians because they had been present at the ceremony of execution. In the first, a doctor expressed doubt as to whether his patient was of sufficient capacity to execute a will, or so an allegation suggests. According to the allegation of the contestants of the will of Edward Wynn, his doctor had prescribed a 'physic a day or 2 before the will which would stupefy.' The doctor was present at the time of the will's execution, and he was reported to have opined that the testator was not of sound mind and told the scrivener that he would so testify.[102] Secondly, one Dr. Brown, William Balle's attending physician, confirmed that Balle was not in 'sensible condition' at the time the will was executed. [103]

The Observations of Witnesses

Counsel for the parties bolstered their clients' contentions by filing interrogatories directed to witnesses that would elicit responses that put at issue the will-maker's sound mind. Thus one contestant's allegation proffered that a will-maker was 'without reason';[104] the written interrogatories posed questions to witnesses about the will-maker's mental state and conduct; and the depositions were calculated to add an unbiased opinion of the dying individual's state of mind.

Because the promoter of the will and its contestant obviously differed on the question of capacity, the observations and conclusions of witnesses elicited through interrogatories was crucial to the outcome. Witnesses were arguably impartial, that is, less interested, at least financially, in the outcome, and the court probably viewed their recollections and conclusions as more reliable

---

100   *Povey contra Povey*, PROB 18/24/15.
101   *Besson contra Jones*, PROB 18/21/92.
102   *Templer con Wynn*, PROB 18/18/98.
103   *Washington contra Balle*, PROB 24/30, 92.
104   *Thyn et Gregory contra Somerset*, PROB 18/6/22.

than those of the parties involved. Witnesses were asked to describe the dying person's state of mind and/or to opine upon the individual's ability to undertake a testamentary act. Contestants framed interrogatories that might solicit descriptions by witnesses of a will-maker as mentally weakened: 'Was Hugh a fickle and uncertain person not fixed in his dealings and performance of things regarding his estate?' 'Was he diminished in his understanding and ran down the street like a madman and was thought to be so?'[105] Of another testator, a witness was asked: 'Was he not a melancholy man and distempered in his braine?'[106]

Questions phrased in this fashion invited statements by witnesses in depositions that related the will-maker's conduct, and some observers also rendered an opinion as to whether the behavior was sufficiently extreme to render a testamentary act invalid. For example, Elizabeth Cock noted that 'though he [Francis Lewin] did extravagant acts ... [the witness] cannot say he was out of his senses.'[107] In other causes witnesses opined that the will-maker was 'decayed,'[108] 'melancholy,'[109] or 'of weak braine ... for little drink make him talk much.'[110]

On occasion the court had evidence of the will-maker's own judgment, albeit filtered through witnesses. For example, Samuel Lanbridge stated that when Anne Vaughn pressed her cousin Anne Mathews to make her will, the latter replied, 'I am not capable to make a will,' and she became 'very angry' at the suggestion that she should do so.[111] Likewise, a witness reported that George Solby said, before the execution of his will, 'my Capacity is gone and my memory fails me.'[112] Yet the reverse might be the case: a testator might refute another's conclusion of incapacity and a witness might report it. The exchange between Edward Wynne and his physician is instructive. When a scrivener arrived to take instructions from Wynne regarding his will, Wynne's attending physician, one Dr. Conquest, was reported to have remarked, 'What a mad man's will; to this charge, the testator responded 'No you are mad.' The following day, however,

---

[105]   *Nauney contra Nauney*, PROB 18/1/35.

[106]   *Fidoe contra Fidoe*, PROB 18/21/35.

[107]   *Aberry con How contra Aldine*, PROB 24/30, 138.

[108]   *Washington contra Balle*, PROB 24/25, 100.

[109]   PROB 24/20, 161. In fact the much considered (and fashionable) malady of 'melancholy' expounded upon at length by Robert Burton in 1621 in his anonymously published *Anatomy of Melancholy* should not have been regarded as sufficient to remove testamentary capacity. I used an American edition (Michigan, 1965).

[110]   *Campion per curitrix contra Thomas*, PROB 24/20, 37.

[111]   *Harwood contra Vaughn*, PROB 24/14, 245.

[112]   *Boles contra Solby*, PROB 24/25, 214.

Wynne was prepared to reconsider his own capacity (or at least the wisdom of his testamentary act), remarking that his will had been made in 'haste.'[113]

Finally, contestants attempted to link age with faulty understanding in order to render a will invalid for want of mental capacity, and the testimony of witnesses was solicited to confirm their contention. One deponent concluded that an aged will-maker was not of sound mind because the dying man had no longer recognized him; in particular the will-maker asked the deponent, one Mr. Boyes, where Mr. Boyes was, and repeated the question 'foure or five times in an houre'; Boyes also deposed that the will-maker in talking to others would 'forget what he saide immediately before and would fall into senseless and impertinent discourse.'[114] Witnesses likewise linked lapses of memory to other frailties or oddities in the will-maker's behavior. For example, it was reported by a witness that Thomas Cocke did not recognize him, even though he had known Cocke since childhood. He also reported that Cocke demanded a number of times to 'let the children be taken away that I may not be disturbed whereas in truth there were noe children in the House.'[115]

The Testimony of Scriveners

The will's scrivener was usually present at a critical moment in the process of testation, and could therefore be a useful witness to the will-maker's mental capacity. The depositions frequently describe a process of will-making that transpired as follows: a scrivener was summoned, took instructions from the will-maker, returned with a draft, and read it over to the will-maker who either approved of its contents or demanded revisions; if necessary the will was altered, but in either case the will was subsequently executed, with the scrivener often serving as a witness. Thus the scrivener could provide evidence of the will-maker's health that was both timely and, because he or she was unlikely to be a legatee or executor, unbiased. Admittedly there was some incentive for the summoned scrivener to conclude that the will-maker was sufficiently robust at the critical moments, otherwise he or she could not write the will, and thus would have to forgo a fee.

A deposition in one of our testamentary causes relates just such a dilemma. When Thomas Owen was called to the deathbed of Robert Stenton, he found him in very poor health, but 'sensible,' and he testified that Stenton asked him to draft his will. But Owen was uncertain of the languishing man's capacity, saying

---

[113] *Templer con Wynn*, PROB 24/25, 188.
[114] *Godfrey contra Delves*, PROB 24/15, 231–2.
[115] *Cocke contra Cocke*, PROB 24/20, 73.

that he preferred to 'draw a few lines of a will … if he comes better to himself he should execute it.' Owen returned to his house with the will, and told Stenton's housekeeper to call him should his condition improve. The following day he was again summoned. Owen remained doubtful of Stenton's capacity, but when Stenton told the housekeeper to pay Owen two guineas, he changed his mind – and not for the reason one might conclude – or so Owen deposed. He reported that he 'apprehended that if he had the presence of mind to know that he should pay him that amount then he must be of sound mind.' Owen then read over the contents of the document to him, and the will was executed and published; Owen remarked, 'it is better to make such a will as the dece[ease]d was capable of this dep[onen]t not being able to judge whether it might be good or not.'[116]

The Court's Dilemma

Unlike the scrivener Owen, the court was unable to shirk the issue of mental capacity. Confronted by the opposing narratives offered by the parties and with little medical evidence to sift, the judges probably regarded lay witnesses' statements as crucial. While they might differ in their version of events, some witnesses struggled in their own minds as to whether a will-maker had been of sound mind at the time the will was made. For example, one Grace Stubbs was unable to be certain whether a dying woman, Mary Burlton, was of sound mind at the precise moment she declared her will because:

> … ye sd dece[ase]d was ye sd Monday some short time before ye speaking of ye said words and some short time after not sensible as this Dept apprehended and soe continued every day after at times to be insensible, but as to any particular words of insanity used by her while she declared she doth not remember.[117]

If Mrs. Stubbs, a disinterest party who was present at the moment of the will's execution, was perplexed, it must have been difficult for the court, removed in time and space, to determine whether the will-maker had had sufficient capacity.

---

[116]   *Ward contra Stinton per curator*, PROB 24/25, 263. Another deponent, John King, present at the execution concurred with the uncertainty regarding Stanton's sound mind. When he was asked whether Stanton had sufficient understanding or not he replied, 'he cannot say.' PROB 24/25, 268.

[117]   *Burlton contra Burlton*, PROB 24/19, 243.

Undue Influence as Grounds for Denying Probate

To have a will set aside on the grounds of undue influence, a contestant had to prove that another person had coerced the will-maker into formulating and executing the testamentary act offered for probate – in short, that someone had substituted his or her testamentary volition for that of the will-maker. There was no shortage of disappointed heirs prepared to contest testamentary acts on the grounds of undue influence. All that was necessary was an aggrieved individual: an heir who would receive more through intestacy or a legatee in an earlier will. Undue influence was raised in about one of four of our actively contested testamentary causes.[118]

Litigation Strategies

As with mental-capacity litigation, counsel formulated allegations by employing a variety of expressions to suggest coercion. Some contestants were succinct in their allegations: one contended that a will had been procured by 'undue means,'[119] another that an individual 'persuaded' or 'importuned' the will-maker.[120] Importuned – meaning persistently solicited, to make or alter a will[121] – was a term that was frequently employed.[122] What did the word mean in the context of the causes? An example can be supplied. Anne Tremhard alleged that the codicils to the will of her husband Thomas that were offered for probate by the executor named therein, one Henley, had been 'importuned.' It was alleged that the deceased's mother, Hannah, had written them and that, although they were signed by her husband, he did so 'to avoid trouble thereof being sicke and in paine and not understanding what he did.'[123] Other language was also used to denote coercion. Contestants of the will of Sir Richard Lloyd seem to have employed nearly all of them. In addition to the use of the word 'importuned' no less than five times in the allegation, it was further charged that Lloyd was 'in fear' of the proponents, that he was 'much able to be imposed upon' and

---

118   See Table 3.1 in Chapter 3.

119   *Conway contra Huddle et Starr*, PROB 18/6/24.

120   For examples, *Fidoe contra Fidoe*, PROB 18/21/35; *Williams contra Phillips*, PROB 18/24/20.

121   According to the *Shorter Oxford English Dictionary* (Oxford, 1973), vol. I, p. 1003.

122   See *Hawkes contra Field*, PROB 18/7/48 where the 'importuning' was regarded by the contestant as 'fierce'. See also *Dixie alias Willoughby contra Slater*, PROB 18/3c/100 and *Owen et.al. contra Lloyd*, PROB 18/9/10.

123   *Henley contra Tremhard*, PROB 25/2/60.

'would act contrary to his inclinations by threats and solicitation,' and that the proponents 'could force or persuade him to do anything whatsoever.'[124]

Litigation on the issue of undue influence was (like capacity causes) largely fact-driven. The strategy adopted by the contestants was to cast suspicion on the context in which the document had been produced, and to highlight the conduct of those who had participated in the drafting and execution of the will. Paramount among contextual factors was that many, if not most of the wills that appear in our collection, were documents fashioned (or words uttered) while the will-maker was languishing on the deathbed. The weakened and the dying, surrounded by various onlookers including family members, friends, servants, acquaintances, and creditors, were particularly vulnerable to coercion.

The Susceptible Will-Maker

In modern law, the susceptibility to coercion of will-makers, particularly those at death's door, is a relevant factor in establishing that a will was procured by undue influence.[125] And so it was in the past. The will of Thomas Hawkes provides an example. The contestant sought to demonstrate that the will-maker was 'distracted in the brain,' and at first had resisted the 'importunings' of his cousin. Witnesses were asked to depose whether the will that was offered for probate had been produced by the promoter from his pocket or, alternatively, whether the will was written in front of the dying man. Was it drafted pursuant to his direction, or did he merely nod his head 'yea or nay' to questions posed? Then they were questioned about his physical state: was his hand guided when he signed the will? But perhaps most damning was the question of whether the attending physician, one Dr. Clitherow, 'did not condemn the persons therein when he heard there was a will.'[126]

This cause suggests the link between mental capacity and undue influence. Weakened physically and mentally, the testator could neither appreciate the significance of his act nor resist the coercion of others. Other causes reflect a similar link. Thomas Goswell's wife alleged that he was an individual who 'in fits of melancholy might be persuaded to sign and seal any writing without reading it.' Indeed it was alleged that he had 'signed blank papers ... to avoid coming to town.'[127] Other contestants asserted that the dying man's hand was guided

---

[124] *Owen et al. contra Lloyd*, PROB 18/9/10 (See also the will of Walter Rea, the terms of which are discussed in *Bombay contra Rea*, PROB 18/13/16).

[125] McGovern, Kurtz, and Rein, *Wills, Trusts and Estates*, pp. 272–7; Kerridge, 'Wills made in suspicious circumstances.

[126] *Hawkes contra Field*, PROB 18/7/48.

[127] *Fisher contra Goswell*, PROB 18/21/3.

when he signed, testimony to the interference of the others as well as to the weakened physical state of the will-maker.[128] Three witnesses even claimed that at the time of execution of one will its maker was already dead. It is not clear that such statements were merely hyperbolic; one witness certainly believed the testator had already died at the time a will was brought to him to sign: 'a pen was put into the dece[ase]ads hand by some p[er]son and as he taketh it by the s[ai]d Wm Corbett and ye dece[ase]d hand was guided by such p[er]son ... and a seal was put by ye same person into ye dece[ase]ds hand and put on ye wax dropped upon ye sheet.'[129]

Undue influence was often alleged to have occurred while the will-maker was isolated from family and friends by those said to have procured the will. One recurring situation alleged was that the will-maker was physically under the control of the proponent at the time the will was drafted and/or executed. In a number of causes, it was insisted, for example, that the will-maker had been confined in the promoter's house and that others were denied access to him.[130] Accordingly, the contestants of the will of Sir William Willoughby, Bart., claimed that he had been sequestered while others 'concocted' the will. According to the allegations of the contestant of the will, the executors even tried to kill him. Because they feared he might recover, the proponents 'caused a great Blackening fire to be made to cause smoke and prevent sleeping' in order to 'increase distemper.'[131]

Even in situations in which the will-maker had not been stowed away, and thus placed physically out of the reach of family and friends, it might be alleged that at the time the will was executed others were kept from the will-maker. For example, the Countess of Somerset's 'friends,' who were attending her in her last illness, were not present at the execution of a codicil that she was alleged to have made. Indeed much was made by the contestant of the codicil of the fact that the publication of the testamentary act was kept secret from them.[132] Likewise, the contestants of one will contended that its promoter had concealed the dying person from his friends and relatives, and did not divulge his illness to 'friends and neighbours,' even though it was 'plague or pox.' When relatives found out the dying man's condition and attempted to visit him, they were told that he was sleeping.[133]

---

[128] For examples, *Walker et Mason contra Grove*, PROB 18/1/50; *Hare alias Elliot et Hare alias Field contra Hare*, PROB 18/21/15; and *Long contra Martin*, PROB 18/21/30.

[129] *Price contra Price*, PROB 24/35, 47.

[130] For examples, *Hill contra Bond*, PROB 18/13/57; and *Seawell contra Harbert*, PROB 18/7/1.

[131] *Dixie alias Willoughby contra Slater*, PROB 18/3c/4.

[132] *Thyn et Gregory contra Somerset*, PROB 18/6/22.

[133] *Moore et Welch contra Ewens*, PROB 18/3c/35.

More commonly, however, the contestant alleged a more subtle form of control over the will-maker and the process of testation. Rather than accusing the will's promoter of stowing the will-maker physically out of reach of others, it was proffered that the promoter had controlled the will-making process in a less direct fashion. For example, a number of allegations contended that the promoter (or another) rather than the will-maker had 'instructed' the scrivener on the terms of the will. Accordingly, the contestant suggested that the will-maker had executed a document prepared by another without his or her active participation; therefore, in the contestant's mind, the will was not the product of the volition of the dying person.[134]

One final cause in our collection can be related to illustrate nicely both elements of control, the physical and the psychological. The will of Miles Martin was alleged to have been procured through the connivance of two unrelated men who had concealed the whereabouts of the physically and mentally debilitated testator from his friends and relatives; central to the plot was the scrivener Mr. Gray, who had included a bequest of £20 to himself, allegedly without the deceased's authorization, for his role in overseeing the plot. Unfortunately for him, the will was nullified.[135]

Conclusion

The 'culture of will-making' in late-seventeenth-century England did not mesh well with the period's closely held ideals of personhood/self-ownership and the freedom of disposition that naturally obtains in a society with individualistic notions of property ownership. Wills were often made late in life, on death's doorstep, executed by those in transition between this life and the one that they either hoped or feared awaited them. The law stood ready to protect their volition and their designs for the disposition of their property, but only for those who were 'rational' and who had acted of their own free will. The wills of those who did not fit into this category must be invalidated. This created a conundrum for the court: in order to protect the society's norm of free disposition, it must at times be removed from some of its members, the weak of mind and character.

While an emerging enlightened consideration of mental disorder as a disease can be recognized in the literature of both medicine and the law, precious little of it seems to have filtered into the Prerogative Court. What can be observed in the records is the difficult task that fell to the judges: to fashion a narrative

---

[134]   *Markham et Carrington contra Markham*, PROB 18/1/35 and PROB 18/1/46.

[135]   *Long contra Martin*, PROB 18/21/30. The sentence is PROB 11/407, 342. A different document was probated: PROB 11/395, 160.

of the factual circumstances surrounding particular will executions that they had to pieced together from the imperfect evidence placed before them, and then to apply the nebulous legal benchmarks of capacity and coercion to the transaction. Because the resolution of causes turned on the narrative assembled from the specific facts of a particular will execution, as related by the parties and their witnesses, the judges were required to form an overall impression of the trustworthiness of the parties and their witnesses. But most of all they were empowered: by accepting or rejecting bits of proffered evidence, the judges could choose the winners and losers of an individual testamentary cause.

Mental-capacity and undue-influence cases abound in modern law, and fact-finders face the same tasks that the judges did in the Prerogative Court.[136] Their struggle can be observed by reading opinions in which the law respecting those doctrines is refined. Unhappily, that luxury is lacking for testamentary causes in early modern England; the opinions of the judges that might explain precisely why a claim of capacity or coercion was upheld or denied were not committed to writing. What was redacted was a formulaic sentence, which does not assist the historian in understanding precisely why a will was probated or excluded. More significantly, it did not provide guidance to will-makers, their scriveners, or their counsel in the Prerogative Court.

Yet the historian may infer from the evidence, as well as report it. The judges rejected three out of four incapacity and undue-influence allegations. Their stance indicates that they were unprepared to allow 'a wide door' to be open for contestants of wills. In short, the judges seem to have been prepared to protect testamentary freedom and to err on the side of personhood/self-ownership, even if their position would allow some wills to be admitted that might have been executed by persons who were unfit to undertake the legal act, or who did so through the 'importuning' of others.

And Parliament was prepared to allow this situation to continue. Many of the wills in the causes were fashioned on the deathbed. When Parliament did not include the proposal to limit the validity of deathbed wills in the final draft of the Statute of Frauds, it tacitly opted to allow the probate court to continue to control the sorting process.

---

[136] Lloyd Bonfield, 'Reforming the Requirements for Due Execution of Wills: Some Guidance from the Past', *Tulane Law Review*, vol. 70 (1995), pp. 1908–9.

Chapter 5
Estate Plans by 'Word of Mouth': The Validity of Nuncupative Wills

Introduction

Tables 3.1 and 3.2 indicated that a significant proportion of the testamentary business of the Prerogative Court of Canterbury in the late seventeenth century was devoted to determining the validity and terms of nuncupative (oral) wills. Nearly one-third of the wills (31.8 percent) offered for probate prior to the enactment of the Statute of Frauds in 1677 involved one or even a second oral will.[1] In 1676, the year for which I transcribed the record in all testamentary causes with surviving allegations, over a quarter of the causes in litigation actually involved oral wills. These causes probably dealt with wills that were more questionable than most others that came before the Prerogative Court because a far greater proportion of oral wills than written ones were nullified (see Table 5.1 – 17.2 percent versus 7.4 percent). This stark fact lends evidence to my hypothesis that, despite only cursory mention in the debate over the adoption of the statute, Parliament tightened up the requirements for the testamentary validity of nuncupative wills in response to vexatious cases involving them that came before the probate courts.[2]

---

[1]   In the three sample years of 1661–65, 1666, and 1671, 12 of the 27 actively contested causes involved oral wills while they appear in 16 of the 59 actively contested causes in 1676. Thus, prior to the Statute of Frauds, 27 of 86 or 31.4 percent of the causes involved oral wills. Only two wills offered for probate after 1676 were by word of mouth. In our discussion here we shall also make reference to nuncupative wills that were not derived from our sample but were nullified. These will form a second collection of wills that were studied, those which were nullified by the court and for which there are surviving allegations, interrogatories and in most causes depositions.

[2]   See Chapter 3, above.

Table 5.1   Disposition of wills: composite (sample years and 1676): written
              versus oral

| | Written wills | | Oral wills | |
	N	percent	N	percent
Admitted to Probate	99	66.8	17	58.6
Nullified	11	7.4	5	17.2
Did not Proceed to Sentence	38	25.7	7	24.1
Totals	148	99.9	29	99.9

This chapter argues that while the adoption of the Statute of Frauds probably limited the number of disputes over oral wills in the Prerogative Court, litigation continued to arise. Although far fewer causes involving wills alleged to have been made by word of mouth were brought before the court after the enactment of the statute (indeed only a pair emerge from our sample),[3] a broader survey of litigation that I undertook (which included all litigation which resulted in wills nullified in the years observed – an additional 40 causes) has uncovered other disputes involving the validity of nuncupative wills. My findings illustrate that disputes over their validity continued after the adoption of the Statute of Frauds. Indeed, these post-1677 causes raise issues strikingly similar to those that surfaced prior to the reforms, suggesting that the law was only partially successful in eliminating this genre of vexing litigation. However, the judges took their cue from the Parliamentary intervention: the Canterbury Prerogative Court does seem to have examined promoted oral wills with a finer lens after the statute.

Parliament's success was limited in effect because it was limited in scope: it did not attempt to alter radically the 'culture of will-making' in early modern England, in which testamentary business was frequently settled shortly before death. Rather it ratified it. After all, early modern society's legal order was in the early stages of transition from the largely oral legal culture of the Middle Ages to

---

[3]   Those of two mariners (who died at sea, and whose wills were therefore exempt from the Statute of Frauds. 29 Car. II, c. 3 (1677), sec. 22: *Williams contra Phillips*, PROB 18/24/20 and text at footnotes 69 – 72; and *Bush contra Couzens*, PROB 18/24/65 and text at footnotes 73–9.

present-day society's reverence for the written word.[4] Thus sections 18 and 22 of the statute respectively exempted wills under £30 in value and those of soldiers and seamen who died abroad. Section 18 also permitted even the wealthier subjects of the realm to make nuncupative wills in their last illness, so long as they did so in their own residence or in another place where they had lived for at least 10 days prior, or indeed anywhere else if they were taken ill by surprise. The modest infringement upon the 'culture of will-making' was twofold: to insist first that a will probated six months after the words were uttered had to have been redacted within six days (Sec. 19), and second, that a written will could not be revoked by an oral one (Sec. 21).

Given the statute's modest reforms, its success in limiting litigation over oral wills seems striking. An investigation into oral wills that were promoted both before and after the statute can assist in understanding both its impetus and its effect. But before I turn to an analysis of the litigation, the disputes must be placed in focus by a survey of the contemporary discussion about nuncupative wills penned by legal commentators of the period.

The Law Respecting the Validity of Nuncupative Wills

That early modern Englishmen and women were aware that the law recognized nuncupative wills can be observed by both word and deed in the Canterbury causes. Some testators clearly expressed a preference for making an oral rather than a written will. For example, proponents alleged that Richard Parsons had made an oral will on his deathbed at the Bell Inn in London. After declaring his will by word of mouth, he was told, according to the allegation, that he should have his directions written out, whereupon he declared, 'I have no land therefore I may dispose orally.'[5] In fact, Parsons was so enamored of oral wills that he may have made more than one: in the course of litigation over the probate of his estate, two persons sought to prove two distinct oral wills, each nominating a different man as executor![6] Another will-maker was counseled by, a layman, on the ability to make wills by word of mouth. According to the promoter of an oral codicil to John Gore's will, one John Osborne, a friend of the will-maker, asked Thomas Burt (the husband of the contestant of Gore's nuncupative will and proponent of a conflicting written will, and therefore a person with an interest against the validity of the oral will) whether the legacies alleged to have been

---

[4]   Jack Goody, *The Logic of Writing and the Organization of Society* (Cambridge, 1986), ch. 5.

[5]   *Ellis contra Parsons*, PROB 18/7/56.

[6]   Ibid., PROB 18/6/23 and PROB 18/7/56.

made by word of mouth were valid. Burt was reported to reply that 'it was ye s[ai]d dece[ase]d[']s will and it would stand good in law.'[7]

In popular culture, then, oral testamentary acts were well ensconced. By the seventeenth century, however, commentators on the law of wills had come to express ambivalence with respect to nuncupative wills. On the one hand, they recognized that permitting an oral declaration of testamentary intent to stand as a valid will of personal property permitted property-owners considerable latitude in devising what modern lawyers would call their 'estate plans.' However, they also warned prospective will-makers of the uncertainty that oral directions brought to wealth transmission.

Sudden death was the primary explanation offered by seventeenth-century legal writers for the recognition of nuncupative wills. In discoursing on oral wills, William Sheppard, writing before the Statute of Frauds, explained their rationale in the following terms. An oral will should be made:

> where a man is sick, and for fear lest death or want of memory or speech should surprise him, that he should be prevented if stayed the writing of his testament, desireth his neighbors and friends to bear witness of his last will, and then declareth the same presently by word before them.[8]

George Meriton concurred, noting that oral wills were resorted to most frequently when the testator was too weak to make a written will and 'past all hope of recovery.'[9] Accordingly, he maintained, some property-owners who were caught unawares and faced imminent death would have their goods descend through the law of intestate succession (or an earlier will) rather than pursuant to last-minute volition unless spoken words could constitute a valid will.

To the justification of exigency John Ayliffe added another: the arcane rules of due execution. According to Ayliffe, the Romans, who had developed the last will as a means of property devolution, recognized that to execute a valid will might be a 'matter of some Difficulty at certain seasons.'[10] Precisely what 'difficulty' he imagined given the less than rigorous due-execution requirements that obtained in early modern England is obscure, but he suggested that cautious property-

---

[7]   *Land et Barnaby contra Burt*, PROB 18/3b/86. In fact, the will was not admitted, though perhaps not because the additions were oral. Sentence is PROB 11/337, 155, 154..

[8]   William Sheppard, *The Touchstone of Common Assurances*, 6th edn (Dublin, 1785), p. 384.

[9]   George Meriton, *The Parson's Monitor Consisting of such Cases and Matters as Principally Concern the Clergy* (London, 1681), p. 12.

[10]   John Ayliffe, *Parergon Juris Anglicani: or a commentary by way of supplement to the canons and constitutions of the Church of England* (London, 1724), pp. 525–6.

owners resorted to oral wills for fear that their written ones might have omitted one or more of these solemnities, and would therefore be deemed invalid.

The testamentary causes observed here confirm the legal commentators' view that oral wills were often uttered on the deathbed, at a moment in which there might be neither the time nor the facilities (a scrivener, pen and ink, witnesses) for a formal written will to be executed. Of the 26 nuncupative wills offered for probate that were uttered prior to the Statute of Frauds, 20 were made on the deathbed. Thus grave illness was not always the explanation for a nuncupative will appearing in my Canterbury data set; three others were clearly made while the testator or testatrix was in good health, while the remaining three were made in circumstances in which it is not clear whether the person in question was seriously ill, let alone at death's door.

Oral wills certainly offered convenience and ease, but they raised serious questions of validity and reliability. While allowing spoken words to have testamentary effect enabled those who might not have ready access to pen and paper (and the ability to use them) to express their volition, permitting oral wills might actually subvert their testamentary intentions through mistake or fraud. In advising property-owners to execute written wills rather than to rely upon oral ones, John Doddridge noted that to commit bequests to pen and paper was preferable to leaving them to the 'doubtful fidelity or slippery memory of witnesses.'[11] Not only might dishonest individuals sabotage testamentary freedom by seeking to probate as nuncupative wills words that were never uttered at all (or, even if spoken, not uttered with testamentary intent), witnesses to an oral will might tamper with the will-maker's estate plan after his or her death. If a witness believed that all or parts of a will were ill-advised (in short, if the witness would have preferred the individual's property to pass otherwise), he might collude to 'redraft' the will through faulty or selective memory.

Thus both the casual character of many oral wills and the whims of witnesses made it necessary for the law to create requirements for their due execution in order to protect testamentary volition, and commentators endeavored to define them. The most important aim of the law was to separate wheat from chaff: to draw a line between mere words or utterances and those that amounted to a will by word of mouth. According to Henry Swinburne, what separated the two was that the words that created a valid disposition had to be uttered by the testator with *animus testandi*, with a 'mind or purpose then and thereby to make his testament.'[12] Circumstances surrounding the utterances, William Sheppard maintained, had to suggest considered thought: 'for if a man rashly unadvisedly,

---

[11] Thomas Wentworth, *The Office and Duty of Executors* (London, 1641), pp. 8–9.

[12] Henry Swinburne, *A Brief Treatise of Testaments and Last Wills* (Garland Reprint of 1590 edition, 1978), p. 8.

incidentally, jestingly, or boastingly, and not seriously, write or say that such a one shall be his executor, or have all his goods ... this is no testament, nor to be regarded.'[13] Indeed, these situations could transpire when a speaker was not at death's door. George Meriton was troubled with the distinction between words and wills, and strove to draw a clear line between mere talk and those utterances that constituted a will made by word of mouth. He noted that it was 'very familiar and common amongst companions' to name a person as executor while in good health. However, he warned that such statements did not constitute an oral will, unless the speaker had had 'full mind and resolute purpose' to have the utterance stand as a will, and that 'he framed himself very seriously ... declaring that those present to beare witness as his will.'[14] While Meriton wrote shortly after the Statute of Frauds was implemented, and the requirement that the will-maker must openly declare that the words uttered should have testamentary effect was in place, the Canterbury litigation that we shall observe below illustrates that even prior to the statute some cautious will-makers and bystanders were urging that will-makers express clearly that their words should be considered a valid will.[15]

As with issues of capacity and coercion, the flexible rules on the authenticity of oral wills empowered the probate courts. These tribunals had the authority to piece together a narrative surrounding the alleged oral will, and by the selective choice of the evidence offered by litigants and their witnesses could determine whether an utterance promoted as an oral will should be admitted to probate. In practice, the Prerogative Court was generally prepared to be flexible in finding testamentary intent in utterances, even in cases in which it seems clear (at least to the modern observer) that the words were not intended to constitute a will. If, for example, the will-maker had given oral directions to another to prepare a written will but death came before the execution of a document, the spoken words could stand as a will of personal property.[16] That the dying person had not intended the words to constitute a will, but they were rather instructions for their scriveners did not matter unless the testator had made it clear that he wanted only a written will. Sheppard, writing shortly before the Statute of Frauds, opined that oral directions might even stand with respect to land if the scrivener had taken notes, committed the words to writing, and read them to the testator who had assented but who died before the writing was duly executed.[17]

---

13   Sheppard, *Touchstone of Common Assurances*, p. 389.
14   Meriton, *The Parson's Monitor*, p. 28.
15   See text accompanying footnotes 47–53, below.
16   For example, *Baden alias Harward et al. contra Skutt*, PROB 18/8/40.
17   Sheppard, *Touchstone of Common Assurances*, pp. 400–401.

Ayliffe concurred, though he was doubtful as to whether this position would hold after the effective date of the statute.[18]

In addition to issues of validity, nuncupative wills also raised thorny issues of interpretation. As Sheppard noted, the spoken word may be 'ambiguous, obscure, and uncertain.'[19] The causes therefore mix questions regarding form with those of content. Issues of validity (whether the words constituted a will) mingle with those regarding interpretation (what its dispository provisions were).

The Context in Which Oral Wills Were Made

The litigation observed here confirms that exigent circumstances often prompted property-holders to make oral wills. Miscalculation or denial of impending death conspired to leave the dying with no choice but to make an oral will. For example, when Mary Wright, who was present while Miriam Langham languished on her deathbed, asked if the dying woman would write a will, Miriam said she 'would when she was better.'[20] Alas, Langham was not restored to good health, and she died with only an alleged nuncupative will, and one of dubious validity at that. Likewise, a witness to the nuncupative will of Frances Arnold deposed that on the morning of her death the languishing woman was ill in bed. When she was asked if a 'scrivener' should be summoned, Arnold replied that she would prefer to wait until tomorrow; she was then told that she might not live that long.[21] Thereafter, according to another witness, she made an oral will: she 'put her hand out of the bed and laid on the hand of ye said Mr. JB and then uttered and declared herself in these or the like words I see I have not time to make my will in writing but all that I have I give to you and make you full Executor.'[22]

Bystanders often prodded property-holders who were in ill health to make their testamentary volition known by word of mouth. For example, those present at Agnes Vignes's deathbed vigil moved her to make her will. Asked to whom she wanted her property to pass on her death, she replied, 'I have nobody to leave my estate to except for Dickey and Daniel.' She was then asked how much should go to each.[23] Similarly, according to the deposition of Lady Elizabeth Harley, proponent of the oral will of Mary Burlton, she came to visit the dying woman,

---

[18] Ayliffe, *Parergon Juris Anglicani*, p. 533.

[19] Sheppard, *Touchstone of Common Assurances*, p. 392.

[20] *Langham contra Langham*, PROB 18/1/5.

[21] *Bull v. Thrushby*, PROB 24/18, 388. The will was offered for probate (PROB 18/7/50).

[22] Ibid., PROB 24/18, 387.

[23] PROB 18/6/76.

who told her that she wished to 'settle what I have.' Lady Harley testified that she had suggested that Mary summon an attorney to write her will, and was told 'Noe my hands are so sore I cannot write.'[24] She then orally declared her will. The prodding need not always have occurred at the last minute. Margaret White testified that she came to Catherine Lipscomb's house three or four days prior to the latter's death. She related that, 'finding her to looke very ill told her that she could not live long and desired her to send for some person to make her will, to which she replied and speaking to this Dep[onen]t said If I dye I give all to ye Boy meaning her stepson.'[25]

Unusual circumstances might conspire with sudden death to require resorting to an oral will. For example, Roger Fiest was forced to utter his will rather than commit it to writing because he selected (as fate would have it) the hour of divine service as the time to settle his worldly affairs. The proponent maintained that when Fiest spoke the words he intended that they be reduced to writing. Indeed one deponent testified that he was on his way to church, and 'as soon as the Sermon was ended he would send for one Samuel Heath, Parish Clerk of Woking to have it put in writing.'[26] A second witness, William Walker, confirmed the testimony.[27] Unhappily, death intervened. Similarly, an otherwise engaged minister required Thomas Yarway to resort to an oral will. The allegation promoting his nuncupative will insisted that Yarway had uttered his oral will only after summoning the minister who was, apparently, nowhere to be found.[28] Even in instances in which a will-maker related the contents to a scrivener, the time lag between directions and due execution could be 'fatal' to the validity of the document if death intervened, the scenario above posited by Sheppard. Promoting the directions that had been expressed to the scrivener of the errant writing as a nuncupative will was the only way to save such a failed attempt at executing a written will.

The plight of Robert Burkenham neatly illustrates how unique particular circumstances might require recourse to an oral will. According to his nephew, Francis, the promoter of an oral will, Robert had been incarcerated by the Spanish in the West Indies where he spent approximately two years in captivity. Along with other English prisoners, he plotted an escape. Again, according to the promoter of the will, Robert told Walter Carson and John Pryor the day before the breakout that if he died and they survived him they should let it be known that he wanted 'his cousin Stannes' to be his executor. John Brown, a deponent

---

24　*Burlton contra Burlton*, PROB 24/19, 242.

25　*Ford et Brown alias Ford contra Lipscomb*, PROB 24/20, 12.

26　*Fiest contra Fiest*, PROB 24/14, 231.

27　Ibid., PROB 24/14, 232.

28　*Quincey alias Yarway contra Yarway*, PROB 18/7/40.

who had been imprisoned with Burkenham, stated that they 'were denied pen ink and paper and not suffered to use ye same neither are they suffered to send or receive letters from any friend.' Brown related the same disposition of the estate, further noting 'w[hi]ch words hee soe uttered with an intent that they should be his last Will.'[29] The court was unprepared to probate the will, in part, perhaps, because there was no clear evidence that Burkenham was dead. According to the contestants, however, 'common fame' held that Burkenham had been killed while making his escape.[30]

But it was not only untimely death or exigent circumstances that prompted the making of oral wills. Some of the alleged utterances were made by those who previously had made wills, often written ones, but were inclined (or urged) to make the last-minute alterations, as the law allowed until the Statute of Frauds was enacted. Thus the prodding that inclined a person to make an oral will might also include entreaties to make amendments to an existing will. According to an allegation, Thomas Bourden was asked if he wanted his written will to stand; he thereafter made some oral bequests, and declared that he wanted both to stand as his will.[31] Likewise, after having executed his will in writing, John Bretton was told that he had not disposed of his books. He then declared that those books housed in the library of Emmanuel College should remain there, while the other volumes should be sold. William Day deposed that after so uttering Bretton confirmed that 'these words shall stand as part of my will.'[32] Oral revocations of written wills might also be alleged, at least until the Statute of Frauds was adopted. Accordingly, an interrogatory filed by a contestant asked witnesses to testify whether the will-maker 'did declare her will to be that she revoke the will herein,' the same document that was offered for probate.[33] An alleged revocatory act could also be more ambiguous. For example, although Robert Tappan, a coachman, had executed a written will, he complicated the disposition of his estate by handing over to his brother his keys with the words 'take my keys I do freely give you all my estate.'[34]

Other oral will-makers, however, could not plead exigent circumstances, and merely seem to have been fond of making impulsive utterances while they were in good health that would later plague the Canterbury court. For example, the contestant of the will of William Grigg alleged that the testator was a person 'who would say to others that he would give them his estate' or sums of money,

---

29   *Stannes contra Burkenham*, PROB 24/25, 48.
30   Ibid., PROB 18/18/17.
31   *Bourden contra Bourden*, PROB 18/1/54.
32   *Bretton contra Bretton*, PROB 24/15, 124.
33   *Cornish contra Antrobus*, PROB 18/3c/85.
34   *Tappan contra Tappan*, PROB 18/1/90.

statements that he never meant, 'mere words given by way of compliment.'[35] Likewise, recall that the contestant of the nuncupative will of Gregory Thorned had noted in his allegation that 'if someone flattered him he might say he would give him estate and if asked the day after Gregory Thorned would smile and say 'you know that when I am merry I doe talk of things I never intend to doe and would bid them not take any notice of w[ha]t hee then said.'[36]

Given the uncertainty that last-minute oral modifications brought to the process of sorting out testamentary intentions, it is not surprising that a Parliament committed to promoting the authenticity of legal acts by requiring writings wished to deprive testators like Mr. Bretton of the ability to 'correct' flaws in their written wills by word of mouth.[37] They also circumscribed the right of the impulsive who were not at death's door to proclaim their wills in public houses. But when it came to the deathbed, Parliament relented: it did not deprive those at death's door from either writing or speaking their testamentary intentions. Probate courts were still empowered to decide who should be a legatee: a rather malleable framework for differentiating between those oral statements admitted to probate and those denied testamentary effect still survived the statute.

Proof of the Validity of Oral Wills and Their Terms

Though in a different context, oral wills, like their written counterparts, raised questions of testamentary intent. Yet, unlike written wills, oral wills also raised questions of their contents: what was given to whom. Although there were alterations to written wills that had to be considered, probate courts had a baseline: the legatees and the property bequeathed to them were stipulated in ink. But when an oral will was admitted to probate, a second issue of proof arose: assuming that the will's promoter convinced the court that the words spoken were intended to be a will, could the promoter prove the terms of the bequests expressed? The contestant set out to prove the contrary: that the person had uttered mere abstract words, and not bequest of personal property, that is, a will. How counsel went about their business in promoting their client's interests, either for or against the probate of an oral will, is the subject of this section.

---

[35]   *Sherman et Pratt contra Green*, PROB 18/5/106.

[36]   *Cooke contra Batty*, PROB 18/3/28.

[37]   29 Car II, c. 3. (1677), sec. 21.

Wills not words

As with offers of probate of written wills, proponents routinely asserted testamentary intent in their allegations. Unlike written wills, in which testamentary intent was assumed, the promoter of an oral will was required to prove its existence to the satisfaction of the court, usually by producing witnesses present at the time the words were spoken. Because witness statements were made in response to interrogatories, the standard for intent to make an oral will may be teased out by closely considering the questions that were posed. In litigation over the oral will of William Grigg, for example, the contestants asked when and where the alleged words had been expressed, how long the witness was present, and whether the witness was with the dying man only once or several times during the day. They were also asked about the dying man's 'posture' (whether he was sitting or lying down) and whether either the witness or the dying man had consumed beer or wine. Other interrogatories asked for what might be regarded as a legal conclusion: did the witness believe that the words expressed amounted to a will?[38] Thus a battery of factual questions with a bearing on capacity culminated in one raising the ultimate issue of purpose: were the words intended to be a valid will?

Witnesses were also asked questions particular to oral wills. Foremost was to repeat the exact words used. Hairs might be split regarding the actual language recalled by witnesses. Written wills are signed and sealed, but words uttered might be a preliminary stage, one which might (or might not) culminate in the execution of a written will. Finality of intention was a critical issue. The questioning of witnesses by contestants was relentless. The tense used by a speaker, present or future, mattered: for example, did the deceased say, 'I make or I will make Samuel Ellis my executor?'[39] Witnesses might be asked whether they believed that the expression was a preliminary 'memorandum' or a 'draft,'[40] words made preparatory to the writing of a will.[41] One interrogatory clearly suggests a twofold question: did the witness believe that when the dying man 'spoke that he declared his will or that he indicated that he intended that he would write a will in the future?'[42] In litigation concerning the validity of Sir Richard Lloyd's written will, a document that was alleged to have been revoked by an oral utterance, the following questions were submitted to the witnesses. Did the witness 'looke upon the said pretended words at the time of the uttering

---

38   *Sherman et Pratt contra Green*, PROB 18/4/104.
39   *Ellis contra. Parsons*, PROB 18/7/71.
40   See *Plydell et al. contra Jones*, PROB 18/24/76 and PROB 18/24/50.
41   *Lee contra Lee*, PROB 18/7/71.
42   Ibid., PROB 18/7/71.

of the same to be a revocation of his will?' 'What was the reason that the said revocation was not putt into writing and signed and sealed?' 'Why did he not the s[ai]d dec[ease]d make a new will, do you think he revoked the same on purpose to dye intestate?'[43] In opposing the probate of a nuncupative will alleged to have been made by Anne Turner, the administrators of her estate asked the witnesses whether they believed that had the woman made a will she would have done so in writing, 'knowing that words doe easily vanish and are forgotten and are very subject to interpretations.'[44]

Some witnesses sought testamentary intent in various aspects of the dying individual's conduct. Will-making was a private act so a witness noted that, when the testator had determined to make his oral will, he had asked those present save two 'to withdraw' from the room.[45] A witness to another nuncupative will, recognizing that wills were solemn acts, noted that the dying person used 'very formal words.'[46] Lack of formality troubled a number of witnesses to utterances promoted as oral wills. Dorothy Hampden deposed that Catherine Lipscomb did not expressly ask her 'to take notice of what she declared, but this Dep[onen]t verily believeth that she did induce and intend by ye speaking of ye said words that ye said John Lipscomb should have her money and her plate.'[47] While this will was uttered after the Statute of Frauds required an explicit declaration, in another cause prior to 1677, one Thomas Stradling deposed that when Jacob Wyam stated that his two brothers were to serve as executors, Stradling had believed that the dying man was making his will. But he expressed some equivocation. In his deposition, he further explained: 'But he did not then say 'I do publish and declare this to be my Last Will and Testament,' or 'declare that it should be his will or that he intended it for his will nor did desire that this Respon[den]t or any other present take notice that it was his Will.'[48] Another witness in this cause, one Elias Fryer, recalled the deathbed scene in less detail in his deposition, but he also noted that the dying man 'did not use the word will nor say it would be his will.'[49] Perhaps it was Wyam's failure to express the legal significance of his act that explains why the court did not admit the will to probate.[50]

---

43   *Owen et.al. contra Lloyd*, PROB 18/8/123.
44   PROB 18/4/99.
45   *Fiest contra Fiest*, PROB 24/14, 231.
46   PROB 24/14, 343.
47   *Ford et Brown alias Ford contra Lipscomb*, PROB 24/12, 14.
48   *Wyam contra Wyam*, PROB 24/11, 261.
49   Ibid., PROB 24/11, 270.
50   Ibid. The sentence is PROB 11/343, 179.

Ascertaining the Dispositive Terms

As noted above, it was also necessary for the proponent of an oral will to prove its contents, the property dispositions uttered by the will-maker. Some of the causes suggest that particular care was undertaken to make certain that witnesses would remember individual provisions. For example, Lady Harley deposed that she had told Mary Burlton that it was 'convenient that some witnesses were called upon to hear what she declared,' and made her recite the words a second time in front of two servants. To make certain that the duo would recall her words, she thereafter 'asked them whether they took notice and remembered what ye dec[ease]d had declared to the intent that they might testify and witness ye same if they were called.'[51] Given the complexity of the dispositions, as reported in the allegation contesting this will, such a precaution was warranted: the dying woman had created successive life estates in trust to her mother and her brother, with the remainder limited to her brother's three children.[52] Likewise, it was reported that individuals present at the making of an alleged nuncupative codicil to the will of Samuel Claphamson were instructed to take particular care to remember its terms. According to a witness, one John Putteford, Mrs. Brown, who was sitting on the dying man's bed, said after the additions were spoken, 'we heare you and then turned herself to ye several p[er]sons named and said pray take notice of it.'[53]

As Doddridge had noted, oral expression might often be ambiguous.[54] While the written word could be vague, the express terms of an oral will might be even less clear. When Mary Webb declared her last will by word of mouth, she limited a remainder over 'to my Brother and Sisters Children.' Although she had a number of siblings who had children, the executor alleged that what the testatrix meant by the expression was only the children of a particular brother and sister-in-law.[55] Likewise, in her deposition, Dorothy Hamden, a witness in another will contest, the Lipscomb will, explained that she had spoken to others about what the dying woman had said, and had to clarify precisely what she heard. Hamden testified that she did not say that the dying woman left all her property to her stepson James, because 'she did not use those words, but gave all her writings to him and said also all money and plate.'[56] The confusion as to the

---

[51] *Burlton contra Burlton*, PROB 24/19, 242.

[52] Ibid., PROB 18/12/28. In fact, the terms of the utterance did not take effect; the Court nullified the proffered oral will. The sentence is PROB 11/368, 109.

[53] *Burford contra Claphamson contra Clamphampson*, PROB 24/25, 323.

[54] Wentworth, *The Office and Duty*, pp. 8–9.

[55] *Beeston contra Webb*, PROB 18/6/16.

[56] *Ford et Brown alias Ford contra Lipscomb*, PROB 24/20, 16.

precise language that the dying woman had used also extended to the executor-beneficiary himself; in his allegation, step-son James noted that she left 'all to James Lipscomb.'[57]

One way of assisting a witness's recollection of an oral will's precise terms was to have the words reduced to writing. After the effective date of the Statute of Frauds, a writing was required for wills of land, and the use of oral wills by the wealthier subjects (personal property over £30) was limited, save in exigent circumstances. But even before the statute had required oral wills probated after six months to have been redacted within six days of their utterance, some executors were sufficiently prudent to have had an oral will reduced to writing. For example, a contemporaneously drafted 'schedule' was attached to the allegation offering the oral will of Elizabeth Stephens for probate.[58] Likewise, again prior to the statute, it was alleged that the overseers of the will of Mary Bourne 'desired to have the will put in writing before intermeddling with the estate,' and proceeded to have the words redacted.[59]

The Crucial Role of Witnesses

Issues of personal interest of witnesses often took on a greater importance in the probate of a deathbed oral will than in a written one. Those present at the deathbed, where most of our oral wills were uttered, were often relatives and friends, persons who were likely to be objects of the dying individual's bounty. Domestic servants, folk of modest means who might be influenced either directly – because they had been remembered in the words – or indirectly – by the promise of reward from others for testifying the 'right way' - also figure prominently as observers. While the same group might be present when a will was written on the deathbed, it is more likely that some disinterested parties, for example the scrivener or the document's witnesses were in attendance. Thus interrogatories filed by contestants of oral wills routinely asked upon whose behalf the witness had been summoned, explored relationships to parties, and queried whether the witness stood to profit from either the will or his or her testimony.[60]

---

[57]   Ibid., PROB 18/13/98.

[58]   *Rawlinson contra Stephens*, PROB 18/7/33.

[59]   *Bourne contra Farthing*, PROB 18/5/94.

[60]   For examples, *Paine et Paine contra Smith*, PROB 18/1/25; and *Poole contra Barker*, PROB 18/1/30. For example of more lengthy set, see *Hare alias Elliot et Hare alias Field contra Hare*, PROB 18/21/15. So frequently were these questions asked that some interrogatories merely directed that the witness be asked the 'usual questions viz. interest.' *Gardner et Moody contra Cumberland*, PROB 18/8/108.

The responses to these questions in the depositions illustrate the struggle that witnesses undertook in drawing inferences from the conduct that they observed. Some witnesses were prompted to make conclusory statements upon considering the drama in which they had been a passive participant: one witness deposed that he 'was persuaded in his conscience' that the dying person 'intended the same to stand for his Last Will and Testament.'[61] Others were more equivocal. A witness to the words of Thomas Yarway, one William Carey, Yarway's servant, deposed that the dying man had told him that he wanted each of his children to receive a legacy of £5, and that he wanted the residue to pass to his wife, Ann. Having so deposed, however, Carey testified that he believed that at the time the words being promoted as an oral will were spoken, the testator was too 'weake and restlesse and in a dying condition to make a will.'[62] Others present seem to have come to a different conclusion. Yarway's daughter, Susanna, put a more positive spin on her father's capacity.[63] Of course, the fact that his utterance included a bequest to her might have accounted for her divergent view.

The Statute of Frauds and its Aftermath

The causes discussed above illustrate the struggle that witnesses undertook to resolve in their own minds whether conduct surrounding the utterance of certain words amounted to an oral will and, if so, to recall its terms. To some extent the Statute of Frauds addressed two of their dilemmas. Section 18 of the statute expressly required that the speaker 'bid the persons present or some of them beare witnesse that such was his Will' for his words to constitute a valid will.[64] Thus formality in oral will-making was channeled: a clear statement of testamentary intent was required. As to the terms expressed, section 21 required a redaction of the words spoken within six days in situations in which an oral will was uttered more than six months prior to probate. Likewise, the venue requirement, – that the words had to be uttered in the residence of the will-maker or where he or she was languishing before death unless an otherwise healthy person was taken ill by surprise – excluded the wills of the merely jolly and generous (or the frequenter of alehouses!). Yet the Canterbury causes discussed above suggest that, to some extent, the statute merely required that which some prudent will-makers, executors, and bystanders were already doing:

---

61 *Jennyns contra Jennyns*, PROB 24/14, 260.
62 *Quincey alias Yarway contra Yarway*, PROB 24/15, 193.
63 Ibid., PROB 24/15, 194.
64 29 Car II, c. 3 (1677), sec. 18.

in particular, the more cautious were already eliciting firm statements that the words spoken constituted a will, and then reducing the words spoken to writing.

To proclaim victory, albeit a limited one, for the statute's promoters would be exaggeration, even in the areas that it directly addressed. A dispute over the probate of Samuel Claphamson's will highlights the statute's mixed impact on the culture of will-making, post-1677. This cause illustrates that the modest reform of requiring a memorandum to be redacted within six days of death if the will was probated more than six months after death could itself raise questions about the will's authenticity. Samuel Claphamson's oral will had been put into writing (as required by the statute because the will was offered for probate more than six months after his death), but a dispute emerged over the memorandum: it was alleged that the scribe, one Daniel Claphamson, 'due to forgetfulness,' had failed to include a bequest of £100 to the will-maker's nephew. A witness present confirmed the omission of the legacy,[65] so the court could have entertained some skepticism about the reliability of the document. Moreover, two witnesses who had signed the memorandum (and attested to the omission because they 'heard' that the £100 had been omitted) actually admitted in their deposition that they were not present when the words Claphamson was alleged to have uttered were spoken.[66] Indeed two other witnesses deposed that at the time the words were uttered they overheard one Mr. Brown say that the words would 'signify nothing.'[67] So much for the reliability of this particular memorandum! A redaction of the words promoted as an oral will might be as questionable as the recollection of the utterance itself.

The lesser incidence of oral wills than written wills in the Canterbury collection after 1677 does, however, suggest that the statute probably took its toll on oral wills. The two nuncupative wills that emerge in the collection were made by mariners who died at sea whose wills were therefore exempt from the statute's mandates.[68] Yet even in these causes the court closely scrutinized the evidence, because in each there was an allegation that the deceased had a duly executed written will in existence at the time he uttered the words promoted as an oral will. Had the words not been those of a mariner, the oral will could not have revoked the written will, because section 21 of the Statute of Frauds explicitly prohibited the probate of oral wills that purported to revoke a will in writing.

These two causes merit detailed analysis because the post-statute court seems to have taken a harder line in examining the validity of oral wills that were outside

---

[65]   *Croke contra Drewry alias Leach*, PROB 24/25, 324.

[66]   *Burford et Claphamson contra Clamphampson*, PROB 24/25, 328, 329.

[67]   Ibid., PROB 24/25, 325, 326.

[68]   29 Car II, c. 3. (1677), Sec. 22.

the statute's ambit. In the first cause, it was alleged that Gerrard Williamson, a Dutchman and a mariner who had died on 16 September 1695 aboard the *Friendship*, had made a nuncupative will 'in his last sickness,' leaving all his property to his shipmate William Phillips, but nevertheless obliging him to pay a debt owing in the amount of 17s. to one Olive Williams.[69] Three witnesses confirmed the substance of the allegation.[70] However, a will alleged to have been duly executed the previous January was offered for probate by its executrix, the same Olive Williams, who claimed to be his landlady and a creditor.[71] The court probated the nuncupative will in Phillips's favor.[72]

In the second cause, John Unity, a carpenter, had also died at sea in July of 1695. About two and a half years earlier, he had written a will in which he left his entire estate to Agnes Bush, coincidentally also his landlady.[73] One witness testified that Unity had 'filled in a Letter of Attorney' in Bush's name.[74] However, according to another allegation, he became gravely ill while on board ship, and made one John Stag, a fellow carpenter, executor of his oral will.[75] It must have been an unhealthy voyage because John Stag died two months later, and the suit to enforce Unity's nuncupative will was brought by Stag's executor. According to the testimony of the ship's surgeon, one Thomas Stodden, Unity had uttered the following words to John Stag in front of four witnesses, 'All I have to you, but pay my landlady I owe no one else.'[76] While a second witness recalled the words in substantially the same terms, his recollection differed with respect to certain particulars. He deposed that Unity had uttered, 'All that I have in the world I give to you Carpenter if I dye to dispose of to your best advantage.'[77] Not surprisingly, the proponent of the written will, landlady Bush, was suspicious of the oral one, and asked the witnesses why an oral will was made when there were persons present who could commit Unity's testamentary wishes to paper.[78] Regardless, the court probated the nuncupative will.[79] Though a scanty two examples allow only a tentative conclusion, the court recognized the exception that Parliament had provided for mariners' wills, though it scrutinized them carefully.

---

[69]   *Williams contra Phillips*, PROB 18/24/20.
[70]   Ibid., PROB 24/35, 123, 124, 125.
[71]   Ibid., PROB 18/24/14.
[72]   Ibid., The sentence is PROB 11/442, 308.
[73]   *Bush contra Couzens*, PROB 18/24/65.
[74]   Ibid., PROB 24/35, 226.
[75]   Ibid., PROB 18/24/69.
[76]   Ibid., PROB 24/35, 196.
[77]   Ibid., PROB 24/35, 209.
[78]   Ibid., PROB 18/24/69.
[79]   Ibid., Sentence PROB 11/433, 338.

Even though the Canterbury sample produced only these two oral wills coming before the court after 1677, a survey of contested wills that were nullified which I undertook indicates that oral wills continued to vex the Prerogative Court after 1677.[80] Mariners at sea uttered only two of eight of these disputed oral wills.[81] While the surviving documentation is scanty in each cause, there was good reason to deny the validity of these mariners' wills: one appears to have been uttered in front of a lone witness[82] and the other may have been denied probate on the grounds of mental capacity.[83]

The causes involving oral wills uttered by will-makers that were not within the mariners' exception suggest that the court rigorously applied the statute. Factually, these causes closely resemble the pre-1677 causes. Many of the same issues surfaced in these will contests despite the tightened rules set out by Parliament. However, the statute made its presence felt. Advocates promoting oral wills were obliged to tailor their allegations to demonstrate that the utterance conformed to the statutory mandate, particularly section 18 (which required that the speaker had clearly asked those present to witness the words as an oral will). Similarly, contestants framed their interrogatories in such a way as to solicit responses that might cast doubt on statutory compliance.

The nuncupative will of Elizabeth Joy, made after the Statute of Frauds, is illustrative. The allegation promoting her alleged will confirmed that the words had been uttered in conformity with the statute: the dying woman had made a 'declaration' disposing of her property, which exceeded £30 in value, by words uttered in her house in front of four witnesses, and the words were redacted 'within four days but at least six days after declaring.'[84] The interrogatories of the contestant focused on the one requirement of the statute that was absent from the allegation which it was alleged justified nullification: 'Did she ask you to beare witness that what she declared was her Will?' However, the contestant also raised the well-worn themes of lack of testamentary purpose, or finality of

---

[80]   My inquiry into wills that were nullified and that left surviving documentation unearthed eight causes involving the validity of oral wills made after the Statute: *Ford et Brown alias Ford contra Lipscombe, Burlton contra Burlton, Stannes contra Burkenham, Burford et Claphamson contra Claphamson, Mullins contra Netter, Besson contra Jones, Moses contra Davie,* and *Belwood contra Smart.* Archival references are supplied when the causes are cited.

[81]   The sentences are for William Walford (*Besson contra Jones,* PROB 11/407, 306), and for Alexander Davies alias David (*Moses contra Davie,* PROB 11/433, 228).

[82]   *Moses contra Davie,* PROB 18/23/5.

[83]   It was alleged that the dying man had suffered from the 'bloody flux' for three weeks (*Besson contra Jones* PROB 18/21/92, PROB 18/21/123).

[84]   *Mullen contra Netter,* PROB 18/21/94.

intention, presented in the causes that we have observed that dealt with wills uttered before the adoption of the statute. In addition to its conformity to statutory requirements, the interrogatories submitted in the cause explored many of the same issues that emerged in litigation prior to the statute. For example, emphasis was placed upon why the will had not been written out: witnesses to the oral will were asked, 'Do you know that there were several attorneys near the Dec[ease]d house skilled in the making of wills who might have been called?' Likewise, they were asked whether 'two or three lines were written for her,' but she had refused to add a signature. Other questions explored the circumstances under which the 'words' were written down.[85] Thus attention was drawn both to the terms of the statute, as well as to factual issues similar to those raised in the pre-statute cases: suspicions touching the circumstances surrounding the will's making and the deceased's questionable testamentary intentions.

A number of other causes that ended in nullification were probably decided because the oral will failed to meet the provisions of the Statute of Frauds. For example, John Belwood offered to probate a nuncupative codicil to supplement John Smart's written will. According to the promoter's allegation, John Smart, 'fearing death,' had gone to a scrivener to have a will drawn up, and that one was produced by a scrivener and signed and witnessed. Shortly thereafter, being 'joyful,' he repaired to a tavern where, according to the allegation, he declared that Belwood should have a bequest of £100.[86] Even if the declaration was not regarded as an oral alteration or change in a written will (which of course it was – and therefore invalid pursuant to section 21) it was certainly not uttered in the dying person's house or residence as required by section 18! The court denied probate to the additional words.[87] Likewise, the oral codicil to Samuel Claphamson's written will was denied probate. The failure to honor its bequests was probably based on the statute, but a reading of the depositions as preserved suggests that a fair amount of pressure had been brought to bear on the dying man. According to a witness present at the deathbed, a dialogue transpired during the last hours of Samuel's life. A number of times Claphamson was asked by various family members, including his wife, 'what would he do for' various relations – his brother John, John's son, her son, and so on. To each query he had responded with a bequest. In fact, some of his responses were met with pleas for additional largesse. Apparently the lease of a house that he bequeathed by word of mouth to his brother John was regarded as insufficiently generous; when it

---

[85]   Ibid.

[86]   *Belwood contra Smart*, PROB 18/13/60.

[87]   Ibid., Sentence PROB 18/368, 109.

was met with the prodding question 'and what give him more?', the dying man
had offered up an additional £100.[88]

Other utterances promoted as oral wills fell victim to the statute. One was
offered for probate that Catherine Lipscomb was alleged to have uttered in the
Three Tuns Tavern about a year prior to her death. Though counsel presenting
the cause was not unaware of section 18 of the statute, he relied upon an oral
confirmation of the words about four days before her death.[89] Why the will
was nullified is not specified, but the court had at least three statutory grounds
based upon section 18 from which to choose, in addition to lack of testamentary
capacity. In the first place, it was not alleged that the tavern was her 'habitation
or dwelling place,' or that she had been suddenly taken ill at the Three Tuns.
Second, the witnesses to the will were somewhat troubled by the fact that the
speaker had never clearly stated that the words uttered were to stand as her will;
section 18 required a more explicit statement by the will-maker than the one
that they recollected. And finally, while three deponents agreed that the now-
deceased did express the desire that her stepson should take her estate,[90] she
made her declarations to witnesses separately; at least one witness stated that she
was alone with her when the words were spoken.[91]

Finally, although the allegation promoting the nuncupative will of Mary
Burlton alleged that the will had been uttered before 'several witnesses,'[92] one
witness who deposed indicated that only she and her husband were present, one
fewer than the statute required.[93] The court might have also been reluctant to
probate the will on the grounds of Burlton's testamentary capacity, because the
same witness was unable to say whether the testatrix was 'sensible' at the time the
words were spoken.[94]

Conclusion

To the modern lawyer, the notion of property transmission at death being
directed by word of mouth might seem anathema. But ours is a society that
has made the transition from an oral to a written legal culture. Early modern
England was in the midst of that journey. Oral wills served a purpose in a

---

88 *Burford et Claphamson contra Clamphampson*, PROB 24/25, 323.

89 *Ford et Brown alias Ford contra Lipscomb*, PROB 18/13/98.

90 Ibid., PROB 24/20, 12; PROB 24/20, 14; PROB 24/20, 18.

91 Ibid., PROB 24/20, 18.

92 *Burlton contra Burlton*, PROB 18/12/28.

93 Ibid., PROB 24/19, 243.

94 Ibid.

society where people were both prone to sudden death and uncomfortable with prospective 'estate planning.' The law struck a different balance between testamentary freedom and the uncertainty in property devolution that oral wills fostered than does modern law. Church-court practice cautiously recognized the validity of verbal estate plans, even though contemporary legal commentators and the court seem to have understood (and our causes illustrate) that wills by word of mouth were 'litigation breeders.'

When Parliament intervened in the province of oral wills by adopting the Statute of Frauds, it did so in a modest fashion, only tightening up around the edges. Many of the pre-1677 Canterbury causes I studied were of oral wills that would probably have satisfied the subsequent statutory requirements anyway. But a smaller number of oral wills appearing in the collection after the statute suggests that either fewer were made or that promoters and their counsel realized that any attempt to probate in the Prerogative Court utterances that did not conform to the statute was futile. Finally, it may well have been the case that the court seized the opportunity provided by the statute to justify a harsher stance even toward wills made by word of mouth that were outside of its ambit. With respect to oral wills made after the statute, the court reversed its position of leniency in the admission of testamentary acts that did not conform to the requirements established by the new law.

Chapter 6

The Sanctity of the Written Word: Testamentary Causes Challenging the Authenticity and Due Execution of Written Wills

Introduction

In contrast to oral wills, one might assume that written wills presented fewer validity issues. After all, promoters were offering for probate documents that were both signed and witnessed. While the testator's mental capacity and any undue influence might be at issue, both testamentary intent and the terms of the bequest were specified in a document purporting to be a will. Though it might be logical, this hypothesis turns out to be incorrect. This chapter sheds light upon the figures presented in Table 3.1, which indicates written documents offered for probate as wills raised authenticity questions even more often than did oral wills.

What accounts for this litigation? The answer to this question is quite simple: both the legal requirements for will validity and the way in which these mandates were implemented in the probate courts. The 'culture of will-making' also had a role to play, for testamentary acts drafted and executed in haste, at death's door, might easily omit a requirement and appear on their face to be of dubious validity. Before observing the Canterbury Prerogative Court's handiwork, let us explore the requirements for due execution of written wills, both then and in our own time.

Due Execution of Wills: Past and Present

Modern Probate Law: Contrasting Approaches to Formalities

As I indicated in the Introduction, the modern tendency in the law of wills, at least in the many of the former colonies, Australian states, Canadian provinces, and much of United States, is to admit a will to probate even in instances in which the document does not meet all of the formalities of due execution stipulated by statute. Probate of these writings is justified in one of two ways.[1] In some jurisdictions, one statutory provision trumps another. The American Uniform Probate Code, for example, sets out the formalities for the due execution of wills, and then allows courts to dispense with them if a judge finds that the will-maker had intended the document promoted to be a will.[2] In other American jurisdictions, courts use sleight of hand. Judges admit wills that do not comport with the requisites of due execution if they find that the will-maker had come close enough to the statutory mandate – in cases in which the will-maker had 'substantially complied' with the statutory requirements.[3]

This indulgent approach to will validity would undo, at least in part, both the 1677 Statute of Frauds and, more particularly, the Wills Act of 1837,[4] the nineteenth-century English legislation that extended the formalities that were required for lifetime and testamentary transfers of land in the Statute of Frauds to all wills. The purpose of both of these statutes was to regularize inter-generational property transmission; they required adherence to specific formalities for a written will to be valid. Accordingly, both the intent to make a transfer and its terms had to be found in the document, and only in the document.[5] Not so with the modern approach: the court can look outside the document for both an intent to devise and perhaps even an explanation of its dispository provisions.

Moreover, the modern colonial approach may promote that which the Statutes of Frauds and of Wills sought to discourage: will contests around the edges. Judicial discretion, rather than strict application of the Wills Act's requirements, might encourage the beneficiaries and/or executors in wills that do not quite adhere to statutory mandates to risk paying litigation costs in the hope that a particular judge will relent, bend a rule, and admit a non-conforming

---

[1]   John Langbein, 'Substantial compliance with the Wills Act,' *Harvard Law Review*, vol. 88 (1975), pp. 489–532.

[2]   Uniform Probate Code, sec. 2–502; sec. .2–503.

[3]   Langbein, 'Substantial Compliance, pp. 489–532.'

[4]   7 Will. IV and 1 Vict., c. 26 (1837). Section 17 of the Administration of Justice Act (1982) modifies the formalities in sec 9 of the Wills Act. For a summary of English law, see Janet Holmes, Lynn Hayes, Jennifer Mason, Judith Masson, and Lorraine Wallis, *Wills, Inheritance and Families* (Oxford, 1996), pp. 22–4, 39–50. A useful summary is provided by Michael Sladen, 'Wills Act 1837: Is it obsolescent?' which I found on the Association of Corporate Trustees website: *http://www.trustees*.org.uk/review-index/Wills-Wills-Act1837.

[5]   Ashbel Gulliver and Catherine Tilson, 'Classification of gratuitous transfers,' *Yale Law Journal*, vol. 51 (1941) pp. 1–10.

will to probate.[6] Regardless of whether these changes actually promote litigation – a difficult contention to substantiate – the ability to bend the rules of due execution empowers the judges in probate causes that come before them. They now have leeway to pick and choose amongst proffered testamentary acts, selecting those to be admitted to probate and those to be nullified by constructing a narrative of the circumstances surrounding a will's formulation and execution from the evidence introduced (or, as some detractors might suggest, according to the 'length of the judicial foot)'.

Church Court Practice and the Statute of Frauds

There is something that smacks of the modern in the transition from the rigid to the indulgent in the approach to will-making rules sketched above: abandoning 'formalistic' requirements when justice so demands, admitting testamentary acts when the court is confident that the will-maker intended the testamentary act being offered for probate to have effect. The causes examined in this study suggest there is in fact also something archaic in this modern transition; we have seen that judges in the Prerogative Court in the early modern period admitted wills to probate even in instances in which it was doubtful that a will conformed to church court law's own minimal due-execution requirements. They did so in the same way as does the modern judge: they created a narrative of what had actually transpired by sifting through the evidence, and then they surmised as to whether the will-maker intended the document to be his or her last will. If they believed that it did, they ignored the defect and proved the will; if they did not, they proclaimed it a nullity.

Church-court law in the seventeenth century required that a will be signed, sealed, and published by the will-maker in front of two or three witnesses who had also affixed their signature to the will.[7] But wills did come before the court in which these formalities had not been observed, and the court was prepared to consider whether these 'irregularly executed' documents should be admitted to probate. Some of the other causes that came before the court raised more specific questions as to whether a document offered for probate was an authentic legal act. In some causes, the judges admitted unexecuted wills to probate if

---

[6]   It must be said that some recent English cases read decidedly 'colonial.' Two for example are *Couser v. Couser* [1996] 1 W.L.R. 1301; and *Weatherhill v. Pearce* [1995] 1 W.L.R. 592.

[7]   Henry Swinburne, *A Brief Treatise of Testaments and Last Wills* (Garland Reprint of 1590 edition, 1978), p. 18.

they believed that the document was in the handwriting of the will-maker.[8] When these holographic wills were offered for probate, the court might have to determine a number of issues: was the document that was alleged to be a holograph actually in the will-maker's handwriting? Was the document offered for probate a draft or memorandum rather than a completed testamentary act? And what should be made of any additions, interlineations, and other alterations that appeared on the face of a written document?

While Parliament was concerned about with the authenticity of legal documents when it adopted the Statute of Frauds, the requisites for will validity it introduced were not comprehensive. Recall that the statute permitted deathbed wills and failed to address written wills of personal property at all.[9] Holographs were still valid. By limiting the reach of the statute, Parliament defended two cultural norms: informal and deathbed will-making. And, like modern 'colonial' legislators, it was prepared to empower the judges, to allow them significant latitude to determine which wills offered for probate should stand. Perhaps Parliament did so for the same reasons modern law has returned to leniency: freedom of disposition of property is a highly valued norm. In order to facilitate such power, only very modest requirements for will validity should be mandatory. Moreover, these provisions ought to be sympathetically, rather than rigorously, applied, even at the risk of encouraging an heir or legatee to promote a will in which some technicality had not been satisfied (and, of course, one in which that individual would receive a larger share of the deceased's property if it were admitted to probate).

Holographic Wills

The Court's Challenge

Even before the Statute of Frauds, church-court law generally required that written wills be signed and witnessed. Henry Swinburne noted, however, that in the early modern period English church courts recognized the validity of wills that were in the handwriting of the will-maker, so-called holographic wills; accordingly, it was not necessary for a written will to be witnessed in order for it to be admitted to probate 'if it be *certaine and undoubted* that the testament

---

[8]   About half of the American states currently allow unwitnessed holographic wills to be probated. For a list see J. Dukeminier, S. Johanson, J. Lindgren, and R. Sitkoff, *Wills, Trusts, and Estates*, 7th edn (New York, 2005), p. 236.

[9]   See the discussion in Chapter 2, above.

is written or subscribed with the testators owne hand.'[10] Practice so confirms: Phillip Floyer cited a number of causes during our period in which the Court of Delegates upheld the validity of holographic wills,[11] and those exhumed in this study confirm that holographs were made and proved in the Canterbury Prerogative Court. This morsel of church-court law was perhaps well known to early modern English will-makers. For example, when the will of Thomas James was offered for probate by his sisters and their children, the promoters alleged that the will should be admitted to probate as a holograph; the testator, it was claimed, had 'relied' on the advice of his sister's husband, an attorney, who had indicated that 'a will in a man's hand without seal' was valid.[12] Eleven of the testamentary causes involve unwitnessed allegedly holographic wills.[13]

Holographs were challenged by contestants on two grounds: first, that the document was not in the will-maker's hand, and second, that if it was, the writing was a 'scroll,' the word of art used in the litigation to indicate a draft or memorandum (or indeed any dubious writing whose legal effect they wished to impugn), from which a more formal document was later supposed to be made. How the Prerogative Court resolved disputes over whether a will was an authentic holograph illustrates both the tribunal's leniency in applying its own law and its general approach to issues of proof in testamentary causes.

In considering the validity of alleged holographic wills, the court had to make two determinations. The first – whether the document had been written by the will-maker – could be resolved in a straightforward manner. Witnesses familiar with the will-maker's handwriting could be summoned and/or documents believed to be penned by him or her could be compared with the proffered will. The second – whether its author intended the document to be a will – was more problematic, because the court was required to ascertain what the now-deceased person had been thinking at some time in the past. What witnesses said he said, or how the writing was thereafter treated, might be some indication of his purpose, yet all the court could do was make an educated guess from the contextual information garnered from the parties and their witnesses.

---

[10]   Swinburne, *Brief Treatise*, p. 191.

[11]   At least seven causes are cited in which holographs were admitted. Phillip Floyer, *The Proctor's Practice in the Ecclesiastical Courts*, 2nd edn (London, 1746), pp. 128–34.

[12]   *Jones contra Hughes et Twaites*, PROB 18/3/6.

[13]   See list of causes in the Appendix. In this chapter they will be cited as referenced in the text.

The Litigation: a Valid Holograph or Scattered Notes?

A useful point of departure here is the will of Thomas Jones, the Keeper of New
Prison in Clerkenwell. It was alleged that he wrote a will in his own hand on 9
January 1696, and that he died of an 'apoplectick fit' almost four months later
on a trip to Whitehall.[14] The document promoted as his last will was found in
his desk. Although it was not witnessed, it could stand as a valid holographic
will if it had been penned by Jones, and its proponent also produced two
witnesses to testify that the writing was in the will-maker's hand.[15] Although she
conceded that point, his wife, Martha, contested the will. In her allegation, she
charged that the 'scroll' exhumed by the other side was only a memorandum.
She relied upon a variety of evidence to support her view that the writing should
not be regarded as her husband's final testamentary act. In the first place, she
maintained that Thomas had mentioned to others that he 'had no will.' Indeed,
she contended that he had told friends that, before he went 'into the country' (a
journey he appears to have taken) he had mentioned that 'he must stay in towne
[London] to write a will.' In addition, she noted that Jones had told others not
provided for in the 'scroll' that he would leave them legacies in his will.[16] Martha
was able to produce two witnesses who had been present when the writing was
found who confirmed her doubts concerning the document. One witness, her
brother Thomas Leeke, (and therefore perhaps a less than impartial witness),
testified that the will was found in a 'pasteboard box,' and he believed his
brother-in-law had intended the writing to be discarded as a 'neglected paper.'[17]
A second witness, one Samuel Tidmarsh, whose connection to the contestant
is less certain, concurred, largely because the now-deceased man had not kept
the document with his 'papers of great moment.'[18] Regardless of their evidence,
the court admitted the document to probate, apparently unconcerned about
its casual safekeeping.[19] Martha certainly had good reason to contest the will:
over £75 was bequeathed to relations in the will, and not a mention of her was
included therein.[20]

The question of whether a will in the hand of the testator was a draft or a
completed legal act arose in other causes involving holographs. For example,
it was alleged that the document offered for probate as the will of Benjamin

14 *Plydell et al. contra Jones*, PROB 18/24/50.
15 Ibid., PROB 24/35, 219, 221.
16 Ibid., PROB 18/24/76.
17 Ibid., PROB 24/35, 222.
18 Ibid., PROB 24/35, 224.
19 Ibid., PROB 11/433, 358.
20 Ibid., PROB 11/436, 78.

Bradbourne was written in his own hand. The promoter, his wife Catherine, relied heavily upon statements that he had made about his 'estate plan.' Catherine maintained that Benjamin had told her that he had made a will prior to their marriage (the tempestuous nature of which will be explored later)[21] 'which should not stand,' and that he was in the course of writing one 'in his own hand.' On another occasion, she contended that when he was asked whether the earlier will should be 'recovered,' presumably so that it could be destroyed, he was heard to say that 'it was unnecessary because he had made another will in writing which would make the other one void.' Moreover, Catherine alleged that Bradbourne had told a neighbor that he had made a will 'with his own hand,' though she conceded that it might be 'unfinished.'[22]

In her own allegation, his sister Elizabeth, the contestant of the will, contended that her brother had told one Thomas Hayton, who was present in Bradbourne's study at the time the document was written, that he could not finish the new will because his hand 'shook.'[23] In her answer to Catherine's allegations, Elizabeth even denied that the 'scroll' offered by Catherine was in fact in her brother's hand.[24] Unfortunately, no depositions survive to enable us to ascertain how each of these litigants was able to support her contentions, but the court sided with the wife, and confirmed its earlier decision to probate the holographic will in common form.[25] A healthy sum was at stake: sister Elizabeth received a modest £50 in the holograph admitted to probate;[26] in her allegation she noted that the bequest in the earlier will amounted to at least £300.[27]

Wills promoted as holographs, however, were not always admitted to probate. In one cause, a holographic codicil was submitted in order to modify an attested will, but was rejected. The court's judgment in this cause anticipates the Statute of Frauds' provision (chapter 21) on unattested modifications of written wills. When the executor of the will of Robert Markham offered a document for probate as his last will, Markham's brother and heir George, contested it. Although he conceded that the will offered was valid, George claimed that his brother had 'instructed' certain legacies to be paid though they were not specified in his will. Witnesses were asked to testify whether they had 'heard Robert Markham appoint property to satisfy such legacies.' George had a letter from Robert to confirm his brother's intent; he submitted it to the court, and in

---

21   See the discussion in Chapter 8, below.
22   *Bradbourne contra Townsend*, PROB 18/8/106.
23   Ibid., PROB 18/8/116.
24   Ibid., PROB 25/2/165.
25   Ibid., PROB 11/355, 212.
26   Ibid., PROB 11/352, 386.
27   Ibid., PROB 18/8/116.

interrogatories asked witnesses whether they were familiar with Robert's hand and could confirm that the writing was in his brother's hand.[28] In this cause, the court was unwilling to be flexible towards an allegedly handwritten testamentary addition; the will was admitted, but without the alleged holographic codicil.[29]

Proving the Will-Maker's Hand

Other wills that were promoted as holographs raised the more straightforward question of whether the document was in fact in the will-maker's own hand. Proof of the will-maker's handwriting was made by recourse to the testimony of those who claimed to be familiar with the author's penmanship, by individuals who asserted that they had actually seen the will written, or by a comparison of the hand in the will with that in other documents that the will-maker had penned.

An example of the first case is the probate of the will of Edward Wakeham. His widow Elizabeth, offered a will alleged to have been in his own hand, a document in which he bequeathed his estate after debts to her as executrix to support the children of his first marriage.[30] Although this will had been witnessed, one of the witnesses had subsequently died and the other was not called to attest to due execution. The promoter nevertheless alleged that the will was valid as a holograph, and therefore claimed that attestation was unnecessary; two witnesses were called to testify that the will was in the handwriting of the deceased. Their deductions were based upon different kinds of evidence. Mary Norbourne, who was married to the testator's bailiff, testified that she 'had occasion to see acquitances and receipts and became well acquainted with his handwriting'; she concluded that the will was in Wakeham's hand by comparing it to other documents that she saw him write.[31] The second witness, one William Coon, concurred. He grounded his testimony in a conversation with Wakeham in which the testator had expressly remarked that the will in controversy had been written in his own hand.[32]

Similarly, Elizabeth Clerke's will was offered for probate as a valid holograph by her two executrices, Eleanor Clarke and Martha Otghar.[33] This cause provides the greatest variety of the sorts of evidence offered to confirm that a document offered for probate as a holograph was actually written in the hand of the

---

[28] *Markham et Carrington contra Markham*, PROB 18/1/46.

[29] Ibid., PROB 11/313, 203.

[30] *Wakeham contra Wakeham*, PROB 18/7/19.

[31] Ibid., PROB 24/14, 403.

[32] Ibid. The cause did not proceed to sentence, nor was a will admitted to probate. Like many other of our testamentary causes, this one was either settled or dropped.

[33] *Walker contra Clark et Otghar*, PROB 18/18/25.

deceased. First, James Wilkinson, who testified that the will was penned by the will-maker, recognized her handwriting because he had previously read letters written by her regarding a legacy that she sought to enforce.[34] Second, Elizabeth Squire and Estera Basse testified that they saw Clerke write the will.[35] While two others who apparently signed as witnesses to the will were not called upon to attest to their signatures, a third witness, Anne Deall, was deposed by the contestant. She admitted that she had signed the will as witness, though not in the presence of the will-maker, because she recognized that the writing was in the testatrix's hand. While Anne testified that she was 'much troubled' by her 'mistake,' she confirmed that the will was in the handwriting of the testatrix.[36] Another witness was less sure: Elizabeth Squire, who maintained that she was present when the will was written by the testatrix, testified that Anne, the errant deponent, could not write, and 'therefore cannot have knowledge of the dece[ase]d hand.'[37] The court was convinced that the will was a valid holograph, and admitted it to probate.[38]

The Problem of Forgery

Other individuals could, and in the court's judgment sometimes did, imitate a will-maker's handwriting. A document promoted as Thomas Hoare's last will was alleged to be holographic. Anne Goswell, his widow, who styled herself as the guardian of Thomas Hoare, minor son and heir of the will-maker, had already taken out letters of administration issued to her when a handwritten will was offered for probate. According to Anne, Hoare's alleged will left two bonds of £1,000 to his three daughters, with the residue of his estate bequeathed to his son.[39] Charity Gallop, the daughters' guardian, challenged the authenticity of the will. According to her allegation, it was a forgery. She contended that Thomas had not written the will. Because he was an 'attorney of such skill,' she surmised that he would never have settled his affairs with an unsealed and unwitnessed document, 'without forme or fashion.' The daughters' allegation explained precisely how the forged document had been produced: Thomas Weblin, Hoare's clerk, had penned the document; it was maintained that he was 'skilled' in the copying of many documents written by his master. To cast further

---

34 Ibid., PROB 24/25, 176.
35 Ibid., PROB 24/25, 177, 178.
36 Ibid., PROB 24/25, 204.
37 Ibid., PROB 24/25, 177.
38 Ibid., PROB 11/389, 252.
39 *Hoare contra Hoare*, PROB 18/13/30.

doubt on the will's validity, Weblin's integrity was impugned.[40] The allegation accused him of coin-clipping, an additional 'skill' that three witnesses confirmed Weblin had mastered.[41] Finally, the contestants, like those in the litigation over the validity of the Leeke will, cast doubt upon the will's authenticity because of the place where it was found,[42] the pocket of the 'breeches' that Hoare was wearing at his death.[43] Upon his passing, a number of individuals searched Thomas Hoare's chamber extensively for a will, but with no success. Thereafter, the will mysteriously appeared in his clothes, even though his maid testified that she had already rummaged through his pockets. Her efforts resulted in a few farthings and a silver tobacco-stopper, perhaps more likely occupants of a gentleman's pockets than a will.[44] While there was certainly sufficient evidence to cast doubt on the authenticity of the will, the court was inclined to accept the promoter's argument, even though the will provided more meagerly for the will-maker's daughters, given their social stature and the size of the deceased's

---

[40]   Ibid., PROB 18/13/11.

[41]   Ibid., PROB 24/20, 77, 81.

[42]   And others: indeed where a will was found after the death of the will-maker it was regarded as relevant to its authenticity. William Sheppard noted that, if a will was found among 'the choice evidences of the testator or fast locked up in a safe place, it is the more esteemed.' William Sheppard, *The Touchstone of Common Assurances*, 6th edn (Dublin, 1785), p. 393. That the will had not been placed with other important papers suggested to some disappointed heirs that the document might not be the now-deceased's will but rather merely a preliminary draft. For example, Thomas Pitts's will was, according to one deponent, John Dunstall, 'found upon a piece of stuffe coverd with a Reame of brown paper lying in ye cords of a bed in ye Dec[ease]d garrett.' Apparently, Dunstall did not find the repository odd, but he did recognize that it was more usual for Pitts to keep papers in a closet next to his bed. See *Lowder et Impey contra Pitt*, PROB 24/17, 136. The will was not admitted to probate. The sentence is PROB 11/338, 323.

[43]   *Hoare contra Hoare*, PROB 18/12/43.

[44]   Ibid., PROB 24/20, 75. Some executors were fortunate enough to have an easier time in finding the documents that they were bound to probate. Richard Richardson, by his own account, was diligently searching for the will of John Isham two weeks after his death, and came upon Isham's will 'sealed up in a sheet of paper in a Cupboard of Drawers where ye Decedent put writings of concern.' *Isham contra Isham*, PROB 24/14, 270. Likewise, according to one witness, the will of Bartholomew Canham was found 'sealed up in a sheet of paper with a seale with these words written on the sd sheete of paper viz. my Last Will and Testament.' *Bourne contra Canham*, PROB 24/15, 270. William Gulstone, the nephew of Edward Twyne, deposed that the latter was so concerned that his will would be destroyed by others that he had ordered his servants to unlock his study and place all his 'loose writings' in a locked trunk. On the Sunday following Twyne's death, the trunk was opened and his will was found. *Rivey contra Twyne*, PROB 24/20, 171–2.

estate. The court revoked the letters of administration that had previously been granted, and probated the will.[45]

Forgery allegations emerged in another cause in which a holographic will was promoted: Lionel Conway claimed that the will of his brother Charles Conway, alleged to have been written in the hand of the deceased and offered for probate by the executors, was in fact penned by another.[46] The contestant charged that a 'person skilled in the art of writing' had drafted the 'scroll.' It was further contended that, given the deceased's employment (Clerk of the Kitchen to the Dowager Countess of Devon), it was not difficult to find examples of his handwriting that could be submitted to the court for comparison, none of which 'appears the same as the subscription of the scroll.'[47] Both sides seem to have presented exhibits to the court for handwriting comparison: the promoters offered letters that they insisted Conway had penned; the contestants produced a deed.[48] Although the cause did not proceed to sentence, the contestant must have dropped his objection; no witnesses were summoned, and the will was admitted to probate.[49]

Thus when a will was alleged to be a valid testamentary act because it was a holograph, proof of the deceased's hand might be made in a number of ways: by summoning witnesses present at the time the alleged will was written;[50] by calling those familiar with the will-maker's handwriting to confirm that the proffered will was indeed in the same hand;[51] by comparison with other documents known to have been written by the will-maker to prove that the one proffered was indeed written by the now-deceased;[52] or by a combination of the above

---

[45] Ibid., PROB 11/374, 368.

[46] *Conway contra Huddle et Starr*, PROB 18/6/79.

[47] Ibid., PROB 18/6/24.

[48] Each side mentions that they had produced the writings in court but I could find no trace of them.

[49] Ibid., PROB 11/342, 522.

[50] In no cause in our collection does the proponent rely exclusively on the testimony of those present at the time of the actual writing of the holograph but, in the probate of Edward Wakeham's will, witnesses testified that they were present at the time the will was written. *Wakeham contra Wakeham*, PROB 24/14, 403.

[51] See the discussion of the probate of the wills of Thomas Jones (footnote 14–22, above), Edward Wakeham (footnote 30-32 above), Thomas Hoare (footnote 39–45, above). See also, *Darrell contra Rowse*, PROB 18/7/21, PROB 24/15, 3; *Billinghurst contra Billinghurst*, PROB 18/7/41, PROB 24/12, 318, 319, and *Lowder et Impey contra Pitt*, PROB 18/10/86, PROB 24/17, 135.

[52] See the discussion of the probate of the will of Richard Markham (footnotes 28 and 29 above) and *Arden contra Schedulthropp alias Tuckys*, PROB 18/7/61.

types of evidence.[53] If the court was satisfied that the document was written in the hand of the will-maker, and manifested his or her testamentary intentions, it was admitted to probate.[54] Even a signature was unnecessary.[55] That Parliament excluded holographic wills from the ambit of the Statue of Frauds suggests that the drafters perceived an ongoing need to allow holographs, and were content with the sorting process that had been developed by probate courts.

The Requirement for a Signature

The Unsigned Will

In legal theory, in our period at least, a written will that was not a holograph – that is one penned by someone other than the will-maker – was an authentic testamentary act only if it was duly executed, that is signed, sealed, and published by the will-maker.[56] As with holographs, the Prerogative Court also assumed a flexible position with respect to unexecuted wills. Indeed even wills that did not bear the will-maker's signature were probated. The will of Joseph Skutt, a London merchant who spent many years in Barbados, provides an example of the circumstances in which a will that was dictated by an individual, but one that remained unsigned and not witnessed owing to intervening death, was offered for, and admitted to, probate. According to the allegation of the will's promoter, his brother and business partner Benjamin Skutt, Joseph had intended to make a will in Benjamin's favor on his return from Barbados. Its purpose was twofold: first, to secure the payment of a debt owed to Sir Ferdinand Gorges, and second, to name Benjamin executor, because Joseph owed (or so his brother believed)

---

[53]   See the discussion of the probate of the will Elizabeth Clerk (footnotes 33–8, above) and Charles Conway (footnotes 46 through 49, above) as well as, *Reeve contra Reeve*, PROB 18/24/75, PROB 24/35, 193–5.

[54]   Witness testimony and handwriting comparison did not always lead to probate. Despite the testimony of witnesses, Thomas Pitt's will (footnote 42) was not admitted to probate (Sentence PROB 11/338, 323), even though (and perhaps because) bonds and bills alleged to have been drawn by the alleged will-maker were exhibited by the proponents. See PROB 24/17, 135, 136.

[55]   In Floyer, *The Proctor's Practice*, a number of causes are cited in which an unsigned holographic will was admitted to probate. Two clear examples are: *Rider v. Rider* (Court of Delegates on appeal from the Prerogative Court of Canterbury, 1704), pp. 128–9, and *Wright v. Walthoe* (Court of Delegates, 1710), p. 132.

[56]   Swinburne, *A Brief Treatise*, pp. 189–92. Or at least in principle; as Perkins noted for the sixteenth century, the requirement existed 'except in special cases.' See John Perkins, *A Profitable Book* (Garland Reprint of the 1827 edition, 1978), sec. 478.

the larger part of his estate to Benjamin's labors. About a month before his death, the two brothers journeyed to Dorset, and Joseph took ill at Poole. In June 1674 (the precise day is left blank in the allegation), Joseph called upon one William Orchard, 'an intimate friend,' to make his will. The two men spent 'two or three hours' together in Joseph's chamber where the will was written down by Orchard, reviewed by the dying man, and finally approved by him. According to the allegation, Orchard left the room to procure wax and witnesses in order to have the will properly executed. Upon his return, he saw that Skutt had fallen asleep. He decided not to disturb him and although Skutt died sometime well thereafter, the will went unexecuted.[57]

A likely story? Perhaps, but Benjamin had another string to his bow. He also offered for probate a holographic will written by his brother while in Barbados. According to the deposition of Sir Ferdinand (who was clearly not without some interest in the matter), he had found this writing when he went with Benjamin to Joseph's chamber shortly after the latter's death.[58] Unfortunately for Benjamin, the alleged holographic will had the word 'cancelled' written on the outside. But both Gorges and another London merchant, James Hooper, deposed that the handwriting in this will was that of Skutt.[59] Perhaps the similarity in terms between the two documents, and the evidence, considerable though not impartial, that Skutt had wanted to die testate influenced the court; the unsigned document (not the cancelled holograph) was admitted to probate.[60]

Likewise, the will of Roger Crow was admitted to probate even though the proponents conceded that it was unsigned.[61] The allegation that was submitted stated that Francis Wise, an attorney, had been summoned to Crow's deathbed and wrote a draft of his will, but Crow died 'before it was finished.'[62] Perhaps the court was moved by the testimony of the scrivener that the dying man had made some notes on the reverse of the will that indicated additional bequests; Wise testified that after he had drafted the will he left it with Crow 'for further consideration.'[63] Finally, the will of George Sherbrooke was admitted to probate[64] even though the contestant alleged that the will was not actually signed.[65]

---

[57]   *Baden alias Harward et al. contra Skutt*, PROB 18/7/2.

[58]   Ibid., PROB 24/15,187.

[59]   Ibid., PROB 24/15, 186.

[60]   Ibid., PROB 11/355, 98, though no will was transcribed in the Will Registers.

[61]   *Crow contra Crow*, PROB 11/45, 358.

[62]   Ibid., PROB 18/21/40.

[63]   Ibid., PROB 24/30, 97.

[64]   Ibid, PROB 11/349, 232.

[65]   Ibid., PROB 18/17/11. Floyer, in *The Proctor's Practice*, cites a cause in which a will penned by another was admitted to probate without the testator's signature. In *Miller v.*

However, the legal requirement of a signature was not always overlooked. The court was more circumspect in causes in which contestants were able to use the signature's absence to cast doubt upon the finality of testamentary intention. For example, the Prerogative Court did not admit the unsigned will of John Ducy to probate,[66] even though his son-in-law deposed that the dying man had read the will over twice but was unable to sign it due to palsy. Arguably the reason why the Court refused to admit the will to probate was because it was incomplete. The same deponent testified that when he had asked his father-in-law if he should call the servants so that they might witness the will, the dying man had said: 'Fold it up and lay it in my closett and if I think of anything else tomorrow well and good or else this is my last Will and Testament.'[67]

The Use of Marks

Illiterate testators might satisfy the signature requirement by making their mark. The use of a mark, however, might raise questions of forgery, particularly if the will-maker could in fact write. Interrogatories submitted by the contestants of the will of Goldwell Hoper asked witnesses to explain why the will-maker did not sign the document himself, since he was literate, and whether the 'mark' that appeared at the bottom of the will was actually made by him.[68] There may have been valid grounds for suspicion regarding the will, because the two witnesses summoned had different recollections of its execution. One witness, Edward Peece, indicated that Hoper was 'ill with palsey,' 'could not move,' and 'could not write.' Nevertheless, when the will was read over to him, he assented to its contents and made a 'mark.'[69] A second witness, David Harwood, testified that the dying man had actually signed the will. In fact, he did not; or so the will

---

Miller, it was alleged that the will was unsigned and also unwitnessed (Court of Delegates on appeal from the Prerogative Court of Canterbury, 1681), pp. 129–30.

[66]   *Boys et Corbett contra Gibbon*, PROB 11/351, 213.

[67]   Ibid., PROB 24/15, 196. In another cause, *Washington contra Balle*, an unsigned will was nullified. According to the proponent's allegation, William Balle's will was complete, but 'never signed by him but only sealed ... because his hand shook.' (PROB 18/21/9; PROB 18/21/7) Witnesses present confirmed that he was in too weakened a physical state to sign, but nevertheless he had sealed and published the will. (PROB 24/30, 40, 49) It was not admitted to probate perhaps due to lack of sound mind or undue influence, given the evidence about the testator's mental state produced by the contestants. (PROB 11/407, 341). See a fuller discussion of the cause in Chapter 10.

[68]   *Hooper contra Hooper per curator*, PROB 18/7/10. The cause refers to the will-maker as Hoper not Hooper.

[69]   Ibid., PROB 24/14, 171.

register indicates. The will was admitted to probate,[70] and the registered copy indicates that a 'mark' rather than a signature was made.[71]

Like a handwritten will or signature, the use of a mark might require authentication. Mary Acton was called upon to identify the mark of Francis Lewin; she deposed that she 'knew his mark among a hundred and she very well remembered the mark w[hi]ch he made to the will.'[72]

Wills Signed by Another

Wills might be regarded as authentic testamentary acts even when signed in the will-maker's name by another person, if there was evidence that the signature had been made at the request of the will-maker.[73] An example comes from the contested probate of the will of Robert Stinton. Once again deathbed estate-planning resulted in issues of will validity, here regarding a document's compliance with the due-execution requirements. In their allegation, the executors of the promoted will conceded that a neighbor, one Thomas Owen, who had drafted the will for the dying man, had also signed the document instead of the testator. The allegation related in detail the surrounding circumstances. Owen was summoned the day before Stinton's death to draft a will according to the dying man's instructions. When he returned the next day with a document in 'proper form,' Stinton was, according to the allegation, too 'weake' to sign. Owen asked him if he should sign instead, and Stinton agreed. Although unable to sign his name, Stinton was able, with the assistance of others, to drop his seal.[74] Owen conceded in his deposition that he was uncertain as to whether the will was valid.[75] The Prerogative Court was not; the will was admitted to probate.[76]

Other documents with dubious signatures were not admitted to probate, even though the affixing of the will-maker's signature by another had been less blatant than in the above example. When Thomas Johnson, an attorney, offered the will of his cousin Sarah Glascocke for probate, her brother Weston Glascocke, contested it. According to his allegation, Johnson, whose character

---

[70]   Ibid., PROB 11/349, 236.

[71]   Ibid., PROB 11/348, 105.

[72]   *Aberry con How contra Aldine*, PROB 24/15, 188.

[73]   The Wills Act of 1837, sec. 7 (7 Will. IV and 1 Vict., c. 26 (1837) so permits, and has not been modified by subsequent statute. Modern American law so permits, for example, the Uniform Probate Code sec. 2–502.

[74]   *Ward contra Stinton per curator*, PROB 18/18/44.

[75]   Ibid., PROB 24/25, 262–4.

[76]   Ibid., PROB 11/383, 299.

was portrayed by the contestant therein as less than pristine,[77] had signed the will using Sarah's mark. Thereafter, he persuaded two individuals, 'later not in the presence of S[arah] G[lascocke], but below stairs' to sign their names as witnesses to the will. Johnson contended that the 'schedule' he sought to promote as her testamentary act had been 'subscribed' by another in her presence, because her hand shook.[78] The will was not admitted to probate.[79] Unfortunately, whether it was the dubious signature or the irregular witnessing that led the court to nullify the will cannot be ascertained.

Is the Signature Genuine?

Just as witnesses were called upon to authenticate that a document was a holograph, they were also sometimes summoned to testify that the signature that appeared on the face of the will was (or was not) that of the will-maker. An example is litigation over the will of George Solby, Citizen and Apothecary of London. A will, allegedly written at the testator's invitation by one Richard Cattell, was probated in common form by the executor of the estate of Anne Boles, daughter of Elizabeth Watgar, who was nominated executrix of Solby's estate.[80] While the contestant, Solby's eldest son Thomas, conceded that Cattell was a scrivener, he contended that he was better known as 'a person who would forge wills ... and lett[e]rs of Attorney.'[81] Thomas was able to find witnesses to corroborate his dismal view of Cattell's integrity. Thomas Summerly agreed with the assertion that Cattell had forged documents, and called him a person of 'very ill principles.'[82] Other witnesses knew firsthand of a Chancery suit in which it was alleged that Cattell had plied his trade, forging receipts relating to the administration of an estate.[83] The will was not admitted to probate, and, as Solby's intestate heir, letters of administration were granted to Thomas.[84]

But evidence could also confirm the authenticity of a signature. It was contended by the contestants of the will of John Digby that the dying man had

---

[77]　It was alleged that he 'practiced as an attorney as one Mr. Kurd, but the real Kurd ordered his serv[an]t to go and inform him not to do sealing of writs in his name.' *Johnson contra Glascocke*, PROB 19/17/84.

[78]　Ibid., PROB 18/17/39.

[79]　Ibid., PROB 11/385, 313.

[80]　*Boles contra Solby*, PROB 18/17/15.

[81]　Ibid., PROB 18/18/50.

[82]　Ibid., PROB 24/25, 211.

[83]　Ibid., PROB 24/25, 210–13.

[84]　Ibid., PROB 11/385, 329.

told others that 'they had put his hand to some writing.'[85] One witness, William Collingridge, testified that he was present with two others when the will was produced and executed by the dying man, and that he recognized the testator's signature because 'he also sent and received letters from the dec[ease]d.'[86] Similarly, Peter Smith, steward to the Countess of Somerset, confirmed his mistress's signature; he deposed that he had seen her handwriting many times and, after perusing the document exhibited, he concluded that it had been signed by her.[87] Another witnesses likewise confirmed her signature.[88] In another cause, William Stretton testified that he 'recognized' the signature on the will presented to him as that of the testatrix Ellen Steele.[89]

Witnessing

To be regarded as an authentic testamentary act, a will written by another person had to be signed and sealed by the will-maker, but also witnessed by at least two persons.[90] Some causes suggest that great care was taken in observing the witnessing requirement. For example, a witness to the will of Walter Rea testified that the testator became concerned during the ceremony of execution that not all of the witnesses could observe the signing of his will. It was reported that he 'bid him to stand aside so that this Dep[onen]t might see him and did ask this Dep[onen]t whether he did see him subscribe his name.'[91]

When a will was offered for probate in solemn form, the party promoting the will was obligated to summon the witnesses to the will to testify that the will had been duly executed, and that it was the authentic testamentary act of the deceased. However, the unavailability of attesting witnesses to a will at the time of probate presented little problem for the Prerogative Court.[92] In four of the

---

85   *Digby contra Digby alias Longueville*, PROB 18/6/44.

86   Ibid., PROB 24/14, 371.

87   *Thyn et Gregory contra Somerset*, PROB 24/15, 58.

88   Ibid., Thomas Cox testified that he was her 'constant person.' PROB 24/15, 61.

89   *Bernard contra Johnson*, PROB 24/14, 225.

90   Swinburne, *Brief Treatise*, pp. 185–6.

91   *Bombay contra Rea*, PROB 24/20, 35.

92   In his discussion of witnesses, Swinburne notes that at least two witnesses were necessary to probate a will in solemn form. Under exceptional circumstances, a testator 'may ordaine that one witness shall make full proof' (*Brief Treatise*, p. 186). But he does not mention a situation in which a witness died after the will was executed, but before probate in solemn form. Because wills were largely deathbed documents, perhaps, it was an uncommon occurrence for a witness to die so soon after the will-maker. But, as we have seen, it was not unknown.

Canterbury causes, the petitioner conceded that one of the witnesses to the will had since died.[93] All of the three causes that proceeded to sentence nevertheless resulted in decrees confirming the will's validity.[94] In three of the four causes, the other witness was called to testify and deposed that he or she had attested to the will in the presence of another witness who had since died.[95]

Although the Prerogative Court in these causes seemed concerned that the witnessing requirement should be satisfied, one cause can be cited in which an unwitnessed, non-holographic will was admitted to probate. Sir Edward Hooper's will was probated even though it was conceded that, after he had signed and sealed the will, 'he put [it] in his pocket intending to have it witnessed,' and he died before so doing. The will was found in his pocket and was 'subscribed by a number of witnesses thereafter.'[96] Regardless of the sequence of 'due execution,' it was admitted to probate.[97] Although no other cause observed concerns a will that was signed, but not witnessed, Floyer cites two causes in the Court of Delegates in which unwitnessed wills were proved. In one cause, it was alleged that witnesses were barred from entering the room where the dying testator was languishing;[98] in the other, witnesses were summoned but did not arrive before the will-maker's death.[99]

---

[93] *Brereton contra Brereton*, PROB 18/13/64; *Bulstrode and Pearse contra Halford*, PROB 18/13/80; *Cooke alias Wright contra Hanson*, PROB 18/24/10; and *Straham contra Roycroft*, PROB 18/24/80.

[94] *Bulstrode et Pearse contra Halford* in the above footnote did not proceed to sentence. The following did: *Brereton*, PROB 11/368, 111; *Cooke alias Wright contra Hanson*, PROB 11/442, 342; and *Straham contra Roycroft*, PROB 11/433, 341.

[95] In *Brereton*, *Bulstrode*, and *Straham* (footnote 93). The proponents of the will of Charles Halford alleged that William and Joanna Windrift witnessed the document, but that William had since died. An interrogatory submitted by the contestant asked Joanna if her husband could read and write, and whether he had signed the will. In her deposition, she testified that both were present at the will's execution, and both had signed the will as witnesses (PROB 18/24/10). Likewise, Sara Smith deposed that Thomas Colclough witnessed the will of William Brereton with her, but that he had since died (*Brereton contra Brereton*, PROB 24/20, 97).

[96] *Hooper contra Hooper*, PROB 18/3c/50.

[97] Ibid., The sentence is PROB 11/343, 137.

[98] Floyer, *The Proctor's Practice*, pp. 129–32, reports *Miller v. Miller*, where it was alleged that the will was unwitnessed, because witnesses were barred by 'persons in whose house the deceased lay.' (1681 Court of Delegates on appeal from the Prerogative Court of Canterbury).

[99] The will-maker died eight days thereafter. Ibid., *Worlick v. Pollet* (Court of Delegates on appeal from the Commissary Court of London and the Court of Arches, 1701).

Alterations

The Suspicious-Looking Document

Finally, the appearance of the document itself might cast doubt on its authenticity. Sir Mathew Hale bemoaned the problems that additions, interlineations, and obliterations raised for will authenticity; a will, he noted, was 'alterable every Hour, and many Times made in Extremity, when there can be no authentick Officer to receive or attest to it.'[100] In a number of causes, the Prerogative Court confronted the issue of whether an alleged 'revision' to a document was the authentic testamentary act of the deceased. If some change had been made to the document offered for probate prior to its execution, then the alteration should stand, but if it was made after execution, by the will-maker or by an interloper, then the will should be probated unaltered. But how could the court be certain precisely when the alteration had occurred?

The process of will-making was conducive to the creation of documents that contained alterations. Scriveners committed many of the wills observed here to writing after conversation with will-makers in which verbal directions were made. The writing was frequently penned elsewhere, and produced subsequently from notes or from recollection. The scrivener would then return to the will-maker's bedside with the draft, and it was read by or to the dying individual, depending upon his or her literacy or physical condition. Having considered the scrivener's handiwork, the will-maker might discern a discrepancy between the instructions given and the document produced, or perhaps the will-maker had a change of heart in the interlude between the scrivener's two visits. Time being of the essence, and paper being perhaps in short supply, an additional bequest (or even more) might be added to the draft, or an existing entry obliterated on the spot. The result was a will of dubious appearance, and therefore one ripe for contest by an eliminated legatee, or by the residuary beneficiaries whose own bequests would be reduced by an additional bequest.

The drafting and execution of the will of John Oxenham closely parallels the model proffered above, and it produced a will in which certain terms were at issue on the grounds that they appeared to have been added sometime after the main section was drafted. The scrivener, Francis Vassal, was called upon to explain the authenticity of the addendum, and he related his recollections to the court. Having been summoned to Oxenham's house by his maid, Vassal conversed with the dying man. Oxenham nominated two executors who were

---

[100] Sir Mathew Hale, *Two Tracts on the Benefit of Registering Deeds in England* (London, 1756), p. 44.

to hold his personal estate in trust for his two younger children. But when he returned, Vassal became concerned that Oxenham's disposition was not complete. More specifically, he was concerned that Oxenham *in extremis* might have omitted a bequest to his eldest son. When he questioned the languishing man, Oxenham replied that his male heir should not have a share. So be it; but Vassal was also concerned that one of the younger children might die before the age of majority, and that provision should be made in the will for just such a contingency. Oxenham told him that in that event the share of the deceased child ought to pass to the survivors.[101] In his deposition, Vassal confirmed that he had made the changes prior to the will's execution. Indeed the altered will was exhibited during the course of his deposition, and he confirmed its authenticity, including the alterations.[102] The will was admitted to probate as amended.[103]

Likewise, the will of Ellen Steele was offered for probate, though according to the contestants it contained 'words blotted out.'[104] Again there was recourse to the recollections of witnesses to determine precisely when the alleged offending act had occurred. In this cause, the scrivener was apparently unavailable to testify, or alternatively, his deposition was lost. The will's witnesses agreed that Steele had duly executed her will, and that the document presented to them by the court was the very same testamentary act. But there were differences amongst them regarding the apparent alteration. One witness deposed to having heard a conversation between the testatrix and the scrivener,[105] while two witnesses denied that she had questioned its contents with the draftsman.[106] William Stretton and Thomas Vicolett were present at the will's execution, and did not report any conversation regarding the contents when the will was read to the testatrix. Gerard Usher, however, did; he testified that she had demanded that bequests of some lands in Stoke Newington pass to her brother Richard for life, and then to his son Phillip for life, with the remainder to Phillip in tail male, rather than to Richard in fee. This alteration, according to Usher, was made prior to the will's execution.[107] Interestingly, however, Vicolett reported a subsequent

---

[101]   Lest it be thought that Oxenham had an aversion to his male heir, the omission was explained by another witness, one Anne Newman, who testified that the exclusion of the eldest son John was due to the fact that lands had been settled upon him in consideration of his marriage. *Oxenham contra Scott alias Oxenham*, PROB 24/20, 145.

[102]   Ibid., PROB 24/20, 144.

[103]   Ibid., The sentence is PROB 11/371, 389, the will, PROB 11/370, 261. John was not entirely excluded from the personal estate; if both sons died he received the residue.

[104]   *Bernard contra Johnson*, PROB 18/7/92.

[105]   Ibid., PROB 24/14, 227.

[106]   Ibid., PROB 24/14, 225, 226.

[107]   Ibid., PROB 24/14, 227.

change of heart regarding other depositions. On the day after the will was executed, Vicolett stated that he was called to Steele's 'chamber' and asked to read the will to her. It was at that point that she raised questions. He reported that she was concerned that her estimation of her net monetary worth (£700) exceeded her bequests by about £50. When asked to whom the residue of her personal property would pass, Vicolett responded that he believed it would pass to the executor, Samuel Bernard (whose relationship to Steele is obscure). According to Vicolett the testatrix told him, 'I doe not intend that Mr. B[ernard] shall be soe much a gainer by me,' and indicated that she wanted the residuary to pass to her nephew Phillip Gower to whom she had bequeathed the remainder of her real property.[108] That change was not made on the face of the will,[109] and the residuary went to the executor, because the document, with the altered interests in land, was admitted to probate without the additional language.[110]

A final cause can be offered to belabor (and illustrate) how the rather haphazard process of will-making prompted much testamentary litigation that raised questions of the authenticity of documents offered for probate as valid wills. Unlike many of our will-makers, Joan Smith made her will well in advance of her death. But again it was its appearance that gave her sisters, one Ayliff and one Hayes (presumably their married names), cause to contest. John Elson offered a document for probate that he alleged had been written by Richard Styles, a clerk to Laurence Alcocke, attorney at law, 'on or about the month of December 1673,' about 10 months before Smith's death. Although she had made an earlier will, it was unclear as to whether it had been duly executed. In the same allegation, Elson claimed that Mr. Newinson, the minister of her neighboring parish of Hambleton, had drawn up this earlier will. However, again according to the same allegation, Smith called upon Alcocke, who deposed that he had assisted her in lending money on bond, to ask him 'to peruse her writings.'[111] She must have been dissatisfied with the provisions therein, because according to Elson's allegation, she asked Alcocke to draft another will.[112]

Given the appearance of the document Elson submitted for probate – rife with a panoply of irregularities, additional pages, alterations, and obliterations, and lacking attestation – Smith's sisters certainly had cause to be suspicious. The allegation explained the will's dubious appearance. According to Elson, Alcocke had drafted the will pursuant to Smith's instructions, conveyed to him on that December day. However, Smith told Alcocke to leave blank the part of the will

---

108   Ibid., PROB 24/14, 226.
109   Ibid., PROB 11/348, 324.
110   Ibid., PROB 11/349, 257.
111   *Elson contra Ayliff et Hayes*, PROB 24/14, 268.
112   Ibid., PROB 18/6/73.

that nominated executors. About a month before her death, Alcocke returned to her lodgings, and read over the will to her. At that time, she indicated that Elson's name should be entered as executor. Other alterations were also made on the face of the draft, after she had determined that she had monetary assets in excess of the bequests made. So a third page was added to the will. She instructed Alcocke that the will as amended should stand as her last will, and that he should take the revised document back to his home to have it rewritten for a subsequent execution. But for unexplained reasons a month passed, and by the time he found a spare moment for redaction, she had died 'before it could be signed.'[113]

In his deposition, Alcocke confirmed the gist of the allegation. He explained that his clerk, Robert Styles, had drafted the will from his notes immediately following the December audience. Thereafter, Alcocke made several additions and interlineations, though he admitted that he had not written in Elson's name as executor. Yet Alcocke affirmed that Smith had wanted Elson to serve. Although she had initially resolved to nominate her nephew, John Hayes, as executor, she recanted, telling Alcocke that 'he being a scholar it was uncertain where he would settle.' Precisely who wrote in Elson's name must remain a mystery. When pressed by way of interrogatory, the attorney admitted that Smith had 'wavered' in settling her estate, and even conceded that she had said that she might prefer to die intestate. Finally, he recalled that when the sisters Ayliff and Hayes asked him after her death if Smith had a will, he had replied with lawyerly caution that she 'had done what he thought did amount to a will.'[114]

Others were summoned by Elson to confirm his version of the events surrounding the drafting of Smith's will. Robert Styles confirmed his master's story. After having 'perused' the writing during his testimony, he confirmed that the document was indeed the one he had drafted, and that Alcocke had made the additions, alterations, and interlineations.[115] Another witness, a domestic servant at the house of Stephen Humphrey where Smith lodged, testified that when Alcocke came to visit her a month before her death, she was told to 'clear the parlour so that business could be transacted.'[116] Likewise, Humphreys testified that Alcocke was summoned to draft a will.[117]

Even though it was conceded that the will was unexecuted, apparently all concerned agreed to abide by the legacies therein. Perhaps this is why the will was admitted to probate, even though it was neither signed nor witnessed.[118]

---

[113]   Ibid., PROB 18/6/73, PROB 18/7/87.
[114]   Ibid., PROB 24/14, 267–8.
[115]   Ibid., PROB 24/14, 272.
[116]   Ibid., PROB 24/14, 244.
[117]   Ibid., PROB 24/14, 248.
[118]   Ibid., PROB 11/349, 266.

According to Alcocke, who seems to have negotiated with the sisters on behalf of Elson, the sisters were satisfied with the disposition of Smith's estate; the only question separating the two sides was who should serve as executor.[119] Elson refused to yield, and the will as proved certified him as executor.[120]

The Evidence of Witnesses

These causes illustrate how reliant the Prerogative Court must have been on the recollections of witnesses. Witnesses might be very specific in their recollections of the appearance of the document to which they affixed their signatures. An example is the will of Stephen Parks, which was offered for probate with alterations.[121] One witness to the will, James Collyer, the dying man's domestic servant, testified that when the will was presented to Parks 'already written,' the testator 'wrote certain words ... and blotted out others,' before it was duly executed.[122] A second witness, Nicholas Collard, was able to go one step further; he testified that line 13 and the first two words of line 31 were obliterated. Collard probably made his numerical calculation after the will was executed; he testified that 'two or three days later' he was summoned to the testator's chamber, and asked to fetch the will. At that time, according to Collard, the will as altered was executed a second time.[123]

But witnesses were not always able to assist the court in determining whether alterations apparent on the face of a will had occurred prior to or after execution. Not all witnesses had actually seen the contents of the document that they

---

[119]   Ibid., PROB 24/14, 268–9.

[120]   Ibid., PROB 11/350, 49. Obliterations were alleged in other wills. When Frances Wells offered for probate the will of her sister, Dorothy Robinson, she charged that a 'scroll' offered for probate by Jasper Wilsher and Thomas Ruffin naming them executors was neither contrived, nor executed, by her sister. *Wilsher contra Ruffin et Wells*, PROB 11/7/90. Moreover, Wells charged that the will had been subsequently altered, likewise without her sister's knowledge. This the executors denied. In their answer, Wilsher and Ruffin explained that a falling-out had occurred between Dorothy and her husband John that had caused her to revoke the previous will, and to execute a subsequent one that they conceded contained some alterations. But 'all Alterations obliterations and interlineations were set downe ... as the dec[ease]d was reading the will' (PROB 25/2/104). The will as amended was read over to her and then duly executed. This was the document they offered for probate. Three witnesses confirmed that she had executed a second will (PROB 24/14, 251, 252, 253). The scrivener, John Billinghurst, testified that the will 'as exhibited' was duly executed (PROB 24/14, 235). It was admitted to probate (PROB 11/349, 142).

[121]   *Parks contra Boughey*, PROB 18/7/68.

[122]   Ibid., PROB 24/14, 384.

[123]   Ibid., PROB 24/14, 361.

signed. For example, Thomas Collingsworth testified that, although he was present at the time of execution, he 'doth not know about the obliterations through the names of beneficiaries.'[124] Nor were suspicious alterations to a document always explained to the satisfaction of the court. The executors of the will of John Eyre, the deceased's brother and a cousin, offered it for probate. According to the contestant, Eyre's widow Sarah, the document contained 'interlineations obliterations and additions' made by the executors. Perhaps the court had sufficient grounds to refuse to recognize the alterations, and indeed the entire will. The scrivener, Giles Eyre (who happened also to be an executor), conceded that he had made the alterations on a copy of the will at the request of the testator, in order to make the will 'stronger,' 'but these changes were not ratified by him because he died suddenly.'[125]

Conclusion

The testamentary causes examined here indicate that the question of the validity of written wills – whether a document offered for probate was the authentic or genuine testamentary act of the deceased – was raised with some frequency. In many respects, the dilemma that the Prerogative Court faced in written wills was similar to that which it confronted with respect to oral wills. Yet there was an important difference. Parliament provided some strict mandates with respect to the validity of nuncupative wills of estates valued in excess of £30 in the Statute of Frauds. Without any strict legislative guidelines on the requirements for the validity of written wills of personalty, the judges were empowered to exercise their judgment, and the causes suggest that the court pondered on a case-by-case basis whether it was reasonably certain that the now-deceased individual intended the writing offered for probate to be a testamentary act.

Nevertheless, the church-court law established certain physical requirements for a document to be a valid will. Moreover, intent and adherence to form were interlinked: executing a document that conformed to the requirements of due execution was evidence that the will-maker had wished the writing to have testamentary significance. But written documents that did not conform to the requirements for due execution came before the court, and the judges had to consider whether these wills ought to be admitted to probate. The culprit was the cultural norms surrounding will-making. Like their oral counterparts, written wills made at or near the deathbed spawned dubious documents. That

---

124 *Digby contra Digby alias Longueville*, PROB 24/14, 371.
125 *Eyre contra Eyre*, PROB 24/16, 214–20.

the words constituting the will were committed to writing, and the document was executed and witnessed, should have made it clearer that its author meant what he or she wrote. But was it a draft, what the allegations were wont to call 'scrolls?' Or was it a holograph, and if not, was it signed by the will-maker and witnessed? Even the precise terms of written wills could be dubious. Arguably, their terms should have been easier to ascertain than those of the oral wills. However, the problem of alterations in some written wills created for the court a similar sense of doubt to what was noted above with respect to oral wills: what precisely were the actual terms of the disposition?

Surveying the Canterbury causes in which authenticity was at issue confirms that Professor Helmholz's view of the mission of probate courts in the sixteenth century also obtained for the late seventeenth:[126] the court was indulgent when a will that did not meet all of the requirements for due execution came before it, if it believed that the document really represented the will of the deceased. The court acted as modern legal commentators (at least in the more lenient 'colonies') have urged courts to do: admit non-complying documents to probate when many/most of the statutory bases have been touched by the will-maker, or if the court is convinced that the will represents the testamentary volition of the will-maker.[127] Perhaps, in this particular regard, the Prerogative Court was slightly – 300 years – ahead of its time. And so too was Parliament. It excluded written wills of personal property entirely from the Statute of Frauds, allowing the court to continue its practice of admitting to probate wills that might be doubtful in form, if it was persuaded that the document manifested the testamentary intent of the deceased.

---

[126] R.H. Helmholz, *Roman Canon Law in Reformation England* (Cambridge, 1990), p. 7.

[127] See Uniform Probate Code sec. 2–503.

Chapter 7
Which Shall It Be? Multiple Testamentary Documents and the Revocation of Wills

Introduction

In this chapter, another distinct type of testamentary dispute is considered. In slightly more than one in eight of our causes (13 percent of all causes; 17.1 percent of our contested causes), a second testamentary act (or even in rare causes a third) was submitted to the court as the last will of the deceased by either the promoter or the contestant, or was alleged by one party or the other to have been made.[1] Having two testamentary acts placed before it at the behest of litigants complicated the Prerogative Court's task. First it had to determine whether each of the wills submitted was an authentic testamentary act. If one or both of the documents (or utterances) offered for probate had not been validly executed, the court had an easy way out of its dilemma: probate the authentic document (or utterance) if there was one; if not, deny probate to the pair and allow the estate to pass by intestate succession. But if both wills were deemed valid testamentary acts, the court faced a second, and a decidedly more challenging task. The judge had to determine the effects of each act upon the other. Did the latter will revoke

---

[1] Archival citations will be provided when the documents are cited. The individual cases discussed in this chapter are: *Marsham contra Cherry, Bourden contra Bourden, Burchett contra Pickes, Cornish contra Antrobus, Price contra Price, Hill contra Bond, Hicks et Meggs contra Singleton, West contra West, Curwin et Short contra Meggot, Bush contra Couzens, Ellis contra Parsons, Thyn et Gregory contra Somerset, Higgins et Higgins contra Stamp, Boys et Corbett contra Gibbon, Bretton contra Bretton, Jones contra Jones, Niblett contra Thonold, Rich et Gayner contra Vernon, Bradbourne contra Townsend, Hodgekinson contra Hodgekinson, Jennyns contra Jennyns,* and *Wilsher contra Ruffin et Wells.* Causes in which multiple wills were involved have already been observed, though not directly addressed, in previous chapters. For example, two documents came before the court each purporting to be the last will of Benjamin Bradbourne (*Bradbourne contra Townsend*), of Agnes Osbourne (*King et Taylor contra Jepp*), and of Joan Smith (*Elson contra Ayliff et Hayes*). At least one cause already observed in which a second utterance was offered for probate as the deceased's oral will. Richard Parsons was alleged to have made two nuncupative wills (*Ellis contra Parsons*, PROB 18/6/23 and PROB18/7/56). Six causes can be cited in which one testamentary act presented to the court was oral and the other written: *Bourden contra Bourden, Cornish contra Antrobus, Bush contra Couzens, Ellis contra Parsons, Bretton contra Bretton,* and *Jones contra Jones.*

the earlier one or should the multiple testamentary acts be read together: was the latter will an addition to or a qualification of the former?

Like the rules of due execution and their application by the court, the legal conventions regarding modification and revocation both limited and promoted a property-owner's freedom of disposition. As life ebbed and their thoughts turned to winding up their temporal affairs, some property-owners sought to update their 'estate plan.' Yet the final hours, and even the last minutes, of life were especially the times that generated dubious wills; questionable amendments to wills might likewise be undertaken under exigent circumstances. The law had to establish guidelines that were calculated to ensure that only those changes that were actually desired by the testator were recognized.

Undertaking multiple testamentary acts was not particular to early modern English will-makers. It also occurs in our own time, and modern wills legislation has established rules to deal with potentially conflicting testamentary acts.[2] A brief (and as far as possible uncomplicated) discourse on probate law, both past and present, is required at this point to pave the way for the historical analysis that follows.

Revocation of Testamentary Documents: Past and Present

Modern Law

Modern law (in jurisdictions whose jurisprudence is derived from English law) regards wills as 'ambulatory': an entire will, or some dispositions therein, may be revoked or amended by a subsequent legal act. Although the particulars may differ in different jurisdictions, the general rule can be simply stated: a later will revokes an earlier one if it so specifies; or, if the second will does not expressly revoke the first will but the documents have inconsistent provisions, the provisions in the second will stand and those of the first will are revoked, but

---

[2]   In the United States, see the Uniform Probate Code sec. 2–507, and Robert Whitman, 'Revocation and Revival: An analysis of the 1990 Revision of the Uniform Probate Code,' *Albany Law Review*, vol. 55 (1991/2), pp. 1035–66. In England and Wales, section 20 of the Wills Act of 1837 (7 Will. IV and 1 Vict., c 26 (1837)) remains in force and reads as follows:

No will or codicil, or any part thereof, shall be revoked otherwise than as aforesaid, or by another will or codicil executed in manner herein-before required, or by some writing declaring an intention to revoke the same, and executed in the manner in which a will is herein-before required to be executed, or by the burning, tearing, or otherwise destroying the same by the testator, or by some person in his presence and by his direction, with the intention of revoking the same.

only to the extent of the inconsistency.[3] In addition, a will may be revoked by some physical act done to it (rather than being replaced by a second disposition), by the will-maker 'cancelling' the document, usually accomplished through physical defacement of the writing, or more simply, by tearing it up, burning it, mutilating it, or otherwise destroying the writing.[4] Finally, provisions can be added to an existing will (or subtracted there from) by a subsequent testamentary act, usually (though not invariably) referred to as a codicil.[5]

Church-Court Law in Early Modern England and the Statute of Frauds

Although their purpose was broadly similar – to allow will-makers the ability to alter an existing will up until their death – the church courts in England during our period approached the issue of subsequent testamentary documents in a different and, unhappily, a more complex fashion. A lengthy passage in Henry Swinburne's treatise on wills confirms the principle that property-owners should be free to alter dispositions in a validly executed will by making a subsequent testamentary act. The latter will should invalidate the former:

> A man may as oft as he will make a new testament even until the last breath neither is there any cautele under the sun to prevent this liberty: but no man can die with two testaments, and therefore the last and newest is in force: so that if there were a thousand testaments, the last of all is the best of all, and maketh void all of the former.[6]

Accordingly, the will of most recent vintage would, in his words, 'infringe upon' the earlier will, even if the subsequent will did not contain express words of revocation, and even if the existing written will was revoked by one uttered by word of mouth (at least prior to the Statute of Frauds).[7] Moreover, even after

---

[3]   The two valid testamentary documents with provisions that do not conflict are read together; in short the provisions of each have effect.

[4]   Jurisdictions differ as to whether a defacement to sections or to individual bequests is valid to revoke the cancelled parts. The Uniform Probate Code sec. 2–507 (a) (2) permits it; New York law does not Estates, Powers and Trusts Law sec. 4–1.1 (a) (2) (A). The English statute seems to be less clearly expressed than is New York, but I read it so as to preclude partial revocation by physical act.

[5]   5 In modern legal parlance, a codicil is deemed to be an addition to an existing will.

[6]   Henry Swinburne, *A Brief Treatise of Testaments and Last Wills* (Garland Reprint of 1590 edition, 1978), pp. 164–5.

[7]   However, a will-maker might undertake not to revoke an existing will by drafting a clause 'derogatorie' into the document. But the effect of the clause was not absolute; under certain

having executed a will, a will-maker could thereafter decide to die intestate, and could revoke all previous testamentary acts by declaring this intention or by destroying the existing will.[8] Thus, if any will at all was to govern the devolution of property, it was the last will that had the final say.

Thus far the law's position on the total revocation of an individual's existing will has been addressed. Suppose, however, that the will-maker was inclined only to tinker, to make modest changes, for example to add (or delete) the odd legacy; might this be done by subsequent testamentary act, either written or by word of mouth?[9] The dispository provisions of an existing will might be altered by a second testamentary act, a codicil. For the subsequent testamentary act to be regarded as a codicil, however, it could not nominate an executor; if it did so it was a will, and the latter document (or utterance) revoked the previous testamentary act in its entirety.[10]

Parliament recognized the problem that multiple testamentary acts could create, but made only two minor modifications of the existing law in the 1677 Statute of Frauds. First, the statute removed from will-makers the ability to alter written wills by oral declaration, but it still permitted probate courts to recognize deathbed alterations by written will; second, it specified the way in which written wills were to be revoked.[11] Even after the statute, however, how an estate was distributed in many successions observed in the Canterbury causes depended upon the narrative of the will's alteration or revocation that the court constructed from the evidence presented by the parties.

---

circumstances the will-maker might still be able to revoke a will with such a clause. See Swinburne, ibid., pp. 166–73.

[8]   This was perhaps easier said than done: there was a presumption, again with detailed exceptions, against a 'bare' revocation, where the will-maker revoked a will without making another. Swinburne notes disagreement amongst writers as to whether a will-maker had to indicate expressly that he or she wished to die intestate. Ibid., pp. 175–6.

[9]   As we observed in both Chapter 5 and 6, above.

[10]   Swinburne, *Brief Treatise*, p.167. While in modern legal parlance, a codicil is considered to be an addition to a will. Clearly the term 'codicil' meant something quite different in Swinburne's time. Harking back to Roman law, Swinburne categorized a document as a testament or a codicil based upon whether a testamentary act (oral or written) nominated an executor: one that named an executor was a will; one that did not was a codicil. The distinction was not merely a technical quibble: if an executor was stipulated, the entire estate was placed in his (or her) hands, charged with the obligation of paying debts and legacies; if no executor was named in a will, the court had to constitute an administrator to perform that function.

[11]   Oral wills could be modified orally, so long as the utterance met the statute's mandate on the validity of oral wills (29 Car. II, c. (1677), sec. 19–23). For a discussion, see Chapter 2, text accompanying footnotes 77–81, above.

Changes of Testamentary Heart: the Culture of Will-Making at Work

'Even until the last breath': the Canterbury causes illustrate, through word and deed, that property-owners were keenly aware of the ambulatory nature of their testamentary acts. Indeed the evidence suggests that will-makers knew a bit about the law of wills dealing with modification and revocation. For example, when Benjamin Bradbourne was asked if he had settled his estate, he indicated that he had made a will 'foure or five years ago which should not stand.' When he was further pressed as to whether that document should be 'recovered he said that it was unnecessarie because he had just made another that would make the other one voyd.'[12] Likewise, Gerard Usher, a witness to the second will of Ellen Steele, deposed that the testatrix had insisted that she had 'cancelled' her existing will prior to the time the superseding document was executed.[13]

Will-makers also realized that the law left them free to modify an existing will, as well as to revoke it. For example, a witness to the execution of the will of Richard Hodgekinson reported that the testator was asked if he wanted to clarify at what point in time a bequest in his will should be paid. Hodgekinson replied that he was not sure, but 'that he might add that to his will by codicil.' He did so; an undated codicil admitted to probate required his executor to pay the stipulated legacies six months after the discharge of his debts.[14]

If an individual was uncertain about whether a subsequent testamentary act could be undertaken, he needed only to ask others for counsel, as it was alleged did John Singleton.[15] In his deposition, William Mason, the curate of St. Leon, Shoreditch, confirmed that he had told Singleton that if he was displeased with the contents of his earlier will, he might 'wish to make another.'[16] Though in this instance the amateur lawyer was correct, laypersons did not always get the law right. Sarah Hill's bad legal advice on revocation (discussed below) nearly thwarted her cousin Clement Pragell's estate plan.[17]

The causes indicate that not only were some will-makers conversant with the law regarding will modification and revocation but that a fair number took advantage of it. Twenty-two of the causes in this study concern multiple testamentary acts: 7 involved a codicil or other addition to an existing will,[18]

---

[12]   *Bradbourne contra Townsend*, PROB 18/8/106.

[13]   *Bernard contra Johnson*, PROB 24/14, 228.

[14]   *Hodgekinson contra Hodgekinson*, PROB 24/12, 310.

[15]   *Hicks et Meggs contra Singleton*, PROB 18/18/15.

[16]   Ibid., PROB 24/25, 138.

[17]   *Hill contra Bond*, PROB 24/20, 136.

[18]   *Bourden contra Bourden, Thyn et Gregory contra Somerset, Bretton contra Bretton, Niblett contra Thonold, Rich et Gayner contra Vernon, Hodgekinson contra Hodgekinson*, and *Jennyns contra*

while in the remaining 15 causes, 2 separate but competing testamentary acts were alleged.[19]

Modification by codicil was undertaken under different circumstances and for different reasons than the execution of a second, conflicting will. Much light can be shed on both the law and the actual practice of modification by relating how the causes were presented and argued by the litigants. Through the causes, the 'law' regarding testamentary amendment and revocation can best be observed (indeed, given the nature of the sources it must be observed). So a report of these 22 causes follows, addressing first those dealing with codicils, followed by others involving conflicting wills.

Multiple Wills: Codicils

Since so many wills of the observed in this study were made on a deathbed, it might seem unlikely that these will-makers would have had the opportunity to undertake a second testamentary act. Having barely managed to execute a single testamentary act before death, how could they have had the time to supplant or to alter it? Of course, not all wills were contrived on the deathbed, and the making of wills in advance frequently explains second testamentary acts, even those with only modest alterations made by way of codicil.

Some indication of whether will-making in good health led to last-minute supplements can be gleaned by calculating the period of time that elapsed between the two proffered testamentary acts, the will and the codicil, in the Canterbury causes observed. For example, nearly a year transpired between the execution of the will and the codicil of Elizabeth Rich. A witness present at the time the codicil was made, one Richard Pauley, testified that he had been summoned to the testatrix's house the day she died 'to add some legacies.' He deposed that he wrote a second document styled, 'A codicile to be annexed to my will bearing the date 6th day of June 1674.' Upon its face there was a further notation, probably also in his hand, 'Memorandum this codicill was made

---

Jennyns. Archival references will be provided when the cause is discussed below.

[19]   *Marsham contra Cherry, Burchett contra Pickes, Cornish contra Antrobus, Price contra Price, Hill contra Bond, Hicks et Meggs contra Singleton, West contra West, Curwin et Short contra Meggot, Bush contra Couzens, Ellis contra Parsons, Higgins et Higgins contra Stamp, Boys et Corbett contra Gibbon, Jones contra Jones, Wilsher contra Ruffin et Wells,* and *Bradbourne contra Townsend.* Archival references will be provided when the cause is discussed below. In some of the causes, the additional testamentary acts are actually offered for probate; in others, the record is insufficiently complete to demonstrate whether a second document was actually offered for probate, though mention is made in the record of another disposition of the will-maker's estate by the contestants of a will being promoted.

twentieth day of May 1675.'[20] The changes to her 'estate plan' embodied in the codicil were modest. In the second document, small legacies to relations who had been ignored in the first will were added,[21] both of which were allowed.[22] Likewise, Samuel Claphamson revised an existing will that he had made while in good health by codicil on his deathbed, or so it was alleged.[23] He chose to do so by word of mouth. The provisions were redacted on the spot, and the alterations were thus within the exception of the Statute of Frauds' general exclusion of oral codicils to written wills.[24] Finally, some time must have transpired between the making of the will and the codicil of John Jennings. Although the time gap between these testamentary acts cannot be ascertained precisely, it was at least long enough for his sister to marry a man who 'displeased' Jennings, prompting him to revoke her bequest by codicil shortly before his death.[25]

Some will-makers, however, changed their minds quickly, and without apparent reason. For example, it was submitted by the proponents of the will and codicil of Thomas Bourden that 'on the s[ai]d day the will made he desired to alter it by nuncupative codicile.'[26] Likewise, James Burton was alleged to have made a written will and a codicil on the same day.[27] Why a quick change of heart occurred in these causes is not clear. Miscommunication between the scrivener and the will-maker on the document's terms might have prompted the need for an alteration. Perhaps a brief addition to a will was necessary when the will-maker realized, upon having the dispositions read over to him, that a bequest was omitted. That was the case with John Bretton's will. William Day, a witness to the will, recalled that Thomas Brown had told the testator upon hearing the provisions of the will read aloud *after* due execution that Bretton had not devised his books. Day reported that Bretton immediately declared a nuncupative codicil remedying the inadvertent omission.[28]

---

20 *Rich et Gayner contra Vernon*, PROB 24/14, 315–16.

21 Ibid., PROB 11/349, 301.

22 Ibid., PROB 11/349, 256.

23 *Burford et Claphamson contra Claphamson*, PROB 18/18/34.

24 The codicil was subject a provision in the Statute of Frauds (29 Car II, c. 3 (1677), sec. 19) requiring the will to written down within a period of six days after the making. Nevertheless, the codicil was denied probate perhaps due to the prodding that others undertook in order to spur his generosity (Ibid., PROB 11/384, 284).

25 Or so it was alleged (*Jennyns contra Jennyns*, PROB 18/2/89). The cause did not proceed to sentence.

26 *Bourden contra Bourden*, PROB 18/1/54.

27 *Brace alias Burton contra Burton*, PROB 18/7/20.

28 *Bretton contra Bretton*, PROB 24/15, 124–5.

In most of the Canterbury causes, the codicil offered was admitted to probate,[29] but it should not be assumed that the execution of a codicil to supplement an estate plan was not without its risks. In the first place, it was probably easier for a codicil to be concealed than in the case of a will. Though witnesses to the codicil would know of its existence, codicils were less frequently executed than were wills. Thus while diligent searches might be made for a will, it might not occur to those surviving, upon finding one testamentary document to rummage through the deceased's effects for a further one. Moreover, the executor or executrix named in the original will had a motive to suppress a codicil: once the debts owed by the will-maker were satisfied and the legacies were paid, whatever remained in his or her hands could be retained. Therefore, an additional legacy in a codicil (as opposed to a swap of beneficiaries) would diminish the residue and limit the extent of the executor or executrix's own 'bequest,' perhaps inclining the greedier among them to suppress the further testamentary act.

An example of the alleged suppression of a codicil by an executor for just that reason can be observed in one cause, though indirectly. When Richard Parsons died in late November of 1674, the estate of his father, John, had yet to be settled, or at least so Samuel Ellis contended. Ellis offered for probate a nuncupative will alleged to have been uttered by Richard, in addition to a written will that he had already proved. In his offer of probate of the oral codicil, Ellis submitted that Richard was indebted to him to the tune of £49, a sum he had paid on Richard's behalf to 'redeem him from prison.'[30] Richard's uncle Anthony also claimed that his nephew had named him executor of a nuncupative will, one that he offered for probate.[31]

Now to the concealed codicil: it was in fact executed by the previous generation of the Parsons family, Richard's father, John. Ellis claimed that uncle Anthony was executor of his father, John's, estate, and that a codicil had been executed in which John had left the bulk of his property to Richard. According to Ellis, both Richard and uncle Anthony had copies made of the codicil, but uncle Anthony did not 'exhibit' the codicil when he took up the estate as executor, and perhaps his dereliction was not entirely inadvertent. As Ellis noted, uncle Anthony was charged in John's will to pay only the testator's debts and a

---

[29]   Three of the seven causes (in footnote 18) do not proceed to sentence: *Bretton, Niblett* and *Jennyns*. Four did: *Bourden*, (PROB 11/351, 172), *Thyn* (PROB 11/355, 96), *Rich* (PROB 11/349, 256) and *Hodgekinson* (PROB 11/351, 196). Samuel Claphamson's codicil, however, was nullified. *Burford et Claphamson contra Clamphamson*, PROB 11/385, 248.

[30]   *Ellis contra Parsons*, PROB 18/6/23. The probate of the will in common form is mentioned in interrogatories that Ellis submitted (PROB 18/7/56).

[31]   Ibid., PROB 18/7/56.

modest legacy to Richard; in the codicil, the bequest to Richard was topped up significantly. Although Richard had pressed his uncle Anthony to probate the codicil, the latter had delayed, blaming his failure to do so on his co-executor.[32] Not surprisingly, uncle Anthony questioned the document's authenticity, or so a witness testified. John Poultney, who claimed to have been present at a meeting in the 'Golden Lyon Taverne' between the three, recalled that uncle Anthony had promised his nephew that he would 'determine whether or not it was a codicile and would determine it in a day or so.'[33] According to Ellis, the executors had refused even to make an inventory of the estate. Indeed, the issue of the codicil was only pressed by Ellis in his action to promote Richard's will.[34] To Ellis, the probate of the codicil would be crucial to his chances for repayment of the debt owed to him because Richard's only property was the interest in his father's estate. It was only if John's codicil was proved that Richard's will (and either the oral or the written one would do) would be worth probating.[35]

Multiple Wills: Conflicting Documents

In addition to alterations by way of codicil, will-makers might undertake a more substantial rewrite, and in particular change the executor (and usually much of the dispository pattern), an act that had to have been done by a second will rather than by codicil. These will-makers were as unpredictable as were codicil-makers regarding the timing of their two testamentary acts. While the time-gap between the alleged execution of the two wills usually exceeded a year, two of our will-makers seem to have changed their minds rather quickly.[36] From the surviving documentation, it is not apparent why they decided to replace their testamentary acts so soon after having executed them, unless, however, one accepts the view of the promoters of the earlier wills: that the subsequent wills were the product of undue influence or were executed by the will-makers when

---

[32]   Ibid., PROB 18/7/22.

[33]   Ibid., PROB 24/15, 18. Another witness present when the matter was discussed at the Golden Lyon and elsewhere had a more blurred account (PROB 24/15, 19).

[34]   Ibid., PROB 18/7/22.

[35]   He probably was not repaid, or at least so we can surmise from the fact that the oral will he promoted was not admitted to probate. In fact neither the oral will nor the codicil was probated, and presumably Anthony pocketed the residue of John's estate (Ibid., PROB 11/351, 180).

[36]   Of 15 alleged conflicting wills (see footnote 19), the dates of both testamentary acts can be ascertained in 8 causes: of these, two of the alleged testamentary acts followed in rapid succession (within the same month and within six weeks); the time spans between alleged execution in the remaining six ranged from 18 months to over three years.

their testamentary capacity had been diminished. In fact, while claims of both undue influence and testamentary capacity are largely absent from the causes in which codicils are promoted, they figure prominently in those in which two separate wills were alleged to have been made.[37]

The distinction between wills and codicils outlined so neatly by Swinburne was not always clearly observed by the litigants in the Prerogative Court or, perhaps in common with their modern brethren, lawyers were prepared to argue in the alternative, that the second testamentary act could be characterized as either. One cause presents an example of two distinct characterizations of the same testamentary act. The contestant of the will of Hannah Antrobus asserted that she had 'corrected' her written will by word of mouth. But precisely how should this second testamentary act be characterized? In her allegation, it was argued that her declaration should stand alternatively: either as a revocation of the written will (and thus as manifestation of an intent to die intestate); as a new will that revoked the previous one, and that constituted her brother George as executor; or, finally, as a codicil that required the executor of the written will, Henry Cornish, to hold the estate in trust for George.[38]

Executing a will well in advance of impending death (as property-owners were implored to do by the legal and spiritual commentators) did result in sets of conflicting wills in the causes. In common with some of the causes in which codicils were contested, the passage of time and the occurrence of particular events led to a change of heart that required a reworking of an existing estate plan. For example, a witness to the will of John West testified that his uncle was 'moved' to make a new will because his existing will was 'outdated.'[39] Likewise, it may have been the time span between the execution of his first will and his death that prompted John Unity to consider a replacement. Unity, a mariner who died at sea, had executed a written will naming his landlady, Agnes Bush, as his executrix. Shortly before his death nearly three years later, however, he was alleged to have revised the disposition of his estate by naming his shipmate John Stag executor and beneficiary, obligating him only to pay debts owing to Bush.[40] Had the relationship between Unity and his landlady soured?

---

[37]   Of the 15 causes in which two conflicting wills were alleged (see footnote 19), all save two, *Burchett contra Pickes* and *Cornish contra Antrobus* involved claims of testamentary incapacity and/or undue influence.

[38]   *Cornish contra Antrobus*, PROB 18/3c/85. The will was admitted to probate (PROB 11/326, 141) as submitted by Cornish, and without mention of George (PROB 11/326, 143).

[39]   *West contra West*, PROB 24/25, 120.

[40]   *Bush contra Couzens*, PROB 18/24/65; PROB 18/24/69. The latter will was admitted to probate (PROB 11/433, 338).

Similarly, William Bradford died leaving two testamentary documents executed over three years apart. His earlier will, dated more than four years before his death, nominated Christopher Marsham as his executor to hold his property in trust for his son, William, who was a factor in the East Indies.[41] While this document was submitted for probate, Richard Cherry, with whom Bradford was lodging at his death, offered a will of more recent vintage naming him executor, a will that was said by Christopher to have been contrived through the exercise of undue influence.[42] The substitution of executors might be explained by Bradford's altered living arrangements, but the explanations of precisely why he modified his will varied according to the party. Marsham proffered that after Bradford began to lodge with Cherry the latter was able to exercise undue influence on him; Cherry, on the other hand, pointed to the kindness he had bestowed upon the aged testator, and the expenses that he had incurred for the elderly man's comfortable support. The stakes for both parties must have been sufficiently high to join battle; although both men agreed that the executor would hold the estate in trust for the testator's son, William, he was living in the Indies where life expectancy was probably short. In addition to his personal estate, Bradford owned some property in London that would pass by his will. Neither document, however, was probated.[43]

Personal differences or reconciliations with executors and beneficiaries arising after the execution of a will might prompt a will-maker to undertake a second testamentary act. Some involved familial rancor. According to the promoters of the 'second' will of Dorothy Robinson, the testatrix revoked a will that nominated her sister Frances Wells executrix by executing a second will. They alleged that she did so because she believed that Frances was responsible for creating serious differences between herself and her husband, a conflict that had arisen subsequent to the execution of her first will.[44] Likewise, two wills were offered for probate as the last will of Benjamin Bradbourne. His wife Katherine alleged that her husband had made his will disinheriting her while he was languishing near death, but that when he recovered he indicated that he wanted to draft another. During the intervening years, she contended, there were serious disagreements with his sister, the executrix of the earlier will, a factor which his wife alleged explained his resort to a second will.[45]

---

[41] *Marsham contra Cherry*, PROB 18/1/10.

[42] The offer for probate does not seem to have survived. Marsham submitted an allegation arguing that the second will submitted was 'contrived' (Ibid., PROB 18/1/52).

[43] No record of a will being probated can be found in the will registers.

[44] *Wilsher contra Ruffin et Wells*, PROB 18/7/90.

[45] *Bradbourne contra Townsend*, PROB 18/8/106.

It was suggested that soured marital relations also prompted the execution of a subsequent testamentary document by William Price. Promoters of his later will claimed that it limited certain bequests that he had made to his wife Jane in a previous will. In the allegation, it was contended that he had expressly revoked the earlier will, largely because the couple had lived apart for long periods prior to his final illness.[46] Instead of leaving his 'lands in London' outright to his wife, as he had directed in his first will, he devised them in a second document to his wife for her life only, with the remainder to an after-born child, if 'she be with child,' and if she was not the remainder was limited to his sisters.[47] But his displeasure with Jane was not total; he retained her as executrix. While she had offered the earlier will to probate, it was the later one that was eventually admitted.[48]

In addition to a change of heart regarding beneficiaries, documents might also go missing, particularly when they were executed in advance of death, leading a will-maker to undertake a second testamentary act. According to Damarie, the daughter of William Jones, the testator's wife, Mary, had burned both his will and a copy thereof without his consent.[49] Mary produced a schedule from which she alleged the will had been drafted, and deposed witnesses who verified the execution of a will and the copy.[50] But, according to Mary, Jones had revoked this will, and made another by word of mouth constituting her as executrix, a will that was admitted for probate.[51]

A final cause merits mention as an example of precisely how conflicting wills could be produced, and the difficulty that the court faced in separating fact from fancy in determining which one (or both) should be given effect as the deceased's last will. In addition, we observe the maneuvering that creditors might undertake to secure the payment of debts by will when their debtor was close to death, another reason why a will-maker might be pressed to alter or revoke a pre-existing will on the deathbed. The attempt to probate three wills alleged to have been executed by Richard Parsons has been already recounted in the discussion of codicils.[52] When Richard died he was indebted to both Samuel Ellis and his uncle Anthony Parsons.[53] As many as four wills may have been made, and as few as none! The first was a written will that was produced by Ellis, and by the time the litigation discussed here transpired it had been proved in

---

[46] *Price contra Price*, PROB 18/13/15.

[47] Ibid., PROB 11/368, 348. The sisters, Mary and Anne, each also received £40.

[48] Ibid., PROB 11/366, 290.

[49] *Jones contra Jones*, PROB 18/7/59.

[50] Ibid., PROB 24/14, 316, 345, 350.

[51] Ibid., The will (PROB 11/349, 98) and the sentence (PROB 11/349, 263).

[52] See text accompanying footnotes 30–35, above.

[53] Fortunately the sums are unimportant because the calculations in each document differ.

common form. Thereafter each party offered different oral wills in solemn form for probate.[54] The deathbed utterance promoted by uncle Anthony was the one best documented, and it was alleged to be a confirmation of a still-earlier will also made by word of mouth about a month prior to Richard's death. According to John Howe, uncle Anthony came to the Bell Inn where Richard lodged in early October of 1674, and at that time Richard constituted him executor by oral will, asking his uncle to pay all his debts, as well as a legacy of £100 to his sister.[55] Only one witness to this utterance was produced, Edward Scott, who testified that he was present and confirmed that he understood that such a disposition was made.[56] But uncle Anthony had another testamentary act, and one better documented; he was able to produce a number of witnesses present while Richard was languishing on his deathbed in Scott's house on 11 November 1674. They confirmed that an oral will naming uncle Anthony as executor was made.[57] Clearly by this time Richard's illness had taken a turn for the worse; and uncle Anthony claimed that he was footing the bill for the medical expenses. Evidence was produced that substantiated uncle Anthony's outlays; Scott's servants testified that they were receiving payments from uncle Anthony, and that he was busily summoning, and paying for, medical advice and nurses.[58]

So Anthony Parsons's position seemed to be secure. As demonstrated in my chapter on oral wills above, testamentary acts by word of mouth were not rare, and in the absence of compelling evidence of lack of testamentary capacity or undue influence, they were frequently admitted to probate. But the rub was all these other wills. Between the two alleged utterances nominating uncle Anthony as executor, it was claimed that Richard had made yet another nuncupative will. Mary Bernie testified that she was present on 28 October in the kitchen of her alehouse when Richard declared his will, nominating Ellis his executor.[59]

And then there was the written will proved in common form. Precisely when and where, and indeed if, this document had been executed was unclear, but there was evidence that Anthony was interested in locating a written will. John Coal, a coffin-maker, deposed that while he was busily pursuing his craft he noted that Parsons was actively searching the deceased's 'trunk' for a will, but was

---

[54]   *Ellis contra Parsons.* Ellis's offer is PROB 18/6/23, that of Parson's, PROB 18/7/56. Ellis's allegation claims that he had proved a written will in common form.

[55]   Ibid., PROB 24/14, 299.

[56]   Ibid., PROB 24/24, 327.

[57]   In particular Edward Scott and his wife, Bridget (Ibid., PROB 24/14, 301; 327). This was the will offered by Parsons.

[58]   Ibid., PROB 24/14, 263; 300; 333.

[59]   Ibid., PROB 24/14,195. Either no other witness to this will was present or Ellis was unable to produce him or her.

'agitated' because he found nothing.[60] Another witness doubted that a written will had been made. Thomas Crosthwaite deposed that he had advised Parsons to make his will a number of times during his last illness, but that the dying man had refused to settle his worldly affairs. Indeed Crosthwaite's testimony shed doubt on whether any will had ever been made, oral or written. On the day he died, Crosthwaite heard another witness 'hitherto examined,' one John Henley, remark that Anthony had asked him if his nephew had made his will; he was told that he had not, and that he 'could not be persuaded to make one.'[61] One may forgive the court, then, for denying probate to any of the wills before it, and instead allowing Parsons's estate to pass by intestate succession.[62]

Conflicting Wills: The Problem of Revocation

Although all of the causes discussed in the previous section implicitly raised the issue of partial or total revocation of an existing will, the proponents of subsequent testamentary documents did not expressly argue that it revoked an earlier will offered for probate. However, in a number of contests observed here that involve 'conflicting wills,' they did. These causes turned on the issue of whether the will-maker effectively revoked one of his or her testamentary acts. Different promoters (or sets of promoters) offered separate testamentary acts for probate, and one or the other (or both of the parties) claimed that the deceased had revoked one of the wills. Once again the seventeenth-century 'culture of will-making' produced an alleged testamentary act which required the court to sort through last-minute transactions to determine whether a will complied with church-court practice and, after the Statute of Frauds had come into effect, Lord Chief Justice North's amendments on the proper method for the revocation of written wills.[63] In addition, both sides usually put forward reasonable claims of a lack of mental capacity and undue influence to the already complicated mix.

One cause that combined revocation, undue influence, and most of all chaos was the offer for probate of two documents, each purporting to be the last will of Clement Pragell of Stepney, who in his will was styled a gentleman. Sarah Hill, a cousin of the deceased, offered one will for probate.[64] According to an allegation submitted in support of this will, the document had been drafted on 21 April 1681 by one Bernard Underwood, a scrivener. The will was delivered to Sarah as

---

60   Ibid., PROB 24/15, 181.

61   Ibid., PROB 24/15, 177.

62   Ibid., PROB 11/351, 180.

63   See the discussion of the evolution of the Statute's provisions in Chapter 2.

64   *Hill contra Bond*, PROB 18/13/68.

executrix.[65] Anthony Bond, another cousin with whom Pragell had from time to time lodged, offered for probate a copy of an earlier will dated 16 February 1680, one that named him as executor.[66] Which will should be probated turned on whether each (or either) was a valid testamentary act and, if both were, whether the second will revoked the first.

Not surprisingly the parties differed on the issue. In his allegation, Bond charged that the will which named him executor had been validly executed, and, although he conceded that it had been destroyed, he contended that it was burnt by Hill rather than by the testator. After having destroyed this will, she then procured the 1681 will, the one that she offered for probate, by coercion after Pragell had been forcibly removed from his lodgings.[67] Thus, according to Bond, the copy of the 1680 will that he offered was Pragell's true last will, and it was revoked neither by a subsequent valid will nor by an effective cancellation pursuant to the statute.

As might be expected, Sarah Hill's version of the events varied considerably from the rendition offered by Bond. While she admitted that she had destroyed the will that Bond offered for probate, she contended that she had done so at Pragell's request. Moreover, she challenged the validity of the will that Bond offered for probate. Hill's allegation contended that it was not a valid testamentary act, because it had been procured by undue influence; she insisted that the earlier will was 'contrived' by Bond, who took advantage of Pragell, the latter being 'aged.' Indeed, Pragell, according to Hill, had shown her the will, and told her that he was 'displeased' by its contents. Pragell then gave it to her with directions to have his 'counsellor,' one Mr. Hights, draft a will which explicitly revoked the 1680 will. Precisely why he was unwilling merely to destroy it immediately was not clear, although one witness seems to have believed that he received some bad legal advice from Sarah Hill. According to Mary Baker, when Hill read the 1680 will over to him, he was 'much troubled and declared that he would make another.' Baker testified that Pragell would have thrown it into the fire, but Hill objected, advising the distressed will-maker to seek advice from 'counsell if he pleased whether or not hee might make away with it without witnesses.'[68] Perhaps she erroneously believed that it was necessary to revoke a written will in writing or else destroy it in front of witnesses. But when Mr Hights traveled to Pragell's lodgings at Wapping, Bond refused to allow him to enter. Finally, Bond relented; but when Pragell announced that he wished to alter his will, Bond 'fell into a passion,' and had the lawyer evicted

65   Ibid., PROB 18/13/55.
66   Ibid., PROB 18/13/57.
67   Ibid., PROB 18/13/57.
68   Ibid., PROB 24/20, 136.

by his servants. Another attempt to alter the will with a different 'counsellor at law,' one John Gee, was likewise thwarted by Bond. Because the 1680 will was not altered according to Pragell's wishes, Hill admitted that she destroyed it. According to her allegation, it was not until Pragell left his lodgings that he was free from the clutches of Bond, and able to write and execute a second will, the one that she offered for probate.[69]

The court admitted the will offered by Hill to probate, and denied probate to the copy of the earlier will submitted by Bond.[70] While the legal niceties meant little to Hill, whether the Bond will was revoked by Hill's cancellation or by the execution of the subsequent will cannot be discerned from the record.[71] Regardless, even though Bond lost the cause, he did not go away empty-handed; in the second will, his cousin left him a bequest of £50.[72]

Whether a previous will was revoked also figures in the probate of a document alleged to be the last will of Sir Thomas Pettus, Bart., of Sutton in Norfolk. Precisely how Sir Thomas may have generated two wills can be gleaned from documents submitted by the parties to the cause, Sir Thomas's wife, Lady Elizabeth, and his daughter (unhappily for us also named Elizabeth), and through witness depositions.[73] Imperfections in the record can be attributed to the fact that the cause brought by daughter Elizabeth was for an account from Lady Elizabeth, who had taken up administration of her husband's estate in the Prerogative Court. According to one of her many allegations submitted in this cause, daughter Elizabeth claimed that Lady Elizabeth had filed an inventory of Sir Thomas's personal property that omitted £5,000 in plate and jewelry from the calculus. According to daughter Elizabeth, Lady Elizabeth had first sought administration on the grounds that her husband had died intestate, and shortly thereafter promoted his will, first in the Common Pleas and then in Chancery, because a trust of land was also included. This will was referred to the Prerogative Court to determine its validity, and was denied probate.[74]

According to daughter Elizabeth, the will that Lady Elizabeth offered had been made about nine years prior to her father's death, and was properly denied

---

[69]   Ibid., PROB 18/13/55. Francesca Brooker, Orlando Gee, and John Johnson deposed that they had witnessed the second will (PROB 24/20, 63, 65).

[70]   Ibid., PROB 11/368, 112.

[71]   Three witnesses were called by Bond to attest to the validity of his will, so it is likely that the court did not nullify the will on the grounds of undue influence (Ibid., PROB 24/20, 161, 162, 163). Revocation is a better bet.

[72]   Ibid., PROB 11/365, 128.

[73]   Because I can find no clear evidence that a second will was actually made, I have not included the cause in the causes that involve multiple testamentary acts.

[74]   *O'Keever alias Pettus contra Pettus*, PROB 18/8/43.

probate. Her lawyer advanced a number of theories: it had been procured by undue influence, and it was drafted at the behest of Lady Elizabeth, who forged her husband's signature to the document and made alterations thereafter without his knowledge and consent. Indeed when the will was shown to 'counsell he told her it was not full enough.' Daughter Elizabeth also alleged that her father was so displeased with the will that he told her to throw it into the fire, and declared 'if she decides to exhibit it I declare that it should not stand.' Indeed shortly before his death he said that he had no will, and that someone ought to draft one that would leave his entire estate to his daughter, with the exception of land already limited to Lady Elizabeth in jointure. Preparations were made to draft such a will, but Lady Elizabeth, so daughter Elizabeth's narrative of the events run, prevented the scrivener from finishing his task.[75]

It is unclear from the surviving record whether a second testamentary act was actually completed. At the very least, daughter Elizabeth used her father's desire to execute a will in her favor to support her contention that the will Lady Elizabeth promoted had been revoked, and that she should receive no less than her intestate share, two-thirds of her father's personal estate. Lady Elizabeth denied that the will that she submitted had been revoked, and dismissed the notion that Sir Thomas had sought to revise the disposition of his estate embodied in the first will.[76] Witnesses were summoned to support the claims of each party. A key witness in the cause was Robert Lord, who, as rector of Sutton, should have been regarded as credible, at least in a church court. Lord confirmed the story that the first will was probably crafted at the insistence of Lady Elizabeth, had been executed by her rather than by him, and in any event had been ordered to be burnt by Sir Thomas. Yet he appears not to have been present at any of the crucial moments, at either the document's execution or its revocation. However, he was prepared to confirm firsthand that Sir Thomas had wished to execute a will that would leave his estate to his daughter, and one that would exclude his wife from any rights in his estate save her jointure. In this matter, Lord claimed to have assisted. He recounted the story of summoning a 'counsellor at law' from Norwich, whom he procured 'to come very private and in ordinary habite.' The disguise was to no avail as 'they had no opportunity to be alone.'[77] The rector's integrity as a witness, however, did not go unchallenged; Lady Elizabeth impugned it by contending that Lord had received 'promises of preferment' from daughter Elizabeth.[78] However, William Hart, styled a 'Citizen of Norwich,' probably had less cause to be biased, and he corroborated in nearly

---

75   Ibid., PROB 18/7/13.
76   Ibid., PROB 18/6/90.
77   Ibid., PROB 24/14, 221–2.
78   Ibid., PROB 18/7/4.

the same terms the hearsay regarding both the execution of the will promoted by Lady Elizabeth and its revocation, as well as Sir Thomas's yearning to replace it with one in favor of his daughter.[79] Which theory the court proceeded upon – that Lady Elizabeth's will was an invalid one or that the document had been revoked – cannot be demonstrated; it was, however, denied probate.[80] Some reconciliation between the two Elizabeths may have occurred, because the issue of the disputed inventory disappears from the court without further trace.

A final cause can be considered in which revocation looms large, as does its frequent companion, undue influence. John Singleton died leaving two documents each purporting to be his last will. One was offered for probate by his wife, Elizabeth,[81] and the other submitted by his nephew, Alexander Hicks, and a stranger, one Marry Meggs.[82] Elizabeth alleged that her husband had made a will nominating her executrix on 15 December 1684. Upon this Hicks and Meggs agreed. Yet they alleged that about half an hour after having made the will he asked if he could make another. According to the allegation, Singleton claimed that he had made the first will only because he was in fear of his wife. In early January, he executed the replacement will, placed it in an envelope, and gave it to one Mrs. Powers for safekeeping. While he told Powers of its contents, he asked that it be kept secret, because if his wife knew he had made another will she would 'murther him.'[83]

If the second will had indeed been duly executed, it would have revoked the first, assuming, of course, the second will could have survived a claim of undue influence lodged by his wife. Three witnesses to the second will were produced, all of whom testified to the will's due execution; Sarah Burrell, Susan Smith, and Bridget Thornton were all present at the time the will was duly executed, and they signed as witnesses. But they were earnestly implored by Singleton to keep 'it private.'[84] Likewise Mrs. Powers confirmed that he had asked her to hold the will in safekeeping, but said that she would only do so if she knew of its contents. He agreed to let her read it, and made her promise to deliver the will to his executors upon his death, that is to Hicks and Meggs, with the message that he had revoked his earlier will.[85] Moreover, William Mason, who had assisted

---

[79] Ibid., PROB 24/12, 329.

[80] Ibid., PROB 11/351, 165.

[81] *Hicks et Meggs contra Singleton*, PROB 18/18/13.

[82] Ibid., PROB 18/18/15.

[83] Ibid., PROB 18/28/15.

[84] Ibid., Or so witnesses were prepared to testify. PROB 24/25, 136 (Burrell); PROB 24/25, 138 (Smith); PROB 24/25, 138–39 (Thornton).

[85] Ibid., PROB 24/25, 139–40.

Singleton in his efforts to make the earlier will, testified that Singleton had asked him to retrieve (surreptitiously, of course) the will in his wife's possession.[86]

The court seems to have been unpersuaded that the second will was valid, and indeed was skeptical of the entire tale of the first will's revocation as presented by Meggs and Hicks. In the first place, much doubt was cast upon the integrity of the witnesses to the second will. Moreover, it was claimed that Singleton had not been present at the Halfe Moone Tavern, the venue where Hicks and Meggs claimed that the will was executed. Deponents were summoned to testify to the dishonest character of the will's witnesses,[87] and the alehouse-keeper and his wife both were doubtful about whether a will had been uttered on the premises on the day in question.[88]

Indeed the widow Elizabeth offered a credible alternative story regarding the appearance of the second will. The executors had contrived it after Singleton's death in concert with 'a fat women known as Susannah Suite.' In addition, a scrivener, one Thomas Jenkins, who wrote the second will (and a bond obligating Singleton to Meggs to boot) was also involved. These two conspirators, in concert with Meggs and Hicks, had had the will drafted, and 'put his name and seal thereto.' They had paid the witnesses to the will generously for their collusion. According to Elizabeth, they received £100, an unlikely sum, perhaps, given the value of the estate. Interestingly, however, although Elizabeth denied that the will she promoted was either forged or was the product of coercion, she was prepared to concede that her husband actually had wanted to revoke the will that she offered for probate. She contended, however, that he, like many of the will-makers we have observed, died before he was able to accomplish his goal.[89]

Conclusion

This chapter concludes our inquiry into the legal issues raised by the will litigation in the Prerogative Court of Canterbury in the later seventeenth century. In causes where multiple testamentary acts were allegedly undertaken, a number of themes that we have previously considered re-emerge, largely due to what I have called 'the culture of will-making' in late-seventeenth-century

---

[86]   Ibid., PROB 24/25, 138.

[87]   Ibid., In particular, Sarah Burrell who was reported by one witness (Joanna Lee) to have told her that she was 'to have £5 or otherwise a Gowne or Petty Coate of Silk or Shift of that value' (PROB 24/26, 312). Another witness (Dorothy Blundel) confirmed the story and called her a 'turbulent spirit' (PROB 24/26, 313).

[88]   Ibid., PROB 24/25, 325, 326.

[89]   Ibid., PROB 18/19/39.

England. Even when property-holders had planned in advance and actually had executed a will, there was a considerable amount of last-minute testamentary activity. Some property-owners waited until they were at death's door to place the finishing touches on their wills. And the law, even after the passage of the Statute of Frauds in 1677, did little to discourage them. 'Estate-planning' on the deathbed allowed others to 'importune' the dying person or at the very least placed individuals into circumstances that might give disappointed legatees a reasonable belief that overreaching had occurred.

In addition to mental-capacity and undue-influence issues, questions of compliance with formality arose. The process of making a written will was sufficiently complicated – from dictation, through redaction and due execution – to allow errors to intrude, either with respect to the content of the dispository provisions or to the requisite adherence to the recognized formalities of due execution. Exigencies of time and his or her physical condition might lead the will-maker to make an addition or amendment by word of mouth. Finally, family quarrels (a topic to be considered in detail in a subsequent chapter) figured prominently in the causes in which multiple testamentary acts emerge. After all, bickering between and amongst siblings, children, and spouses, as well as with other more distant relatives, easily set the stage for the more organized rancor in the Prerogative Court.

In these causes, as with those previously explored, the court patched together a narrative of what the judges believed had actually happened. Indeed, where an allegation of multiple testamentary acts was raised, other legal and factual wrinkles generally entered into the story. The court was obliged to give effect to the deceased's last will, so the sequence of the testamentary acts was crucial. In terms of the law, the court had to determine which acts executed by whom were sufficient to undo an existing testamentary act. The malleable rules and the controverted facts empowered the judges; it allowed them ample latitude to select to whom the property in question should pass.

PART III
Windows into Social Relationships

This monograph has thus far treated the legal issues raised in will contests in the Prerogative Court of Canterbury in the latter half of the seventeenth century. The three chapters that conclude the narrative provide evidence about some of the personal factors that prompted the litigation that I have charted: where the will-maker was allegedly married to one of the parties, and the fact of that union was in dispute; or where the will-maker had serious conflicts with family members who had been disinherited; or where women were engaged in the will-making process or became enmeshed in the litigation as heirs or executrices. In each genre of dispute, the law had a role to play.

The records produced by the testamentary litigation provide evidence about the context in which each will was drafted and then disputed, as well as the circumstances in which petitions to administer the goods of a person who died intestate were challenged. They also help explain why heirs apparent might be excluded, and other individuals substituted. The documents produced in the course of this litigation – the allegations, answers, interrogatories and depositions – focus on the life and death of the will-maker and provide us with windows, a unique vantage point, into the dynamics of family relations that often escape the historical record, but that frequently inform the otherwise enigmatic human conduct.

Chapter 8

Contested Successions and Contested Marriages: Evidence from the Records of the Prerogative Court of Canterbury

Introduction

Early modern English folk frequently selected their spouse as executors or executrices and left them substantial legacies in their wills, and the law dictated that a surviving spouse had priority in being appointed administrator or administratrix should a husband or wife die intestate.[1] Thus, in the testamentary litigation observed, whether an individual was married to the will-maker or the individual who died intestate was relevant evidence in determining if a will that was offered for probate was genuine and valid, or whether an individual who petitioned to administer an estate should be granted letters of administration.

The fact of a marriage – whether a legal union had in fact occurred – might have been a simple matter for the Prerogative Court to determine, except for the flexible marriage-formation law that obtained in England in our period. Prior to the 1753 'Act for the Better Preventing of Clandestine Marriages,' commonly referred to as Lord Hardwick's Marriage Act,[2] many English folk married 'clandestinely,' that is, not in their parish church and after the calling of banns. These 'clandestine marriages' were valid, but had often been celebrated in secret.

Historians have suggested that the practice of clandestine marriage generated wrangles over property rights.[3] And why not? The logic runs as follows: notice

---

[1]   The Statute of Distributions (23 and 24 Car. II, c. 10, sec. 3) directed that one-third of the personal estate of an individual should pass to the surviving widow and two-thirds to the children, the surviving heirs of a deceased child taking the ancestor's share by representation. If the intestate died without there being children or their representatives, one-half of the estate passed to the surviving widow and the remaining one-half to the next of kin. If the intestate had no widow, then the entire estate passed to his children and their representatives or to his next of kin.

[2]   26 Geo II, c. 33 (1753).

[3]   For a discussion of the literature, see Lloyd Bonfield, 'Developments in Family Law,' in David Kertzer and Maurizio Barbagli (eds.), *Family Life in Early Modern Times*

of such a clandestine marriage might easily escape family and friends, those who were most likely to be named executors, administrators, and legatees in the absence of a marriage; some of these disappointed individuals might be sufficiently surprised, and disconcerted, to learn that an otherwise unfamiliar person was proving a will or asserting the right to take up administration of a deceased's estate that they would contest the petition. To persuade the court that the will nominating him or her as executor or executrix was valid, or the administration petition justified, it was critical for the putative spouse to establish the fact of marriage to the satisfaction of the Prerogative Court.

This chapter commences with a historiographical outline of clandestine marriage and its implications for property transmission, and then proceeds to uncover considerable evidence from the Canterbury causes to argue that 'irregular marriage' did indeed spawn disputed inheritances.[4] This evidence highlights an ongoing theme of this book. The contemporary 'culture of will-making' and the flexible law of will validity that was fashioned by the Prerogative Court empowered its judges to create their own narrative for each individual alleged testamentary act, and to rule on the will accordingly. This untidy process of judicial scrutiny, compounded by the equally muddled one of marriage formation, is illuminated in this chapter.[5]

(New Haven, 2001), pp. 110–12.

[4]   Eight causes in the Canterbury collection were petitions to take up the administration of goods brought by a party who alleged that a marriage had been validly contracted between the promoter and an individual who died intestate, while a ninth cause raised the issue of whether the promoter's parents were married, thereby allowing her to take up intestate administration of her maternal uncle's goods: *Dudley contra Roberts* (1662), *Mynors alias Treadway per curator contra Davis* (1675), *Kyme contra Kyme* (1680), *Gibson alias Birchenhead et Morris et Birchenhead contra Woodhall alias Newstead* (1681) (the case in which proponent is not a spouse), *Baxter contra Baxter* (1690/1), *Hawkins contra Pierce* (1691), *Naylor alias Mossman contra Mossman* (1691), and *Read contra Read alias Rogers* (1696). To these 'sample' causes I can add *Golding contra Cage* (1672) which I happened upon by chance. Further, in six will contests, the question of whether a valid marriage occurred was also raised by executors/executrices and legatees: *Thornton contra Stockman* (1663), *Digby contra Digby alias Longueville* (1674), *Weedon contra Draper* (1675), *Halley contra Halley* (1676), *Wise contra Woodward* (1696). To these cases we may add *Briggs contra Briggs* (1679), also fortuitously discovered. Archival references (National Archives, London) will be given when reference is made to actual documents, and hereafter the causes will be cited by the name of the proponent.

[5]   Three of the above causes proceeded to sentence: *Digby*, *Kyme*, and *Halley*. The disputed wills were probated. In the other causes, there is no evidence that it proceeded to sentence. That a cause does not end in a judgment does not mean the converse: that a marriage was regarded as not proved. The parties may have settled outside of court. It is possible that, upon hearing the witnesses in these causes, the contestant of a will, or the opponent to an

Clandestine Marriage in Early Modern England: The Historical Context

In his study of marriage in early modern England, Brian Outhwaite noted the difficulties in establishing in precise quantitative terms the numbers of Englishmen and women who married clandestinely, that is, outside of the strict requirements for entry into marriage established by canon law, as it obtained in post-Reformation England, as to place, time, and procedure.[6] However, late-seventeenth and early-eighteenth-century marriage registers of the so-called 'peculiar jurisdictions' like the Chappel of Holy Trinity in the Minories and St. James, Duke's Palace, or the infamous Fleet Prison, and the healthy trade in licenses (which permitted marriages to be held without reference to the canonical requirements) suggest that large numbers of couples were avoiding getting married in their parish church in regular fashion, that is to say, after the calling of banns and at the times specified by canon law and during the seasons prescribed by the church.[7]

Historians are at a loss to explain precisely why so many individuals chose to marry clandestinely.[8] Dr. Outhwaite ably explored the reasons: financial (it may have been cheaper); social (the 'quality' were so doing); familial (parental objections to the match); and individual (some impediment might have existed, or the party or parties might not have wished to exhibit themselves due to some physical deformity).[9] He cautiously offered, however, no definitive conclusions

---

application to take up administration, decided to withdraw his or her opposition. Hereafter the causes will be cited by the name of the moving party instead of the full case name given above: the proponent of the will or the individual seeking to take up intestate succession.

[6] R.B. Outhwaite, *Clandestine Marriage in England* (London, 1995).

[7] E.M. Thomlinson, *A History of the Minories* (London, 1907); J.S. Burn, *The History of Parish Registers in England* (London, 1982); J.S. Burn, *The Fleet Registers* (London, 1833). For a discussion of clandestine marriage, see J. Boulton, 'Clandestine marriage in London: an examination of the neglected union variable,' *Urban History* (20) (1993), pp. 191–210, and Outhwaite, *Clandestine Marriage*, ch. 2. Clandestine marriages, of course, were also contracted outside London. See for example E.A. Wrigley, 'Clandestine Marriage in Tetbury in the late Seventeenth Century,' *Local Population Studies* (10) (1973) pp. 15–21; R.B. Outhwaite, 'Sweetapple of Fledborough and clandestine marriage in eighteenth-century Nottinghamshire,' *Transactions of the Thoroton Society for 1990*, vol. 94 (1991), pp. 35–46; and Outhwaite, *Clandestine Marriage*, pp. 22–4, 31–49.

[8] For example, Lawrence Stone stressed the desire of some to children to avoid the choices of their parents, *The Family, Sex and Marriage in England 1500–1800* (London, 1977), pp. 35, 317; while John Gillis, focusing largely upon the lower classes, adds economy and privacy as reasons to 'countering the power of patriarchy,' For Better, *For Worse: British marriages 1600 to the present* (Oxford, 1985), pp. 93–6.

[9] Outhwaite, *Clandestine Marriage*, ch. 3.

that explain recourse to clandestine marriage. Doubtless each clandestine marriage had its own justification, and some combination of the considerations here mooted may have weighed on the minds of couples who chose not to marry publicly in their parish church.

The contemporary objections to clandestine marriage, on the other hand, are easier to fathom. Aside from the fact that the ability to marry secretly might diminish parental control over choices of marriage partner, consternation was manifested for decades over the unseemly nature of clandestine marriage, and in particular, the activities of the aforementioned clandestine marriage centers.[10] The rather casual way in which such unions were created could, and did, lead to disputes over whether a couple had been legally joined. Indeed the immediate impetus for Lord Hardwicke's Act may have been a case heard in the House of Lords in the preceding year in which a marriage of 30 years' duration was challenged as invalid on the grounds that one of the parties had not been free to enter into marriage at the time of its celebration.[11] While the preamble to Lord Hardwicke's act cited 'great Mischiefs and Inconveniences' that current marriage law occasioned, it did not enumerate them. Perhaps, given clandestine marriage's ill repute, it would have been seen as a superfluous exercise to rehearse them.

One frequently asserted reason for opposition to clandestine marriages was the legal mischief that it engendered with respect to rights in property. Marriage outside the parish church, and therefore without the notoriety that accompanied it, rendered the property rights that arose out of marriage the subject of 'legal tangles.'[12] Yet, as Outhwaite noted, historians of the church courts have suggested that the quantity of litigation over the validity of marriages declined in the early modern period,[13] and few cases are offered by him, or indeed by others,[14] in which a property dispute turned on the issue of whether a person was legally married.

A number of the testamentary causes that we have observed in this study, however, do raise the fact of marriage and its validity. While the primary issue in these causes was the validity of a will or the right to take up administration of the estate of an intestate, whether the individuals concerned believed they were married, and whether that marriage was valid in the eyes of the law, could

---

[10]   Ibid., p. 94.

[11]   Outhwaite, *Clandestine Marriage*, p. 76.

[12]   Ibid., p. xvii, 87.

[13]   Ibid., pp. 41–3, citing the work of M. Ingram, *Church Court, Sex and Marriage in England, 1570–1640* (Cambridge, 1987); and R. Houlbrooke, *Church Courts and the People during the English Reformation, 1520–1570* (Oxford, 1979).

[14]   Lawrence Stone is the exception; *Uncertain Unions: marriage in England 1660–1753* (Oxford, 1992), pp. 15–16 and the cases cited therein.

be central to its disposition. From the allegations, answers, interrogatories, and depositions in these causes, crucial information that is useful to legal historians can be discerned, in particular descriptions of how marriages which gave rise to such disputes were contracted, and how issues regarding their validity were raised and proved in the Prerogative Court of Canterbury.

The Causes: The Legal Context

Nine petitions to take up administration of an intestate's goods raised the issue of marriage validity in the Canterbury causes.[15] With the exception of one cause, each involved an individual claiming to be a surviving spouse who either sought to take up administration, or had already received letters of administration, or resisted the claim of another petitioning to do so.[16] In each cause, then, the petitioner's legal right to take up administration turned on whether the couple had been lawfully married, because statute granted the surviving spouse priority over the contestant in such appointments.[17] The petition in the remaining cause was also based upon the statute; it was brought by a woman requesting letters of administration of the goods of her uncle, claiming that she was the child of his sister and his next heir.[18]

Six of the testamentary causes that raised the fact and/or the validity of marriage involved wills.[19] In four of them, an individual alleged that there had been a marriage between the proponent and the now-deceased to support his or her nomination as executor/executrix in a will being promoted,[20] and in another a marriage was alleged to justify a considerable bequest to a woman who claimed

---

[15]   See footnote 4 above.

[16]   Cases are followed by the archival reference for the initial allegation by the spouse except where noted: *Dudley* (PROB 18/1/40), *Baxter* (PROB 18/21/55), and *Hawkins* (PROB 14/21/70) (where administration had already been granted to a creditor of the deceased and the wife wished to have it revoked and granted to her), *Naylor alias Mossman* (PROB 18/21/80) (where the administration had already been granted to the wife, but no record survives, and children of the deceased sought to have it revoked), *Read* (PROB 18/24/25) and *Mynors alias Treadway per curator* (PROB 18/7/79).

[17]   21 Hen.VIII, c.5 (1529), sec. 2. See also William Nelson, *Lex Teatamentaria, or a Compendious System of all the Laws of England* (London, 1714), pp.14–17.

[18]   *Gibson*, PROB 18/14/30.

[19]   See footnote 4 above.

[20]   *Thornton*, PROB 18/1/20 (1663); *Digby*, PROB 18/7/52(1674); *Weedon*, PROB 18/7/31 (1675); and Halley, PROB 18/7/28 (1676). To these cases we may add *Briggs*, PROB 18/12/68, the case fortuitously discovered.

to be the dead man's spouse.[21] In the final testamentary cause that involved questions of marriage validity, a will was contested by a woman who alleged that she had been married to the deceased and that he had wished to make a will in her favor but had been prevented from doing so by others.[22]

Each of these six offers for probate became a will contest because the promoter of the will was bound to serve the will-maker's intestate heir or co-heirs with notice of the proceeding when the will in question was offered for probate in solemn form.[23] In each cause, the contestant denied that there had been a marriage or its validity for one or both of two interlinked reasons: first, if, as the contestant claimed, the now-deceased and the promoter were not married, why did the will-maker choose the promoter, a stranger, rather than a relative, the contestant, to serve as executor or executrix or to leave that individual a substantial bequest? Second, if the promoter was a stranger rather than a relative, as was the contestant, had the aberrant testamentary act been procured by the promoter's undue influence or had it been undertaken by an individual who lacked mental capacity to do so?

Although the logic of each the contestants' arguments might be compelling, it was not conclusive. Individuals in the past could and did disinherit heirs and choose strangers as beneficiaries in their wills of their own volition, as they do in our own times.[24] In the absence of some local custom,[25] a property-owner had the right to choose anyone – regardless of family relationship – to be a beneficiary or executor. The charge by an heir that a marriage was invalid – that promoter and the will-maker were not married – was launched only because it might be suggestive that something was amiss.

---

[21]   *Digby*, PROB 18/7/52.

[22]   *Wise*, PROB 18/24/70.

[23]   See Henry Swinburne, *A Brief Treatise of Testaments and Last Wills* (Garland Reprint of 1590 edition, 1978), pp. 223–5.

[24]   In most American jurisdictions which adhere to the system of separate marital property, the surviving spouse has a right to an 'elective share', a proportion of the deceased spouse's estate. The will leaving property to others is, however, valid; it operates on the deceased estate less the 'elective share'. J. Dukeminier, S. Johanson, J. Lindgren, and R. Sitkoff, *Wills, Trusts, and Estates*, 7th edn (New York, 2005), pp. 425–65. For England and Wales see Janet Finch, Lynn Hayes, Jennifer Mason, Judith Masson, and Lorraine Wallis, *Wills, Inheritance, and Families* (Oxford, 1996), ch. 2.

[25]   Henry Horwitz, 'Testamentary practice, family strategies, and the last phases of the custom of London, 1660–1725', *Law and History Review*, vol. 2 (1984), pp. 223–39.

The Canterbury Causes: Allegations of Marriage

In this sub-set of our testamentary causes, the petitioner's strategy would be first to allege and then to document the marriage. Some allegations of marriage were succinct. Richard Golding's petition to take up administration of his wife's estate specified that 'he did obtain consent and married in Trinity in the Minories near the Tower according to the book of Common Prayer in front of credible witnesses and in confirmation of marriage had Carnal copulation of each others body and lived together as man and wife.'[26] Similarly, the petition of Anne Hawkins to take up administration of John Hawkins's estate cited the following: date (14 March 1688/89); venue ('Chappel of the Blessed Trinity in the Minories'); fact of consummation; subsequent cohabitation; and reputation as married.[27]

Other allegations, particularly petitions to take up administration by a surviving spouse, paint a rather more complete portrait of the courtship process, the marriage, and the couple's subsequent domestic life. However, the date, venue, and even the officiating minister were usually specified. For example, according to the allegation submitted by Frances Phipps alias Kyme, she was married by one Mr. Stone, a 'minister in Holy Orders and Chaplain to the Hon. Lord Goring in the parish church of Steptney, M[i]dd[le]sex on 10 Sept 1659.'[28] But Frances's allegation offered far more detail about her marriage and indeed her domestic life. According to the allegation, Frances was given in marriage by a 'friend,' one Mr. Stokes. Further, consummation occurred on the marriage day at the house of one Mr. Cox in Trinity Lane, and this was 'true public and notorious.' The ensuing domestic arrangements were also illuminated; Frances alleged that the couple took a house in Hampton where they lived together for at least 11 years. However, and this final statement might explain the doubts in the minds of the dead man's heirs as to whether there had indeed been a legally-binding union, the couple thereafter 'repaired' to the house of her father due to Frances's illness. According to Frances, however, they were still 'reputed' to be married during their sojourn. In fact, she alleged that upon the death of her father the couple took out administration of his goods together, which was certainly suggestive that the couple were joined.[29]

Likewise, Anne Read's petition to take up administration of the goods of her husband George, a mariner, provided some details of their marriage. In addition to setting out the date and the place of their marriage, as well as details of their wedding breakfast and the place of consummation of the marriage, she alleged

---

26 *Golding*, PROB 18/4/42.
27 *Hawkins*, PROB 18/21/70.
28 *Kyme*, PROB 18/13/63.
29 Ibid.

that the couple had spent a fortnight together at her house in Newcastle, at which time George wrote his elder daughter informing her that he was married, and that his wife Anne would travel to London to reside in his 'dwelling house.'[30]

The Canterbury Causes: Proof of Marriage

Alleging marriage was one thing; proving it to the court was another. How did parties prove alleged marriages in the Prerogative Court of Canterbury?[31] Three types of evidence of the fact of marriage were produced in the causes. First, some spouses had recourse to what might be called 'official' written documentation: a marriage certificate, or all or part of a marriage register. Second, there was resort to 'non-official' documents to which a party had access, such as letters or other writings. Finally, and most frequently, marriage was proved by the parole testimony of deponents called before the court: witnesses recollecting the ceremony, recounting a variety of statements made to them, and reminiscing upon connubial occasions at which they had been present.

Marriage Registers and Certificates

First, we should examine the six causes in which 'official' documentation – the actual marriage register or a marriage certificate or copy thereof – was submitted as evidence.[32] Richard Golding, who claimed to have married Christian Lenthall at Holy Trinity in the Minories,[33] deposed one John Linn, who kept the chapel's marriage registry book. Linn, perhaps even with the relevant volume in hand, testified that he had 'checked in the book for better memory,' and discovered that the couple were indeed joined in marriage in January of 1670. His memory may well have required some rejuvenation; not only was his testimony taken more than two years after the alleged celebration, but in his deposition Linn claimed to be 74 years of age. William Clayton, who styled himself as clerk to

---

[30]   *Read*, PROB 18/24/25.

[31]   At the outset, it should be noted that the court considered itself competent to determine the fact of marriage of individuals whose wills or administrations were before it. In none of the causes does it appear that the issue of whether the deceased had in fact been married was resolved by reference to another church court in a separate proceeding.

[32]   Causes in which a will was promoted by an alleged spouse or where an alleged spouse claimed that his or her deceased spouse had died intestate and sought to take up administration of the estate.

[33]   *Golding*, PROB 18/4/42.

Linn, corroborated the latter's recollection.[34] Anne Hawkins also produced both the marriage register of Holy Trinity in the Minories and its then keeper, John Tracy, to document her marriage.[35] Finally, Ambrose Dudley had recourse to the marriage register book in a cause in which he sought to take up administration of the estate of a woman whom he asserted was his wife. In his allegation, Dudley claimed to have been married to the deceased Mary Dudley, and exhibited 'a Register booke wherein hee entered down with his owne hand the names and surnames of all persons he married' of one Mr. Payne, who according to Dudley, 'was a prebend, Dean or subdean of Chichester Cathedral.'[36]

All the same, in the last two causes the marriage register was not regarded as conclusive proof of marriage, at least to the contestants. Mary Dudley's heirs denied that she was married to Ambrose. They countered with the following: Mary Dudley had always been reputed to be a widow by the name of Johnson; she had put money out at interest in the name of Johnson; Ambrose Dudley called her by the name of Johnson; they lived apart – and perhaps the clincher – she had had him imprisoned for debt.[37] Ambrose Dudley explained the confusion by the fact that their marriage did not conform to the Interregnum ordinance that required marriages to be celebrated by Justices of the Peace. While Mary had told others that she was not married, what she meant (or at least so Dudley proffered) was that she was not married in accordance with the law at the time of the celebration. This fact explained why she was 'called by her wydows name and paid scot and lot.'[38]

In the three other causes, there was recourse to a marriage certificate in order to prove that the alleged union had indeed transpired. In her petition to take up administration of the goods of Thomas Birchenhead, Mary Woodhall alias Birchenhead alleged that she was the lawful issue of William and Elizabeth Newstead; Elizabeth was the deceased man's sister, and therefore as nearest kin his niece Mary should be granted letters of administration. Her parents' marriage certificate was produced but, as in the previous cause, the contestants were undaunted. Although only a single deposition survives, the contestants submitted a number of interrogatories questioning the marriage and the authenticity of the certificate. Witnesses were to be asked: 'Were you present when the certificate herein exhibited was taken out of the Register?', 'Were they married by license?', and 'Do you know who was the minister of the church of

---

34   Ibid., PROB 24/11, 134–5.

35   *Hawkins*, PROB 24/30. 288.

36   *Dudley*, PROB 18/1/40.

37   Ibid. These issues are surmised from the Interrogatories submitted which are filed in the archive with the Allegation.

38   Ibid.

Edmonton?' Of course, the outcome of the cause also turned on Mary's birth
date. Even if her parents had been married, the right to take up administration
under the statute turned also on her legitimacy; witnesses were asked whether
they believed that Mary's parents were married by the date of her birth.[39] To
confirm her legitimacy, Mary called three witnesses to her parents' marriage
who testified that she was born in the year following the marriage.[40] Their
recollections corroborated both the authenticity of the marriage certificate and
the allegation of date of birth supplied by Birchenhead's niece Mary. In addition
to this evidence, one of the witnesses also acknowledged that the deceased
'owned her to be his niece.'[41]

Similarly, Mary Baxter offered a marriage certificate to prove the existence of
her union with John Baxter, a fact contested vigorously by his mother, Anne.[42]
The marriage certificate was allegedly written by one Thomas Hipsley, clerk of
the 'Chappel at Knightsbridge,' who was called into court by her to authenticate
it. His testimony gives a full picture of the mechanics of producing such writings,
at least in that clandestine marriage center:

> before completeing the Ceremony of Marriage aforesaid the said Mr. Coatts
> [the minister] delivered to this Dep[onen]t the Cert[ificate] in the said ninth
> Art[icle] mencioned with a Blanck therein for the names to be inserted and
> thereupon this Dep[onen]t inserted the names of John Baxter and Mary Jacob
> in the Blanck left in the Cert[ificate] in the manner as appears and he looks at
> the s[ai]d Cert[ificate] to be wrote by Mr Coatts he having some writings as
> supposed to be his.[43]

Perhaps it was Hipsley's further testimony that emboldened the deceased
mother, Anne Baxter. Hipsley, who moonlighted as a 'joyner,' impeached his
own testimony. He was prepared to state only that he thought that the couple
had been married; although he believed he recognized Mary, he wavered in his
identification of her, and conceded that he could not recall the deceased.[44]

Finally, Anne Halley sought to probate in solemn form the will of William
Halley, whom she alleged was her husband.[45] She asserted in her allegation the fact

39   *Gibson alias Birchenhead et Morris et Birchenhead*, PROB 18/13/40.
40   Ibid., PROB 24/20, 174, 188, 203.
41   Ibid., PROB 24/20, 203.
42   *Baxter*, PROB 18/21/55.
43   Ibid., PROB 24/30, 142.
44   Ibid., PROB 24/30, 142–3.
45   *Halley*, PROB 18/8/27. Prerogative Court procedure required her to notify his heirs
in solemn form probates, in this cause his siblings; although no counter-allegation or answer

of their marriage and their subsequent cohabitation, and, in order to support the existence of her union to the now-deceased, Anne produced a document styled a 'marriage certificate' issued on 31 May 1671 at St. James, Dukes Palace. The interrogatories offered by the deceased's brothers and sisters suggested that the siblings believed that the certificate had been fraudulently obtained. Witnesses summoned by the promoter were asked if they had seen the marriage register actually being signed. But further and more telling questions were posed: 'Was there an argument between the minister who was alleged to have performed the ceremony and his clerk?' and 'Whether when the clerk was asked to write out the certificate, did an argument transpire between the minister and his clerk, and the clerk was struck when the clerk asked Mr. D if he remembered marrying them?'[46] Unfortunately, the depositions in response to the interrogatories were either never taken or else they do not survive.

Other Writings as Evidence of Marriage

These causes demonstrate that the production in court of 'official' evidence of marriage in the form of a marriage certificate or the actual marriage register was not regarded as conclusive by either party. Other writings were also submitted. After setting out the date and place of marriage, and the fact of consummation, Mary Baxter explained the need for her recourse to a clandestine marriage with John Baxter: it was kept secret in order for her husband to maintain his position as servant to a barrister.[47] In addition to her marriage certificate, Mary Baxter exhibited letters written to her both before and after the marriage by her alleged husband.[48]

Although formal documentation was not present in an action to take up administration of the goods of George Read, a mariner who had died at sea, by a woman who alleged that she had been married to the deceased, another document was instead submitted.[49] Anne Read claimed that she had been married to George Read in a 'Chappel of the Church of England.' According to her allegation, they were 'treated' at a wedding dinner, after which the marriage was consummated at her house. Thereafter, he remained at her house for a fortnight, during which time he was said to have written to his daughter informing her of the marriage, and forewarning his children that his wife was

---

survives, they probably entered an objection, because a second allegation was subsequently submitted, and they submitted interrogatories.

[46]   Ibid., Interrogatories.

[47]   *Baxter*, PROB 18/21/55.

[48]   Or so the abovementioned allegation stipulates.

[49]   PROB 18/24/25.

coming to London. This she did and, according to her allegation, the children brought her to Read's house in London 'and treated her with respect as their mother.' Now to the writing produced: she had a 'letter of attorney' which purported to empower her to take control of his goods while at sea.[50]

In addition to the testimony of witnesses present at the marriage, this cause certainly produced the most interesting form of documentation of a marriage, albeit not in writing. Allan Brought, George Read's friend and fellow seaman on the *Albemarle*, testified that 'upon his owning to the s[ai]d marriage a Garland was put upon the Maine top mast stay of the s[ai]d Trader as is usual when a seaman belonging to a shipper is married.'[51]

The Testimony of Witnesses

In most of the causes, however, written documentation was not offered, and, as we have seen, even in causes in which marriage certificates were proffered opposing parties were quick to contradict physical evidence by allegation. The most common way to prove their contention expressed therein was through witnesses. In both the Baxter and Read causes just discussed, each side called witnesses to support their position. In opposing Mary Baxter's petition to administer the estate of her alleged husband, his mother, Anne Baxter, argued that it was not possible for the couple to have been joined in marriage at the time alleged. According to Anne Baxter, her son John was a servant to a barrister, one Mr. Tufton, and at the time Mary alleged that their union was celebrated at St. Martin in the Fields, Baxter 'did attend on him from his house in Red Lyon Fields and his chambers in the Temple.' Thereafter, Anne claimed that John accompanied Tufton to Staffordshire, and that when John returned to London, he 'never left his house until his death.' Moreover, according to Anne Baxter, her son, subsequent to the alleged date of the marriage, 'courted several women,' 'declared himself a bachelor,' and 'never owned her [Mary] as his wife.'[52]

A number of deponents corroborated Baxter's mother's contentions. While conceding that Mary came to see Baxter on the day he died, Deborah Tawse, one of Tufton's domestic servants, deposed that she never heard them 'acknowledge each other as man and wife.' Furthermore, according to her deposition, Mary called Baxter 'brother,' though Tawse also stated that he had never previously mentioned a sister.[53] Two other domestic servants, Sarah Mosely and Christopher

---

[50]   Ibid. Seamen routinely executed such letters which empowered the holder of the power of attorney to collect debts, especially wages due, in the event of their death at sea.

[51]   Ibid., PROB 24/36, 39.

[52]   *Baxter*, PROB 18/12/45.

[53]   Ibid., PROB 24/30, 59.

Graunt, confirmed Deborah's evidence of a sibling relationship, though both testified that they heard him call her sister, and not the reverse.[54] However, a fourth domestic servant, William Latnor, seemed to disagree. He testified that it was 'publickally discoursed he the s[ai]d B[axter] did Court the s[ai]d Mrs. Howard and this Dep[onen]t. observed and understood that he did court her.'[55]

Not surprisingly, Mary could count on the testimony of her family. Her uncle, William Jacobs, deposed that Baxter had asked him for consent to marry her, that he had been present at the marriage ceremony, and that he had advised her to take up administration as widow. He confirmed the reason for secrecy, that Baxter would lose his position with the barrister. Moreover, he testified that he knew Baxter 'from childhood,' and attested that the letters submitted by Mary were in the 'hand of John Baxter.'[56] His wife, Sabilla, confirmed his testimony, adding that the night after their marriage the couple 'lay naked in bed together at the house of this Dep[onen]t.'[57] And there was Mary's brother Robert: he 'observed him [Baxter] to court [Mary],' and saw them 'undressed in bed.'[58] To this intimate portrait of cohabitation, Susan Jacobs, Mary's sister, added that she had 'heard him [Baxter] say he would never have or never marry with any other person.'[59] In addition to relatives, Mary had recourse to a less interested witness. Another Sabilla, the widow Sabilla Carew (who appears to be unrelated to the parties but claimed she knew the deceased 'since she can remember') testified to knowing of 'meetings and treatys concerning a marriage,' that Baxter had 'courted' Mary, and that she 'followed next after the Corps of the s[ai]d Dec[eased] as his widow and Relict.'[60]

Witness statements likewise figure prominently in Anne Read's petition to probate her alleged husband's will. In her interrogatories, Read's daughters questioned the regularity of the marriage and, in particular, whether the minister was in 'clerical habit.'[61] They also raised the question of whether her father had been drunk at the time of the marriage. Read was able, however, to produce two deponents present at the ceremony. One, Anne Forster, testified to a modest level of acquaintance with the woman who called upon her to depose; she admitted that she had known Anne Read for a scant six weeks prior to the marriage. Yet she was able to clear the air, or at least so it would seem, regarding the regularity

---

54   Ibid., PROB 24/30, 60–61.
55   Ibid., PROB 24/30, 62.
56   Ibid., PROB 24/30, 143–4.
57   Ibid., PROB 24/30, 148.
58   Ibid., PROB 24/30, 152–3.
59   Ibid., PROB 24/30, 151–2.
60   Ibid., PROB 24/30, 145–6.
61   Ibid., PROB 18/24/25.

of the ceremony, a point raised by George's daughters in their interrogatories. She testified that she was present at the wedding, at which George Read was 'very sober,' the minister was in 'clerical habit,' and 'a ring [was] used and all things usual at marriages' were present. Another 'thing usual' reported by deponents after a marriage (as subsequently discussed cases will reveal) seems to have been consummation: Anne Forster deposed that after the marriage she returned to Anne Read's house, and 'saw her undress herself ready to go to bed but this Dep[onen]t did not see her in bed.'[62] A second witness, Mary Baxter, was able to testify that she had known William Ladler, the clergyman present, for 15 years and that 'he was reputed to be a minister.' In fact she swore that she had seen him 'marry several persons according to the Book of Common Prayer.' Perhaps her testimony was tinged with self-interest, because one of those whom he was alleged to have married was Mary herself![63]

Similarly, Anne Hawkins also called upon witnesses to corroborate her reference to the marriage register when contestants denied the fact of her marriage to John Hawkins. One Jane Hitchcock deposed that about two years prior to her testimony the couple had come to her house 'newly married' and asked for lodging. They shared a furnished room for 'three or foure months ... after which he went to sea and died at sea.'[64] In addition, they 'owned each other' as husband and wife. Two other witnesses confirmed her testimony.[65]

Testimony of witnesses who were present during courtship, marriage, and married life was particularly critical in causes in which there was no documentary evidence of marriage available. When Elizabeth Stockman offered to probate the nuncupative will of Sarah Shelhorne, one Mr. Thornton (Christian name not given) claimed that the will was invalid, and that as Sarah's husband he should take up administration of her estate. Stockman alleged that there was an agreement between the two women, Sarah and Susan, that if Susan survived Sarah, Susan, and not Thornton, would receive her estate. That arrangement, she alleged, was confirmed on 24 September 1662 when one George Styles came to visit. According to the allegation, Styles asked Shelhorne if she had made her will. When she replied that she had not, she orally confirmed the agreement in the following terms:

> There was an agreement between me and my mistress [meaning Elizabeth Stockman] with whom I live since my estate was given to me by her she should have it returned if she survives me but if I outlive her then I was free to dispose.

---

62 *Read*, PROB 24/36, 40.
63 Ibid., PROB 24/36, 39.
64 *Hawkins*, PROB 24/30, 279.
65 Ibid., PROB 24/30, 279, 288.

So there will be no mistake I declare it my will that all my est[ate] save my clothes
I [have already]'disposed of to E[lizabeth] S[tockman]. I name her ex[ecu]trix.[66]

While no witnesses were called to attest to the words, or at least, no depositions
confirming the concord survive, two men, Charles Stenton and Charles Croare,
testified that Sarah and Thornton had indeed been married 'by the form of
the book of Common Prayer' by a 'minister dressed in a [clerical] habit.'[67] The
testimony reveals a discrepancy in dates: while the alleged nuncupative will was
said to have been uttered in 1662, the deponents testified that the marriage did
not occur until November of 1664.

Likewise, the only evidence offered to substantiate the allegation of marriage
in the administration of the estate of Thomas Mossman was oral testimony. The
guardian of Thomas's children petitioned to revoke an administration granted
to a woman styled Mary Mossman, who claimed to have been the now-deceased
man's wife.[68] According to the guardian's allegation, the proponent, if married to
Mossman, was a bigamist: Mary Mossman was actually Mrs. Naylor, the wife of
one J. Naylor (full Christian name not given), and this couple had lived together
as man and wife in Horwood in Buckinghamshire until 1682. Although she had
left her husband and had come to London by 1684, the guardian claimed that
after 1685 she cohabited with Mossman, even though her husband was still living
until 1687. According to the guardian, however, Mary was merely employed by
Mossman as a housekeeper and only pretended to be his wife; while he admitted
the same privately, he publicly represented her as his wife to save her reputation
(and perhaps his own as well!).

Fortunately, depositions in this cause survive, and not surprisingly, the
witnesses summoned by the opposing parties disagreed as to the fact of marriage.
One Rebecca Davis claimed to have been present at a marriage ceremony
between Mary and Thomas. While she did not address the issue of a previous
marriage, she testified that the couple 'did live and cohabit together as man
and wife,' although she conceded that she 'hath knowne the Dec[ease]d and
the Producent to have some fallings out, but never heard the Dec[ease]d say he
was not married to her.'[69] Rebecca described the wedding that occurred at 'St.
James House' with some specificity. The marriage took place in a 'large room,'
conducted by 'a gentleman in a black habit,' who 'read the formes of matrimony
to them.' She was later told that the 'gentleman' was a 'Romanish priest' (she
believed that Mary was a Roman Catholic) who 'ordered' Thomas:

---

66   *Thornton*, PROB 18/1/20.
67   *Thornton*, PROB 24/6, 406–7. The error might be one of transcription.
68   *Naylor alias Mossman*, PROB 18/18/80.
69   Ibid., PROB 24/30, 166–7.

To putt the Ring on the fourth finger of the s[ai]d Mary's left hand and to give her a piece of silver which hee accordingly did and holding the s[ai]d Mary by the hand on w[hi]ch the s[ai]d Ring was and in which she had the piece of silver hee the s[ai]d dec[eased] did repeat after the s[ai]d priest these words viz. With this Ringe and Silver I thee wed.

Four other witnesses – Thomas Stockman (who testified that he had known Thomas Mossman for over twenty years), Obadia Warwick, Catherine Spackman, and Martha Calthrup – all recalled 'fallings out' between the couple, but had rather a different view on the issue of whether there was a valid marriage. In the first place, while none of the witnesses mentioned Mary's alleged pre-existing marriage, all four agreed that Thomas never held himself out as married to Mary.[70] But Martha qualified her statement; Thomas had claimed that he was not married by the 'lawfull church of England,' but that 'he was drawne in to take her into his house by her popish crew and that their Ceremonies of their Wax Candle signified nothing,' and that he could 'lawfully turn her away w[hi]ch he would because she was not his lawful wife.'[71]

Bigamy was also alleged, but then summarily disappeared from the record, in a second cause in our collection of Canterbury causes.[72] Again, the only evidence of marriage was provided by witnesses. Mary Briggs sought to probate the will of Richard Briggs, whom she alleged was her husband of at least 18 years, and asked to have letters of administration that were issued to one Anne Briggs alias Fox revoked.[73] It is likely that Anne took up the administration of Richard's estate by claiming that she was his spouse. In her interrogatories, Anne asked witnesses the following questions: 'Whether they were present at the marriage of Richard and Mary?' 'Whether Richard had formerly been married to one Sherman?' (a serial bigamist or had she died?); and finally, 'Whether prior to his 'cohabitation' with Mary Briggs, was he not married to Anne?' She also queried the witnesses as to whether Mary was 'formerly going by the name of Mollie and a common strumpet?'[74] The only witnesses who were deposed, Thomas and Jane Ingle, who were also witnesses to the will, did not respond to the litany of questions, but merely testified that the couple (Mary and Richard) were taken to be man and

---

70   Ibid., PROB 24/30, 186–93.

71   Ibid., PROB 24/30, 193.

72   Another cause in which bigamy appears involved the probate of Thomas Day's will by his wife Dorothea (*Day contra Day*, PROB 18/3/37). After five years of marriage, Thomas was alleged to have moved from London to Devon and married Honor Pollard, by 'a minister in Holy Orders,' though it is not certain whether the union was clandestine.

73   *Briggs*, PROB 18/12/68.

74   Ibid. Interrogatories.

wife. They also confirmed Mary's allegation that Briggs had received £500 that had been left to Mary as a legacy by her brother, one Captain Winters, a tidy sum which if it had been collected by Briggs and remained in his hands would have made pursuing the litigation decidedly worthwhile.[75]

As in Anne Read's cause, there was also conflict between the deceased's children and the proffered step-parent in litigation over the estate of Joseph Kyme. Mary Kyme, Joseph's daughter, sought to have a will that she alleged her father had executed probated in solemn form.[76] One Frances Phipps alias Kyme, who claimed that she had been married to the deceased, had already taken up administration of Joseph's goods in the Commissary Court of the Bishop of London, or so testified James Ellis, the clerk of the court, upon examination in court of a copy of the letters of administration.[77] In her allegation, Frances specified the name of the minister, and also the place where the marriage was consummated. To bolster further her assertion of marriage, she noted that the couple had lived together in her father's house, and that they had served together as co-executors of her father's estate.[78] In a subsequent allegation, Frances attempted to discredit witnesses to the 'scroll' that Joseph was said to have executed, and denied that she was acquainted with one Sergeant Burton, to whom (according to Mary Kyme) a letter alleged to be the last will of the deceased had been sent.[79] For her part, in her interrogatories which were filed with Frances Kyme's initial allegation, Mary questioned the witnesses to the ceremony, and asked whether they had ever heard Joseph Kyme declare that he was married.[80]

Testimony of Consummation

Although the consummation of a marriage was not required for a marriage to be legally valid, regardless of whether the union was clandestine or otherwise, James Brundage has noted that in Western Christendom, even as late as the Reformation, popular belief and learned clerical commentary generally considered it essential for marriages to be binding.[81] Our causes suggest that it was ensconced in popular culture in late-seventeenth-century England.

---

[75] Ibid., PROB 24/19, 66–7.

[76] *Kyme*, PROB 18/13/58.

[77] Ibid., PROB 24/20, 78.

[78] Ibid., PROB 18/13/63.

[79] Ibid., PROB 18/13/20.

[80] Ibid., PROB 18/13/58.

[81] James Brundage, *Law, Sex, and Christian Society in Medieval Europe* (Chicago, 1987), pp. 502–5.

Consummation was almost invariably noted by spouses in their allegations,[82] and even when it was not witnesses, as we shall see, made frequent reference to consummation and sexual relationships between those alleged to be married, suggesting that in even in learned circles, within the church courts, witness substantiation of sexual relations was also some evidence of marriage.

Two of the causes address consummation most directly. One J. Davis (full Christian name not given) sought to take up administration of his alleged wife Mary's estate.[83] To support their own claim to take up administration, the contestants, the dead woman's two sisters and heirs, disputed the fact of marriage and therefore a grant of administration to Davis, denying that the union had been contracted or solemnized on the days proffered by the proponent.[84] According to the contestants, the now-deceased was 'a diseased person who was confined to her chamber.' Further, they asserted that Davis paid for neither Mary's doctors nor her funeral, and that she was buried under the name of Treadway and not Davis. Finally, it was alleged that she was 13 years old at her death, and under the tutelage of her aunt, who had not consented to any union.

In his allegation, Davis contended that in May, June, and July of 1673, the couple 'being free from all marital Contracts did treat together concerning a marriage to be had and contracted between them.' Further, Davis maintained that a contract was entered into in early August, and that the marriage was solemnized at St. James, Duke's Palace on the 12 August. But Davis went further:

> in consummation ... [they] did lodge together in one and the same bed *solus cum sola et nudus cum nuda* and had the Carnal Knowledge of each others body ... several times but at least once on 12 August 1673.[85]

Mary's sisters, concerned that intercourse might weaken their contention that the couple had not been joined in marriage, asked witnesses that if they deposed of 'carnal knowledge ... how they might come to know it?'[86]

---

[82]   In addition to the two causes discussed below, consummation was alleged in: *Golding* (PROB 18/4/42), *Hawkins* (PROB 18/21/70), *Kyme* (PROB 18/13/63), *Read* (PROB 18/25/75), and *Baxter* (PROB 18/21/55).

[83]   *Mynors alias Treadway per curator*, PROB 18/5/116.

[84]   Ibid., PROB 18/7/79.

[85]   Ibid, PROB 18/5/116.

[86]   Ibid., Interrogatories. See also her allegation files, PROB 18/7/79. Other questions posed to the witnesses in the cause were directed toward the particulars of the ceremony of marriage rather than to its consummation. Was the minister in holy orders? Did you see the license? Were banns spoken? In addition, the contestant asked if the deponent knew that the

Likewise, consummation was alleged to support the existence of a valid marriage when Bernard Weedon attempted to probate the nuncupative will of his wife Jane.[87] In an answer to the allegations filed, the validity of the will was contested by the guardian of William Draper, Jane's minor son by a previous marriage.[88] Indeed William had reason to object to the will, because he received no bequest therein. According to Weedon's allegation, Jane had specifically intended to disinherit him because she believed 'he hath enough estate already.'[89] In his interrogatories, Draper asked witnesses a number of the usual questions that raised the issue of whether the parties were in fact married: how long did they live together; did he call her 'wife' or Mrs. Draper, and she, 'husband'; when did you hear them declare that they were married; did they not 'lie together' after the date of the marriage?[90]

There may have been a reason for this marriage to be celebrated and kept secret. According to John Applebee, a deponent, Bernard and Jane were indeed married; he testified that Bernard 'did rule and govern the s[ai]d Jane's house as Master thereof.' The reason for the secrecy was that Jane was heavily in debt, and 'he did not want his estate to be charged for it.'[91] Another deponent, Barbara Clark, testified that Jane had told her that she was married to Bernard, but kept it under wraps due to her indebtedness. While they may have concealed their marriage, they did little to cover their bodies. Clark also testified that Jane asked her to place another pillow on her bed for Bernard, and 'the said Jane and Bernard went into bed naked together while this Dep[onent] was in ye Roome.'[92] Another witness, one Richard Clarke, a servant (though it is not clear to whom) also saw them naked in bed together.[93]

---

young woman was under a guardianship, and if the guardians had consented 'or was it done privately so that they might not know.'

[87]   *Weedon*, PROB 18/7/31.

[88]   Ibid., PROB 25/2/124.

[89]   Ibid., PROB 18/7/31.

[90]   Ibid., PROB 18/7/30.

[91]   Ibid., PROB 24/14, 399.

[92]   Ibid., PROB 24/14, 347.

[93]   Ibid., PROB 24/14, 349. Clark also testified that he believed that the Weedons were married by a 'Romanish priest.' He deposed that he had observed a ceremony through a window. Although he could not make the parties out with certainty, he did hear words spoken, hands joined, and either the priest or Bernard was kneeling. The alleged priest may have been either George Bease alias Lason or Mr. James Ayres. Both were described as 'tailors' by one Lawrence Smith, who deposed that they were regarded as priests although he never saw either 'perform office of a priest' (PROB 24/14, 347).

In his answer, William's guardian, William Gannock, responded that he had spoken of the matter with Jane, and she had denied that she was married.[94] According to him, although there was 'friendship' between the two, there was also 'formality.' Actually, he seems to have been one of the few witnesses who did not have a glimpse of them in bed together; he deposed that:

> in case there was any Copulation between them (of which this Respondent knoweth nothing) the same (if any such were the same being Clandestine and Concealed from this Respondent) he believeth it to be illegal as he hopeth he may be able to proove.

Whether in fact he was able to do so remains uncertain, because the case did not proceed to sentence. The failure of the will to be probated was probably a victory for the ward to whom his mother's estate would descend by intestacy.

The Court's Dilemma: Sorting Fact from Fancy

Thus while not conclusive of marriage, consummation must have been one type of evidence that the court considered in trying to determine whether a couple was married. The probate of the will of Joseph Digby illustrates the dilemma that the court confronted in causes that involved disputes over a marriage: making sense out of inconsistent allegations and contradictory depositions. One Mary Digby alias Longueville, along with Nicholas Hollis, offered for probate a document purporting to be the will of Joseph Digby.[95] The will was allegedly executed on 18 August; Digby died on 3 September.

Probate of the will was opposed by George Digby, the testator's great-uncle, on the grounds of undue influence and lack of testamentary capacity. But the central issue was the marriage: were Joseph and Mary husband and wife? In a lengthy allegation, Digby denied that his great-nephew had in fact married.[96] To support his position, he noted the following: Digby had avoided her company; in correspondence he referred to her as Mrs. Longueville; she was not called, 'Mistress,' by the servants 'nor did she pay them wages therein'; and she brought an action against her brother for her portion in the name of Longueville. In fact, the last matter, an unpaid marriage portion, might have been the primary point of contention between herself and the now-deceased and his relatives. According to the contestant, Mary was told by one Mrs. Nicholas Hollis (presumably the

---

94   Ibid., PROB 25/2/124.
95   *Digby*, PROB 18/7/52.
96   Ibid., PROB 18/7/44.

co-promoter's wife) that since Digby had now recovered her portion she could be called Mrs. Digby. But her great-uncle George Digby alleged that she had confided in Mrs. Hollis that they were not married; in fact it was suggested that Mary was 'melancholy' over the matter, and Hollis had pressed Digby to marry her.

The reason for Mary Digby alias Longueville's anxiety with regard to a union may well have been the fact that Joseph Digby was the father of her two children. It was perhaps for that reason that it was not necessary for her to allege consummation. This fact Digby's great-uncle strenuously denied; the two girls who were named in the 'scroll' offered by the proponents were 'brought to Bed... in London,' and were not baptized in the name of Digby.[97] No marriage certificate was produced by the proponents, so the court had only the allegations of the interested parties and the testimony of the witnesses upon which to rely. In her answer to the allegation of Great-Uncle George, Mary Digby alias Longueville denied charges of undue influence. With respect to the girls, she explained that the now-deceased had paid for his daughters' nurse, but wished to keep the fact of their birth private. She further alleged that he had indeed publicly acknowledged their marriage.[98]

Whether the two were married seemed unclear to a number of deponents. William Collingridge, a husbandman who had witnessed the will, testified that he had never heard the will-maker declare himself to be married, and he could not be certain that Joseph and Mary were husband and wife.[99] With respect to the two girls, he had heard the deceased talk about them, but never saw them reside together or recalled them visiting the house. The other witness to the will, William Fontaine, a yeoman, was likewise uncertain as to the marital state of the duo, though he knew that Mary had gone by the name Longueville.[100] Yet both witnesses were aware of the dispute with her brother over her portion. Indeed another witness, John Harbert, a servant, deposed that the promoter had told him that the reason that she did not marry was that she would have to start the legal proceedings over her portion again in the name of her husband.[101]

The question of whether the promoter of the will had charge of the alleged deceased spouse's affairs, and therefore might more likely be married to him, was addressed by Nicholas Hollis, who was named executor in the disputed will.[102] He did concede that Mary had 'command of the house and keys,' and that she

---

[97]　Ibid.
[98]　Ibid., PROB 25/2/108.
[99]　Ibid., PROB 24/14, 371.
[100]　Ibid., PROB 24/14, 372.
[101]　Ibid., PROB 24/14, 375.
[102]　Ibid., PROB 24/2, 87.

'sat at the table as Mrs of the family.' Although Digby at times called her Mrs. Longueville, he did so only because of the law suit.

The cause did proceed to judgment; like the wills in the causes of Kyme and Halley, the will was admitted to probate.[103] These sentences suggest that the court likely considered the alleged marriages valid. None of the other causes discussed here proceeded to sentence. That a cause does not end in a judgment does not mean the converse: that a marriage was regarded as not proved. The parties may have settled outside of court. It is possible that, upon hearing the witnesses in these causes, the contestant of a will, or the opponent to an application to take up administration, decided to withdraw his or her opposition.

Conclusion

The marriages of those embroiled in this probate litigation were 'clandestine,' supporting the view of both contemporaries and of modern historians, that such unions did indeed give rise to disputes over property. People entered into such marriages for a variety of reasons. While it is not possible to gauge the frequency of the disputes that arose with quantitative precision, a fair number have been exhumed, and the fact that even the rather humble – a seaman's wife for example – were prepared to petition the court to take up an administration on the basis of a clandestine marriage (and for relatives to resist it) suggests that controversy was not uncommon. Given the number of probate jurisdictions that existed in England before the reforms of the nineteenth century, this inquiry may have only touched the tip of a litigation iceberg.

The causes I have surveyed highlight the ways in which litigants in the court attempted to prove the fact of marriage. These disputes differed from spousals' litigation, causes to enforce a marriage or contract to marry, in that one party to the marriage was dead, and it is therefore not surprising that the methods used to prove a marriage might differ in form. The ways in which the causes are presented is certainly suggestive of what was regarded as relevant evidence that a valid marriage had been celebrated. The evidence – documentary, written, and oral – that litigants presented, and that presumably the court was prepared to consider, varied. Marriage certificates and actual register books were hauled into court and offered by individuals who claimed to be married as evidence of a union, but they seem not to have been regarded (at least by their opponents) as conclusive of marriage validity. Reference was also made by litigants to letters

---

[103]   Ibid., The sentence is PROB 11/351, 220. I could, however, find no copy of the will.

and other writings. And oral testimony, often hearsay, abounded. Amongst the most widely proffered kinds of 'impressionistic' evidence was that of reputation and consummation. Consummation and reputation continued to matter to the law as proof of marriage, if not in the law of marriage itself.

The causes discussed in this chapter confirm the contention elaborated in previous chapters about the process of decision-making in the Prerogative Court. Once again the judges were required to construct a narrative, that of a marriage, from the evidence produced. That narrative assisted them in determining (at least in part) to whom the property in question should pass. Like a flexible law of will execution and revocation, the malleable law of marriage-formation empowered the judges to follow their consciences and their predispositions in guiding them to a decision on succession to property.

Chapter 9

Discord and Disinheritance:
Windows into Family Relations from
Testamentary Litigation

Introduction

The execution of a will was a crucial moment in the process of property transmission between generations in past time. In a will, early modern English folk could apportion their property amongst kin and friends, considering first and foremost the surviving members of their nuclear family. Yet the will-maker could, absent local custom limiting freedom of disposition, disinherit the lot and select another beneficiary; our wills provide examples that both ungenerous bequests to heirs and their total disinheritance occurred. Of course, the disappointed spouse or heir could challenge the offending will, and if successful claim his or her intestate share of the deceased ancestor's estate. The testamentary causes indicate that they did do so. Then, as now, what greater incentive could there be to contest a will than frustration on being excluded from a legacy or disappointment over the value of one actually made?

The testamentary causes observed in the Canterbury records illustrate that one frequent explanation for meager bequests to or disinheritance of close kin was a breakdown in rapport between will-maker and his or her heir or spouse. While the wills themselves often explain the factors that led to a paltry legacy or complete disinheritance, the testamentary litigation that ungenerous wills engendered provides a much more detailed glimpse into the motives, assisting the historian in understanding the reasons for meager bequests to close family members. Unlike the will left by the deceased, the allegations, interrogatories, and depositions allow others to speak: both legatees and disappointed heirs (and their witnesses) could report on conduct that might explain the will's contents.

The 'facts' offered in the court documents were ammunition in a legal battle, so I can make no argument that the stories of family relations and their breakdowns actually occurred as related. Indeed, as one might expect, the other side – the contestants of these wills – vigorously challenged most of the contentions of discord offered by will proponents. Yet even if the parties and their witnesses embellished their accounts, the stories related must at least have been regarded as plausible by those who offered them up to the court; litigants relating these often time grim family histories were, after all, aiming to persuade a judge that what was related had actually transpired.

These causes, which focused on family discord and disinheritance, also shed light on an issue that has vexed historians for some time: the level of violence that obtained in pre-modern England. In early modern English society, where life was (at least as argued by Thomas Hobbes) 'nasty, brutish, and short,' historians might expect to find levels of intra-familial discord and, in particular, violence that at the very least would rival our own.[1] Recent research considers the issue of spousal violence. Elizabeth Foyster has uncovered more examples of physical abuse in an examination of separation cases than have others who have focused largely on criminal records,[2] but she concludes that 'threats not blows' were what were more commonly hurled at spouses and other family members.[3] She has invited historians to discard their limited concept of marital violence as exclusively made up of physical abuse, and to broaden its definition to include 'verbal cruelty' and economic deprivation. Using a wider range of sources, Joanne Bailey concurs: by the beginning of the eighteenth century, wife-beating was no longer regarded as acceptable 'correction,' and was considered a form of madness. But even by the late seventeenth century, the quarter sessions records in Oxfordshire and North Yorkshire that Bailey studied reveal only a couple of cases of physical violence against spouses per decade.[4]

It will be argued here that while family discord, particularly among spouses, is documented in a significant number of our testamentary disputes, and helps to explain some meager bequests or disinheritances, these causes similarly provide scant evidence of physical violence between family members. Indeed a lone case can be offered, the improbable case of a mother on her deathbed

---

[1]   Alan Macfarlane (*The Justice and the Mare's Ale: law and disorder in seventeenth century England* (Oxford, 1981) challenged Lawrence Stone's (*The Family, Sex and Marriage in England 1500–1800* (London, 1977)) paraphrase of Thomas Hobbes' *Leviathan*, p. 231. See Introduction footnote 33.

[2]   Or so one would conclude from the work of James Sharpe, 'Domestic homicide in early modern England,' *Historical Journal,* vol. 24 (1981), p. 31; Peter King, Punishing assault: the transformation of attitudes in the English courts,' *Journal of Interdisciplinary History*, vol. 27 (1996) p. 54; and C. Emsley, *Crime in England, 1750–1900* (Harlow, 1996), pp. 44–6, which is cited in Elizabeth Foyster, *Marital Violence: an English family history* (Cambridge, 2005), p. 23.

[3]   Foyster, *Marital Violence*, p. 30.

[4]   Joanne Bailey, *Unquiet Lives: marriage and marriage breakdown in England, 1660–1800* (Cambridge, 2003), pp. 120–22; 195–202; 125–7.

attacking her adult son.[5] Without doubt, our forebears ranted and raved verbally against their family members (oft times quite poetically), and they believed that enmity justified disinheritance. But in that time of nasty, brutish, and short lives, if will-maker and kin did strike each other, litigants in will contests were not prepared to allege it, even if either side was an 'innocent' victim. Likewise, their witnesses did not report much violence, only threats: words rather than deeds were unleashed. While it is difficult to argue a negative, that the lack of mention proves the absence of violence, it is nevertheless telling that people who were prepared to recount vivid tales of verbal abuse were unwilling to report physical altercations, if they had witnessed such conduct.

The Contexts of the Disputes

Evidence of disinheritance of kin due to family discord emerges from both sides in probate disputes. The typical scenario is as follows. A will is offered for probate. A disappointed family member decides to contest it. Through either an answer or a counter-allegation submitted, the contestant depicts a sense of familial harmony that would render disinheritance inconceivable *if* the will-maker had been of sound mind or free from undue influence. Interrogatories are submitted to witnesses who were aware of family intimacies, and depositions are taken to support the claim of either concord or coercion. The will's promoter, on the other hand, responds by justifying the will's pattern of disposition in an allegation relating the disaffection with the disappointed contestant that accounts for either exclusion from a will or an ungenerous bequest. To substantiate the contention, the promoter might also produce witnesses whose response in depositions to questions posed through interrogatories confirms the alleged family discord. Thus a narrative about the nature and quality of familial relations, whether depicted as being in concord or in conflict, was a useful weapon in the arsenal of probate litigants on either side of a will contest.

One approach to categorizing the family discord that emerges from the Canterbury records is by reference to its participants. Because the descendants of the nuclear family had priority in intestate succession, and therefore probably had expectations of substantial bequests, disputes between parents and their children and stepchildren will be considered first, followed by tiffs between spouses. Thereafter, the discussion moves to siblings, because in the absence of surviving members of a nuclear family, siblings and their descendants would benefit through intestate succession. These groupings are not mutually exclusive:

---

[5]   Even in the lone case (*Rawlinson contra Stephens*) the physical violence has to be surmised. One witness claimed that the testatrix attacked her son when he took away her pewter (PROB 24/15, 161).

for example, spousal conflict might arise from dissension between step-parent and stepchild; children might object to one parent's treatment of their other parent; and more distant relatives might join in a fray between spouses or between parents and their children. Then as now, family discord knows no predictable bounds: each individual enmeshed in this litigation believed that he or she had a moral claim on the will-maker's bounty, and in each cause there was disappointment over the contents of a will.

Parent–Child Disputes

Proponents of wills generally blamed parental disinheritance of children upon disobedience and distrust. 'Undutiful' seems have been the preferred catchword used in the allegations to characterize parental displeasure with a child's conduct. Accordingly, in her allegation in support of her offer for probate of her husband's will and codicil, Elizabeth Hodgekinson stated that Richard had disinherited his son Thomas because he was 'undutiful' and had 'disobliged' him.[6] The scrivener of the will had testified that the testator asked him to draft a will to protect his wife from his 'undutiful' son who would 'disturb' his wife after his death.[7] While none of the three witnesses whose depositions survive related specific instances, all three agreed that they had heard the testator describe Thomas as 'undutiful.'[8] Thomas begged to differ; in his interrogatories, he asked witnesses if they 'did ever see signs of disrespect' between the two.[9] Similarly, the will of Bartholomew Canham referred to his son Thomas as 'undutiful.' Canham probably objected to Thomas's exploits in Barbados, because the will conditioned a bequest of land to him on his returning to England.[10] Likewise, in their offer to probate the will of Thomas Pitt, two of the three executors alleged that the will-maker had expressly stated that he did not want his 'undutiful son,' the third executor, to come into possession of his house, because 'he did not trust him.'[11]

The distrust between parent and child that led to a contested will was frequently bitter and longstanding, but the abuse that ensued, at least so the evidence reveals was verbal, rather than physical. For example, there had been a long history of unpleasantness between Richard Barrett and his son Dacre when Richard wrote his will disinheriting his son. The allegation that was submitted

---

[6]   *Hodgekinson contra Hodgekinson*, PROB 18/7/74.

[7]   Ibid., PROB 24/14, 310.

[8]   Ibid., PROB 24/14 305, 310–13.

[9]   Ibid., PROB 18/7/14.

[10]   *Bourne contra Canham*, PROB 11/348, 237.

[11]   *Lowder et Impey contra Pitt*, PROB 18/10/83.

to accompany the offer for probate of the document explained the father's conduct: Dacre had had a 'lunacy order' entered against his father; the father had appealed; and, according to the allegation of the proponent of Richard's will, the order was discharged. Thereafter, Dacre had come to his father's house and ransacked it looking for 'deeds.'[12] Witnesses also had a more detailed story to relate. The breakdown in the relationship between father and son probably began when Richard appropriated the marriage portion of Dacre's wife in order to endow his own daughters.[13] Another witness, John Field, who had been a domestic servant for the family for 14 years, recounted the filial relationship in more graphic terms. In fact, there were some discrepancies in financial 'accounts' that had led to 'words of difference' between father and son. More specifically, Field recalled a particular disagreement in which Dacre called his father an 'Old Beast and an Old Rogue,' and told his father 'that he did not care a fart for what he could give him.' According to Field, Richard told Dacre to 'hold his tongue,' or he would have him 'turned out.' Apparently Dacre did not do so, at least to his father's satisfaction, and father expelled son, who returned sometime later with the abovementioned 'Commission of Lunacy.'[14]

Another detailed picture of longstanding filial conflict, replete with verbal abuse, can be observed in allegations challenging the will of Francis Lewin, in a document that disinherited his daughters. Disobedience in choice of marriage partner seems to have been the initial explanation for the breakdown in the filial relationship, to which a more recent dispute regarding property dealings was added. According to the allegation submitted by the proponent, the will's executor George Aberry, the dying man had summoned his neighbor John Rewe and asked him to write his will. 'Perceiving no gift to a child,' Rewe asked Lewin to explain the omission. Apparently, Lewin first replied that it was his own will rather than that of Rewe, and if Rewe would not draft it as instructed, Lewin would call upon another person to do so; but according to a witness, Lewin thereafter replied (and not without some degree of expressed irritation), that if Rewe had the right to know another man's business, that his children, Mary Aldine and Jane How, had 'abused' him and 'tried to poison him.'[15] The allegation also claimed that Mary, who had married without his consent and had been threatened with disinheritance for so doing, 'did try to purloin and get sums of money'; both his daughters and their husbands, it was claimed, acted 'undutifully … saying scandalous things about him and calling him nasty names and wearied him of his life.' All these incidents led him to conclude that he was 'discharged of

---

12 *Owen contra Barrett*, PROB 18/24/28.
13 Ibid., PROB 24/35, 77.
14 Ibid., PROB 24/35, 267.
15 *Aberry con How contra Aldine*, PROB 18/21/20.

any kindness towards them.' Two witnesses confirmed the disharmony between father and daughters, unpleasantness that they confirmed was accompanied by threats of disinheritance.[16] Another witness, Thomas Brewer, who was alleged to have served as a mediator between father and daughters, conceded that there had been conflict, but claimed that a reconciliation had occurred.[17] In his deposition, Brewer denied that he had heard the will-maker say that he would disinherit them.[18] The latter statement was challenged in another allegation submitted by Aberry in which it was claimed that when Brewer heard that his son-in-law William Alden had received only 5s. in Lewin's will, Brewer was reported as saying 'now hes done what he said he would.'[19] Perhaps in his testimony Brewer was drawing a fine distinction between complete and substantial disinheritance. Regardless, the meager gift must have been a disappointment to his son-in-law, given that Lewin's personal estate was alleged to exceed £1,800.

The allegation noted two other sources of conflict between Lewin and his daughters. One was the treatment of their mother, Joanne, who, after 48 years of marriage, had been forced by Lewin to leave the marital home, and move in with daughter Jane.[20] In addition, there were also disagreements over property; apparently Lewin had renewed a lease of some lands at a low yearly rental (because he had pocketed a large entry fine), contrary to an earlier agreement that he had made with his children.[21] Thus longstanding animosity between parent and child, mixed with more current concerns over the disposition of property, figured prominently in this dispute between parent and children.

Mothers, as well as fathers, were capable of expressing dissatisfaction with a child by threatening disinheritance. According to the proponent of the will of Elizabeth Stephens, the will-maker had claimed that her son John had been 'undutiful.'[22] When John appeared at his mother's deathbed as she was making her will, he asked her if he or his siblings would receive a legacy. Upon hearing his plea, she 'called for a shilling' and gave it to him, allegedly saying, 'Take this it is more than you deserve. I will give you nothing. You have been a wretch.' His reply, at least as reported by the proponent suggests something less than grief at the impending passing of his mother; he was reported as exclaiming, with apparent sarcasm, 'I shall drink to your health with it.' Two witnesses, who confirmed the above dialogue, specified that the drink that he said he would

---

16   Ibid., PROB 24/30, 122, 138.
17   Ibid., PROB 18/21/20.
18   Ibid., PROB 24/30, 121.
19   Ibid., PROB 18/21/20.
20   Ibid., PROB 18/21/16, PROB 24/30, 17.
21   Ibid., PROB 18/21/16.
22   *Rawlinson contra Stephens*, PROB 18/7/33.

imbibe would be a pint of sack.[23] Likewise, one witness to the oral will testified that when Martha Rawlinson, the will's executrix, had arrived at the dying woman's bedside, Elizabeth had told her in John's presence, 'I am glad you have come ... this Reprobate my son ... hath carried my goods away and if it were not for my infirmity hee would take my bed from under me.'[24] According to witnesses, the testatrix said that she had made Martha Rawlinson her executrix rather than son John, because she believed that her son would not pay for a proper funeral and would bury her 'like a swine.'[25]

Likewise, Mary Spenser's will expressed antipathy towards her 'unnatural' daughters, Margaret and Elizabeth, whom she charged were possessed by 'unbridled and violent humours.'[26] The will charged that they had undertaken 'horrid practices against my life,' and even 'went to witches to know the tyme of my death.' In her will, she left them only her prayers, so that they might 'repent and mend their wayes.' Apparently such bounty was insufficient to deter their contest of her will.

The step-parent-stepchild relationship might also give rise to conflict. Such discord can best be viewed in a cause disputing the validity of Thomas Yarway's will. It was alleged that Thomas Quincey, the second husband of Anne, Thomas Yarway's widow, was cruel to his nine stepchildren, eight of whom were minors at their father's death. According to his son John, Yarway had died with a considerable estate, one worth somewhere in the range of £600 to £800.[27] In their reply, Anne and Thomas Quincey claimed that the figure suggested by John Yarway was an exaggeration, estimating the value of Yarway's estate at a mere £50.[28] Moreover, there was a difference of opinion on the financial arrangements that the now-deceased father had made for his family. John, the lone male amongst eight sisters, claimed that his father had left his entire estate to his children, subject only to an annuity of £14 for his widow, Anne, provision that perhaps might be regarded as ungenerous given the magnitude of the estate as he valued it (in the £600 to £800 range).[29] According to Anne's current husband (Thomas Quincey), each child had been left with a bequest of £5 with the residuary to the widow, terms that were equally implausible if the estate was worth as much as £800, but that would

---

[23] Ibid., PROB 24/15, 162.

[24] Ibid., PROB 24/15, 161.

[25] Ibid., PROB 24/15, 162–3.

[26] *Sandys et al. contra Gee et Spenser*, PROB 11/350, 182.

[27] *Quincey alias Yarway contra Yarway*, PROB/18/7/37.

[28] Ibid., PROB 25/2/127.

[29] Ibid., PROB 18/7/37.

be consistent with Quincey's contention that Yarway, a horse soldier, had a more modest estate in the neighborhood of £50.[30]

Not surprisingly, the allegation of cruelty to his stepchildren was denied by Quincey in an Answer. His response is a masterful monologue of self-justification, and perhaps embodies a common step-parental lament.[31] Quincey maintained that he treated his stepchildren well, in fact 'better than what he could be compelled to do by law'; perhaps he was speaking figuratively when he added that 'in truth he hath been a very slave to them.' Further, Quincey charged that John Yarway was issuing 'cunning insinuations,' and 'manipulating' his wife (John's mother) to defraud him of money. Deponents seemed to support Quincey's version of his paternal devotion, his grim assessment of the deceased man's estate, and Yarway's testamentary disposition. According to four witnesses, Thomas Yarway (having unsuccessfully summoned his minister) 'called up all his children about him and left £5 to each child and the rest to his wife by word of mouth.'[32] Some doubt about the deponents' version might reasonably be expressed; it had all happened some time ago: Yarway had died in January 1656, and two of the deponents were unable to date his death more specifically than '16 or 17 years ago.'[33] Even wife Anne in her answer asserted, not without ambiguity, that her deceased husband 'did try to propound a nuncupative will.'[34] Quincey asserted that the oral will was never probated because the guardian of the minor children, their paternal uncle, was satisfied that Quincey would be a righteous step-parent.[35] Why John surfaced nearly 15 years after his father's demise to attempt to promote his will is unclear; perhaps it was because one (or more) of his sisters had just come of age, and demanded a share in the inheritance.[36]

---

[30]   Ibid., PROB 25/2/127.

[31]   Ibid.

[32]   Ibid., PROB 24/14, 380; 381; 390; 391.

[33]   Ibid., PROB 24/14, 380; 381.

[34]   Ibid., PROB 25/2/132.

[35]   Ibid., PROB 25/2/127.

[36]   Not all step-parent/stepchild relationships were contentious. Catherine Lipscomb left her entire estate to her deceased husband's son, James, of whom she was heard to say that 'if she had born ye said James of her owne body he could not have been more dutiful to her than he was.' Her statement is even more compelling because it came from a woman who was not without the ability to be frank: when it was mentioned to her that other relatives and friends might 'expect something ... she replied this: 'Let them work as I have done before' (*Ford et Brown alias Ford contra Lipscomb*, PROB 24/20, 12). Apparently relations had not always been so cozy between stepmother and stepson. Another witness related a less amicable incident, the lone example of alleged physical violence that emerges from the causes that had transpired between the two shortly after the death of her husband. The witness recalled that the testatrix 'fell upon ye sd James in a great fury and beat him and pulled him by ye haire

Sibling Conflict

Quarrels between siblings can also be observed in the causes that comprise the Canterbury collection. Many of the same themes observed in filial relationships, such as distrust and disobedience, likewise soured the sibling bond. Indeed a breakdown in trust between siblings might actually explain resort to a will. For example, Sarah Smith, a witness to the will of William Brereton, deposed that the testator had been concerned about his wife's well-being, and explained that 'he made his will for fear of mortality saying hee did it to prevent trouble adding that his Brothers would deal worse with his wife after he was gone.'[37]

Likewise, disobedience in choice of marriage partner might provoke disinheritance by a sibling, as well as by a parent. A complicated example can be offered in conflicting documents offered for probate as the will of James Jennyns. When his sister Barbara had married without his consent, it was alleged that Jennyns had revoked a bequest of £1,000 to her by tearing up his will, and then throwing the scraps into the fire at the Sun Tavern in Holborn. Not satisfied with mere physical destruction, Jennyns was said to have thereafter made a 'codicil' that revoked the bequest to Barbara in the previous will (now presumably in ashes), and nominated his uncle, Ralph, as executor.[38] Upon so doing, it was reported that he had declared 'that if his sister should go barefoot in the streets he would not releave her or give her a farthing.'[39] Alas a copy of the earlier will survived, or so a witness who was present at the revocation testified.[40] Jennyns's sister and his mother offered the copy for probate;[41] Uncle Ralph, on the other hand, promoted the subsequent document, which contained a substantial bequest to the will-maker's brother, also (unhappily for the purposes of piecing together the drama) called Ralph.[42] Thus the sibling conflict was three-cornered, with brother Ralph insisting that the bequest to sister Barbara by brother James had been revoked.[43] Ralph was prepared to go to the Court of Chancery to establish that his brother had created an oral 'settlement' of his

---

of ye head and hath heard that ye sd James defending himself happened to throw her down.' According to the deponent, however, reconciliation had followed (PROB 24/20, 15).

[37] *Brereton contra Brereton*, PROB 24/20, 97.

[38] *Jennyns contra Jennyns*, PROB 18/7/89. Strictly speaking, the document should have been styled a will, since the executor was changed.

[39] Ibid., PROB 24/14, 255.

[40] Ibid., PROB 24/14, 254.

[41] Ibid., PROB 18/6/42.

[42] Ibid., PROB 18/7/89.

[43] Ibid., Or so he told a witness. See PROB 24/14, 257.

estate in his favor.[44] And Ralph's alleged disdain for his family members knew no neat bounds. One deponent in the cause, James Downers, indicated that Jennyns had also been less than enamored of his own mother. According to his testimony, the will-maker had said that his mother 'was as wicked and unkind a mother [as] a man ever had.'[45]

In contesting the will of Benjamin Bradbourne, offered for probate by his sister Elizabeth, and in promoting a conflicting one purportedly handwritten by Bradbourne in his last illness, his widow Catherine painted a rather dismal portrait of relations between her husband and his sister.[46] To explain the subsequent will, Catherine cited 'disagreements' that had arisen in the last illness of their mother. The widow did not mince words in relating conversations between the couple in which Badbourne had referred to Elizabeth as 'my old tormenting sister.' Moreover, according to wife Catherine, his sister's very presence made him 'melancholy' and 'disquieted him.'[47] So acrimonious were the sibling relations that he referred to her as 'his unnatural sister and said that she should not be a penny the better for his Estate.'[48] Not surprisingly, Elizabeth denied Catherine's characterization of their sibling relationship, accusing the witness who substantiated the widow's rendition of their discord as 'deposing falsely.'[49] This cause will be revisited when considering examples of marital discord, because Elizabeth's strategy was to respond to her sister-in-law's depiction of sibling conflict with even more dire reports about her brother's marital relations.

In other causes, the source of the sibling conflict is less apparent, but reference to the causes is useful because third parties can be seen to meddle in the sibling relationship. Financial concerns may have explained the bad blood between William Walford and his sister Mary Jones, if it indeed did exist; as in other causes, there was an interloper who related the tale. In this case, it was his former master, John Besson. What is clear is that both Walford's sister and Besson had advanced money to the testator; which one would be repaid depended upon the validity of a will that he had made. According to Besson, Walford, who died at sea, had uttered a nuncupative will leaving him all his property.[50] To have selected a stranger rather than his sister was not in his view 'untoward,' because 'he had

[44]   Ibid., PROB 18/6/45. The date of the case is 1674, prior to the Statute of Frauds.

[45]   Ibid., PROB 24/14, 255.

[46]   *Bradbourne contra Townsend*. Elizabeth's offer is PROB 18/8/66, Catherine's PROB 18/8/106.

[47]   Ibid., PROB18/8/106.

[48]   Ibid., PROB 25/2/186.

[49]   Ibid., PROB 18/7/66.

[50]   *Besson contra Jones*, PROB 18/21/92.

been like a father to him,' and he had 'preserved him from being arrested.' And, according to Berron, this attempted arrest was made at the behest of none other than his own sister! Mary, Walford alleged, had been disinherited because she and her husband, an attorney, had attempted to have her brother imprisoned for debt. As he lay dying, Walford was said to have uttered: 'I have a sister unkind and all I have I leave to my Master John Berron.' For her part, Mary categorically denied that their relationship had been strained, citing numerous letters and presents that she had received from her grateful brother. Moreover, according to Mary, there never was any question of an arrest, even though a debt of £5 5s. was overdue and she had not been reimbursed for additional moneys that she paid on his behalf to others.[51] Not to be outdone, Berron noted that a number of letters accompanied by gifts had been sent from the now-deceased sailor to him; one letter stipulated that, if Walford died at sea, all that he owned ought to go to Berron, and that his 'sister Mary wife of a lawyer who had been cruel shall have nothing.'[52]

One final cause brings a number of the themes of sibling discord together. Once again debts are involved and a third party was alleged to have intermeddled in a will-making for his own benefit and exaggerated the breakdown in a sibling relationship to explain his own generous treatment in the resultant testamentary document. And once again, the abuse was with words rather than acts. Our testator, William Balle, an aspiring lawyer, was injured in a fall as a young man. Thereafter, he was regarded as incapable of managing his financial affairs, an obligation that was undertaken by his father, with whom he lived. Subsequently, Balle was befriended by a coffeehouse-owner called Washington. According to Balle's father and brother, Washington was a scoundrel who had 'prevailed upon him by indirect means' to lodge at his coffeehouse where on his deathbed he made a will naming Washington his executor. Washington's allegation tells a different tale. Balle was in need of a home and 'necessaries,' which he, rather than his relatives, was prepared to provide. In fact, he alleged that Balle 'complained of unkindness of son and brother.'[53] Richard Strode, Balle's 'cousin,' corroborated this view. According to Strode, Balle told him that his relatives would prefer to have him 'lye in prison' rather than in Washington's coffee shop, and that 'he was more beholding to Washington' than to any of his relatives.[54]

---

[51]   Ibid., PROB 18/21/123.

[52]   Ibid., PROB 18/21/92.

[53]   *Washington contra Balle*. Both Washington's offer to probate and a counter-allegation submitted by his son are filed as PROB 18/21/7.

[54]   Ibid., PROB 24/30, 34.

Marital Discord

Perhaps the most comprehensive glimpse into seventeenth-century marital discord that emerges from the testamentary litigation can be patched together from the evidence submitted in cause of the disputed will of Sir Thomas Pettus. Here the abuse related was again verbal rather than physical. Lady Elizabeth Pettus, Sir Thomas's wife, offered his will for probate.[55] His daughter, Elizabeth O'Keever, contested the will on the grounds that it had been procured by undue influence or, alternatively, that the will submitted had been revoked or perhaps even that the document was a forgery.[56] To bolster her claim that a will executed by her father in favor of his wife must have been of dubious provenance, Elizabeth alleged that her father and 'his lady lived in discontent, that she was disrespectful, and that many times he said that she had intermeddled in his estate and would not allow him necessaries.' Accordingly, it was inconceivable that he would leave a will with bequests in her favor. Indeed, it was reported that he had stated during his last illness that he wanted her to receive only her jointure at most, and 'if he knew how to make it less he would.' To support her contention that the will promoted by her stepmother should be denied probate, Elizabeth (who actually had sought administration of his goods on the grounds that Sir Thomas had died intestate) submitted interrogatories to witnesses that probed the 'differences' between Sir Thomas and Lady Elizabeth, and solicited evidence of her 'unkindness.'[57] She further asked the same witnesses for a conclusion: to opine whether it was 'racionally probable' that, given their relationship, he would leave his entire estate to his wife.[58]

These interrogatories produced depositions in which a number of witnesses gave quite detailed statements on the strained relationship that obtained between the couple. Philip Pitcher of Hingham, who styled himself a yeoman, testified that Sir Thomas had told him that Lady Elizabeth 'did scold him and pinch him with her elbow so that he could not lie in bed.'[59] He further stated that, according to Sir Thomas, their time in bed together was infrequent; he also complained to Pitcher that 'he did lye apart' from her for a month. Again according to Pitcher, Lady Elizabeth also managed her husband's business affairs to a greater degree than he liked; Sir Thomas had complained to him that she 'intermeddled' by paying in and receiving money, including debts and rents. Lady Elizabeth brought him papers to sign, and they quarreled over whether

---

[55]   *O'Keever alias Pettus contra Pettus*, PROB 18/6/90.

[56]   Ibid., PROB 18/7/13.

[57]   Ibid, PROB 18/6/90, Interrogatories.

[58]   Ibid.,

[59]   Ibid., PROB 24/14, 304.

he should be made aware of their contents. Not only did she meddle with his income, but she also controlled his expenditure; he was reported to have objected to the fact that she would not even allow him 'necessaries.'

Henry Collins, husbandman and tenant of Sir Thomas, confirmed Pitcher's testimony, particularly regarding the extent of Lady Elizabeth's control over, and interference with, Sir Thomas's business affairs. Collins furnished a specific example; he recounted an involved transaction with Lady Elizabeth in which he charged that she had altered the amount on a bond that he had entered into with Sir Thomas.[60] Like many other witnesses, his testimony should perhaps be read with caution: the transaction related might have left some residual bad feeling between the witness and Lady Elizabeth.

William Hart, however, confirmed both the couple's marital discord and Collins's claim that Lady Elizabeth had interfered with her husband's legal affairs. In a deposition in which he described himself as Sir Thomas's attorney, Hart deposed that about a year prior to his death, while they were together in Norwich, Pettus had pulled out some pieces of paper and exclaimed, 'Look what that damn whore my wife would have me do.'[61] Hart confirmed the facts alleged by daughter Elizabeth, that Sir Thomas's wife had tried to have a will drafted for him but that he had not approved of the provisions of that will, the one drafted by 'Sargent Earle.' Revisions were never made, and the will went unexecuted, though Hart claimed to be uncertain whether the unwanted will was the one that Lady Elizabeth offered for probate.

Naturally, Lady Elizabeth countered. In her interrogatories she asked witnesses whether Sir Thomas had expressed to them that he was grateful to her for 'preserving' his estate.[62] Moreover, she implied that Sir Thomas was rather a difficult fellow to live with; she asked witnesses whether he was a 'passionate man and at times did speak ill of his friends and express sorrow if he spoke ill of his Lady.'[63] Either her witnesses were not summoned or their depositions were lost, because no trace of them remains. Which narrative of the couple's married life did the court ultimately accept? Probably the one offered by the daughter, because the will that the wife promoted was nullified.[64]

Other causes in which alleged marital discord led to spousal disinheritance contain less rich documentation. Yet the flavor of marital discord, and how it was presented, grudgingly surfaces from the record. One cause suggests that it might have stemmed initially from (or perhaps been exacerbated by) disputes

[60] Ibid., PROB 24/14, 312.
[61] Ibid., PROB 24/14, 329–30.
[62] Ibid., PROB 18/7/13, Interrogatories.
[63] Ibid., PROB 18/7/13 Interrogatories.
[64] Ibid., PROB 11/351, 165.

over the amount and payment of a marriage portion. Anthony Tatham offered for probate the nuncupative will of John Wilmott, one in which he was named as executor.[65] According to Tatham, he had secured employment for the will-maker, and Wilmott had 'acknowledged his care over him as a father ... and [they] called each other father and son.'[66] In order to shed light upon why Wilmott had selected an outsider as executor rather than his widow, Tatham noted that there had been differences between Wilmott and his wife Abigail and her mother over her marriage portion. Wilmott had been forced to sue to recover the sum; Tatham alleged that Wilmott had had to spend £45 in legal expenses to recover a portion of £50. Alice Page, Wilmott's domestic servant and a witness to the oral will, confirmed both the surrogate paternal relationship and the lawsuit over the marriage portion. According to Alice's testimony, however, the ill feelings were between Wilmott and his mother-in-law, and not the will-maker and his wife. She believed that the residuary estate after the payment of Wilmotts's substantial personal and business debts, owed in part to Tatham, was bequeathed to the widow Abigail. But there was a 'condition': 'he desired his mother-in-law should be put out of his house.'[67]

Other causes that illustrate marital discord can be cited. The testamentary litigation over the will of Benjamin Bradbourne has been already been considered in our discussion of sibling discord. Catherine, Bradbourne's spouse, and Elizabeth Townsend, his sister, each offered to probate a different will. According to sister Elizabeth, marital discord between the couple explained a will naming her as executrix that she offered for probate, one that had been executed during the early years of her brother's marriage, a document that she contended was never revoked and was confirmed by her brother at his death.[68] Catherine, however, offered for probate a later will,[69] composed (according to Elizabeth) while her brother was not of sound mind.[70] In her allegation, Elizabeth asserted that there were 'great variants' between husband and wife.[71] She further maintained that the wife was a 'cross woman,' whose 'ill carriage had caused him to spend many a hundred pound abroad.' Moreover, it was noted that

---

65   *Tatham contra Tatham*, PROB 18/7/9.

66   Other causes likewise suggest that kinship terms were employed in non-kinship relations. For example Thomas Hatton called Benjamin Bradbourne 'father' and the latter called him 'son' though they were unrelated by blood (*Bradbourne contra Townsend*, PROB 25/2, 187).

67   *Tatham contra Tatham*, PROB 24/14/280–82.

68   *Bradbourne contra Townsend*, PROB 18/8/106.

69   Ibid., PROB 18/7/66.

70   Ibid., PROB 25/2/165.

71   Ibid., PROB 18/8/116.

she had brought 'noe Porcion to the s[ai]d Dece[ase]d nor ever had any Child or Children at least none that lived.' In addition, Elizabeth made much of the physical separations of the couple during their tempestuous union. In particular, she noted that she was in Bath during his last illness. This Catherine conceded, though in one of her answers, Catherine alleged that, although entreated to do so, the dying man had refused to send for her.[72]

Catherine, as one might expect, justified her conduct; during her absence, the couple had corresponded 'with kind letters'; and she immediately returned from her sojourn upon hearing of the seriousness of the illness.[73] Catherine blamed the intermeddling of his sister Elizabeth as the source of any marital discord. And a battery of clauses in the allegation so maintained: her arrival at the deathbed 'disquieted him'; it made him 'melancholy'; and he continually referred to her as 'my tormenting sister.'[74] Witnesses corroborated this charge.[75] In her interrogatories posed to one Thomas Hayton, a confidant of the now-deceased Benjamin, Catherine asked if Elizabeth had tried to 'blow the Coals and beget a difference' between the couple; were they (the couple) 'not taken by neighbours to have friendly relations?'[76] For her part Elizabeth impeached the credibility of Hayton's testimony by asking witnesses whether they believed that Thomas had 'designs' on the widow.[77]

Likewise, Thomas and Priscilla Rogers had a tumultuous union, and they exchanged unpleasant words, or at least so the three executors of Priscilla's will – a document that left her husband no bequest – would have the court believe. The testatrix married Thomas in April 1685, about 13 months prior to her death. According to the allegation submitted by the executors, Thomas became 'unkind' to her, did not 'allow her meate and drinke and other necessaries,' 'abused' her and 'called her an old witch.'[78] When he learned that she had written a will that disinherited him, he burned it in front of her, and tried to prevent her from making another, even though a marriage agreement had been executed that allowed her full power to dispose of goods to the value of £700 to £800. Thereafter, however, she was able to summon one Charles Perkins, an 'attorney,' to draft another will 'whilst he [Thomas] was out ... though during the consultation she was in great fear of him returning.' When Thomas found out that a second will had been drafted, he became angry and prevented its

---

72   Ibid., PROB 25/2/187.
73   Ibid., PROB 18/9/13.
74   Ibid., PROB 18/8/106.
75   Ibid., PROB 18/7/66.
76   Ibid., PROB 18/8/116.
77   Ibid., PROB 18/8/106.
78   Ibid., PROB 18/19/22.

execution for some time. Eventually, however, it was both signed and witnessed. So overbearing was Thomas that it was alleged that he had kept Priscilla under lock and key.[79] Interrogatories submitted by the executors solicited confirmation by others of her husband's violent words. One witness, a servant, was asked whether, when Priscilla directed her to summon William Davis, one of the will's executors, Rodgers had threatened to shoot her if she did so.[80]

Of course, Thomas's version of their marriage was decidedly rosier. In his allegation, he characterized himself as a 'kind loveing husband.' Moreover, Thomas noted that he had provided his wife with medical attention during her last illness. According to the allegation, one witness, Elizabeth Brown, who testified that Thomas 'drunk to her [his wife's] damnation' and 'called her an old witch,' was importuned by William Davis, the will's proponent. Indeed Thomas Rodgers claimed that it was Davis who used the nasty epithets; he had called her 'an old bitch.' Finally to the substance of the case: the will had been burned by Thomas at Priscilla's direction when she came to the realization that its executors were alienating her from her husband.[81]

In another cause, marital discord probably led Thomas Day, described as a 'chirgeon,' to leave his wife Dorothea Day's 'company and live apart,' after four years of marriage, at least according to an allegation submitted by his daughter Elizabeth's guardian.[82] Elizabeth made her contention to cast doubt upon the validity of an oral will offered for probate by Dorothea. It was alleged that Dorothea had remained in London when Thomas had moved to Devon, where in 1659 he married one Honor Pollard, 'by a minister in Holy Orders of the Church of England.' Thomas had, it was reported, 'professed himself to be unmarried,' although he had in fact been married to Dorothea for about a quarter of a century. After the wedding, the newly united, though perhaps bigamist, couple 'cohabited' until Honor's death some three to four years thereafter, during which time Elizabeth was produced and, according to her guardian, baptized as the child of Thomas and Honor. It was conceded, however, that Dorothea had commenced a suit in the Court of Arches to confirm the existence of her union with Thomas. Although Thomas contested their marriage, a sentence confirming its validity was entered and was sustained on appeal to the Court of Delegates. According to his daughter's allegation, Thomas continued to deny the marriage and 'tried to obtain a Commission of Review.'[83]

---

79   Ibid., PROB 18/19/31.

80   Ibid., PROB 18/19/30.

81   Ibid.,

82   *Day contra Day*, PROB 18/4/37.

83   Ibid.

Dorothea Day, however, had another story. In her allegation, she claimed that there had been reconciliation between her husband Thomas and herself. Recognizing that he had 'much abused' her, Thomas decided to make a nuncupative will in her favor. Thereafter, he came to visit her at her lodgings, and offered to 'cohabit'; at the same time he indicated to her that he would not leave his estate to his daughter by his second marriage because she was a bastard. Further, she claimed that he had written a letter to one John Jones (said to be of Lincoln's Inn) that contained a last will.[84]

Witnesses produced in the cause differed as to whether Thomas had ever claimed to be married to Dorothea. Although he testified that he was aware of the cause in the Court of Arches, John Etheridge, who claimed to have known Thomas 10 years before his death, testified that he was unaware that Thomas and Dorothea had cohabited, noting that after Honor's death he remained in their marital home.[85] Richard Wimbold, who was Thomas's apprentice and therefore in a position to know, was of the same opinion. Prior to the marriage with Honor, he reported that Thomas had lived as a bachelor.[86] However, two other witnesses testified that they knew of the first marriage to Dorothea, and had been aware that he had written a letter to confirm his nuncupative will that named her as his executrix.[87] John Small deposed that Thomas had confessed that he had 'very much wronged his wife Doro[thea].'[88] That he might have done, but the Court was unmoved; the will was denied probate.[89]

Other causes provide additional examples of marital discord and spousal disinheritance, though they present evidence of the antagonism less graphically. In common with the marriage of Thomas and Dorothea Day, separation is a recurring theme. For example, the proponents of the will of Thomas James – a document that disinherited his wife – claimed that Thomas had come to London at least eight years earlier and had lived with his sisters 'and was content there which his wife knows to be true.'[90] According to the will's promoters, his two nieces, James had provided for his wife by way of jointure, and the will that they offered for probate intentionally omitted her. Indeed it was alleged that she had previously agreed not to claim a portion of his estate, but apparently had a change of heart. Likewise, John and Dorothy Robinson had also lived apart for about a year prior to Dorothy's death. It was alleged that Dorothy had

---

[84]   Ibid., PROB 18/3/49.
[85]   Ibid., PROB 24/11, 54–5.
[86]   Ibid., PROB 24/11, 302.
[87]   Ibid., PROB 24/10, 410, 411.
[88]   Ibid., PROB 24/10, 411.
[89]   The sentence is PROB 11/346, 137.
[90]   *Jones contra Hughes et Twaites*, PROB 18/3/6.

retained upon marriage the 'power to make an estate.'[91] Two wills were offered for probate, one submitted by her sister Frances and the other brought forward by two unrelated executors.[92] The validity of each will was questioned by the promoter of the other, but both parties to the litigation agreed, and witnesses confirmed, that John had 'much cheated and abused [Dorothy].'[93] John was not included in either will. Indeed, he was called as a witness and testified that he had known Dorothy for 20 years but he did not indicate the length of their union. John conceded that Dorothy had retained the power to make a will, and noted that they lived apart for 'three-quarters of a year.' Even though he attributed their marital breakdown to Frances's intermeddling, he deposed that he favored her victory in the cause, because he believed that the other side had 'endeavored to cheat her.'[94] Finally, recall also that Francis Lewin (whose less-than-happy relationship with his children we have already explored) had 'turned out' his wife of 48 years for reasons that remain obscure.[95]

Sorting Fact from Fancy: The Court's Dilemma

This survey of the Canterbury litigation may aptly be concluded with a cause that illustrates ongoing family discord involving a variety of relationships, and the probate of two documents that each purported to be the last will of Henry Raven, who died in the Fleet imprisoned for debt.[96] The dispute began, or so it is alleged, as a quarrel between uncle and nephew over Henry's parental inheritance, and concluded with litigation between uncle and Henry's spouse over Henry's estate. Before probate of the will was granted, it had to withstand charges of spousal discord and the meddling of a mother-in-law. The narrative that can be stitched together is as follows. It began with the death of Henry's father who left a will nominating his brother Robert as executor. According to its terms, Uncle Robert was obligated to pay nephew Henry an annuity of £50 per annum. This arrangement must not have been an uncommon one, for a dying testator with young children to entrust his estate to a sibling in this

---

91   *Wilsher contra Ruffin et Wells*, PROB 18/7/90.

92   Ibid. Francis's offer is PROB 18/7/90. That of the two executors, Ruffin and Wells, who describe themselves as 'ancient and intimate acquaintances' (PROB 25/2/104) is PROB 18/6/80.

93   Ibid. The interrogatories are filed with PROB 18/6/80. The statements of the witnesses are PROB 24/14, 235, 251.

94   Ibid., PROB 24/14, 253.

95   *Aberry con How contra Aldine*, PROB 18/21/16.

96   *Peyton contra Raven*. Uncle Raven's offer for probate is PROB 18/7/17, and the widow Elizabeth's petition to revoke and probate a nuncupative will is PROB 18/8/53.

manner. But of course there was the danger that the stipulated sums might not be paid, at least not without the threat of legal action. Thereafter, nephew Henry made a will leaving his estate to his uncle. Some time later, however, he married Elizabeth and by the time of his death had produced 'several children' with one on its way, or so his spouse maintained.[97] Whether the initial annuity had been paid, to whom, and the extent of the arrears was all very much in dispute. According to Uncle Robert's allegation, nothing was due. Indeed he charged that Elizabeth, at the prompting of her mother, 'being covetous and desirous of receiving them [the annuity] or at least one half' conspired to imprison her husband for debt. Although Henry was 'nearly starved to death,' he gave power of attorney to Elizabeth's mother to receive all or part of the sum on a weekly basis. Uncle Robert produced a letter (not submitted to the court) in which Henry expressed 'dislike for the two,' and bitterly admitted to having been 'ill used.' Shortly before his death, Henry indicated that he wanted his earlier will to stand. When asked 'how he had taken care of his wife,' Henry had made it clear that he wanted her to receive nothing, and was reported as saying 'as for my children let their grandmother provide for them Robert has been my best friend.'[98]

Elizabeth Raven, not surprisingly, had a different view of both her marriage and the property affairs of her husband. Although she conceded that a will had been made in uncle Robert's favor, she contended that it had been revoked, because the now deceased Henry Raven had married and produced children after the will was executed. In her answer, she maintained that Henry had a personal estate of £700, and held interests in real estate to the value of £550 per annum.[99] She alleged that on his deathbed Henry had made a nuncupative will in her favor, and witnesses supported her claim, though it is not clear that they were present at the actual moment that the words were uttered.[100] According to the allegation, Henry was not without malice toward his uncle; he 'raged against him,' and said that he 'hoped that he lived a year longer and be revenged of his uncle.'[101] Numerous witnesses confirmed his hostility towards Robert. William Sheldon testified that Henry believed that his uncle had his father's estate in his hands, and that Robert refused to pay his nephew's legacy. According to Sheldon, Henry had called his uncle a 'rogue'; because he had cheated him out of what he believed to be his legacy. He also deposed that Raven told him that 'if

---

[97] Ibid. By interrogatory, she asked witnesses whether they knew of the will, the subsequent, marriage, and the children (PROB 18/7/17).
[98] Ibid., PROB 18/8/92.
[99] Ibid., PROB 25/2/162.
[100] Ibid., PROB 24/15, 211, 243, 258.
[101] Ibid., PROB 18/8/53.

it were not for fear of being hanged he would kill him.'[102] Another witness, Mary Maxwell, testified that so much did he despise his uncle that getting even with him provided Henry with the determination to go on; he told her that he hoped to live longer 'to be revenged of ye damned Dogg my Uncle.'[103] Unfortunately, the case, like so many others, did not proceed to sentence so we can only surmise that the parties entered into some compromise.

Conclusion

The causes observed here illustrate the disappointment of some heirs and spouses over legacies. Displeasure with a testamentary plan often prompted a will contest by the disappointed individual. A will proponent explained the will-maker's conduct by introducing evidence of significant quarrels between the will-maker and his kin. The portrait of spousal discord confirms the obvious: not all marriages in early modern England were without rancor. Because divorce was not an alternative and judicial separation was a long, unwieldy, and expensive exercise, couples probably just separated. Others stuck it out and lived together, but neighbors, friends, and domestic servants certainly seem to have been aware of these unhappy unions. It was a spouse's parting shot – disinheritance or a niggardly bequest in a will – that brought the unhappy relationship into the public domain. Likewise litigation ensued when children and siblings were excluded from wills. Yet the abuse that we have discerned was largely verbal rather than physical. There seems to be no end to the abusive names disaffected spouses, and indeed other relatives, were prepared to fling at each other. But they seemed disinclined towards physical violence (though on occasions they threatened it) or else were unprepared to allege it in court documents, and their witnesses rarely mention it in their depositions. The historian would have expected the record to yield more examples of actual violence in a society in which life was supposedly so nasty, brutish and short. The sword that was brandished in these causes took the form of the pocket book.

Not surprising, quarrels over property, particularly the repayment of debts, figure prominently in disputes between siblings and other relatives. In a society in which kin had only very loose economic relations, property disputes amongst them are less likely to arise. However, the will-makers observed here were linked to their kin economically, not infrequently borrowing money from their

---

[102] Ibid., PROB 24/15, 230.
[103] Ibid., PROB 24/15, 257.

relatives and ultimately disagreeing on whether repayment had occurred. Such links often sparked ill feelings, nasty epithets, and finally a will contest.

Chapter 10

The Myriad Roles of Women in Will-Making and Testamentary Litigation in Late Seventeenth-Century England

Introduction

The foregoing chapters have been replete with narratives of seventeenth-century lives related through probate litigation in the Prerogative Court of Canterbury. The stories recounted about the lives and deaths of will-makers were frequently told by women. This abundance of women appearing in an early modern English court is unusual. Indeed, the court appearance of married women is particularly remarkable because, through the doctrine of coverture, a wife's legal personality was supposed to be merged into that of her husband.[1] As a result, a husband rather than his wife usually appeared as the party to a legal transaction or dispute.

But coverture was unknown to the civil law, and therefore to the English ecclesiastical law upon which it was based.[2] Thus women, married and unmarried, could appear, sue, and be sued in their own name in church courts in testamentary disputes. The vibrant role that women played in the Prerogative Court confirms the argument of Amy Erickson, who perceives women as vigorous participants in the probate process, both in and outside church courts.[3] In her view, women were often able to manipulate probate law in their own interest, and to participate actively in the process of property transmission at

---

[1]   Sir William Blackstone is sometimes paraphrased as having written that the husband and wife are one person in law and that person is the husband. See for example, J.H. Baker, *An Introduction to English Legal History*, 4th edn (London, 2002) pp. 483–9). His rendition (and Baker's) is in fact far more guarded. In the first place, his discourse on coverture is specifically stated to deal with personal rather than property rights. Indeed, much of his presentation is given over to exceptions to the rule. A major exception was the ability to sue and be sued in ecclesiastical court. See Sir William Blackstone, *Commentaries on the Laws of England* (Chicago, 1979) Reprint of 1765 edition), vol. I, pp. 430–33. A useful discussion of married women's legal capacity can be found in Sara Mendelson and Patricia Crawford, *Women in Early Modern England* (Oxford, 1998), pp. 34–42.

[2]   Blackstone *Commentaries*, vol. I, p. 442.

[3]   A.L. Erickson, *Women and Property in Early Modern England* (London, 1993).

death. Accordingly, Erickson has concluded that women should not necessarily be viewed as passive victims of the largely male-dominated legal system. Others scholars concur and recognize that coverture in practice differed from its theory; they have produced a more nuanced, and a decidedly more complex, view of its operation.[4] This depiction of 'women and the law' is in stark contrast to the views of some historians who regard women in pre-industrial England as passive victims of juridical oppression.[5]

This chapter both confirms the more textured view and argues something more. It uses the testamentary litigation observed to document that by the late seventeenth century women figured in oft-times critical roles in guiding property transmission between the generations, in particular in will-making, as well as in will probate and testamentary litigation. With respect to the making of wills, one can observe women executing their own wills, documents that subsequently feature in testamentary causes. Women were also active in directing the testamentary destinies of others – their friends, neighbors, and relations, indeed even their betters, such as their employers – by serving as scriveners,[6] witnesses to wills,[7] and executrices.[8] They also managed the will-making process for others.[9] Finally, and perhaps most significantly, women appeared as witnesses in will contests and disputes about estate administration (see Table 10.4). It was often their testimony that was crucial in determining the validity

---

[4]   Indeed married women, though more scarce than men in the records, have been observed both in and out of court as early as the Middle Ages. They undertook legal acts, sometimes without their husbands joined, though in matters of property transmission, and debt and contract, the concept of unity of person was generally respected. Marjorie K. McIntosh, *Autonomy and Community: the Royal Manor of Havering, 1200–1500* (Cambridge, 1986), pp. 170–76; L.R. Poos and Lloyd Bonfield, *Select Pleas in Manorial Courts* (Selden Society, London, vol. 114, 1997), pp. clxxvii–clxxxi.

[5]   Eileen Spring is the most vigorous advocate of the position that the legal principle coverture in practice controlled property relations between the spouses to the detriment of women (at least in the aristocracy), both married, and unmarried (*Land, Law and Family: aristocratic inheritance in England 1300– 1800* (Chapel Hill, 1993)).

[6]   Jane Bennett was alleged to have penned the will of Abigail Hardwick (*Hardwick contra Holland*, PROB 18/1/15), and Vere Gerrard had a will drafted for Somersett Fox with blanks left for the exact amount of legacies, and was instructed by the testatrix to fill in the exact amounts (*Gerard v. Blackston*, PROB 24/14, 391).

[7]   Because wills were executed on the deathbed it was not uncommon for domestic servants and nurses to serve as witnesses. See the discussion in the two 'case studies' below.

[8]   See the discussion in Chapter 1, text at footnotes 53, 60, 64, and 84–7.

[9]   Many examples can be cited. A good one is Mary Heads who summoned a scrivener and then set out the dying man's personal property in writing so that they could be easily included (*Price contra Price*, PROB 18/13/15). She was also present when Mary Edwards, a domestic servant, witnessed the will (Ibid., PROB 24/30, 154).

of a proffered testamentary act: whether the requisite mental capacity had been present; coercion absent; signature made; interlineations present at the time of execution. In previous chapters I have argued that the established norms of will-making empowered judges to select which wills should be admitted to probate and which fell by the wayside. This chapter argues that witnesses were likewise empowered: they provided the facts to which the norms were applied, and these crucial voices were often those of women.

Women as Parties in Probate Litigation

First, let us consider the overall presence of women in the Prerogative Court. Table 10.1 indicates that the Canterbury court may be justly regarded as the 'women's court', because nearly as many female litigants figured in the causes therein as did males. The reason for the frequency with which they appeared is easy to explain. Probate practice required the executor or executrix to notify the heirs of the will-maker when he or she probated a will in solemn form.[10] Because our male will-makers frequently chose their spouses as executrix (40 out of 150, or 26.7 percent), a widow often offered her deceased husband's will for probate, and thus appeared in the record as proponent.[11]

Table 10.1   Litigants in the Prerogative Court of Canterbury, 1660–1700: gender of parties

	Male		Female	
	N	percent	N	percent
Proponents	100	53.5	87	46.5
Respondents	105	53.8	90	46.2

Note: The data are derived from 184 causes investigated in the PCC. The numbers exceed 184 because some causes involved multiple parties.

---

[10]   See discussion in Appendix.

[11]   The actual percentage of married will-makers who chose their wives is larger since some male will-makers were probably unmarried, a fact that the researcher is not able to ascertain in all causes.

Moreover, because a widow would be an interested party in the estate should a will offered for probate be nullified, a widow who was not chosen as executrix was required to be cited by the will's promoter (28 out of 150, or 18.7 percent). Likewise, will-makers selected 22 female relatives to serve as executrices. Sisters and daughters were most numerous.[12] Two will-makers choose their mothers.[13] However, more remote female kin appeared. Cousin, that generic term for a kinswoman, similarly appear as executrixes.[14] Other remote kinswomen were selected. Mary Spenser, for example, chose her niece as a co-executrix.[15] Even the selection of female in-laws were not unknown.[16] Another will-maker chose her female friends.[17] These women (like widow-executrices) frequently offered the will in which they were nominated executrix for probate. Finally, because will-makers often left female heirs, promoters were required to cite them if they chose to probate a will in solemn form. Thus, for all the above reasons, women were present as parties in the solemn-form probates in the Prerogative Court nearly as frequently as were men.

Women also 'appeared' in the court as will-makers, or more precisely as deceased will-makers, as the testatrixes whose wills were the subject of contest

---

[12]   Darrell Johnson named his 'sisters' (*Wingfield et Johnson contra Johnson*, PROB 18/1/60) as did John Kyme, his sister Mary (*Kyme contra Kyme*, PROB 11/369, 270); John Young, his sister Ann (*Kinaston contra Young*, PROB 11/368, 381); Daniel Palmer, his sister Hannah Walker (*Walker alias Palmer contra Baker alias Palmer et al.*, PROB 18/13/50); George Sherbrooke, his sister and co-executrix Rebecca (*Sherbrooke contra Sherbrooke*, PROB 11/349, 278). Thomas Gold selected his daughter Jane (*Mascall contra Spenser*, PROB 18/3c/40); as did Sir Richard Neale, daughter Frances (*Setton alias Neale contra Neale*, PROB 18/24/30); James Burton, daughter Catherine (*Brace alias Burton contra Burton*, PROB 11/352, 40); Elizabeth Rich, daughter Mary (*Rich et Gayner contra Vernon*, PROB 11/349, 301); Andrew Tebbat, daughter Margaret (*Slatter contra Tebbat*, PROB 11/348, 416); Sir John Lee, daughter Katherine (*Lee contra Lee*, PROB 11/342, 59); and Frances Belgrave, daughter Eleonore with her brother (*Blagrave contra Quarrington*, PROB 11/349, 129).

[13]   Richard Upsdale selected his mother (*Tribe alias Upsdale contra Hearsey*, PROB 18/3c/80) as did Elizabeth Stephens (*Rawlinson contra Stephens*, PROB 11/351, 7).

[14]   Hugh Naunay chose a cousin Ann (*Nauney contra Nauney*, PROB 11/130, 164), as did Clement Pragell, who selected cousin Sarah Hill (*Hill contra Bond*, PROB 11/365, 128). John Harbert, nominated his cousin, Rebecca Seawell (*Seawell contra Harbert*, PROB 11/351, 297).

[15]   *Sandys et al. contra Gee et Spenser*, PROB 11/350, 182.

[16]   Robert Markham choose his sister-in-law Ann (*Markham et Carrington contra Markham*, PROB 11/313, 283) and Christopher Pim chose his mother-in-law Mary Thatcher (*Pim contra Thatcher*, PROB 18/18/54).

[17]   Elizabeth Clarke chose two female 'friends' Clarke and Otghar (*Walker contra Clark et Otghar*, PROB 11/384, 18).

or, more infrequently, as intestates whose estate administration was the subject of dispute.[18] Nearly one in five of the contested wills and administrations (34 out of 184, or 18.5 percent) in the data set were those of women. This figure, given

Table 10.2   Wills probated in the Prerogative Court of Canterbury 1671–81: gender of deceased

Year	Female		Male		Totals
	N	percent	N	percent	
1671	267	17.5	1,259	82.5	1,526
1676	298	19.5	1,230	80.5	1,528
1681	333	18.5	1,463	81.5	1,796

the percentage of women's estates that were probated or administered in the Prerogative Court, suggests (perhaps surprisingly) that their estates were no more likely to have been contested than those of men (see Table 10.2).[19] Table 10.3 illustrates that the estates subject to litigation were evenly divided between widows and spinsters, and that even the wills and intestate estates of married women could be the subject of controversy.

Table 10.3   Marital status of women whose wills or administrations were in dispute in the Prerogative Court of Canterbury, 1660–1700

N = 34					
Married		Unmarried		Widowed	
N	percent	N	percent	N	percent
4	11.8	15	44.1	15	44.1

[18]   Four of the 34 causes involving the estates of women dealt with matters of administration. The rest were contested wills.

[19]   When I surfed the Index Library's Will Register Canterbury volumes for the period many years ago, I counted only probates. Thus I must correct my observed figure to exclude the four administrations. My data set consists of 176 will probates, 30 of which were those of women or about 17 percent.

Women as witnesses

In addition to the roles of litigant and testatrix, women also were present in another capacity in the Prerogative Court: as witnesses. Slightly less than one out of every three witnesses examined in the causes observed were women (see Table 10.4). Women appear as witnesses because, as the narratives produced in

Table 10.4   Gender of witnesses: testamentary litigation in the Prerogative Court of Canterbury, 1660–1700

	N	percent
	N = 530	
Male	380	71.7
Female	150	28.3
Totals	530	100

previous chapters illustrate, they were active, and indeed often crucial, participants in the will-making process. Women were witnesses to the documents themselves,[20] and they were also called on to attest in court that the will produced by its promoter was (or was not) indeed the now-deceased's last will and testament, duly executed. Where a will was challenged on the grounds of lack of mental capacity or undue influence, or on whether the will (oral or written) complied with the formalities of due execution, the testimony of those present was vital. The social and economic organization of early modern society was such that women were well placed to observe the conduct that would be legally relevant in probate disputes. Because wills were frequently prepared at or near the deathbed, a realm where women were often present as servants, nurses or care-givers, their observations on the circumstances in which a will was conceived and executed were often crucial. Examples can be offered. Who was better placed to know whether John Baxter, a clerk to Lord Tufton, was married than his lordship's two domestic servants, Deborah Tause and Sarah Mosely?[21] Or who could give

---

[20]   The sheer number of female witnesses to wills, and the facts that women were called on to be witnesses when men were available, and that some testators were willing to have only female witnesses suggest that there was very little reluctance to have women serve as witnesses to wills.

[21]   *Baxter contra Baxter*, PROB 24/30, 60.

more credible evidence of John Chapman's mental faculties on his deathbed than Alice, his attending nurse?[22] Who were more likely to authenticate marks and handwriting than housekeepers, like Susan Seacomb, who dealt regularly with tradesmen using written directions from their masters?[23]

So women served frequently as witnesses, and often testified about conduct that must have been crucial to the outcome of a cause. Furthermore, women do not appear to have been unwilling to call into question the testimony of men, even across class lines. Good examples are Mary Vaud, a domestic servant, who challenged the credibility of the scrivener of the will of Thomas Brown,[24] and Ann Richardson who testified to contradict her husband's testimony.[25] These witnesses seem not to have been reluctant to be assertive. Nor was nurse Emma Smith who admitted the audacity to question the dose of laudanum that was prescribed by a doctor to her patient.[26] Indeed many of the causes leave the researcher with the impression that it was the testimony of women that greatly influenced, if not controlled, their outcome.

Case Studies

How may this proposition – that there was at least a modicum of female control of the outcome of will contests – be further demonstrated, given the evidence available? Had the Prerogative Court judges delivered opinions, there would be no doubt as to the effect of a particular witness's testimony on the court's judgment. But they did not, and the researcher must proceed by way of inference. One way of assessing the role of women in determining an outcome is to sketch in more detail their role as seen through their own testimony and that of others. Of the two hundred or so causes I have considered in detail in this study of probate litigation, two have been isolated by way of example. While no argument is made that these causes are typical of those observed, they are of a

---

[22]   Ann Chapman (*Seawell contra Harbert*, PROB 24/14, 355) attested to John Harbert's mental capacity. See also the deposition of Alice Cooper, Richard Sherbrooke's nurse (*Sherbrooke contra Sherbrooke*, PROB 24/14, 188) and Bridgett Scott (PROB 24/14, 183, 302).

[23]   Richard Barrett's housekeeper, Susan Seacomb (*Owen contra Barrett*, PROB 24/35, 265). See also the following women attesting to handwriting and marks: *Wakeham contra Wakeham*, PROB 24/14, 403; *Slatter contra Tebbat*, PROB 24/14. 266; *Aberry con How contra Aldine*, PROB 24/15, 188.

[24]   *Hovingham contra Vossins*, PROB 24/14, 295.

[25]   *Aberry con How contra Aldine*, PROB 24/30, 86.

[26]   *Templer con Wynn*, PROB 24/30, 358.

type: causes in which the observations of women witnesses were crucial to the outcome.

Probate of the Will of Thomas Gollibrand

The first cause is the contest over the will of Thomas Gollibrand. Though not a wealthy man, Thomas was not without some substance. According to his brother Samuel, he possessed tenements in London worth over £50 per annum, real property that had been devised to him by his grandfather, in addition to a substantial personal estate.[27] The parties to the testamentary litigation – the proponent, his widow Margaret, and the contestant, his brother Samuel – offered decidedly different narratives of his will-making, which occurred shortly before his untidy death.

Because it seems more factually complete, Samuel's version – cobbled together from surviving allegations that he submitted to the court – will be presented first. Samuel charged that at least a few weeks before his brother Thomas's demise, his sibling was not a healthy man. Although he was living in Lea in Kent, Thomas had traveled to London to consult a physician, and lodged there at Samuel's expense. Unfortunately, Thomas's health did not improve. While Samuel was himself too ill to care for Thomas when his brother returned to Lea, he sent his **half-sister, Mrs. Cole**, to his brother's bedside instead. The day before he died Thomas wrote to his brother begging him to come immediately. Samuel, however, reported that his own health had taken a turn for the worse, and he could only dispatch **his wife and daughter, and 'another kinswoman.'** Thus Thomas was blessed with **four female care-givers**, and therefore four women who might be able to testify to the events surrounding the alleged will-making.

As to the document offered by the widow for probate, Samuel conceded that a 'scroll'[28] had been contrived the day before Thomas's death, largely by one John Langworth, his brother's fellow lodger. While he conceded that Langworth had gone up to London to have the document drafted at Thomas's direction, he alleged that Thomas had been 'senseless' at the time it was executed. Nevertheless, Langworth 'commanded everyone in the room to leave' and the will was 'executed,' though without doubt while Thomas was 'not of sound mind.' Accordingly, the writing offered for probate should, in Samuel's view, be nullified.[29]

Not surprisingly, the **widow Margaret**'s version of the events surrounding the will-making differed considerably in detail, and therefore in conclusion.

---

[27]   *Gollibrand contra Gollibrand*, PROB 18/7/81.

[28]   Recall that a scroll was a 'word of art 'frequently used by contestants to characterize writings that believed should not be probated as a valid will.

[29]   Ibid., PROB 18/7/81.

The most significant divergence was with respect to Thomas's mental state; she alleged that at the time the will was executed 'it was a great mercy that he [Thomas] had his understanding.' Although Margaret conceded that Thomas's health was failing, she reported that he was insistent that he should make his will despite his weakened physical state. Indeed Thomas, believing he was not long for this world, had urged Langworth to journey to London to engage a 'lawyer' to draft his will, knowing that he might soon die. Langworth returned on 3 November with a 'rough draft,' a document with the monetary value of some bequests left blank (tantamount to a modern 'form will') which would allow Thomas to fill in the desired amounts. After consulting with Langworth while he was reclining on a 'pallet bed' in the dining room, Thomas insisted that Langworth go off into the adjoining kitchen to amend the will according to his directions. This Langworth did. The will was read over to Thomas, and it was duly executed at about seven in the evening: signed and sealed by the dying man, and witnessed in Margaret's presence.[30]

Of course each party's rendition of the circumstances surrounding Thomas's devising and then dying was tinged with interest. Thus the court was fortunate to have the witness depositions of some individuals who were arguably less partial. Like the parties to the litigation, however, some of the witnesses observed very different deaths of the same man. Other witnesses had been so preoccupied with mundane chores that they were able to render only very sketchy accounts. **Mary Molentfort**, who described herself as a 'cozen in the third or fourth degree' and was probably the **kinswoman** whom Samuel alleged to have had accompany his wife and daughter to Thomas's lodgings, stated that she had arrived there at about five in the evening. Her account supported Samuel's allegations.[31] When she reached Thomas in his chamber, she found him 'lying in a Low Room on his trundle bed with his clothes on.' She reported that she heard 'rattles in the throat in a very violent manner,' and that 'he had difficultie breathing.' When she 'asked him how he did he made no answer.' During the hour and a half she remained with him, he did not speak; nor did he respond to Langworth's questions. Molentfort also reported upon the making of the alleged will. Early in the evening, Langworth went to the kitchen, returned with a document, and asked everyone to leave the room, except **a servant, Sarah Stokes**. This Mary did, then she had supper and returned to sit with Thomas until he died at about 11 in the evening.

---

[30] Ibid., PROB 18/7/83.
[31] Ibid., PROB 21/14/, 276.

While **Margaret Cruttenden**, a neighbor, corroborated the gist of Mary's version,[32] others present at the demise of Thomas disputed the two women's version of his death, and recalled a quite dissimilar will-making drama. **Margaret Hutchinson**, for example, presented a more sedate scene. She deposed that Thomas had been dressed in his clothes while lying on a pallet bed, and about 5 o'clock in the evening he said, 'Now I desire all friends to withdraw.' Along with others present, she left the room, and sat with Thomas's wife Margaret in the kitchen. Shortly thereafter, Langworth entered the kitchen looking for a pen, and told her that 'he was put upon a business that he was unacquainted with.' Sometime thereafter she returned to the deathbed, and Thomas 'took her by the hand and asked her how she did and afterwards they had discourse together touching spiritual things.'[33]

Two other female witnesses who were present confirmed the widow's version. **Bridget Saunders,** Thomas's domestic servant, concurred that Gollibrand had been of sound mind until his death which occurred at about 11 or 12 o'clock that same evening. During the will-execution ceremony, she was occupied adjusting the pillows supporting the dying man. She recalled that he was 'troubled with palsey,' and that his hand shook. But she was so engaged with her task that she could not say whether he had actually dropped his seal himself. However, she did recall that Thomas Hutchinson and **Sarah Stokes** had signed the will as witnesses.[34] **Stokes** confirmed that there was considerable dialogue between the dying man and those who gathered at the deathbed. She deposed that Thomas had actually insisted on his wife's presence at the execution ceremony, and when the will had been read over to him, he asked her if she was satisfied with her bequest. According to Stokes's version, he sat up in his bed and asked for his spectacles so he could sign and seal the document, and he was able to do so without the assistance of others.[35]

Now there were men around as well, and they corroborated the narrative fashioned by the latter two female witnesses. Two men of the cloth present during the deathbed drama seem to have confirmed the dying man's mental capacity. William Colett, a 'minister,' claimed that he 'discoursed with him before six according to his Duty.'[36] Likewise, Thomas Hutchinson, a Professor of Theology in the University of Cambridge and Rector of All Saints' London, and a witness to the will, visited Thomas that fateful evening. In his witness statement, Hutchinson noted that the dying man was 'weake,' but he recounted

---

[32] Ibid., PROB 24/14, 277.

[33] Ibid., PROB 24/14, 213.

[34] Ibid., PROB 24/12, 179–80.

[35] Ibid., PROB 24/12, 180–81.

[36] Ibid., PROB 24/14, 214.

in no uncertain terms that Thomas 'gave orders for instructions' for his will.[37]
For those who might doubt his memory, Hutchinson claimed that a written
record confirmed his recollections. He testified that he 'keeps a diary and set
down that he signed the dec[ease]d will as witness.'[38]

Finally, there was the testimony of the scrivener, John Langworth. Thomas's
friend for over 20 years, Langworth confirmed that he had consulted at length
with him over a month before his death concerning the various ways in which
Thomas might dispose of his estate.[39] He recalled that Thomas was in particular
troubled about the proper disposition of his London tenements, and that he had
finally resolved that they should pass to Samuel after the death of his wife. But
he also wanted to use this property to care for his sisters during their lives. In the
course of their discussions, Langworth took down notes, and then proceeded
to see one Mr. Wickham, an attorney who practiced in St. Bartholomew's Lane
in London. According to Langworth, Wickham advised him to create a trust.
When Langworth returned to Lea with a draft, he was unhappily surprised to
note that his friend's physical condition had deteriorated so rapidly. Regardless,
Langworth raised the issue of a trust with his dying friend. Thomas concurred
with the arrangement, and selected trustees. But Langworth hoped that a lawyer
would arrive in time to redraft the will according to the terms of the trust, as
advised by Wickham and agreed to by Gollibrand. When it seemed as if the
dying man was fading, Langworth decided it was dangerous to dally any longer,
and resolved to take matters in hand. He went into the kitchen and wrote the
will himself 'from memory.' Thereafter, it was read over to Gollibrand, and duly
executed by him. Although Thomas was weak, he was 'raised up on the bed,' and
was told 'to take time to sign cleerly.' This he was able to do, and without his
hand being guided. After the will was executed, the summoned attorney arrived
and was asked to 'draw it up into better form.' Upon perusing the document,
however, the lawyer, deemed a rewrite unnecessary.

The Prerogative Court admitted the will of Thomas Gollibrand to probate.[40]
While the court may have preferred a disposition that left his surviving spouse
a life estate during her widowhood, and was aware that the probating of the will
would lead to that outcome, it was ostensibly charged with deciding a different
issue: was the will offered for probate a valid testamentary act of a man of sound
mind? By admitting the will to probate, the court must have been convinced
that Margaret's rendition of events surrounding her husband's death, a version
corroborated by witnesses – the majority of whom were female – rather than

37 Ibid., PROB 24/12, 175.
38 Ibid.,PROB24/12, 176.
39 Ibid., PROB 24/12, 176–9.
40 Ibid., PROB 11/349, 253. The will is PROB 11/349, 299.

that of his brother Samuel was a more plausible, if not totally accurate narrative of the last few days of the life of Thomas Gollibrand.

The Probate of the Will of William Balle

A second example is also the will of a man, one William Balle. Richard Washington, the executor named therein, offered the will for probate. In his allegation, it was conceded that the will, though dictated by Balle, had been reduced to writing and sealed, but was not signed: 'by reason of the shaking of hand he did not sign but did offer to and declared the same to be his will.'[41] Although his brother Charles and the will-maker's son William had been summoned to the dying man's bedside to observe the will's execution, they did not arrive until an hour after it was 'published' in the manner specified by church-court law. When they did arrive at Washington's coffeehouse, the place where Balle lodged, and subsequently died, they asked to see the will. Apparently, they read it over and then left without comment.

Oddly, the contestant, son William who was not provided for in the will, made little of the missing signature in his allegations. Rather, he strongly opposed its probate on two other grounds. First, he charged that the dying man had lacked sufficient mental capacity to write a will, and second, that the will was the product of undue influence, interlinked claims that surfaced frequently in the causes observed in this study.[42] However, unlike Thomas Gollibrand's brother, Balle's heir claimed that his father's incapacity had been longstanding, rather than the result of his last illness. About 30 years earlier, it was asserted that Balle, an aspiring young man studying for the bar, had suffered a fall that ended his budding legal career and 'impaired his memory and judgement.' The accident left him 'a stupid unfit and melancholy person.' Balle subsequently 'contracted debts,' and when hounded by creditors, he took 'refuge in Whitefryers some years before his death' under the protective wing of the Washingtons, the coffeehouse owners. Thereafter, he was prevailed upon 'by some indirect means' to lodge with them in rooms above their establishment. While it was conceded that sums of money might have been spent by the Washingtons for Balle's support, it was alleged that his host also had received some payments from the deceased; Washington had 'prevailed upon him' to allow him to collect rents owed to Balle on his own account for several years, sums amounting to between £4,000 and £10,000. Shortly before his death, which occurred either late in the evening of 20 October 1690 or early in the morning of the following day, Balle's ill health

---

[41]　*Washington contra Balle*, PROB 18/21/9.

[42]　See Chapter 4, above.

took a turn for the worse: he was 'violently seized by disease ... lost senses ... and could not get out of bed.'[43]

According to a further allegation, it was at that point that pressure was brought to bear on the unfortunate man. Regardless of his weakened state, and 'in the extremitie of sickness,' **Mrs. Washington** (her Christian name is left blank in the document) 'contrived dec[ease]ds will' without benefit of instruction from the dying man. To corroborate the assertion of Balle's debilitated condition, the contestant offered the following assertions: first, when Dr. Brown, Balle's physician, came to attend the dying man about an hour after the 'pretended will' was made, Balle could not respond to his questions; second, **nurse Dorothy Chebsey,** who attended Balle, had refused to witness the will; and finally, 'in order to prevent fraud' Chebsey had summoned the contestant and the dying man's brother Charles to observe and to object to the entire charade.[44]

While the question of whether Balle had long ago lost his reason in the fall was not without relevance, Balle's son, as contestant, had to prove one of two issues: either that at the time the will was executed Balle had lacked capacity, or that the will represented the volition of the Washingtons rather than that of the dying man. In order to do so, the contestant summoned four witnesses to shed light on Balle's mental state. All (two males and **two females**) were related to the contestant, and were perhaps therefore biased but, more significantly, their testimony was not directly relevant because they had not been present at the time of the will's execution. Thus, rather than being able to describe Balle's condition when the testamentary act was being undertaken, they could only confirm that the now-deceased had had a fall long ago, an accident that had left him senseless. The witnesses, however, could confirm that young William, who had long believed that he would receive his father's estate, was deserving of his father's bounty: all four witnesses agreed that the young man had always been 'dutiful.'[45] Thus, at least in their view, there was no reason for Balle to have disinherited his son in the will.[46]

In sum, the depositions of the four witnesses summoned by the contestant, though helpful, were neither entirely disinterested nor was their evidence pertinent. That they could not claim to have been present at the moment of the

---

[43]   *Washington contra Balle*, PROB 18/21/9.

[44]   Ibid., PROB 18/21/7.

[45]   Ibid., The witnesses were Joyce Balle (PROB 24/30, 100–101); Henrietta Balle (PROB 24/30 101–2); and Charles Balle (PROB 24/30, 103–4). A fourth witness, Dr. Milo Cook, Balle's sister's husband, attested to his brother-in-law's prowess as a student, and the sad tale of how his fall from a scaffold had terminated his career at the bar (PROB 24/30, 105).

[46]   Ibid., PROB 24/30, 104 and PROB 24/30, 102.

will's execution was crucial. Though Balle had been of weakened intellect since his fall, the will might have been executed in a lucid moment, when the dying man was able to understand that he was undertaking a testamentary act.

But the contestant had another witness, **Dorothy Chebsey,** the unhappy William's nurse, who was in attendance at the crucial moment that the alleged will was made. She, in common with many others who plied that trade, hovered about a deathbed, in this case during the course of Balle's last illness, and was therefore able to testify to his condition at the time of 'execution.' According to her testimony, about a fortnight before Balle died, he was 'taken ill.' From that point on until his death 'he was kept in his chamber.' The day before Balle expired she reported that he was 'insensible.' While she tried to get him up out of his bed, 'he was grown so weak that he made water and it run through the seate of his breaches.' When his son William came to see him to 'ask for his blessing,' Balle's responses were 'senseless.' Nor was Balle able to converse with Dr. Brown, his physician, who was summoned to the deathbed and who had questioned the dying man about his condition.[47]

According to Chebsey, Balle had really played no role in either the drafting or the execution of the document propounded by Washington as Balle's last will.[48] Not only did he not sign the document, he also did not dictate its terms. About seven in the evening, the Washingtons, accompanied by one Joseph Washington of the Middle Temple (whom she knew was the promoter's half-brother) and Richard Strode entered Balle's chamber. A 'Paper' was read to him, but 'asked did he like it he made no answer and was unable to hold the pen to sign.' Although Joseph Washington then indicated that he did not want to continue with the ceremony of execution, Strode proceeded to drop Balle's seal on the document. When asked if she would sign as witness, Chebsey refused on the grounds that 'he was insensible and she would sweare so before a thousand Judges to that effect.' In his interrogatories addressed to her, however, Richard Washington suggested that her reluctance to sign was based on other grounds; she was asked if she had refused to sign the document because she was 'upset there was no gift to her.'[49]

Washington's witnesses produced far different versions of the physical and mental state of Balle, and of the drama that surrounded the execution of the dying man's will. Perhaps the most detailed vignette was offered by Richard Strode, who seems to have orchestrated the production of the document and

---

[47]   Ibid., PROB 24/30, 92–3.

[48]   Ibid., PROB 24/30, 94.

[49]   Ibid., PROB 18/21/7. We have no response in her deposition to this rather pointed question.

who signed the will as a witness.[50] Although he did not specify in what degree, in his deposition Strode claimed kinship with Balle. Perhaps it was on that basis that Strode raised the question of a will with Balle on the day that he died. Strode claimed that when he had come to the Washingtons' coffeehouse on the morning of the 20 October, he recalled that **Washington's wife and daughter** were both overcome with grief at the turn for the worse that Balle's condition had taken, and distraught at their inability to summon a doctor to his bedside. Strode, on the other hand, appeared to be more concerned with lawyers than he was with doctors. He stated that he had asked Balle if he had made his will. When Balle replied that he had not, Strode 'thought that it was necessary that he put him in mind of it.' He left, subsequently returned, and when he queried Balle again, he told him 'that it was best for satisfaction of all his friends to make a will.' Strode claimed that Balle had agreed; the dying man replied, 'I wish it with all my heart.' Balle asked Strode to draft the will, but he declined; rather Strode suggested that 'cozen Washington' be summoned. Strode confirmed that he was present when Joseph Washington read the will to Balle, and heard Balle say in an 'audible voice that he liked it.' Although the will 'was delivered to him to subscribe his hands shook so he could not sign.' But Strode dropped wax on the document, and Balle was able to affix his seal thereto. During the transaction, Balle was 'aguey,' but nevertheless of sound mind. Indeed, as the will was being 'executed,' Balle remarked to him that he 'was better than he had been for some time.' Even after the document was sealed, Strode claimed that Balle was 'weake but still capable.' He boldly asserted that Balle had freely made the will; in his view his dying kinsman was 'not pressed.'

The other witness to the will, Joseph Hasselwood, confirmed that Joseph Washington had 'plainly and distinctly' read over the will to Balle. Hasselwood indicated that, upon hearing the dispository provisions, Balle had remarked 'Let it be so.' Hasselwood's recollection of the execution of the will paralleled the narrative offered by Strode: Balle could not sign his will because his hand was shaky, but he was able to drop his seal on the melted wax. However, he noted that Strode and Washington expressed some doubts about validity at the time the will was executed; Strode reportedly told Washington, 'if it do you no good it do you no hurt.'[51]

Although she was not present at the bedside at the time the will was executed, **Mary Boucher,** a domestic servant, confirmed that Balle had been a 'hearty man,' and of 'sound mind.' She stated that she had gone up to Balle's chamber after the will was made and shortly before his death to 'see if hee wanted anything.' Nurse

---

50   Ibid., PROB 24/30, 34.
51   Ibid., PROB 24/30, 34–5.

Chebsey was sitting beside Balle's bed; she heard her 'ask him if he remembered what he had done,' and he responded affirmatively. Boucher reported that Chebsey asked 'what care have you made that I am paid'; and when he did not respond, she added 'I hope to be reimbursed.' Again there was silence. All things considered, Boucher's evidence indicates both mental capacity shortly after the will was executed and a lack of coercion regarding the dispositive terms of the document. Indeed she confirmed that the exclusion of Balle's son and brother from his will was possibly intentional; she testified that both 'came to the house very seldom.'[52]

Washington's final witness was the scrivener, Joseph Washington, who admitted that he was promoter Washington's half-brother. One might expect him to support the cause of his half-sibling, and to confirm Strode's version of the will-making drama, and indeed he did. Washington related the details of the conversation that he had had with the dying man, and in particular he recounted Balle's desire to secure payment of the debts that he owed to the Washingtons. The lawyer claimed that he had advised Balle that the 'best way to do so was to make him [R. Washington] executor.' Balle then asked him to draft the will with such a provision. Washington did so and he read it over to Balle. Washington concurred with the other witnesses present that Balle had been too weak to sign the will, but that the dying man was physically able to drop his seal. As to Balle's general condition, Washington reported that, while he was confined to bed, he was 'capable.'[53]

The court, however, disagreed. The deathbed will of William Balle was not admitted to probate.[54] In common with all the causes, the legal grounds for the decision were not specified in the sentence. Two issues had been raised: the blend of unsound mind and undue influence and the fact that the will was unsigned. A lawyer might conclude that the latter omission was fatal, though there is little evidence in the surviving record that the contestants actually pressed this technicality. Perhaps they realized that court was less concerned with form than with intent, or maybe it was conceded that the seal sufficed. The contestant, however, strenuously pursued the issues of mental capacity and undue influence. Both sides offered evidence to support their view as to whether the will was a valid testamentary act of the dying man. It was a matter of whom the court believed, and of the standard of capacity and the level of coercion required to nullify a will on the grounds of lack of mental capacity and undue influence. Perhaps the court believed that the Washingtons had overreached and contrived the will for their own advantage. Certainly there was sufficient evidence for the

52   Ibid., PROB 24/30, 40.
53   Ibid., PROB 24/30, 49.
54   Ibid., PROB 11/407, 310.

court so to hold. But if the court did believe the narrative Balle's son fashioned, it must have valued the evidence of a female nurse over that of the scrivener and two male witnesses.

Conclusion

In this chapter, I argue that women were empowered by the 'culture of will-making' that obtained in early modern England. Women played vital roles in both testamentary acts and testamentary litigation. Some made their own wills and others orchestrated the testamentary acts of their kin, friends, and neighbors. Women also served as scriveners and as witnesses. As administrators and executrices, they offered wills for probate. And, when it came to probate disputes, their testimony as witnesses was often critical. The two causes rehearsed in detail in this chapter do not prove that the testimony of women had directed the court's ultimate sentences. One can only speculate as to the reasons that actually moved the court in each of these causes. But if we assume that the judges were attempting to fathom what actually transpired at the deathbed in order to make their decision on will validity, they had to construct a narrative of the will-making from the testimony of the witnesses. In these causes, and indeed countless others, women frequently supplied that evidence, because their gender roles placed them in the perfect position to observe the dramas that surrounded will-making. Their presence, both in and out of court, indicates no preference for males either to serve as witnesses to wills or to be called upon to testify to events surrounding the execution of an alleged testamentary act. Thus women were not only will-makers, executrices, witnesses to testamentary acts, and litigants, they were also, at least at times, crucial arbiters of the facts that governed the outcome of many testamentary causes.

Conclusion

By the time of the Restoration, most landed estates held by the aristocracy and gentry came to be transmitted between generations by family settlements, written documents crafted by skilled conveyancers executed most frequently on the marriage of the an individual family's presumptive male heir. This tendency in inheritance practice, *inter vivos* land settlement, was widespread and can be observed even amongst lesser landholders, the yeomanry and urban landowners, though perhaps not as markedly. Precisely how these arrangements were fashioned is unclear. Drafts were undoubtedly first penned, but the final writing to emerge was likely the product of days or weeks, and no doubt in some cases, even months of negotiation and reflection in solemn conclave between a mix of family members with interests in the property concerned. The bride and groom were involved to be sure, but so too was the senior generation; perhaps even both sets of parents were represented if they were alive. Roles might vary, in part depending upon whether the land was the groom's patrimony or that of the bride. And familial participation might be ongoing, because both generations could continue to hold interests in the patrimony, even after the settlement took effect. Moreover, under the classical strict settlement, others family members were also involved, the portions of siblings (in some cases brothers and sisters of both parents and children) were often dictated in the settlement. Intergenerational transfer of land thus became an orderly process rather than a single event, with detailed consideration of inheritance strategy culminating in a writing. Disputes that arose over these settlements were consigned to Chancery where the terms could be unraveled with due deliberation in cases that might take years to reach conclusion. With respect to inheritance of land, then, early modern England to all intents and purposes had completed its transition from a society in which legal directions were oral to one in which transfers were embodied in a writing.

As the preceding chapters illustrate, this sedate picture sketched above, admittedly idealized for the purposes of comparison, did not obtain with respect to the intergenerational transfer of personal property. Unlike the transmission of land, personal property passed from the dead to the living on an event, the death of its owner, by will or intestate succession. There were no periods of overlapping generational interests similar to those posited above with respect to land. The very nature of the will-making process during the period was haphazard. Even amongst the wealthy, as our example of the Countess of

Somerset illustrates, due deliberation seems to have been in short supply. No doubt the process was complicated in part because death was less predictable, and probably more gruesome than it is today. But it seems odd to the observer that so many individuals gave little thought to the devolution of their personal property at an earlier point of the life course. Our period coincides with the commercial revolution. As the value of personal property began to increase, at least for some, the will became a more economically significant vehicle for intergenerational wealth transfer. That the passage of significant amounts of personal property seemed so chaotic must have been troublesome, even to men and women who organized their affairs in a more tidy manner than those whose stories grace the preceding chapters.

That the Statute of Frauds addressed wills of land therefore comes as no surprise. Not all landholders executed settlements; and land acquired after execution somehow had to be transmitted. That Parliament in the statute went beyond land, and for the first time addressed will-making with respect to personal property as well is more perplexing. Surely Parliament's goal must have been to bring order and a greater degree of efficiency to the probate of wills. I have suggested, although I cannot prove, that Parliament's discussion of deathbed will-making and the detail in which it addressed oral wills demonstrates a link between debate in the high court known as Parliament and litigation in the more modest jurisdiction called the Prerogative Court of Canterbury. The compromise reached in the statute, allowing the practice of deathbed will-making to continue to be valid while tightening the requirements on oral wills, to my mind demonstrates the sort of deference legislatures frequently exhibit towards societal norms. Efficiency concerns often give way to other societal values. After all, then as now with wills, it was not the Crown's property that was at issue. Rather, it was that of the will-maker.

So, as we have seen, the dramas that played out in the Prerogative Court survived the Statute of Frauds. Probate of wills was not unaffected by its mandates, but the sort of counterpoised interests that led to litigation before the statute continued. Those discontented with legacies pursued other issues like undue influence and lack of mental capacity, ones left untouched by the statute. Before chastising Parliament too harshly, recall that will contests plague the courts in our own time, and modern law reformers have been less than successful in addressing shortcomings in current law.

If the vignettes of devising, dying, and dispute which the causes observe produced do not reveal to us enough about the law of wills, which we readily concede seems to have reposed largely in the minds of the judges and applied on a case-by-case basis, it certainly tells us much about the lives of our forebears. They seemed disinclined to believe that their lives were ending, uncertain who really deserved their bounty, unsure of how to transmit it, and quite angry at the end with some of their family members. In short, they **were** like we **are**. And like many of us, they were content to allow the probate court to sort it all out after they were elsewhere.

Appendix

A primer on probate jurisdiction in early modern England, probate procedure in the Prerogative Court of Canterbury, the sources used in this study, and how the evidence was assembled

Introduction

The purpose of this appendix is to place in a straightforward fashion, make easily comprehensible, the jurisdiction studied, its procedure, the nature of the records employed in this study, and how they were assembled. In accomplishing the first aim, I shall err on the side of simplicity, in order to provide the non-specialist reader with only basic information needed to understand how the records observed were produced. Thereafter, I shall discuss in detail the documents produced by the court that have been the evidentiary source of this study, and how I selected the causes that were observed.

Jurisdiction

Those even vaguely familiar with civil jurisdiction in pre-modern England will not be surprised to learn that English probate jurisdiction was reposed in a variety of courts with overlapping competence. Nor will they be shocked to discover that, while in the abstract this seamless jurisdictional web was fixed and its rationale perhaps even explicable, its logic may not appear obvious to the modern eye. The historian is not alone; contemporaries may have been likewise confused. Indeed, even Henry Swinburne, whose volume was calculated to guide contemporaries on will-making and probate, noted 'diverse opinions' over the interpretation of the jurisdictional requirements of particular probate courts.[1]

At the onset, two legal terms of art must be distinguished: probate and administration. Probate means proof – proof that a will, a legal act undertaken by a person now-deceased, is legally valid, and therefore should direct the

---

[1]   Henry Swinburne, *A Brief Treatise of Testaments and Last Wills* (Garland Reprint of 1590 edition, 1978), p. 222. The *Briefe Treatise* was first published late in the reign of Elizabeth I, and was frequently reprinted in the seventeenth and eighteenth centuries and referred to by other contemporary legal writers.

distribution of his or her property after death. Once the will was offered for probate, the executor (executrix if a woman) was authorized to take up administration of the property of the deceased. Once probated, the executor could distribute the deceased's property. The jurisdiction that probated the will would oversee the executor's administration of the deceased goods. However, disputes over land bequeathed generally were taken to royal or borough courts. The term administration was used in successions in which no valid will was proved, where an individual died 'intestate.' The prescribed probate jurisdiction appointed an administrator (or administratrix) and supervised the distribution of the deceased's personal property. As with testate successions, it did not hear disputes over hereditary rights in land.

Where a will should be probated during our period was directed by two interrelated factors: geography and wealth. First, to geography: both where a person died and where that person held property were relevant in determining the proper venue for probate. The probate of wills and the administration of personal property (as opposed to lands and tenements) were largely lodged in ecclesiastical jurisdictions. England and Wales was divided into two provinces, the Archbishoprics of Canterbury and York. Archbishoprics were in turn divided into dioceses, and these were sub-divided into archdeaconries. A person who died with goods situated in only one archdeaconry had his or her will probated or administration granted in the archdeacon's court in that locale. But those with goods in two or more probate jurisdictions were subject to different courts. A deceased with personal property in more than a single archdeaconry had a will probated (or administrations granted) in the Bishop's diocesan court; and those with *bona notabilia*, goods in excess of £5 in more than one diocese, had their wills proved (and again administrations in the event of intestacy) in one of the two Archbishop's court (depending upon geography): the Prerogative Court of Canterbury or the Prerogative Court of York. For those with goods in both provinces, two probates or administrations were required, one in each Archbishop's court. Finally, to make matters more complicated, some areas were outside the jurisdiction of an archdeacon, and subject to 'peculiar' jurisdiction; the power to probate wills and grant administrations in a specific geographical area was held by someone other than the archdeacon, perhaps the dean of a cathedral, a clergyman, or even the lord of a manor.

An investigation of probate litigation in the Prerogative Court of Canterbury will necessarily be skewed towards the more wealthy members of early modern English society, those with *bona notabilia*. Such a bias may not be unwarranted with respect to understanding Parliament's concern to tighten probate procedure, a core objective of this study. During the Interregnum, Parliament's concern was largely directed to the probate of the wills of wealthier property owners. To be sure, focus upon the records of the Canterbury court may have an effect upon the types of causes that emerge from the record, and described herein. The lesser subjects of the realm, however, are not entirely excluded. The threshold monetary level for probate in the Prerogative Court, £5, was by 1660 decidedly modest. Moreover, because the Prerogative Court had jurisdiction over the wills of those who died abroad, there are a number of cases that involve the probate of wills and the granting of administration of the humbler sort, in particular, seamen. The sample therefore will not be totally skewed towards the wealthy.

Finally the Prerogative Court should be characterized as a busy jurisdiction. Of course some days the pressure of business was greater than others. Death, and therefore probate, was seasonal in early modern England.[2] Thus, as one might expect, very late autumn was an active time for the court. For example, on 2 December 1676, 51 separate entries were made in the Act Book: witnesses were summoned; other witnesses were deposed; still others were witnesses cited for failing to appear; allegations, answers, exhibits were submitted. In addition, six sentences were issued that day and eight wills were offered for probate.[3] When the court convened a week later (10 December), it dealt with causes at only a modestly more subdued clip: nine sentences were issued; four wills were offered; and the court dealt with another 13 miscellaneous items.[4] There were, however, less hectic times. For example, on the previous 4 May 4 only six entries were made, no sentences were issued, and only two wills were offered for probate.[5] A month later, on 5 June, only a single entry was made.[6]

Probate Procedure

Most of the testamentary business in the Prerogative Court observed concerned probates in solemn form.[7] In his *Briefe Treatise*, Swinburne succinctly summarized probate procedure:

---

[2] E.A. Wrigley and R.S. Schofield, *The Population History of England, 1541–1871: a reconstruction* (London, 1981), pp. 293–98, especially Figure 82.

[3] PBOB 29/57, 655–64.

[4] PROB 29/57, 666–78.

[5] PROB 29/57, 453–7.

[6] PROB 29/57, 495.

[7] Some of the testamentary causes observed were applications to take up administration (5.4 percent) and others demands for accounts by executors or administrators of the deceased's property (8.2 percent).

When the testament is to be prooved in forme of lawe, it is requisite that such persons as have interest (that is to say) the widow and next of kinne to the deceased, to whom the administration of his goods ought to be committed, if he had died intestate, are to be cited to be present at the probation and approbation of the testament, in whose presence the will is to be exhibited to the judge, and the petition to bee made by the party which perferreth the will, and enacted for the receiving, swearing and examining of the witnesses upon the same, and for the publishing or confirming thereof: whereupon witnesses are received, and sworne accordingly, and are examined everie one of them secretly, and severally, not onely upon the allegation or articles made by the partie producing them but also upon interrogations ministered by the adverse partie, and their depositions committed to writing: afterwards the same be published, and in case the proof be sufficient the Judge doth by his sentence or decree, pronounce for the validitie of the testament.[8]

Although the passage from Swinburne does not set out precisely who would offer the will for probate, the promoter of the cause was in most cases the executor of the will, an individual 'interested' in the estate (that is to say a legatee), or the person who had custody of the document. Indeed, it was possible for the promoter to be an amalgam of all three: he or she had the will in hand, was executor/executrix, and was a primary will beneficiary. In offering the will for probate, the promoter asked the court to regard the will as a valid exercise of testamentary volition and to empower the executor to gather the deceased's personal estate, pay debts, and a distribute of what remained to legatees.[9]

Actually, as students of the early modern legal order will not be surprised to learn, the process was a good bit more complicated. First, not all wills were probated in solemn form (if they were probated at all), what Swinburne called 'form of law.' Instead, the will's promoter might elect a less formal process, probate in common form. In common-form probate, the parties with an adverse interest (the intestate heirs who would take the estate if the will was found to be invalid and the deceased's spouse) were not served with notice, and therefore not

---

[8]   I have relied heavily on Swinburne's *Briefe Treatise*. Though first written in the reign of Elizabeth, it was the standard work on wills and was reprinted into the nineteenth century. In fact the copy I most frequently consulted, the one in the Cambridge University Library, is a 1677 edition. My references, however, are to the Garland Reprint of 1590 edition, 1978, p. 224.

[9]   *The Special and General Reports made to His Majesty by the Commission appointed to Enquire into the Practice and jurisdiction of the Ecclesiastical Courts in England and Wales 1831–32*, pp. 199– 215.

likely present at probate proceedings. The court acted solely upon the petition of the will's promoter and authorized administration based exclusively thereon.

Wills offered for probate in common form thus leave scant record. Though more expeditious and less costly an option, there was a greater risk for promoters who decided to take the easy way out. Probate in common form left the executor and the heirs vulnerable, because a grant of probate in common form by the court was open to a subsequent challenge by a party with an interest in the estate.[10] Indeed, as Philipp Floyer noted in his manual of church court practice published in the first part of the eighteenth century, much of the Prerogative Court's business was 'setting aside wills exhibited or otherwise proved in Common Form.'[11]

In Chapter 3, I address the factors that moved individuals to elect to probate testamentary acts in solemn form: to establish conclusively the right to take possession of the will-maker's goods, and to distribute them according to the will-maker's testamentary directions. If a will's promoter believed that his or her right to take possession of the deceased goods could become contentious, promoter might conclude that it would be prudent to bear the inconvenience and the greater expense of solemn form probate. Moreover, to come forward with the will immediately would be a sensible strategy. Arguably the court might be more sympathetic to an individual who sought its authority in advance (and therefore be more likely to confirm the validity of the testamentary act in question), rather than after having been hauled before it by a disappointed heir. Thus one might expect that the promoters were less likely to be the deceased's heir, particularly his sole heir, and more likely to be entangled in an estate in which there were conflicting interests between those (heirs, co-heirs and spouses) who believed that they had a claim to the deceased's property. Floyer concurred. He noted that an executor who was in 'no ways kin ... hath the Greatest Part of the Deceased Effects bequeathed to him' might cite the widow and heirs, and having proved the will in solemn form a 'definitive sentence for the Force and Validitiy' of the will would be entered which could not be set aside 'unless some Nullity doth appear in the Proceedings.'[12]

Of course, most early modern Englishmen and women probably died with a variety of surviving relations (children, siblings, parents and spouses) each who believed that they had claims to their individual bounty. And they did so in varying and unknown configurations, so it is not a simple matter to determine whether the relations exhumed from the documents submitted in the causes

---

[10] Swinburne, *Briefe Treatise*, pp. 223–5.

[11] Phillip Floyer, *The Proctor's Practice in the Ecclesiastical Courts* 2nd edn (London, 1746), p. xxxviii.

[12] *The Proctor's Practice*, pp. xxxix.

discussed above varied greatly from the norm, and therefore explained why these particular wills were probated in solemn form while most other wills escaped the process. Suffice it to say that a significant number of causes commenced when an outsider came to the court will in hand, and an even healthy number involve clashes between spouses and heirs, a traditional fault-line in social relationships then and now.

The study, however, focuses on contested wills; and to expand on Swinburne's exposition, procedure ran roughly as follows. Promoter offers a will for probate in solemn form; an individual cited disputes the validity of the will or the accuracy of its terms in an answer; objections are often times elaborated upon in an allegation, particularly in causes in which contestant sought to promote a different will. Interrogatories to witnesses are filed by both sides, though in the more actively contested causes second (or even additional) rounds of questions are submitted. Sometime thereafter depositions are taken. Judgment follows, unless one side or the other elected to drop the cause. While most of the causes follow this pattern, others observed raise different issues: a creditor who entered a caveat, claiming an interest in the property of the deceased; an heir who sought an accounting from an executor; a party who wished to take up administration of an intestate's estate. In these causes, however, the same process of answer, interrogatory, depositions, judgment follows if the cause is pursued to conclusion.

The more actively contested the cause, the more documents produced by the parties, the more useful it is in the enquiry. Thus it was the hotly contested cause that yielded more detailed interrogatories, and therefore resulted in more elaborate depositions. From these depositions much may be learned about the deathbed, illness, how wills were drafted and executed. In a number of causes, the questions submitted go beyond merely the circumstances under which the will was produced but explore matters relevant to the distribution in the will. For example, if a child was disinherited, witnesses might be called upon to opine upon justifications; if a person seemingly unrelated was named executrix, witnesses might explain that the choice was made because she was married to the dead man; and if joined, reveal the circumstances that surrounded their union. These depositions illuminate marriage practices, family discord, and gender relations.

Documentary Sources

The litigants in the Prerogative Court of Canterbury, be they the promoters or the contestants of wills, told stories to the judges. In court papers, in their allegations and answers, they set out in detail the precise reasons for either their support for the validity of wills promoted, or the logic that supported their contest. Unlike most pre-modern courts, they did so using language largely intelligible to the lay person. Moreover, they produced witnesses to corroborate their version of the saga that they related. From both litigants and witnesses, detailed vignettes of the now deceased's last moments were provided: when, and in what manner, and from what causes, he or she expired. Often their story details the will's execution: who drafted it; who was present at the signing; to whom it was given for safekeeping. Legal causes of action are stated: undue influence, testamentary capacity, and a myriad of authenticity issues were raised. Other matters also emerge from the record. The specific questions posed by the legal dispute, for example, was the will a product of undue influence, might give way to ancillary matters of marriage formation, criminality, family discord, areas of tremendous interest to social historians, but spheres of social contact that frequently produce only scant record.

The Prerogative Court of Canterbury generated the following sources (all housed in the National Archives) used in this study: Act Books,[13] Allegations,[14] Answers,[15] Interrogatories,[16] Depositions,[17] and Exhibits[18] to name the most important. Their utility has been of mixed value to this study.

Act Books provide the most complete picture of the course of testamentary litigation, because they contain entries of all business that came before the court in the course of each session. In the well-indexed volumes, offers of probate were redacted, notations made that witnesses were summoned, appeared to testify, or were absent as the case may be. That a sentence was issue was also recorded. Act Books are invaluable in filling in the gaps that occur because of missing documentation. For example, where the original offer of probate is missing from a bundle of allegations, a notation that it was submitted can usually be located in the Act Book. Likewise, if there is a question as to whether a witness testified, but no deposition located, the record in the Act Book will allow the research to determine that it was somehow lost. Thus, when and who offered the will for probate in one of the causes and when and who opposed probate can be ascertained, and if the cause proceeded to sentence, precisely when it was issued.

Yet complete as they should be, Act Books are a vexing source for the legal historian who wishes to understand the subject matter of testamentary disputes. Because the Act Book is a procedural record of the transactions of the court, the will contest is only set out formulaically therein; the legal basis of the dispute

---

[13]   PROB 29.
[14]   PROB 18.
[15]   PROB 25.
[16]   Generally filed with allegations, PROB 18.
[17]   PROB 24.
[18]   PROB 28.

is not expressed in sufficient detail for one to be certain of the essence of the controversy. Moreover, offers recorded seemed to have been dropped because one frequently finds only the initial entry. There is no further process. Thus an entry in an Act Book that indicates that a cause was commenced does not always mean that litigation actually ensued, because many causes do not seem to have gone further than the initial stage, the offer for probate. Moreover, not all the causes initially entered in the Act Book have surviving allegations.

There are, however, other sources from which to draw a more complete picture of the essence of probate disputes. First, there are the 'allegations,' the document which Swinburne described as 'the petition to be made by the partie which preferreth the will,'[19] preserved in bundles in the National Archives. The allegations provide a richer, more informative source than do the Act Books to discern the substance of testamentary business. Although most causes that were resolved by sentence in the Prerogative Court of Canterbury have left scant record, about one-third have left surviving allegations. In most of these causes, the initial document filed, the 'offer to probate,' which commenced an individual cause survives. In some causes, a subsequent allegation supplemented the offer, perhaps in response to the contestant's 'answer.' In other causes, however, the initial offer to probate appears to be missing, and only an allegation by the promoter in which he or she denied some or all of the points raised in the contestant's allegation survives. The contestant opposed the promoter's allegation either by 'answer' or by filing what I have called 'counter-allegations.' The latter seems to be the choice most often taken by advocates who litigated testamentary causes, if one may surmise from documentary survival. Few answers are archived, while the files of contested probates are replete with 'counter-allegations.' Their occurrence cannot always be explained by the fact that a contestant was offering up an alternative document for probate. Why the contestant filed a counter-allegation rather than an answer is not clear; contestant might have done both, and the answer was not recorded in the act book and is lost.

Additional information concerning the substance of testamentary causes can be gleaned from other documents produced by the litigation. Perhaps the most informative are the interrogatories and the depositions taken in response thereto. In the National Archives, interrogatories are often catalogued with the corresponding allegation. The initial interrogatories filed were those questions that the party cited wished to ask of promoter's witnesses. For example, consider a simple cause in which the promoter offered to probate a will in solemn form; the promoter was required to bring forward the attesting witnesses. Those witnesses might be asked a battery of questions. Were they aware of the danger of perjury

---

19   Swinburne, *Brief Treatise*, p. 224.

and advised of its consequences? How long did they know the deceased, and their 'producent'? Were they lodgers, servants or of other 'mean stature'? How much were they worth debts paid? Were they instructed how to testify? To whom they would give victory if it was in their power to do so?[20] So common was this litany that some interrogatories merely state that the witness should be asked the 'usual questions.'[21] If, for example, a party cited wished to challenge the will on the grounds of undue influence or lack of testamentary capacity, contestant directed questions to those witnesses that might establish coercion or cast doubt upon the mental faculties of the will-maker. Interrogatories in cases of testamentary capacity or undue influence that were frequently posed include: At whose request was the will drawn? Who wrote down the words? Who was present during the ceremony? Was the deceased's hand guided when he or she signed the will or made a mark?[22] Oral wills produced their own particularized battery, focusing on whether the words spoken amounted to a will, and if so, what were its precise terms.[23] Indeed, so detailed were interrogatories submitted that they might occupy many sheets of paper, leading some commentators to doubt their effectiveness. Floyer cautioned that 'Long and Multiplex Interrogatories often hurt the Cause of the Party Ministrant and make for the Producent –*Ergo cavete Procuratores*!'[24] Doubtless in some causes Floyer was correct, but the historian does not have the same agenda as the advocate. Much can be ascertained about the circumstances under which the will was executed by recourse to opposing party's interrogatories.

The responses to the interrogatories, the witness depositions, likewise illuminate the precise issues in dispute, and are a major documentary source in this study of testamentary litigation. Much evidence on the context in which wills were drafted and executed, information that corroborates, conflicts or elaborates upon the allegations and answers of parties to the cause, and allows us to probe further issues of mental capacity, undue influence, authenticity and the like is derived from witness depositions. The depositions provide 'contextual' evidence of the lives of the will-makers and their social circle: they provide windows into marriage processes, vignettes of family discord, and observations on the role of women. Moreover, witness testimony was useful to the church courts in resolving

---

[20]   Rather 'typical' examples are *Cooke contra Neades*, PROB 18/7/72; *West contra West*, PROB 18/18/35; *Kinaston contra Young*, PROB 18/13/35.

[21]   *Gardner et Moody contra Cumberland*, PROB 18/8/108.

[22]   For example, see *Walker et Mason contra Grove*, PROB 18/1/50. See Chapter 6 for an extensive discussion.

[23]   For example, *Gardner et Moody contra Cumberland*, PROB 18/8/108. See Chapter 7 for an extensive discussion.

[24]   Floyer, *The Proctor's Practice*, p. 107.

a cause, or so contemporary commentators suggest; John Ayliffe noted that:
'Among all the several Species of Proof that is deem'd most effectual is made by
Witness whose Credit and Evidence is involved for the Confirmation of some
doubtful matter.'[25] Because depositions figure so prominently in this study it is
useful to consider in more detail precisely who might qualify as a witness.

At civil law most persons were regarded as competent to testify with the
exception of those who exhibited 'dishonestie in manners,' 'want of judgement,'
or 'affection more to one partie than to the other.' Straightforward as the above
benchmark seems, Swinburne conceded that the learning on the matter of
witness competence 'should far exceed the quantitie of this small volume.'[26]
Ayliffe considered incapacity of witnesses in more detail, and noted that
individual judges had wide discretion to 'repel and set aside unfit and improper
Witnesses.'[27] Accordingly, those of doubtful character should be excluded, 'since
a good Name and Reputation for Credit and Integrity is the Foundation of all
Testimony.'[28] Witnesses should be 'free not bond,' above the age of 14 (though
20 was 'full' age at civil law), and 'not an infamous person or the like.' Women
could be (and as Chapter 10 demonstrates indeed often were) witnesses in
testamentary causes. Wealth was a consideration in determining credibility;
'whether he be a Pauper and an Indigent Person?'; as was religion, 'whether he
be a Pagan, Infidel, Heretick, Christian or the like?'.[29] And above all there was
the question of interest. Neither 'Friends' nor Eneemies' should be witnesses,
though it was recognized that in testamentary causes it might be necessary to
admit testimony of persons close to the deceased because they were often present
at the time the will was executed.[30] Likewise, they ought not to be hired, though
the party who summoned a witness often paid their expenses. Above all, they
should not be 'instructed' on how to testify.[31]

The truthfulness of the response of witnesses to the questions proffered by
the parties cannot be assumed. And while perhaps comforting, fidelity is not
required. While the court may have been concerned with veracity, the historian
is content with the story that is told, so long as it is plausible. Indeed there is
some reason to doubt the truthfulness of the testimony. Witnesses are more
likely to be truthful when they are disinterested, and those summoned were

---

[25]   John Ayliffe, *Parergon Juris Anglicani: or a commentary by way of supplement to the
canons and constitutions of the Church of England* (London, 1724), p. 535.

[26]   Swinburne, *Brief Treatise*, p. 186.

[27]   Ayliffe, *Parergon Juris Anglicani*, p. 535.

[28]   Ibid., p. 538.

[29]   Ibid., p. 537.

[30]   Ibid., p. 541.

[31]   Ibid., p. 543.

not without connection to the parties. In testamentary causes they were called to court by one party or another, and therefore not unknown to the litigants, at least to the summoning party. It was not uncommon in the interrogatories for a witnesses to be asked at whose behest the witness was called, whether she had been instructed on how to testify, received any payment for testimony, and whether and whom they favored in outcome. Witnesses frequently conceded in their testimony that they were linked to one or the other parties (or even both parties) in varying degrees: as relatives, friends, servants, and apprentices.[32]

Although research has focused primarily upon the allegations, interrogatories, and depositions, the judicial process in the Prerogative Court produced other documents that aid the researcher in the quest to understand more fully the nature of probate litigation. The 'answer,' the contestant's formal response to the promoter's offer of probate, has been mentioned. In the National Archives, answers have been filed separately, but do not survive for most causes. Those that have been preserved shed further light on the nature of the controversy. In addition to the answer, cause papers and exhibits were submitted to the court and remain as part of the record. Unfortunately, few of this class of documents survive.

Having discussed the sources available, the historian of probate must reveal that which is not at his disposal. It would have made an investigation into probate law and practice in early modern England more satisfying if the judges furnished written opinions in which they explained their decisions. This they did not do. In causes that were pursued to conclusion, the Act Book usually notes judgment, a sentence recorded, and the will registers[33] indicate whether the contested will was admitted to probate (or nullified) by sentence of the court. Thus although it is easy to discern which party prevailed it is not easy to know why, because the sentence merely indicates whether the will promoted was admitted to probate (a sentence of *pro valore testamentum* or *pro confirmacion testamentum*) or denied probate (*pro nullitate testamentum*). Thus no extant source details the reasons for judgment. Substantive legal principles might explain a sentence in a particular cause. Judgment likewise might have been controlled by the facts: a party might have prevailed because the opposing side's witnesses did not persuade the court of due execution or testamentary capacity, and/or because the application of a principle of law supported his or her claim.

---

[32]   Interrogatories were addressed to witnesses who admitted that they were beneficiaries under the will. Yet in some cases, individuals who viewed the execution of a will declined to witness on the grounds that they were legatees, but were deposed regarding the circumstances under which the will was executed (*Eyre contra Eyre*, PROB 24/16, 16; *Gerard v. Blackston*, PROB 24/14, 391).

[33]   Archived as PROB 11.

That 'reporters' in the modern (or even in the contemporary) sense do not exist is unfortunate to the legal historian of probate. However, this study is not at a loss for law. A variety of commentaries on the law of wills were produced during the period that set out probate law and practice in considerable detail,[34] and a compendium of decisions in testamentary causes was printed in the mid-eighteenth century that also draws upon decisions made during the period under study.[35] The focus of this study, then, is upon the dynamics of testamentary litigation, the issues raised, and how advocates raised and proved their contentions. Moreover, from the resolution of some of the cases, some (if not most) aspects of the law governing probate may be deduced. Aside from the few manuals of probate practice, these disputes are the best evidence that historians have of the legal process by which early modern Englishman transmitted personal property by will.

The Process of Assembling the Evidence

It remains to describe the data set of late seventeenth-century causes upon which analysis was based. To construct it, a sampling technique that was hardly sophisticated was used. Each year, many hundreds of wills were probated the Prerogative Court of Canterbury; but about 300 appear to have been solemn form probates. Allegations survive for only about one-third of these causes: 100 per annum. Constraints of time (and patience) would not allow this researcher to scrutinize every cause commenced in the 40 years after 1660 for which an allegation has been preserved. Causes were observed at five-year intervals, from 1660 to 1696, and a sample was constructed within the selected year. The survey begins with the period 1660–1666 considered as a group, because these years saw relatively few causes, and the allegations were placed together by the archivist in the same bundle. Thereafter, bundles catalogued for 1671, 1676, 1681, 1686, 1691, and 1696 were selected, and every fifth cause was included, with the exception of 1676, a year in which every cause with an allegation in the bundle was read. Because the testamentary causes in the Prerogative Court have a nominal index by deceased, the cause could be followed if it continued in subsequent or began in a preceding year. If, for example, there were further allegations submitted by proponent or contestant in the next year, they were

---

[34]   The commentaries are cited discussed in Chapter 1.

[35]   Floyer, *The Proctor's Practice*. A survey of manuscript will be the subject of a companion study. In addition, a number of cases in Lord Nottingham's manuscripts deal with testamentary matters. D.E.C. Yale (ed.), *Lord Nottingham's Chancery Cases*, 2 vols. (Selden Society, vols. 73 and 79, 1954, 1961).

found; and if a cause commenced in 1670 produced an allegation in 1671, it was included in the sample and the earlier allegation was also read.

One hundred and eighty-four causes emerged through this rough and ready 'sampling' technique.[36] Because somewhere in the order of 10,500 (300 × 35) causes came before the court during the last 40 years of the seventeenth century, of which about 2,635 (75 × 35) to 3,500 (100 × 35) left surviving allegations, the sample is a mere 0.18 percent of all probates, but between 5 to 7 percent of the causes initiated for which allegations have survived. The data set therefore may be regarded as an adequate body of causes, but one can always argue that the researcher should have delved more fully into the bundles!

---

[36] I also have included in this study, though not in the Tables produced in Chapters 3 and 5, a number of other causes, most notably those probates that were nullified during the period that left allegations. The odd cause also came to my attention. All told, I have read the surviving record of 224 causes, and cited 215.

Bibliography

Manuscript Sources: Testamentary Causes

A. 'Sample' Cases[1]

Case No.	Case title	Details
1	Aberry con How contra Aldine (1690)	Allegations: PROB 18/21/16, 18, 20, 29, 90. Depositions: PROB 24/15, 188–90, 214; PROB: 24/30 17, 32, 83–90, 121–2, 138–9. Sentence: PROB 11/407, 349.
2	Adkins contra Bowles (1696)	Allegation: PROB 18/24/60. Sentence: PROB 11/433, 331. Will: PROB 435, 158.
3	Almond contra Almond (1675)	Depositions: PROB 24/14, 313. Sentence: PROB 11/349, 261. Will: PROB 11/349, 1.
4	Arden contra Schedulthropp alias Tuckys (1676)	Allegation: PROB 18/7/61. Answer: PROB 25/2/69. Depositions: PROB 24/14, 303. Will PROB 11/350, 218.
5	Ashendon contra Ashendon (1675)	Allegation: PROB 18/7/53 Deposition: PROB 24/15, 2, 164–5, 197. Sentence: PROB 11/351, 182. Will: PROB 11/351, 335.

---

[1]   For methodology used in selecting these cases, please see the Appendix. Please note also that surnames are not spelled consistantly in the records. I have standardized the names of parties in the text by using the surname found in the case index in the National Archive.

6	Austin contra Smith con Atkinson (1691)	Allegations: PROB 18/21/75, 63. Depositions: PROB: 24/30, 261, 266, 332, Will: PROB 11/18, 142.
7	Baden alias Harward et al. contra Skutt (1675)	Allegations: PROB 18/7/2; PROB 18/8/40. Depositions: PROB 24/15, 186–8, 280, 311. Sentence: PROB 11/355, 98.
8	Baxter contra Baxter (1690)	Allegation: PROB 18/21/45, 46, 55. Depositions: PROB: 24/30, 42, 59–63, 142–54.
9	Beeston contra Webb (1674)	Allegation: PROB 18/6/57, 61; PROB 18/7/69. Answer: PROB 25/2/101. Deposition: PROB 24/14, 93, 239. Sentence: PROB 11/349, 237. Will: PROB 11/348, 36.
10	Beresford contra Beresford (1681)	Allegation: PROB 18/13/45. Sentence: PROB 11/366, 289. Will: PROB 11/365, 131.
11	Bernard contra Johnson (1675)	Allegation: PROB 18/7/92. Depositions: PROB 24/14, 225, 227. Sentence: PROB 11/349, 257. Will: PROB 11/348, 324.
12	Billinghurst contra Billinghurst (1675)	Allegation: PROB 18/7/41. Depositions: PROB 24/14, 318–19. Sentence: PROB 11/351, 206.
13	Bingham contra Wakefield (1686)	Allegation: PROB 18/18/70. Depositions: PROB 24/25, 86–7.
14	Blagrave contra Quarrington (1686)	Allegation: PROB 18/7/80. Depositions: PROB 24/14, 273, 275–6. Will: PROB 11/349, 129.

15	Boles contra Solby (1685)	Allegation: PROB 18/7/15, 27, 50, 53. Depositions: PROB 24/25, 210–14, 221, 229-31, 240, 251. Will: PROB 11/349, 129.
16	Bourden contra Bourden (1663)	Allegation: PROB 18/1/54. Sentence: PROB 11/312, 334. Will: PROB 11/310, 360. Codicil: PROB 11/312, 334.
17	Bourne contra Canham (1675)	Allegation: PROB 18/7/49. Deposition: PROB 24/15, 171–3. Sentence: PROB 11/351, 186. Will: PROB 11/348, 237.
18	Boys et Corbett contra Gibbon (1675)	Allegation: PROB 18/7/39. Depositions: PROB 24/15, 195–6; 265. Answer: PROB 25/2/136. Deposition: PROB 24/15, 195, 266. Sentence: PROB 11/351, 213. Will: PROB 11/349, 28.
19	Brace alias Burton contra Burton (1675)	Allegation: PROB 18/7/20. Depositions: PROB 24/14, 136. Sentence: PROB 11/351, 163. Will: PROB 11/352, 40.
20	Brace contra Reresby (1675)	Allegation: PROB 18/7/55. Deposition: PROB 24/14, 335, 395–6. Sentence: PROB 11/349, 265. Will: PROB 11/347, 9.
21	Bradbourne contra Townsend (1676)	Allegations: PROB 18/7/66; PROB 18/8/116, 106; PROB 18/9/13. Answers: PROB 25/2/165, 186, 186, 188. Sentence: PROB 11/355, 212. Will: PROB 11/352, 386.
22	Bradford contra Crisp (1663)	Allegation: PROB 18/1/70. Sentence: PROB 11/310, 351.

23	Brereton contra Brereton (1681)	Allegation: PROB 18/13/64. Depositions: PROB 24/20, 97. Sentence: PROB 11/368, 111. Will: PROB 11/368, 129.
24	Bretton contra Bretton (1675)	Allegation: PROB 18/7/46. Depositions: PROB 24/14, 322–3; PROB 24/15, 124–6. Sentence: PROB 11/351, 172. Will: PROB 11/357, 45.
25	Brinsden contra Levett (1675)	Allegation: PROB 18/7/83. Depositions: PROB 24/14, 259–60. Sentence: PROB 11/349, 241.
26	Brire et Chamberlayne contra Bryant (1680)	Allegation: PROB 18/12/39, 93; PROB 18/13/95. Depositions: PROB 24/20, 17, 21.
27	Briscoe contra Briscoe (1696)	Allegation: PROB 18/24/45. Depositions: PROB 24/35, 20, 22. Sentence: PROB 11/433, 333. Will: PROB 11/435, 160.
28	Bull contra Thrushby (1675)	Allegation: PROB 18/7/50; PROB 18/8/36. Depositions: PROB 24/15, 186, 197–9; PROB 24/18, 323, 387–8. Sentence: PROB 11/351, 183.
29	Bulstrode et Pearse contra Halford (1680)	Allegation: PROB 18/13/80. Deposition: PROB 24/20, 42.
30	Burchett contra Pickes (1671)	Allegation: PROB 18/3c/54, 64.
31	Bush contra Couzens (1696)	Allegation: PROB 18/24/65, 69. Depositions: PROB 24/35, 196, 209–10, 226. Sentence: PROB 11/433, 338.
32	Campion per curitrix contra Thomas (1680)	Allegations: PROB 18/12/84; PROB 18/13/90. Depositions: PROB 24/20, 37–9.

33	Clarkeson contra Darcy alias Warwick (1686)	Allegation: PROB 18/18/30.
34	Clerke contra Clerke (1675)	Allegation: PROB 18/7/95. Depositions: PROB 24/14, 199–200. Sentence: PROB 11/349, 233. Will: PROB 11/349, 280.
35	Cocke contra Cocke (1680)	Allegations: PROB 18/12/86; PROB18/13/85. Depositions: PROB 24/20, 10–11, 73. Sentence: PROB 11/368, 36. Will: PROB 11/366, 322.
36	Collier alias Hussey et Walls alias Hussey contra Hussey (1675)	Allegation: PROB 18/7/47. Depositions: PROB 24/14, 401–2.
37	Collingwood contra Collingwood et Collingwood (1670)	Allegation: PROB 18/3c/95. Sentence: PROB 11/337, 191. Will: PROB 11/335, 253.
38	Colwell contra Colwell (1675)	Allegation: PROB 18/7/97. Depositions: PROB 24/15, 12 Sentence: PROB 11/351, 190. Will: PROB 11/349, 320.
39	Comber contra Comber (1674)	Allegation: PROB 18/7/6. Deposition: PROB 24/14, 72. Sentence: PROB 11/349, 243. Will: PROB 11/349, 295.
40	Conway contra Huddle et Starr (1675)	Allegations: PROB 18/6/24, 79; PROB 18/7/34. Depositions: PROB 24/4, 35, 71, 143. Will: PROB 11/342, 522.
41	Cooke alias Wright contra Lawes et Hanson (1696)	Allegation: PROB 18/24/10. Sentence: PROB 11/442, 342. Will: PROB 11/437, 83.
42	Cooke contra Batty (1671)	Allegations: PROB 18/3c/28, 30, 41. Depositions: PROB 24/10, 502–4, 517, 526.

43	Cooke contra Neades (1676)	Allegation: PROB 18/7/72. Depositions: PROB: 24/14, 323, 328–9. Sentence: PROB 11/351, 177.
44	Cornish contra Antrobus (1671)	Allegation: PROB 18/3c/85. Sentence: PROB 11/337, 431. Will: PROB 11/366, 143.
45	Cox et Tompkins contra Cox (1686)	Allegations: PROB 18/18/85, 88, 90. Sentence: PROB 11/385, 337.
46	Croke contra Drewry alias Leach (1686)	Allegations: PROB 18/18/20; PROB 18/19/74. Depositions: PROB: 24/25, 324–5, 351, 353. Sentence: PROB 11/389, 276.
47	Crow contra Crow (1691)	Allegation: PROB 18/21/40. Deposition: PROB 24/30, 97. Sentence: PROB 11/403, 357. Will: PROB 11, 403, 358.
48	Curwin et Short contra Meggot (1686)	Allegation: PROB 18/18/85. Depositions: PROB 24/25, 14, 17.
49	Darrell contra Rowse (1675)	Allegation: PROB 18/7/21. Depositions: PROB 24/14, 117; PROB 24/15, 3.
50	Davis et al. contra Rogers (1685)	Allegations: PROB 18/18/10; PROB 18/19/17, 22, 30, 31, 44. Depositions: PROB 24/25, 244–51, 258–60. Sentence: PROB 11/389, 301. Will: PROB 11/390, 58.
51	Deene alias Collins contra Deane alias Collins (1675)	Allegation: PROB 18/7/26. Sentence: PROB 11/349, 266. Will: PROB 11/349, 305.
52	Dickinson contra Boughley (1671)	Allegation: PROB 18/3c/70. Sentence: PROB 11/337, 450. Will: PROB 11/336, 361.

53	Digby contra Digby alias Longueville (1674)	Allegations: PROB 18/7/15, 44, 52. Answers: PROB 25/2/87, 89, 108. Depositions: PROB 24/14, 63, 371–8. Sentence: PROB 11/351, 220.
54	Dixie alias Willoughby contra Slater (1671)	Allegations: PROB 18/3b/4; PROB 18/3c/4, 87, 100.
55	D'laune et Colly contra Wentworth (1686)	Allegation: PROB 18/18/80. Depositions: PROB 24/25, 97–9. Sentence: PROB 11/385, 336. Will: PROB 11/383, 343.
56	Draper contra Clay (1696)	Allegation: PROB 18/24/35. Depositions: PROB 24/35, 188. Sentence: PROB 11/433, 340. Will: PROB 11/428, 33.
57	Dudley contra Roberts (1662)	Allegation: PROB 18/1/40. Depositions: PROB 24/5, 129.
58	Dyamond alias Webber contra Collyer et Skinner (1673)	Allegation: PROB 18/7/42. Depositions: PROB 24/14, 208–9, 227.
59	Ellis contra. Parsons (1674)	Allegations: PROB 18/6/23; PROB 18/7/14, 22, 56, 76. Answers: PROB 25/2/125, 133, 135. Depositions: PROB 24/13, 248; PROB 24/14, 47–58, 148, 195–7, 263–4, 299–303, 317–18, 327–8, 333–4, 382–4; PROB 24/15–20, 177–83. Sentence: PROB 11/351, 180.
60	Elson contra Ayliff et Hayes (1674)	Allegations: PROB 18/6/73; PROB 18/7/29, 87. Answers: PROB 25/2/ 91, 94, 110, 120. Depositions: PROB 24/14, 244–5, 248–50, 267–9, 272. Sentence: PROB 11/349, 266. Will: 11/350, 49.

61	Fidoe contra Fidoe (1691)	Allegation: PROB 18/21/35. Depositions: PROB 24/30, 94, 106. Sentence: PROB 11/407, 337. Will: PROB 11/405, 349.
62	Fiest contra Fiest (1675)	Allegation: PROB 18/7/78. Deposition: PROB 24/14, 231–5. Will: PROB 11, 350, 233.
63	Finch contra Finch (1675)	Allegation: PROB 18/7/45. Depositions: PROB 24/14, 324–5. Sentence: PROB 11/351, 167. Will: PROB 11/349, 315.
64	Foster contra Alsoby alias Slatford (1691)	Allegation: PROB 18/21/10. Deposition: PROB 24/30, 46–7. Sentence: PROB 11/407, 328. Will: PROB 11/405, 210.
65	Foster contra Thurston (1675)	Allegation: PROB 18/7/36. Deposition: PROB 24/15, 173. Will: PROB 11/351, 131.
66	Frassier contra Frassier (1681)	Allegation: PROB 18/13/75. Deposition: PROB 24/20, 84. Sentence: PROB 11/368, 97. Will: PROB 11/367, 91.
67	Frere contra Frere per curator (1675)	Allegation: PROB 18/7/24. Deposition: PROB 24/14, 135. Sentence: PROB 11/349, 264. Will: PROB 11/349, 303.
68	Gerard v. Blackston (1675)	Allegation: PROB 18/7/51. Depositions: PROB 24/14, 338–40, 391–4. Sentence: PROB 11/351, 179. Will: PROB 11/350, 125.
69	Gibbs et Gouge contra Wiggens (1675)	Allegation: PROB 18/7/88. Depositions: PROB 24/14, 260–61. Sentence: PROB 11/349, 249. Will: PROB 11/349, 296.

70   Gibson alias   Allegation: PROB 18/13/40.
      Birchenhead et Morris   Depositions: PROB 24/20, 174, 188, 203.
      et Birchenhead
      contra Woodhall alias
      Newstead (1681)

71   Godfrey contra Delves   Allegation: PROB 18/7/58.
      (1675)   Answer: PROB 25/2/94.
                        Depositions: PROB 24/14, 202–3; PROB
                        24/15, 170, 231–2.

72   Gollibrand contra   Allegations: PROB 18/7/81, 93.
      Gollibrand (1675)   Depositions: PROB 24/ 12, 175–81;
                        PROB 24/14, 175–80, 213–17, 276–8.
                        Sentence: PROB 11/349, 253.
                        Will: PROB 11/ 349, 299.

73   Halley contra Halley   Allegations: PROB 18/7/28, 30, 31;
      (1675)   PROB 18/8/27.
                        Sentence: PROB 11/351, 189.
                        Will: PROB 11/349, 319.

74   Hardwick contra   Allegation: PROB 18/1/15.
      Holland (1667)

75   Hare alias Elliot et Hare   Allegation: PROB 18/21/15.
      alias Field contra Hare   Depositions: PROB 24/30, 117–18.
      (1691)   Sentence: PROB 11/407, 346.
                        Will: PROB 11/409, 149.

76   Harwood contra Vaughn   Allegation: PROB 18/7/77, 82, 86.
      (1675)   Answer: PROB 25/2/119.
                        Deposition: PROB 24/14, 269–73,
                        245–7.

77   Hawkes contra Field   Allegation: PROB 18/7/48.
      (1675)   Depositions: PROB 24/14, 319, 335–7,
                        358–60, 364–5.
                        Sentence: PROB 11/351, 162.
                        Will: PROB 11/352, 114.

78   Hawkins contra Pierce   Allegations: PROB 18/21/60, 70.
      (1691)   Depositions: PROB 24/30, 279, 288.

79	Hawley contra Pride (1675)	Allegation: PROB 18/7/91. Depositions: PROB 24/14, 253–4. Sentence: PROB 11/349, 240.
80	Henley contra Tremhard (1675)	Allegation: PROB 18/7/5. Answer: PROB 25/2/60 Sentence: PROB 11/349, 247.
81	Hovingham contra Vossins (1675)	Allegations: PROB 18/6/9, 26, 27; PROB 18/7/8, 16. Depositions: PROB 24/14, 168–70, 184–6, 200, 290–98. Will: PROB 11/344, 9.
82	Hicks et Meggs contra Singleton (1686)	Allegations: PROB18/18/13, 15; PROB 18/19/37, 38, 39. Depositions: PROB 24/25, 136–9; PROB 24/26, 3–5, 12, 279–83, 298–301, 313–15, 324–7. Will: PROB 11/385, 151. (Revoked PROB 11/385, 353).
83	Higgins et Higgins contra Stamp (1675)	Allegation: PROB 18/7/35. Deposition: PROB 24/14, 265. Sentence: PROB 11/351, 214. Will: PROB 11/352, 283.
84	Hill contra Bond (1681)	Allegations: PROB 18/13/55, 57, 68. Depositions: PROB 24/20, 63–9, 136–9, 160–67. Sentence: PROB 11/368, 112. Will: PROB 11/365, 128.
85	Hoare contra Hoare (1680)	Allegations: PROB 18/12/43; PROB 18/13/11, 30, 76. Depositions: PROB 24/20, 75, 77, 81. Sentence: PROB 11/374, 368. Will: 11/356, 191.

86 Hodgekinson contra Hodgekinson (1675)

Allegation: PROB 18/7/74.
Depositions: PROB 24/14, 305, 309–11, 313.
Sentence: PROB 11/351, 196.
Will: PROB 11/350, 409.

87 Holland contra Mallet alias Geurdain (1675)

Allegation: PROB 18/7/43.
Depositions: PROB 24/15, 278–80.
Sentence: PROB 11/351, 209.
Will: PROB 11/347, 67.

88 Hooper contra Hooper (1671)

Allegation: PROB 18/3c/50.
Sentence: PROB 11/343, 137.

89 Hooper contra Hooper per curator (1675)

Allegation: PROB 18/7/10.
Depositions: PROB 24/14, 170–72.
Sentence: PROB 11/349, 236.
Will: PROB 11/348, 105.

90 Hornby contra Hornby (1691)

Allegation: PROB 18/21/65.
Depositions: PROB 24/30, 301–3.
Sentence: PROB 11/407, 343.

91 Horton et al. contra Bland (1675)

Allegation: PROB 18/7/98.
Sentence: PROB 11/349, 239.
Will: PROB 11/ 349, 288.

92 Isham contra Isham (1675)

Allegation: PROB 18/7/84.
Depositions: PROB 24/14, 270–71.
Sentence: PROB 11/349, 243.
Will: PROB 11/349, 291.

93 Jennyns contra Jennyns (1674)

Allegations: PROB 18/6/42, 45; PROB 18/7/89.
Depositions: PROB 24/14, 254–63.

94 Jones contra Jones (1675)

Allegation: PROB 18/7/59.
Depositions: PROB 24/14, 316–17, 345–6, 350–51.
Sentence: PROB 11/349, 263.
Will: PROB 11/349, 98.

95	Kinaston contra Young (1681)	Allegation: PROB 18/13/35. Depositions: PROB 24/20, 125–8. Sentence PROB 11/ 386, 114. Will: PROB 11/368, 381.
96	King et Taylor contra Jepp (1676)	Allegations: PROB 18/6/52; PROB 18/7/64. Depositions: PROB 24/14, 203, 237–8, 283–9, 379–80. Sentence: PROB 11/351, 202. Will: PROB 11/351, 115.
97	Kirby contra Marwood (1675)	Allegation: PROB 18/7/38. Depositions: PROB 24/14, 264–5.
98	Kyme contra Kyme (1681)	Allegation: PROB 18/13/20, 58, 63. Depositions: PROB 24/20, 61–3, 74–8; PROB 24/21, 31, 153–5. Sentence: PROB 11/371, 365. Will: PROB 11/369, 270.
99	Lambert contra Watkins (1666)	Allegation: PROB 18/1/80.
100	Langham contra Langham (1666)	Allegation: PROB 18/1/5. Will: PROB 11/322, 319.
101	Layer contra Duncomb (1675)	Allegations: PROB 18/4/69; PROB 18/7/85. Depositions: PROB 24/14, 257–8.
102	Lee contra Lee (1675)	Allegation: PROB 18/7/71. Depositions: PROB 24/14, 333–4. Sentence: PROB 11/349, 255. Will: PROB 11/342, 59.
103	Lewger contra Lewger (1675)	Allegation: PROB18/7/67. Depositions: PROB 24/14, 331–2, 337–8. Sentence: PROB 18/349, 256.
104	Loane contra Loane (1691)	Allegation: PROB 18/21/50. Depositions: PROB 24/30, 43–4. Sentence: PROB 11/407, 317. Will: PROB 11/405, 297.

105   Lodge contra Lodge et   Allegation: PROB 18/18/60.
        Lodge (1686)   Depositions: PROB 24/25, 74–5.
                                     Sentence: PROB 11/385, 334.
                                     Will: PROB 11/382, 343.

106   Long contra Martin   Allegations: PROB 18/21/30, 34, 110.
        (1691)   Depositions: PROB 24/30, 50, 114.
                                       Sentence: PROB 11/407, 342.
                                     Will: PROB 11/395, 160.

107   Markham et Carrington   Allegations: PROB 18/1/45, 46.
        contra Markham (1664)   Sentence: PROB 11/313, 283.
                                       Will: PROB 11/313, 203.

108   Marshall contra Oakley   Allegation PROB 18/18/40.
        (1687)   Depositions: PROB 24/25, 186–7.
                                       Sentence PROB 11/389, 269.
                                     Will: PROB11/387, 49.

109   Marsham contra Cherry   Allegation: PROB 18/1/10, 52, 53.
        (1663)

110   Mascall contra Spenser   Allegation: PROB 18/3c/40.
        (1671)

111   May contra May (1675)   Allegation: PROB 18/7/7.
                                       Sentence: PROB 11/349, 241.
                                     Will: PROB 11/349, 284.

112   Medlicott contra   Allegation: PROB 18/7/25.
        Medlicott (1675)   Sentence: PROB 11/349, 271.
                                       Will: PROB 11/349, 180.

113   Mitchell contra Mitchell   Allegation: PROB 18/18/96.
        (1696)   Depositions: PROB 24/25, 90, 139–41.
                                       Sentence: PROB 11/385, 354.
                                     Will: PROB 11/382, 346.

114   Moore alias Tither   Allegation: PROB 18/3c/90.
        contra Tither (1671)   Sentence: PROB 11/337, 419.

115   Moore et Welch contra   Allegation: PROB 18/3c/35.
        Ewens (1671)   Sentence: PROB 11/338, 316.

116	Mynors alias Treadway per curator contra Davis (1673)	Allegations: PROB 18/5/116; PROB 18/7/79. Depositions: PROB 24/14, 278–80.
117	Nauney contra Nauney (1662)	Allegation: PROB 18/1/35. Sentence: PROB 11/310, 89. Will: PROB 11/310, 164.
118	Naylor alias Mossman contra Mossman (1691)	Allegation: PROB 18/21/80. Depositions: PROB 24/30, 166–7, 186–8, 193.
119	Needham contra Pulter et Buxton (1681)	Allegation: PROB 18/13/70. Depositions: PROB 24/20, 106–9.
120	Niblett contra Thonold (1675)	Allegations: PROB 18/6/104; PROB 18/7/60.
121	O'Keever alias Pettus contra Pettus (1674)	Allegations: PROB 18/6/90; PROB 18/7/4, 13, 32; PROB 8/8/43. Depositions: PROB 24/13, 146–8, 153–4; PROB 24/14, 55, 150, 221–2, 304, 312, 329–31, 355. Sentence: PROB 11/351, 165.
122	Owen contra Barrett (1696)	Allegations: PROB 18/24/5, 28. Depositions: PROB 24/35, 77–81, 197–230, 265–87.
123	Oxenham contra Scott alias Oxenham (1662)	Allegation: PROB 18/13/59. Depositions: PROB 24/20, 144–5. Sentence: PROB 11/371, 389. Will: PROB 11/370, 261.
124	Paine et Paine contra Smith (1662)	Allegation: PROB 18/1/25. Will: PROB 11/310, 71.
125	Parks contra Boughey (1674)	Allegation: PROB 18/7/68. Answer PROB 25/2/126. Depositions: PROB 24/14, 361, 384–5. Sentence: PROB 11/349, 273. Will: PROB 11/349, 190.
126	Partridge contra Samwaies et al. (1691)	Allegation: PROB 18/21/85.

127	Pearce contra Pearce (1675)	Allegation: PROB 18/7/62. Depositions: PROB 24/14, 341–5. Sentence: PROB 11/349, 270. Will: PROB 11, 348, 269.
128	Pettyward contra Pettyward (1675)	Allegation: PROB 18/7/96. Depositions: PROB 24/14, 218–19. Sentence: PROB 11/349, 235. Will: PROB 11/349, 281.
129	Peyton contra Raven (1675)	Allegations: PROB 18/7/17; PROB 18/8/53, 92, 117. Answers: PROB 25/2/136, 158, 162. Depositions: PROB 24/15, 209–10, 230, 243–4, 257–8. Sentence: PROB 11/355, 120. Will: PROB 11/355, 120.
130	Piggot contra Ley (1675)	Allegation: PROB 18/7/57. Deposition: PROB 24/14, 322–3.
131	Pim contra Thatcher (1686)	Allegations: PROB: 18/18/54, 55. Sentence: PROB 11/385, 344.
132	Pitt contra Knowle (1671)	Allegations: PROB 18/3c/60, 65. Sentence: PROB 11/338, 323.
133	Pleydall contra Hales (1681)	Allegations: PROB 18/13/25; PROB 18/14/9. Depositions: PROB 24/29, 21, 49. Sentence: PROB 11/371, 460. Will: PROB 11/374, 122.
134	Plydell et al. contra Jones (1696)	Allegations: PROB 18/24/50, 71, 76. Depositions: PROB 24/35, 219–24. Sentence: PROB 11/433, 358. Will: PROB 11/436, 78.
135	Poole contra Barker (1662)	Allegation: PROB 18/1/30.
136	Povey contra Povey (1696)	Allegations: PROB 18/24/15, 26. Depositions: PROB: 24/35, 51–6. Sentence: PROB 11/442, 339.

137   Price contra Price (1681)   Allegations: PROB 18/13/15; 62.
Depositions: PROB 24/20, 129, 133–5;
PROB 24/30, 154; PROB 24/35, 47–8,
65.
Sentence: PROB 11/366, 290.
Will: PROB 11/368, 348.

138   Price alias Williams contra Price (1675)   Allegation: PROB 18/7/18.

139   Quincey alias Yarway contra Yarway (1675)   Allegations: PROB 18/7/37, 40.
Answers: PROB 25/2/127, 132.
Deposition: PROB 24/14, 380–82, 390;
PROB 24/15, 193–4.
Sentence: PROB 11/351, 197.
Will: PROB 11/352, 197.

140   Rawlinson contra Stephens (1675)   Allegation: PROB 18/7/33.
Answer: PROB 25/2/117.
Sentence: PROB 11/351, 211.

141   Read et Boulby contra Fettiplace (1675)   Allegation: PROB 18/7/75.
Answer: PROB 25/2/117.
Sentence: PROB 11/351, 211.

142   Read contra Read alias Rogers (1696)   Allegation: PROB 18/24/25.
Depositions: PROB 24/36, 39–40.
Will: PROB 11/430, 152.

143   Reeve contra Reeve (1696)   Allegation: PROB 18/24/75.
Depositions: 24/35, 193–5.
Will: PROB 11/430, 152.

144   Rich et Gayner contra Vernon (1675)   Allegation: PROB 18/7/63.
Deposition: PROB 24/14, 314–16.
Sentence: PROB 11/349, 256.
Will: PROB 11/349, 301.

145   Rivey contra Twyne (1682)   Allegation: PROB 18/13/5.
Depositions: PROB 24/20, 79, 85.
Sentence: PROB 11/374, 357.
Will: PROB 11/374, 341.

146 Roope et Wakeham contra Jones et al. (1686)

Allegation: PROB 18/18/65.
Depositions: PROB 24/25, 215–19.
Sentence: PROB 11/385, 319.
Will: PROB 11/383, 53.

147 Roth contra Roth (1696)

Allegation: PROB 18/24/45.
Sentence: PROB 11/439, 336.
Will: PROB 11/435, 163.

148 Saltmarsh contra Saltmarsh (1675)

Allegation: PROB 18/7/73.
Depositions: PROB 24/14, 377–9.
Sentence: PROB 11/351, 162.

149 Sandys et al. contra Gee et Spenser (1675)

Allegation: PROB 18/7/23.
Sentence: PROB 11/351, 175.
Will: PROB 11/350, 182.

150 Seawell contra Harbert (1675)

Allegations: PROB 18/7/1, 44; PROB 18/8/6.
Answers: PROB 25/2/156, 157.
Depositions: PROB 24/14, 352–6, 362–5; PROB 24/15, 173, 259, 267, 271.
Sentence: PROB 11/351, 216.
Will: PROB 11/351, 297.

151 Setton alias Neale contra Neale (1696)

Allegation: PROB 18/24/30.

152 Sherbrooke contra Sherbrooke (1675)

Allegation: PROB 18/7/11.
Depositions: PROB 24/14, 188.
Sentence: PROB 11/349, 232.
Will: PROB 11/349, 278.

153 Sherman contra Millner (1675)

Allegation: PROB 18/7/54.
Depositions: PROB 24/ 14, 320–21.
Sentence: PROB 11/351, 161.
Will: PROB 11/350, 50.

154 Slatter contra Tebbat (1675)

Allegation: PROB 18/17/65.
Depositions: PROB 24/14, 266, 351–2.
Will: PROB 11/348, 416.

155   Staley contra Staley
       (1686)

Allegation: PROB 18/18/75.
Depositions: PROB 24/25, 57.
Will: PROB 11/383, 145.

156   Strahan contra Raycroft
       (1696)

Allegation: PROB 18/24/80.
Depositions: PROB 24/35, 243–4.
Sentence: PROB 11/433, 341.
Will: PROB 11/433, 242.

157   Stowe contra Dicks
       (1686)

Allegation: PROB 18/18/5.
Depositions: PROB 24/25, 354.

158   Tappan contra Tappan
       (1666)

Allegation: PROB 18/1/90.

159   Tatham contra Tatham
       (1675)

Allegation: PROB 18/7/9.
Depositions: PROB 24/14, 280–82.
Will: PROB 11/349, 220.

160   Templer con Wynn
       (1686)

Allegation: PROB 18/18/98, 99, 100.
Depositions: PROB 24/25, 188–95, 201,
357–8.
Sentence: PROB 11/389, 258.
Will: PROB 11/388, 338.

161   Thimbleby contra
       Thimbleby (1673)

Allegation: PROB 18/3c/45.
Depositions: PROB 24/10, 359, 495.
Sentence: PROB 11/343, 128.
Will: PROB 11/341, 398.

162   Thornton contra
       Stockman (1663)

Allegation: PROB 18/1/20.
Depositions: PROB 24/6, 406–7.
Sentence: PROB 11/ 312, 340.

163   Thyn et Gregory contra
       Somerset (1674)

Allegations: PROB 18/6/22; PROB
18/7/27; PROB 8/66, 69, 111, 113, 114.
Depositions: PROB 24/15, 49–54, 58–63.
Sentence: PROB 11/355, 96.
Will: PROB 11/355, 296.

164   Tomkins contra Pooley
       (1675)

Allegation: PROB 18/7/12.
Depositions: PROB 24/14, 198.

165   Tribe alias Upsdale
       contra Hearsey (1671)

Allegation: PROB 18/3c/80.

166 Turgis contra Hunt (1671)

Allegation: PROB 18/3c/74.
Sentence: PROB 11/337, 193.
Will: PROB 11/337, 64.

167 Turner contra Fretwell (1666)

Allegation: PROB 18/1/84.

168 Wakeham contra Wakeham (1675)

Allegation: PROB 18/7/19.
Depositions: PROB 24/14, 403.

169 Walker alias Palmer contra Baker alias Palmer et al. (1681)

Allegation: PROB 18/13/50.
Depositions: PROB 24/20, 192.
Sentence: PROB 11/368, 118.

170 Walker contra Clark et Otghar (1668)

Allegation: PROB 18/18/25.
Depositions: PROB 24/25, 176–8, 204–5.
Sentence: PROB 11/389, 252.
Will: PROB 11/384, 18.

171 Walker et Mason contra Grove (1663)

Allegation: PROB 18/1/50.
Sentence: PROB 11/310, 341.

172 Ward contra Stinton per curator (1685)

Allegation: PROB 18/18/44.
Depositions: 24/25, 262–76.
Will: PROB 11/383, 299.

173 Webb contra Allen (1691)

Allegation: PROB 18/21/25.
Depositions: PROB 24/30, 123.
Sentence: PROB 11/407, 347.
Will: PROB 11/390, 213.

174 Weedon contra Draper (1675)

Allegations: PROB 18/7/30, 31.
Answer: PROB 25/2/124.
Depositions: PROB 24/14, 346–50, 363–4, 398–9.

175 Wingfield et Johnson contra Johnson (1663)

Allegation: PROB 18/1/60.

176 West contra Stone et al. (1675)

Allegation: PROB 18/7/2, 3.

177	West contra West (1686)	Allegation: PROB 18/18/35. Depositions: PROB 24/25, 120–21, 325–6, 362. Sentence: PROB 11/389, 166. Will: PROB 11/389, 213.
178	Whitelocke contra Hulburd (1696)	Allegation: PROB 18/24/55. Depositions: PROB 24/35 9–15, 185–5.
179	Williams contra Phillips (1696)	Allegation: PROB 18/24/20. Depositions: PROB 24/35, 123–5. Sentence: PROB 11/442, 308. Will: PROB 11/436, 148.
180	Wilsher contra Ruffin et Wells (1674)	Allegations: PROB 18/6/80; PROB 18/7/90. Answer: PROB 25/2/104. Depositions: PROB 24/14, 235–6, 222, 251–3. Sentence: PROB 11/349, 245. Will: PROB 11/348, 142.
181	Wise contra Woodward (1695)	Allegation: PROB 18/24/70. Depositions: PROB 24/35, 205–8. Sentence: PROB 11/433, 33. Will: PROB 11/435, 158.
182	Wood contra Hopkins (1663)	Allegation: PROB 18/1/65.
183	Wormall et Jenkins contra Holman et Spence (1675)	Allegation: PROB 18/1/75. Sentence: PROB 11/ 320, 331. Will: PROB 11/320, 202.
184	Wymondesold contra Wymondesold (1675)	Allegation: PROB 18/7/94. Depositions: PROB 24/14, 229. Sentence: PROB 11/349, 235. Will: PROB 11/349, 231.

B. Additional Cases Consulted

Case No.	Case title	Details
1	Belwood contra Smart (1681)	Allegation: PROB 18/13/60. Sentence: PROB 11/368, 109.
2	Besson contra Jones (1690)	Allegations: PROB 18/21/92, 123. Sentence: PROB 11/407, 306.
3	Bombay contra Rea (1680)	Allegation: PROB 18/13/16. Depositions: PROB 21/19, 302; PROB 21/20, 34–5.
4	Bourne contra Farthing (1672)	Allegations: PROB 18/4/70; PROB 18/5/94. Will: PROB 11/342, 284.
5	Briggs contra Briggs (1679)	Allegation: PROB 18/12/68. Depositions: PROB 24/19, 66–7.
6	Burford et Claphamson contra Clamphampson (1686)	Allegation: PROB 18/18/34. Depositions: PROB 24/25, 323–9. Will: PROB 11/384, 284.
7	Burlton contra Burlton (1690)	Allegation: PROB 18/12/28. Depositions: PROB 24/19, 242–3. Sentence: PROB 11/368, 109.
8	Compton contra Compton (1674)	Allegation: PROB 18/6/84.
9	Day contra Day (1671)	Allegations: PROB 18/3/49; PROB 18/4/36, 37, 39; PROB 18/5/6, 10. Depositions: PROB 24/10, 302–3, 410 11; PROB 24/11, 54–6.
10	Eyre contra Eyre (1677)	Allegation: PROB: 18/2/77. Depositions: PROB 24/16, 120–25, 214–20, 255–56.
11	Fisher contra Goswell (1690)	Allegations: PROB 18/21/2, 3. Depositions: PROB 24/30, 137. Sentence: PROB 11/407, 310.

12	Ford et Brown alias Ford contra Lipscomb (1680)	Allegation: PROB 18/13/98. Depostions: PROB 24/20,12–20, 140, 196.
13	Gardner et Moody contra Cumberland (1676)	Allegations: PROB 18/8/108; PROB 18/8/30. Depositions: PROB 24/16, 15. Sentence: PROB 11/3. Will: PROB 11/352, 155.
14	Golding contra Cage (1672)	Allegation: PROB 18/4/42
15	Johnson contra Glascocke (1684)	Allegations: PROB 18/17/39, 84, 86. Sentence: PROB 11/385, 313.
16	Jones contra Hughes et Twaites (1670)	Allegation: PROB 18/3/6.
17	Land et Barnaby contra Burt (1670)	Allegation: PROB 18/3b/40. Depositions: PROB 24/10, 160, 208–10, 254. Sentence: PROB 11/337, 155, 154.
18	Leslow alias Jones contra Jones (1673)	Allegations: PROB 18/5/10; PROB 18/6/10. Depositions: PROB 24/13, 50–56, 61, 65.
19	Lowder et Impey contra Pitt (1678)	Allegation: PROB 18/10/83. Depositions: PROB 24/17, 135–7. Sentence: PROB 11/338, 323.
20	Moses contra Davie (1694)	Allegation: PROB 18/23/5. Sentence: PROB 11/433, 315. Will: PROB 11/415, 228.
21	Mullen contra Netter (1690)	Allegation: PROB 18/21/94. Sentence: PROB 11/407, 340.
22	Osbourne contra Jeep (1676)	Allegations: PROB 18/6/52; PROB 18/7/44. Sentence: PROB 11/251, 116.

23 Owen et.al. contra Lloyd   Allegations: PROB 18/8/122, 123; PROB
    (1676)   18/9/10.
                                Depositions: PROB 24/15, 378.

24 Pierce contra Pierce (1690) Allegation: PROB 18/21/44.
                                Sentence: PROB 11/407, 324.

25 Prise contra Seawen alias   Allegation: PROB 18/24/72.
    Prise (1695)   Sentence: PROB 11/433, 340.
                                Will: PROB 11/421, 7.

26 Sherman et Pratt contra   Allegations: PROB 18/4/104; PROB
    Green (1672)   18/5/106.

27 Sheppard contra Sheppard   Allegation: PROB 18/21/45.
    (nd)   Depositions: PROB 24/25, 215.

28 Stannes contra Burkenham   Allegation: PROB 18/18/17.
    (1685)   Depositions: PROB 24/25, 48–56.

29 Washington contra Balle   Allegations: PROB 18/21/7, 9.
    (1692)   Depositions: PROB 24/30, 34–5, 40–42
                                49–52, 90-94, 100–105.
                                Sentence: PROB 11/407, 310.

30 Williams contra Williams   Allegation: PROB 18/18/87.
    (1686)

31 Wyam contra Wyam   Allegations: PROB 18/4/3, 103.
    (1671)   Depositions: PROB 24,/11, 260–62,
                                270–71; PROB 24/12, 382.
                                Sentence: PROB 11/343, 179.

Primary Printed Sources

Adams, Norma, and Donahue, Jr., Charles, *Select Cases from the Ecclesiastical Courts of Canterbury c.1200–1301* Selden Society, vol. 95 (London, 1981).

Anon., The Visitation of the Sick, *The Book of Common Prayer* (London, 1669)

Anon., *A Rationale upon the Book of Common Prayer of the Church of England* (London, 1668).

Anon., *Of the Original of Ecclesiastic Jurisdiction of Testaments* (London, 1683).

Anon., *Theological Discourse of Last Wills and Testaments* (London, 1696).

Anon., *The Office and Duty of Executors* 5th edn (London, 1663).

Anon., *A Rationale upon the Book of Common Prayer of the Church of England* (London, 1668).

Anon., *A Familiar Plan and Easy Explanation of the Law of Wills and Codicils* (London, 1785).

Ayliffe, John, *Parergon Juris Anglicani: or a commentary by way of supplement to the canon and constitutions of the Church of England* (London, 1724).

Blackstone, William, *Commentaries on the Laws of England*, 4 vols. (University of Chicago Reprint, 1979).

Bray, Gerald (ed.), *The Anglican Canons 1529 –1947* (Woodbridge, 1998).

Brydall, John, *Non Compos Mentis: or the law relating to natural fools, mad folks and lunitick persons explored* (London, 1700).

Burn, J.S., *The Fleet Registers* (London, 1833).

Burn, Richard, *Ecclesiastical Law* 3rd edn (London, 1775).

Fincham, Kenneth, *Visitation Articles and Injunctions of the Early Stuart Church* (Church of England Record Society, 1994).

Firth, C.H., and Rait, R.S. (eds.), *Acts and Ordinances of the Interregnum 1642–1660*, 3 vols. (London, 1911).

Hale, Sir Matthew, *Two Tracts on the Benefit of Registering Deeds in England* (London, 1756).

Hall, G.D.G. (ed.), *The Treatise on the Laws and Customs of the Realm of England Commonly called Glanvill* (2nd edn Oxford, 1993).

Law Reform Committee's 22nd Report, *The Making and Revocation of Wills* cmnd. 7902, 1980.

Meriton, George, *The Parson's Monitor consisting of such Cases and Matter as principally concern the Clergy* (London, 1681).

Nelson, William, *Lex Teatamentaria, or a Compendious System of all the Laws of England* (London, 1714).

Ninth Report of the Royal Commission on Historical Manuscripts, Part II, Appendix.

Parker, Henry, *Reformation in Courts and Cases Testamentary* (London, 1650).

Perkins, John, *A Profitable Book* (Garland Reprint of the 1827 edition, 1978).

Peters, Hugh, *Good Work for a Good Magistrate* (London, 1651).

Poos, L.R., and Bonfield, Lloyd, *Select Pleas in Manorial Courts1250–1550: family and property law* (Selden Society, London, vol. 114, 1998).

Restatement (Third) of Property, Wills and Other Donative Transfers sec 3.3 (1999).

Ridley, Thomas, *A View of the Civil and Ecclesiastical Law* (Oxford, 1675).

Sabine, George H. (ed.), *The Works of Gerrard Winstanley* (Ithaca, 1941).

Shapiro, Ian (ed.), *Two Treatises of Government and a Letter Concerning Toleration* (New Haven, 2003).

Sheppard, William, *England's Balme* (London, 1656).

—, *The Touchstone of Common Assurances* 6th edn (Dublin, 1785).

Spelman, Henry, 'Of the Origins of Testaments and Wills,' in *The English Works of Sir Henry Spelman, Kt.* (London, 1727).

Swinburne, Henry, *A Brief Treatise of Testaments and Last Wills* (Garland Reprint of 1590 edition, New York, 1978).

Taylor, Jeremy, *The Rule and Exercise of Holy Dying* (London, 1674).

Thorne, Samuel E., trans., *Bracton On the Laws and Customs of England* (Cambridge, MA, 1968).

Vaughn, Rice, *A Plea for the Common Laws of England* (London, 1651).

Woodward, Thomas, *The Office and Duty of Executors* 5th edn (London, 1641).

Yale, D.E.C. (ed.), *Lord Nottingham's Chancery Cases*, 2 vols. (Selden Society, vols. 73 and 79, London, 1954 and 1961).

Secondary Sources

Addy, John, *Death, Money, and the Vultures: inheritance and avarice 1660–1750* (London, 1992).

Amussen, Susan, *An Ordered Society: gender and class in early modern England* (Oxford, 1988).

Aylmer, G.E., 'The meaning and definition of property in seventeenth-century England,' *Past and Present*, vol. 86 (1980), pp. 87–97.

Arkell, Tom, Evans, Nesta, and Goose, Nigel (eds.), *When Death Do Us Part: understanding and interpreting the probate records of early modern England* (Oxford, 2000).

Bailey, Joanne, *Unquiet Lives: marriage and marriage breakdown in England, 1660–1800* (Cambridge, 2003).

Baker, J.H., *An Introduction to English Legal History*, 4th edn (London, 2002).

Bonfield, Lloyd, 'Reforming the Requirements for Due Execution of Wills: Some Guidance from the Past,' *Tulane Law Review*, vol. 70 (1995), pp. 1893–1920.

—, 'Developments in Family Law,' in David Kertzer and Maurizio Barbagli (eds.), *Family Life in Early Modern Times* (New Haven, 2001).

—, 'Seeking Connections between Law and Kinship in Early Modern England,' *Continuity and Change*, vol. 24 (2009), pp. 49–82.

—,"Normative rules and property transmission," in Lloyd Bonfield, Richard Smith, and Keith Wrightson (eds.), *The World We have Gained* (Oxford, 1985), pp. 155–76.

Bonfield, Lloyd, Smith, Richard, and Wrightson, Keith (eds.), *The World We have Gained* (Oxford, 1985).

Boulton, J., 'Clandestine marriage in London: an examination of the neglected union variable,' *Urban History*, vol. 20 (1993), pp. 191–210.

Brace, Laura, *The Idea of Property in the Seventeenth Century* (Manchester, 1998).

Brokowki, Andrew, 'Reforming section 9 of the Wills Act,' *Conveyancer and Property Lawyer* (2000), pp. 31–42.

Brooks, C.W., *Law, Politics and Society in Early Modern England* (Cambridge, 2008).

Brundage, James, *Law, Sex, and Christian Society in Medieval Europe* (Chicago, 1987).

Burn, J.S., *The History of Parish Registers in England* (London, 1982).

Cox, Jane, *Affection Defying the Power of Death: wills, probate, and death duty records* (Birmingham, 1993).

Dukeminier, J., Johanson, S., Lindgren, J., and Sitkoff, R., *Wills, Trusts, and Estates* 7th edn (New York, 2005).

Emsley, C., *Crime in England, 1750–1900* (Harlow, 1996).

Erickson, Amy, *Women and Property in Early Modern England* (London, 1993).

Finch, Janet, Hayes, Lynn, Mason, Jennifer, Masson, Judith, and Lorraine Wallis, *Wills, Inheritance, and Families* (Oxford, 1996).

Floyer, Phillip, *The Proctor's Practice in the Ecclesiastical Courts* 2nd edn (London, 1746).

Foyster, Elizabeth, *Marital Violence: an English family history* (Cambridge, 2005).

Gibson, J.S.W., *Wills and Where to Find Them* (Chichester, 1974).

Gillis, John, *For Better, For Worse: British marriages 1600 to the present* (Oxford, 1985).

Goody, Jack, *The Development of the Family and Marriage in Europe* (Cambridge, 1986).

—, *The Logic of Writing and the Organization of Society* (Cambridge, 1986).

Goose, Nigel and Evans, Nesta, 'Wills as an historical source', in T. Arkell, N. Evans and N. Goose (eds.), *When Death Do Us Part: understanding and interpreting the probate records of early modern England* (Oxford, 2000).

Green, I.M., *The Re-Establishment of the Church of England, 1660–63* (Oxford, 1978).

Gulliver, A.G., and Tilson, C.J., 'Classification of gratuitous transfers', *Yale Law Journal*, vol. 51 (1941), pp. 1–39.

Hamburger, Philip, 'The Conveyancing Purposes of the Statute of Frauds', *American Journal of Legal History*, vol. xxvii (1983), pp. 354–85.

Heath, Peter, *Church and Realm, 1272–1461* (London, 1988).

Helmholz, Richard, *Canon Law and the Law of England* (London, 1988).

—, *Roman Canon Law in Reformation England* (Cambridge, 1990).

Henning, Crawford, 'The original drafts of the Statute of Frauds (29 Car. II c. 3) and their authors', *University of Pennsylvania Law Review*, vol. 61 (19–13), pp. 283–316.

Hill, Christopher, *The World Turned Upside Down* (New York, 1972).

—, *The Intellectual Origins of the English Revolution* (Oxford, 1997).

Holmes, Janet, Hayes, Lynn, Mason, Jennifer, Masson, Judith, and Wallis, Lorraine, *Wills, Inheritance and Families* (Oxford, 1996).

Horwitz, Henry, 'Testamentary practice, family strategies, and the last phases of the custom of London, 1660–1725', *Law and History Review*, vol. 2 (1984), pp. 223–39.

Horwitz H., and Polden, P., 'Continuity or change in the Court of Chancery in the seventeenth and eighteenth centuries?' *Journal of British Studies*, vol. 35 (1996), pp. 24–57.

Houlbrooke, Ralph, *Church Courts and the People during the English Reformation* (Oxford, 1979).

—, *Death, Ritual and Bereavement* (London, 1988).

—, *Death, Religion and the Family in England, 1480–1750* (Oxford, 1998).

Hunter, Richard, and MacAlpine, Ida (eds.), *Three Hundred Years of Psychiatry, 1535–1860* (London, 1963).

Ingram, M., *Church Court, Sex and Marriage in England, 1570–1640* (Cambridge, 1987).

Kerridge, Roger, 'Wills made in suspicious circumstances: the problem of the vulnerable testator', *Cambridge Law Journal*, vol. 59 (2000), pp. 310–34.

King, Peter, 'Punishing assault: the transformation of attitudes in the English courts', *Journal of Interdisciplinary History*, vol. 27 (1996).

Kitching, Christopher, 'The Prerogative Court of Canterbury from Warham to Whitgift', in Rosemary O'Day and Felicity Heal (eds.), *Continuity and*

Change: personnel and administration of the Church of England, 1500–1642 (Leicester, 1976).

Langbein, John, 'Substantial compliance with the wills Act,' *Harvard Law Review*, vol. 88 (1975), pp. 489–532.

Laslett, Peter, 'Demographic and microstructural history in relation to human adaptation: reflections on newly established evidence,' in D.J. Horner (ed.), *How Humans Adapt: a biocultural odyssey* (Washington, 1983), pp. 343–70.

Leslie, Melanie, 'The Myth of Testamentary Freedom,' *Arizona Law Review*, vol. 38 (1996), pp. 235–90.

MacDonald, Michael, *Mystical Bedlam: madness, anxiety and healing in seventeenth-century England* (Cambridge, 1981).

Macfarlane, Alan, *The Origins of English Individualism* (Oxford, 1978).

—, *The Justice and the Mare's Ale: law and disorder in seventeenth century England* (Oxford, 1981).

Macpherson, C.B., *The Political Theory of Possessive Individualism: Hobbes to Locke* (Oxford, 1962).

McGovern, William, Kurtz, Sheldon, and Rein, Jan Ellen, *Wills, Trusts and Estates* (St. Paul, MN 1988).

McIntosh, Marjorie K., *Autonomy and Community: the Royal Manor of Havering, 1200–1500* (Cambridge, 1986).

Maine, Henry, *Ancient Law* (London and New York, 1864).

Marsh, Christopher, 'In the Name of God? Will-making and Faith in Early Modern England,' in Tom Arkell, Nesta Evans, and Nigel Goose (eds.), *When Death Do Us Part: understanding and interpreting the probate records of early modern England* (Oxford, 2000), pp. 158–75.

Mendelson, Sara, and Crawford, Patricia, *Women in Early Modern England* (Oxford, 1998).

Miller, J. Garth, 'Substantial compliance and the execution of wills,' *International and Comparative Law Quarterly*, vol. 36 (1987), pp. 559–88.

Millon, David, '*Circumspecte Agatis* Revisited,' *Law and History Review*, vol. 2 (1984), pp. 105–23.

Outhwaite, R.B., 'Sweetapple of Fledborough and clandestine marriage in eighteenth-century Nottinghamshire,' *Transactions of the Thoroton Society for 1990*, vol. 94 (1991), pp. 35–46.

Outhwaite, R.B., *Clandestine Marriage in England* (London, 1995).

Pollock, Frederick, and Maitland, Frederick W., *The History of English Law* (Cambridge, 1968).

Porter, Roy, 'Madness and the Family before Freud,' *Journal of Family History*, vol. 23 (1998), pp. 159–72.

—, *Madness* (Oxford, 2002).

Prior, Mary, 'Wives and wills 1558–1700,' in John Chartres and David Hey, *English Rural Society, 1500–1800: essays in honour of Joan Thirsk* (Cambridge, 1990), pp. XXX.

Radin, Margaret, 'Property and Personhood,' *Stanford Law Review*, vol. 34 (1882), pp. 964–70.

Reeve, Andrew, *Property* (Atlantic Highlands, NJ, 1986).

Riden, P. (ed.), *Probate Records and the Local Community* (Gloucester, 1985).

Shapiro, Ian (ed.), *Two Treatises of Government and a Letter Concerning Toleration* (New Haven CN, 2003).

Sharpe, James, 'Domestic homicide in early modern England,' *Historical Journal*, vol. 24 (1981), pp. 29–48.

Sheehan, Michael, *The Will in Medieval England from the Conversion of the Anglo-Saxons to the Thirteenth Century* (Toronto, 1963).

Spring, Eileen, *Land, Law and Family: aristocratic inheritance in England 1300–1800* (Chapel Hill, 1993).

Spufford, Margaret, 'Religious preambles and the scribes of villagers' wills in Cambridgeshire,' in Tom Arkell, Nesta Evans, and Nigel Gose (eds.), *When Death Do Us Part: understanding and interpreting the probate records of early modern England* (Oxford, 2000), pp. 144–57.

Spufford, Peter, 'A printed catalogue of the names of testators,' in G.H. Martin and Peter Spufford (eds.), *The Records of a Nation* (Woodbridge, 1990).

Stone, Lawrence, *The Family, Sex and Marriage in England 1500–1800* (London, 1977).

—, *Uncertain Unions: marriage in England 1660–1753* (Oxford, 1992).

Sutherland, D.W., *Quo Warranto Proceedings in the Reign of Edward I* (Oxford, 1963).

Takahashi, Motoyasu, 'The number of wills proved in the sixteenth and seventeenth centuries: graphs, with tables and commentary,' in G.H. Martin and Peter Spufford (eds.), *The Records of a Nation* (Woodbridge, 1990), pp. 187–214.

Thirsk, Joan, 'Unexplored sources in local records,' *Archives*, vol. vi (1963) 29, pp. 8–12.

Thomas, Keith, *Religion and the Decline of Magic* (New York, 1971).

Thomlinson, E.M., *A History of the Minories* (London, 1907).

Tully, James, *A Discourse on Property: John Locke and his adversaries* (Cambridge, 1980).

Veale, Donald, *The Popular Movement for Law Reform 1640–1660* (Oxford, 1970).

Whitman, Robert, 'Revocation and Revival: An analysis of the 1990 Revision of the Uniform Probate Code,' *Albany Law Review*, vol. 55 (1991/2), pp. 1035–66.

Wrightson, Keith, and Levine, David, *Poverty and Piety in an English Village: Terling 1525–1700* (Oxford, 1995).

Wrigley, E.A., 'Clandestine Marriage in Tisbury in the late Seventeenth Century,' *Local Population Studies*, vol.10 (1973), pp. 15–21.

Wrigley, E.A., and Schofield, R.S., *The Population History of England 1541–1871: a reconstruction* (Cambridge, 1982).

Wynne, William, *The Life of Sir Leoline Jenkins*, 2 vols. (London, 1724).

Index